T0375066

THE I TATTI
RENAISSANCE LIBRARY

James Hankins, General Editor

PONTANO

DIALOGUES

VOLUME I

ITRL 53

GIOVANNI GIOVIANO PONTANO

✦ ✦ ✦

DIALOGUES

VOLUME I ✦ CHARON AND ANTONIUS

EDITED AND TRANSLATED BY

JULIA HAIG GAISSER

THE I TATTI RENAISSANCE LIBRARY

HARVARD UNIVERSITY PRESS

CAMBRIDGE, MASSACHUSETTS

LONDON, ENGLAND

2012

Printed in the United States of America

Series design by Dean Bornstein

Library of Congress Cataloging-in-Publication Data

Pontano, Giovanni Gioviano, 1429–1503.
Dialogues / Giovanni Gioviano Pontano ;
edited and translated by Julia Haig Gaisser.
volumes. cm. — (The I Tatti Renaissance library ; 53)
Latin and English on facing pages.
ISBN 978-0-674-05491-2 (v. 1)
I. Gaisser, Julia Haig. II. Pontano, Giovanni Gioviano, 1429–1503.
Dialogues. English. 2012. III. Pontano,
Giovanni Gioviano, 1429–1503. Dialogues. Latin. 2012.
IV. Title. V. Series: I Tatti Renaissance library ; 53.
PA8570.P5D53 2012
871′.04 — dc23 2012007924

Contents

Introduction

PONTANO AND NAPLES

Giovanni Pontano (May 7, 1429–September 17, 1503) served five kings of Naples as a courtier and diplomat and earned even greater fame as a scholar, prose author, and poet.[1] Pontano was born in the Umbrian hill town of Cerreto but grew up in Perugia, where his mother had moved with her children after the death of his father in a local civil disturbance. In 1447, at the age of eighteen, he was lucky enough to find a place in the entourage of King Alfonso of Aragon, who was then campaigning in Tuscany, and in 1448 he accompanied the king when he returned to Naples. There he spent the rest of his career. At Alfonso's court he found several good patrons and friends. The most influential was Antonio Beccadelli, called Panormita (1374–1471), who became his political and literary mentor.[2] The young Pontano was soon writing poetry in the racy manner of Panormita, accompanying Panormita on diplomatic missions for Alfonso, and taking part in the gatherings of Panormita and other Neapolitan humanists.

Pontano made his career in Naples in the employment of Alfonso and his successors, whom he served in positions of ever increasing delicacy and responsibility for over forty-five years.[3] He suffered hardships in the First Barons' War (1458–65), campaigning with Alfonso's illegitimate son, Ferrante, as he fought to secure his title to the throne. He became the tutor of Ferrante's sixteen-year-old son and heir, Alfonso Duke of Calabria, who at first proved to be a difficult and ungrateful charge; after Alfonso's marriage to Ippolita Sforza (1465), he served as secretary to both for many years. He traveled with Alfonso during both the War of Ferrara (1482–84) and the Second Barons' Revolt (1485–86), and finally negotiated a peace between Ferrante and the barons and their

ally, Pope Innocent VIII (1486). In 1486 he became Ferrante's first secretary, or as we would say, prime minister, after the execution of his predecessor, Antonello Petrucci, who had been one of the leaders of the revolt. When Ferrante broke the terms of the first peace with Innocent, Pontano negotiated a second (1492).

But by this time Naples was already moving inexorably toward catastrophe. The French kings had had their eye on the kingdom from the moment that King Alfonso I wrested control of it from the Angevins in the 1440s, periodically pressing their claims through alliances with the pope and various Italian cities. Now they were ready to strike. As the French threat increased, the throne of Naples passed in quick succession to Alfonso Duke of Calabria (Alfonso II, 1494) and to his son Ferrandino (Ferrante II, 1495). Pontano continued in his post as prime minister, working desperately to stave off the inevitable. On February 22, 1495, the French army of Charles VIII took possession of Naples. Ferrandino had to abandon the city, and Pontano was left to hand over the keys of the Neapolitan fortresses to the invader, his last act as prime minister.[4] Although Ferrandino was able to retake his kingdom within the year, he did not live long to enjoy it. He died in October 1496 and was succeeded by his uncle, Federico, for whom Pontano, now officially retired from politics, performed occasional services until the kingdom of Naples was finally retaken by the French in 1501.

Pontano's public duties, heavy and exhausting as they undoubtedly were, did not prevent him from enjoying an affectionate domestic life, although by modern standards he was anything but an exemplary husband. In 1461 he married Adriana Sassone, a seventeen-year-old girl from a wealthy noble family, who bore him three daughters and a son within the decade. He lovingly celebrated his wife in his poetry, especially in a collection entitled *De amore coniugali,* which also includes a dozen lullabies to his son Lucio (b. 1469). But other women were also the subject of his

erotic and poetic attentions, particularly the girl he calls Stella, whom he met in Ferrara in 1482 and celebrated in many poems.[5] He humorously refers to his extramarital affairs in a comic vignette in *Antonius* in which his son, Lucio, tells how his mother jealously upbraided him for his unfaithfulness (*Antonius*, 100). Nonetheless, when Adriana died (1490), Pontano seems to have felt profound and bitter grief. He mourned her loss in many poems and built a chapel next to his house as a family mausoleum.[6] The building still stands on Via dei Tribunali. Adriana is buried there, along with Pontano himself and their children, as well as Lucilio, his son by Stella.

Pontano's literary and intellectual accomplishments would be impressive even if we did not know of his heavy public responsibilities. He was a humanist to the core, studying, transcribing, correcting, and annotating the texts of ancient authors, as well as imitating and building on their ideas in his works. He was deeply interested in the usage and orthography of classical Latin — expertise that he brought to bear both in studying and correcting ancient texts and in his own writing. (Unlike many humanists, he wrote only in Latin.) He discussed Latin usage at length in several works, including his dialogues. His passion for orthography has made him the despair of editors, since he often changed his mind about a spelling if he had (or thought he had) new information about it.

He was a distinguished and elegant poet — arguably the best Latin poet of the Renaissance, although his much younger contemporaries Michele Marullo and Jacopo Sannazaro and the sixteenth-century poet Johannes Secundus would also be in contention. Pontano wrote in conventional genres (lyric, bucolic, epic, didactic epic, elegy), but he was also an innovator, creating styles and genres that spoke to his own time. He wrote Latin lullabies, celebrated married love in elegiac verse (the combination of marriage and eros is unthinkable in classical elegy), and made the Ca-

tullan hendecasyllable the basis of a new genre that would be imitated all over Europe for the next two hundred years. He used hendecasyllables for several poems in his first poetic collection, *Pruritus* (Titillations), which he composed in 1449 in the manner of Panormita's scandalous *Hermaphroditus* (Panormita used only elegiacs), used them again in his *Liber Parthenopeus sive Amores* (1457), and came back to them in his brilliant late collection *Hendecasyllabi sive Baiae* (printed posthumously in 1505).[7] Pontano was also a prolific prose author. His prose works fill three tightly packed quarto volumes of over six hundred pages each in the 1518–19 Aldine edition. He wrote treatises on virtues and vices, astrology, conversation, and Latin orthography, as well as a history of the First Barons' War (*De bello neapolitano*). He also wrote five dialogues: *Charon, Antonius, Actius, Aegidius,* and *Asinus*. *Charon* and *Antonius* are the subject of the present volume; the rest will appear in volume 2.

From his first days in Naples, Pontano enjoyed the friendship of his fellow humanists and the gatherings that were the centerpiece of their intellectual and social life. Originally these gatherings took place in the royal library, but after Alfonso's death (1458), the humanists met out of doors, under an arcade near Panormita's house on Via Nilo; they called both the arcade and the group itself *Porticus Antoniana* after their leader.[8] On Panormita's death in 1471 Pontano became head of the sodality, which is generally but anachronistically called either Accademia Napoletana or (more often) Accademia Pontaniana, a term first attested in the 1480s and in general use only after Pontano's death. Sometimes Pontano and his friends met in places near the palace and the Porticus Antoniana, whether at Pontano's house on Via dei Tribunali or later on in the nearby *tempietto* he built in 1492 as a shrine and family chapel. But they also went farther afield, to the monastery of San Giovanni a Carbonara or to Pontano's pleasant Villa Antiniana on the

Vomero, a hill west of the city.[9] The main activities of the group seem to have been conversing on moral and intellectual topics, reading aloud and discussing ancient and modern texts, observing each others' birthdays and anniversaries, and dining together.[10] Meetings were frequent and regular, particularly after Pontano's retirement from public life in 1495; and, although the group was not rigidly organized, it observed certain customs. Everyone present was obliged to take part in the conversation, and in a predetermined order; and each member of the sodality was awarded a Latin name. Sannazaro, for example, was called Actius Syncerus; Pontano's lifelong friend Pietro Golino was called Petrus Compater. At an unknown date Pontano himself was awarded the name Jovianus (Gioviano); he is generally called Giovanni Gioviano Pontano.

PONTANO'S DIALOGUES

Pontano wrote his five dialogues over a thirty-year period, from around 1469 (*Charon*) to 1501 (*Aegidius*).[11] The content, tone, and cast of characters are different in each. *Charon,* set in the underworld of classical mythology, takes a long view of the tribulations and folly of humanity, but with particular attention to fifteenth-century Italy. *Antonius,* a Menippean satire named for the recently dead Antonio Beccadelli, is set in the Portico Antoniano, where members of his sodality remember and emulate their deceased leader, conversing on favorite topics and stopping from time to time to interrogate passersby. *Asinus* (The Ass) is an allegorical comedy on ingratitude starring Pontano himself, worn-out and half-crazed after making peace between Ferrante and Innocent VIII. *Actius,* named for Sannazaro, its principal interlocutor, presents discussions of poetic meter and style and of the art of writing history. *Aegidius,* named for the famous Augustinian Egidio da

Viterbo (Giles of Viterbo), presents a serious discussion of philosophy and religion that David Marsh has called "Pontano's literary and spiritual testament."[12]

In spite of their obvious differences, however, the dialogues also show a strong family resemblance, all bearing the unmistakable stamp of their author's interests and sensibilities. They are constructed along similar lines and with similar elements and themes.

Each of the dialogues uses a contemporary historical crisis or event to precipitate the discussion. These events have furnished important clues for dating and chronology, although we cannot always distinguish between the dramatic date of a dialogue and its actual time of composition.[13] But their true role is literary — to place the interlocutors in a real historical moment, providing not only a jumping-off point but also a context for their exchanges. In *Charon* the crisis is an impending war in Italy. The conflict is not specified, but Monti has plausibly identified it as the war undertaken in 1469 by Pope Paul II to claim Rimini from Roberto Malatesta.[14] The pope was allied with Venice; opposing them was a league consisting of Milan, Florence, and Naples. Within a few months the pope was forced to give up his claim, and a major conflict was averted; but the crisis is an appropriate backdrop for the interlocutors' discussion of human folly and especially for Mercury's angry denunciation of the madness of war. Men complain, he says, about the deaths caused by natural disasters like earthquakes but think nothing of killing each other:

> Because in a single night, after several centuries, around twenty thousand people have been crushed under their houses, they are all horrified. . . . But is there any art they don't use to bring about wars, which in the space of a single hour, almost every year, wipe out many thousands of men, and sometimes obliterate whole kingdoms and populous na-

> tions? It is with wars that they busy themselves; this is their sport, this their delight; it is considered the greatest honor to bring back the head of an enemy impaled on a spear. (*Charon* 30)

Since the impending conflict never materialized, perhaps Pontano thought naming it would seem anticlimactic, especially long after the event. In terms of the dialogue itself, however, there were also good reasons to leave it unspecified. The discussion is prompted by the apprehension and threat of conflict, not by the conflict itself; the dread of war rather than any particular war is what matters, especially in the underworld, where events are viewed from the perspective of eternity.

In the other dialogues, however, the precipitating event is identified. In *Antonius* it is the death of Panormita. The dialogue is set at the moment when the sodality is no longer Panormita's but not yet Pontano's. Neither appears in the dialogue, but both are present in the minds and conversation of the interlocutors. The work opens with the interlocutors at the Portico Antoniano; at the end of the discussion they disappear into the house of Pontano. *Asinus* is set in motion by the peace that Pontano was able to negotiate in August 1486 between Ferrante and Innocent VIII, or rather by the toll of the effort on the weary negotiator. Mentally and physically exhausted, Pontano takes a holiday from serious matters and even from rationality at his villa, where he makes a pet of an ungrateful ass, discourses on country matters, and worries his friends (the other interlocutors). In *Actius*, as in *Antonius*, the starting point is also a death, that of the devout Neapolitan abbot Ferrando Gennaro at an unspecified date between 1484 and February 1495.[15] Sannazaro's affectionate memories of Ferrando and his relation of a dream in which the dead Ferrando appeared to him and spoke of the afterlife set off a wide-ranging conversation about religion, poetry, and history. But Ferrando soon disappears from the discus-

sion; he is the trigger that puts the dialogue in motion, not one of its central subjects. The dialogue has another real event as its background, for it is set in the dark days after the first French invasion of Italy. The extremely technical discourses on poetic style and the art of writing history that dominate the work are not escapist, but rather an effort by the interlocutors to come to grips with the truth and art of language, which they see as basic to all understanding. Pontano's last dialogue, *Aegidius*, has its starting point in the recent death and departure of several important members of the sodality. Pontano's old friends Pietro Golino (Compater) and Gabriele Altilio died in 1501, and Jacopo Sannazaro went into exile in the same year; Elisio Calenzio died in 1502.[16] The losses prompt a discussion that ranges over several topics, including immortality of the soul, poetic truth, hopes for a Christian philosophy, and a sermon by Egidio da Viterbo.

Important as it is, however, the precipitating event is not the subject of a dialogue. It motivates the discussion, but it is not what the discussion is about. The dialogues have no single subject or issue to debate. Rather, they are staged as free-flowing conversations taking place in the context of a particular historical situation. Except for the mythological *Charon*, the dialogues are presented as idealized portrayals of the Neapolitan sodality, showing its members as they move naturally from topic to topic in their usual courteous and leisurely exchanges. The spontaneity of the discussion, of course, is only a fiction, and one that Pontano does not always take much trouble to maintain, for often an interlocutor will hold forth for many pages, presenting not a comment but almost a treatise on his theme. These long disquisitions, so unnatural in real conversation, are found particularly in the dialogues treated most like actual gatherings of the sodality (*Antonius, Actius,* and *Aegidius*) and may reflect its actual practice. Since each member had not only the opportunity but the obligation to speak at a

gathering, those in attendance no doubt prepared some—perhaps all—of their discourses in advance.

The settings of the dialogues vary, but all take place out of doors: on the Styx and its banks in *Charon*, at the Portico Antoniano in *Antonius*, in the countryside and streets of Naples in *Actius*, in an inn near Naples and at Pontano's villa in *Asinus*, and in the courtyard of his house on Via dei Tribunali in *Aegidius*. The open-air settings give a certain movement and internal energy to the dialogues, allowing both sudden arrivals of new interlocutors and chance encounters with characters outside the group. Sometimes the strangers are fellow humanists who participate as interlocutors, like the Sicilian traveler in *Antonius* who has come to see the Portico Antoniano, or Suardo and Peto in *Aegidius* who have traveled from Rome to visit Pontano.[17] The true outsiders, however, are figures who have no part in the humanist world and do not share its interests or preoccupations. These outside characters, whether serious or comic, add variety and interest, but their encounters with the interlocutors can also provide new topics and direction to the discussion.

Interaction with outsiders is essential to the structure of *Charon*, *Antonius*, and *Asinus*. In *Charon* the outsiders are souls of the dead, some long dead, like Diogenes and Crates who swim eternally in the Styx, some recently arrived with news of the contemporary world and its follies. As he encounters these souls, Charon, the principal interlocutor, comes closer to understanding the meaning of *sapientia* (wisdom). In *Antonius* the interlocutors accost and interrogate a parade of passersby. In the first part of the dialogue the outsiders are types, whose folly is exposed and held up to ironic criticism; but as the work progresses, the outsiders are presented as individuals, and their interaction with the interlocutors becomes a real exchange. *Asinus* features two sets of outsiders—the first a group of characters around an inn, commenting on

the recent peace, and the second Pontano's gardener and a young servant. Both sets are essential: the group at the inn to show the good results of Pontano's exhausting efforts (the benefits of peace include an expected uptick in the landlord's trade in drink and tarts), that at Pontano's villa to witness his doting attentions to the ungrateful ass.

In *Actius* and *Aegidius*, however, encounters with outsiders are more restricted and the setting itself becomes less open, as if mirroring an increasing separation of the sodality and its discussions from the everyday world.[18] In *Actius* the outsiders, a group of ignorant rustics, appear only briefly at the beginning of the dialogue; they have a short exchange with the ironic and disdainful interlocutors and are not heard of again. The setting is not clearly specified. The encounter with the rustics seems to take place in the countryside; the interlocutors leave them behind, begin their discussion, and then, apparently having moved into the city, sit down under a portico to continue it. One of the speakers suggests that they challenge passersby to discussion, but the suggestion is empty: no one comes by, and the interlocutors continue to address only each other. In *Aegidius* there are no true outsiders at all, and the setting is only nominally out of doors. The discussion takes place in an enclosed and private space, the courtyard of Pontano's house, protected from chance encounters with anyone not part of the group.

Conversations in the dialogues shift from topic to topic, but the interlocutors come back again and again to certain themes, presenting them from different points of view and with different emphasis, like musical variations played in different keys and at different volumes. Among the most prominent recurrent themes are religion, poetry, and language — each large enough to subsume diverse and sometimes antithetical subtopics, and each of lifelong interest to Pontano.

Religion is important throughout the dialogues, but its treatment changes over time. In *Charon, Antonius,* and *Asinus* the tone is satirical and the talk is less of religion itself than of its disreputable associates, superstition and clerical misconduct; but the interlocutors of *Actius* and *Aegidius* move into a less ironic mode, treating religion primarily in its positive aspects and examining serious theological questions.

In *Charon* superstition exists in a symbiotic relationship with clerical misconduct. Mercury makes the connection in an exchange with Charon (36–37):

> *Mercury.* If you want to learn the truth, no worse evil has befallen men than superstition. . . . The gods are more troubled by superstition than they are gratified by true religious awe. Judge from this how detestable superstition is: as if we were being fattened up with blood and gore, man slaughters man for us, and even sheds his own blood.
>
> *Charon.* What an unspeakable crime! Tell me, how can it be that even priests and pontiffs do not oppose this wickedness? . . .
>
> *Mercury.* No men are less concerned about true religion, since their aim is to increase their property, pile up money and keep busy fattening up their bodies. . . .
>
> *Charon.* If only I lacked ears to hear these things! Do other mortals allow so great a crime to go unpunished?
>
> *Mercury.* They are held back by superstition.

Examples of superstition are listed and satirized: praying to religious pictures for the recovery of a sick chicken, hanging images of ailing body parts as votives in churches, committing nonsense on saints' days, like being drunk or chasing a greased pig (*Charon* 38–39). The greatest ferocity, however, is reserved for wicked clergy.

Almost the first sinners we see in the dialogue are a cardinal and a patriarch whom Mercury characterizes as "the most depraved priests in the world" (16). The unspecified war that sets off the discussion is caused by priests through the "desire to increase their kingdom" (45). The crowd of shades that Charon loads on his boat at the end includes a cardinal priest and his mistress, a thievish monk, and a bishop who diverted the wealth of his church into his belly (54–55). The list culminates with the worst clerical sinner of all, a still living parish priest whose story demonstrates the unholy union of superstition and clerical wickedness. The priest's crime is told by the shade of his victim, a naive young girl whose ignorant piety he had used to deceive her when he raped her in church in a feigned religious ceremony (56–57). She subsequently died in childbirth; the priest, however, did give her absolution, apparently his only legitimately religious action in the episode.

In *Antonius,* religion, less prominent than in *Charon,* is still treated by satirizing superstition and clerical misconduct. But the satire is lighter and more varied. The vices are shown as similar to other examples of human folly—deplorable enough, to be sure, but not significantly worse than the rest. Their treatment depends on the personality of the interlocutor reacting to them. At the beginning of the dialogue, Compater, modeling himself on Antonio, reacts with ironic amusement to a case of superstitious delusion, a man hurrying to warn the king that the population of Naples faces imminent destruction from a plague of basilisk serpents (*Antonius* 7). He dismisses him with sarcastic courtesy ("Depart, excellent citizen; you have served your country well"), characterizes his delusion as both ridiculous and pitiful, and—still playing the part of Antonio—tells another story to illustrate the extent of human foolishness. An example of clerical misconduct a few pages later gets a very different reaction from Enrico Poderico (Herricus Pudericus). Enrico, a generation older than Compater, is shown from

his first appearance to be both highly critical of the present and nostalgic for what he sees as a nobler and better past. When he meets a young man on his way to fetch a prostitute for his randy bishop, his reaction is predictable:

> What an age we live in! What morals! Once, once, continence and chastity existed in Christian priests, while innocence was honored and poverty esteemed. Now—for shame!—what sewer is not cleaner than the priesthood? (*Antonius* 14)

Still different in tone is the treatment of a story illustrating the mutual reinforcement of superstition and clerical wickedness told near the end of the work. The speaker this time is the cheerful and irreverent raconteur Suppazio, a latecomer to the discussion, just arrived from his travels through Italy looking for wise men. (The search, of course, was in vain.) He tells of meeting a widow who supported herself by selling charms to gullible women but faced severe competition from the local monks horning in on her business (*Antonius* 91). As if that were not bad enough, she complained, the monks were guilty of sexual misconduct. They visited the fishermen's wives at night when their husbands were at sea, and one even seduced a girl's good-looking fiancé, put a cowl on him, and brought him into his cell. But the story ends with a twist. When Suppazio warns the widow that offending the monks could be dangerous, she quickly reassures him. "Please stop worrying," she says. "From girlhood I have been on intimate terms with the warden of the monastery, and, unless I'm mistaken, he is the man you see coming this way." Suppazio's breezy and ironic tale is far different from the tragedy of the girl and the priest in *Charon*. Everyone in it seems equally unchaste and venal, and outrage is far away—that is, until the next paragraph, when Suppazio sees the poor fishermen piously saving their best fish for the good monks as an offering to God (92).

In *Asinus* religion appears briefly in a satirical reference to a notorious example of clerical misconduct. A group of pious Irish pilgrims on their way to Jerusalem has just had a shock. Unable to believe it possible that the pope at Rome had children, they found him seated on a golden throne presiding over his son's wedding, while his daughter led the dances.[19]

In *Actius* and *Aegidius*, however, religion is important and serious. In *Actius* Sannazaro's first speech begins on the usual anticlerical note. "Don't you know," he says, "that only the priests as agents of the gods have the right to put heaven up for sale, and that they alone are permitted to deal with the inmost parts of the earth, since it is in their power to consign anyone they like to the lower regions?"[20] Like Enrico in *Antonius*, Sannazaro goes on to contrast the disgraceful present with a simpler and better past. Unlike Enrico, however, he uses the contrast to lead into a serious theological discussion. He returns to religion at the end of the dialogue in his praise of poetry as a means of glorifying God and conveying His truth to mankind. In *Aegidius* religion is central; in this final dialogue Pontano's interests have moved far beyond satirizing superstition and malfeasant clerics to real religious devotion and the importance of theological and philosophical understanding.

Pontano was both a practicing poet and a sophisticated student of classical poetry. He incorporates his own poetry into each of the dialogues: songs of the blessed and condemned shades in *Charon*, ten poems in various genres and meters in *Antonius*, a short hymn to peace in *Asinus*, snippets from his didactic epics *Urania* and *Meteororum liber* in *Actius*, and a hymn to Fra Mariano in *Aegidius*. But he also quotes other poets—particularly Vergil in *Antonius* and *Actius* and Sannazaro in *Aegidius*. Poetry is most important, however, in *Antonius* and *Actius*. In *Antonius* Pontano mingles prose and verse in a kind of Menippean satire. Scenes at the beginning

and end of the dialogue are punctuated with Pontano's poems; the work concludes with an epic of over six hundred verses that functions as an epilogue. The scenes heavy with Pontano's poetry frame a long section whose centerpiece is a detailed discussion and defense of several passages from the *Aeneid* that had been criticized by ancient scholars. *Actius* also includes both Pontano's poetry and a discussion of Vergil, but in a different way and in different proportions. *Antonius* quotes whole poems of Pontano, ascribes them to several speakers, and places them at a distance from the discussion of Vergil, but in *Actius* only a few bits of Pontano's poetry are quoted, and by a single speaker, Sannazaro, who uses them, along with lines from various ancient poets, to illustrate points about Vergilian metrics and poetic style. In both dialogues, however, the presence of Pontano's poetry along with Vergil's implicitly puts the ancient and modern poet on the same plane—presenting Pontano not as a rival but as a worthy descendant of Vergil and other poets of antiquity. Pontano always aspired to a place in the Latin poetic tradition, and hints of his ambition are not unique to the dialogues. He made the claim openly in his poetry, and he began to do so very early in his poetic career. In a poem from *Parthenopeus* (ca. 1457–58), for example, he explicitly presents himself as a successor to Catullus:

> Surely you won't have seen anyone naughtier since Catullus, or more wanton—to say nothing of more elegant? But certainly this book of mine is second to its learned Catullus alone, and Calvus and the ancient discipline. It is not much less than the modern poets. It dances, singing in tiny verses a strain that the Muses' lyres and the girls of Bacchus have not sounded for a thousand years.)[21]

Pontano made his living with words—as a scribe in Alfonso's chancellery, as a secretary to the Duke of Calabria and Ippolita

Sforza, and finally as a diplomat and prime minister. But words were his passion as well as his livelihood, for he was both a textual and a literary critic of ancient authors, a student of Latin usage, and a prolific author in both prose and verse. Language, broadly conceived and in all its aspects, was the basis of his interests and activities; and the Latin language above all was at the heart of his intellectual and literary life. In every dialogue except the comic *Asinus* he gives it his urgent attention. His interlocutors care about what words mean, how they functioned in ancient usage, and how they are put together in prose and verse to achieve their rhetorical and artistic effects. To the modern reader their discourse sometimes seems too long, too technical, and too polemical, but we must remember the nature of the humanist enterprise. The humanists wanted not merely to read the ancient Latin authors, but to have the knowledge to understand their every nuance and to bring that understanding into the expression of ideas in their own fifteenth-century world. They wanted, paradoxically and impossibly, to turn themselves into native speakers of a dead language. The task was particularly urgent for someone like Pontano, who made Latin the sole medium for his entire literary production. For him and his like-minded interlocutors, the tiny details of style and usage that sometimes dominate the discussion are not trivia or technicalities, but the fundamental components of communication — the nuts and bolts of meaning, we might say — and their precise and correct use was essential to thought as well as understanding. But correctness for its own sake is not everything. Pontano was a master of Latin, but a modern master. Unlike many of his contemporaries, he treated the language not as a fossil to be preserved in the amber of pious Ciceronianism but as a medium of contemporary expression allowing — and benefiting from — the addition of neologisms and coinages, as well as occasional influence from Italian.[22]

Language, then, is a central, if not *the* central preoccupation of most of the dialogues, primarily because it is a central preoccupa-

tion of Pontano himself. But it is also a fundamental concern of dialogues in general, as Virginia Cox reminds us:

> The most fundamental distinguishing feature of the dialogue is a concern with communication, with the problem of what people do with language and what they do with knowledge. Every dialogue . . . shares the generic trait of self-consciously embodying a conception of the relation between language, social practice and cognition.[23]

Pontano comes at this major theme in different ways. In *Charon* the interest is primarily in words themselves, with interlocutors and outsiders alike defining, punning, pouncing on solecisms, and playing with etymologies. The tone ranges from philosophical seriousness to irony to slapstick, sometimes leaving the reader hard put to decide which is which. Since the diverse population of Hades includes a gaggle of ignorant grammarians, satire is sometimes also in play, provoked by their lofty pretensions and penchant for quarreling. As modern scholars have observed, some of this satire of pedants is directed at contemporary humanist targets.[24] Ignorant pedantry is also attacked in *Antonius*. The interlocutors deride contemporary ignoramuses — heaping scorn on foolish show-offs pretending to a knowledge of Greek, satirizing ignorant grammarians who start fights over trifles, and impugning the understanding of modern critics who would argue that Quintilian is superior to Cicero. But they also attack ancient authorities whom they consider deficient in judgment and taste for their criticism of Vergil. All of these targets, both modern and ancient, lack real understanding of language and are simply too ignorant to know it. As in *Charon*, they are sometimes proxies for contemporary humanist opponents.[25] But the real concern with language in *Antonius* is not solely, or even predominantly, polemical. Pontano's primary interest is literary and philological — that is, he wants to demonstrate the workings of language, not in the abstract, but in relation to

particular classical texts: Cicero, Quintilian, and, above all, Vergil. In the last case, of course, the themes of language and poetry intersect, as they inevitably must when a philologist poet discourses on a poetic text. We see the same overlapping or intersection of themes in *Actius* when Sannazaro presents his technical discussion of the ways in which diction and rhythm in poetry produce their artistic effects. Only a poet who was also a philologist would (or could) present such a demonstration. *Aegidius* shares some of the linguistic interests of the other dialogues (correct diction and usage, the relation of language and poetry), but it moves into a larger and more exalted conception. The focus now is on the sacred power of language as the highest medium of both God and man. On the one hand there is the word of God in creation ("in the beginning was the Word") and His promise of salvation to mankind through the word of Gabriel to Mary.[26] On the other, there is the need expressed throughout the dialogue for Pontano and his friends to cultivate Christian eloquence in the service of philosophy and theology.

The dialogues were composed and revised over a long period that saw great changes in Naples, in humanism, and in Pontano himself. Pontano wrote *Charon* as a relatively young man, *Aegidius* in his old age, a generation later. From dialogue to dialogue his interlocutors come back to favorite themes, but the direction, tone, and emphasis of their discussion shift as Pontano's own perspective alters. The mood and focus of the dialogues changed over time, and it could hardly be otherwise. But within each dialogue there is also great variety, especially variety of subject. The interlocutors do not discuss one or two topics from several points of view and come to a resolution. Rather, they move — sometimes it feels that they jump — from one topic to another, bringing up several sides of several issues, and leaving the reader to decide what their conversation has accomplished. There is no simple, single result: it is much easier to summarize any one of the dialogues

than to say succinctly what it is about. But *variatio* is not the same thing as chaos. Pontano can keep several ideas going at once; coherent threads run through the discussions, intelligible as separate strands, but also intersecting with each other to develop complex and subtle arguments.

NOTES

1. For Pontano's life see Monti Sabia, "Giovanni Gioviano Pontano," 307–14; eadem, *Un profilo moderno*, 1–27; Kidwell, *Pontano*. (Full references may be found in the Bibliography.)

2. For Panormita see Resta, "Beccadelli, Antonio"; Ryder, "Antonio Beccadelli." Panormita's *Hermaphroditus* has been translated by Holt Parker for the I Tatti Renaissance Library: Antonio Beccadelli, *The Hermaphrodite*, ITRL 42 (Cambridge, MA, 2010).

3. For a succinct account of Pontano's political career, see Bentley, *Politics and Culture*, 127–41.

4. The Florentine historian Francesco Guicciardini, writing forty years after the event, famously charged Pontano with warmly welcoming the French and censuring the Aragonese dynasty (*Storia d'Italia* 1.3). Modern scholars reject his assertion; see Bentley, *Politics and Culture*, 130; Monti Sabia, *Un profilo moderno*, 22–23; Kidwell, *Pontano*, 1–14.

5. Stella is the principal subject of *Eridanus*, but she also appears in *Hendecasyllabi* 1.28, *Urania* 4.157–63, 5.293–98, and *Tumuli* 1.43.

6. Among the poems mourning Adriana are *Eclogue* 2, *Lyra* 9, *Tumuli* 2.24, 25, 60, 61, *Eridanus* 2.1 and 32 (which also mourns his son Lucio). Pontano's chapel ("tempietto") is illustrated in Kidwell, *Pontano*, 216. For bibliography see Monti Sabia, *Un profilo moderno*, 16; see also Luigi Fusco, "La Capella Pontano. Storia di una fabbrica e della sua decorazione," in *Atti della giornata di studi per il V centenario della morte di Giovanni Pontano*, ed. Antonio Garzya, Quaderni dell'Accademia Pontaniana 39 (Naples, 2004): 65–72.

7. Gaisser, *Catullus*, 220–33, 242–47. See also the essays in Thomas Baier, ed., *Pontano und Catull* (Tübingen, 2003). Rodney Dennis has

translated the *Baiae* for the I Tatti Renaissance Library: ITRL 22 (Cambridge, MA, 2006).

8. For the names and meeting places of the humanist gatherings, see Furstenberg-Levi, "Fifteenth Century Accademia Pontaniana," 40–41; Hankins, "Humanist Academies," 36.

9. For the Villa Antiniana see Kidwell, *Pontano*, 50, 104–7.

10. For the activities of Pontano's sodality, see Furstenberg-Levi, "Fifteenth Century Accademia Pontaniana," 44–50.

11. Monti, "Ricerche sulla cronologia."

12. Marsh, *Quattrocento Dialogue*, 101.

13. Monti, "Ricerche sulla cronologia."

14. Ibid., 270–72.

15. Ibid., 288–89.

16. For the dates, see ibid., 291–96. Compater is an interlocutor in *Antonius* and *Actius*, Altilio and Sannazaro in *Actius* and *Asinus*, and Calenzio in *Antonius*.

17. The strangers in both dialogues are present throughout. The Sicilian traveler is unidentified. Giovanni Battista Suardo (called Suardino Suardo) and Francesco Peto were late arrivals in Pontano's sodality. *Aegidius* shows them as newcomers to Naples (Suardo was from Bergamo, Peto from Fundi), attending their first meeting of the group.

18. See Marsh, *Quattrocento Dialogue*, 100–101.

19. In January 1488, the son of Innocent VIII married a daughter of Lorenzo de' Medici. Monti, "Ricerche sulla cronologia," 299.

20. *Actius*, 130 (Previtera).

21. Pontano, *Amores* 1.28.4–14. See Gaisser, *Catullus*, 225. For poems in which Pontano presents himself as a successor to Tibullus and Propertius, see Gaisser, "Giovanni Gioviano Pontano and the *Triumviri Amoris*" (forthcoming).

22. On the influence of Italian see especially Mariotti, "Per lo studio dei *Dialoghi* del Pontano." Coinages and neologisms appear in both *Charon* and *Antonius*; see, e.g., *Charon*, nn. 9, 28, 30, 40; *Antonius* 16 and n. 25.

23. Cox, *Renaissance Dialogue,* 6.

24. The argument between the grammarians Theanus and Pedanus at *Charon* 51 parodies a dispute between Valla and Poggio. See Ferraù, *Pontano critico,* 13–14 n. 1.

25. The most obvious target is Valla, especially since the dialogue honors his old enemy Panormita. Valla famously claimed both a preference for Quintilian and some disdain for Vergil. See Ferraù, *Pontano critico,* 37–41. For a specific refutation of Valla's grammatical arguments, see *Antonius* 82 and n. 136.

26. *Aegidius,* 269 (Previtera).

DIALOGUES

CHARON

Minos, Aeacus interlocutores

1 *Min.* Qui magistratum, Aeace, gerunt, iis nunquam sine negocio ocium esse debet.

Aeac. Prudenter atque e re dictum a te est, Minos; nam et in ocio cogitare oportet de negocio et ubi liberior aliquanto factus est curis animus, quia tum longe maxime quid verum sit cernit, exercendus hic est, a sene praesertim, cui non ut ineunti aetati pila et trochulus, sed rerum optimarum cognitio atque scientia curae esse debeat.

Min. Scilicet non dies noctesque aut dormienti tibi aut potanti optatum illud a diis optigit, nati ut sint Myrmidones, sed animum colenti et prudenter ac pari iure moderanti populos.

Aeac. Sunt haec, Minos, ut dicis, quae diis immortalibus tribuere solebam, quorum erat muneris ut boni prudentesque haberemur. Eorum ergo benivolentiam non thure et extis magis quam recte agendo, prudenter consulendo, iuste imperando conciliare studebam mihi.

2 *Min.* Deorum profecto, deorum est, ut dicis, ista benignitas; quos non hedorum sanguis aut frugum primitiae placatos faciunt, sed innocentia, veritas, castitas, fides, continentia, quae sunt illorum munera; quibus qui utantur, iis consilia ipsi sua aperiunt seque inspiciendos praebent; quin, quod deorum est proprium, non abstinentes modo et moderatos quos noverint in coelum ad se, ut scimus, evocant, verum incontinentius qui vixerunt, dum poeniteat, dum in viam redeant, in eos quoque clementes sunt atque benefici. Etenim deus ille optimus maximus non tam

CHARON

Minos and Aeacus, interlocutors

Minos. Those who hold office, Aeacus, should never be idle in their free time. 1

Aeacus. What you say is sensible and timely, Minos, for even in spare time one ought to think about the business of the state,[1] and when the mind has been released somewhat from cares, it should be kept active, because then it has by far the clearest perception of the truth. This is especially the case for an old man, who should be interested, not in a ball and a hoop as in his boyhood, but in the study and knowledge of the best things.[2]

Minos. Clearly you were not sleeping or carousing night and day when the gods granted your wish for the birth of the Myrmidons, but cultivating your mind and governing the peoples with foresight and equity.[3]

Aeacus. These are things, as you say, Minos, that I was in the habit of ascribing to the immortal gods, by whose gift I was considered foresighted and good. And so I strove to win their goodwill, not with incense and entrails, but by right action, good counsel, and just rule.

Minos. This benevolence of yours is from the gods, as you say— 2
surely from the gods, who are appeased not by the blood of kids or first fruits, but by the innocence, truth, chastity, loyalty, and continence that are their gifts. They reveal their counsel to those who employ these qualities, and allow themselves to be seen by them. In fact—for this is the special property of gods—as we know, they not only summon to themselves in heaven those they have found to be temperate and self controlled, but they are also merciful and kind to those who have lived with

peccata ulciscitur quam miseratur et parcit. Amat hominum genus; et dum aut pestem illis aut tempestates immissurus est, in iram eorum sceleribus provocatus, nunc monstris praemonet, nunc per ostenta declarat, et cum maxime iratus est, per crinitas stellas, ut procurationem adhibeant, qua placatus ipse sententiam mutet. Et certe maximas fore in terris discordias et calamitates auguror. Meministi enim ut excussa est nuper terra, ut movit ab imis usque sedibus et quam saepe! Pessima quaedam videntur portendi mortalibus et animus scire avet. Quamobrem, si videtur (ferias enim agimus et collega Rhadamanthus hodierno satis est muneri), concedamus ad ripam et sub amoena cupressorum umbra consideamus tantisper, dum e terris aliquis ad nos eat; ad quod vel invitare laenis aquarum decursus potest, vel, quod nostra scire interest quid agant homines, ut ad illorum actiones iudicia comparemus.

Aeac. Recte, Minos, et commode; nam et mens ipsa praesagit triste nescio quid ac periculosum imminere mortalibus, et ipse meministi, nuper dum in sacerdotes illos sententiam diceres, queri eos et aegre ferre laborare Italiam seditionibus magnosque in ea legi exercitus. Quamobrem in pratum hoc descendamus, si placet.

Min. Descendamus, et, si tibi videtur, Charontem ad nos vocemus; nam et ipse ociosus est.

Aeac. Et ocium agit et oratio eius erudita et gravis est.

less restraint—provided that they repent, provided that they return to the path. For the best, greatest god does not so much punish sins as pity and forgive them. He loves the race of men; even when he has been provoked to wrath by their crimes and is about to send a pestilence or tempests against them, sometimes he gives advance warning with prodigies, sometimes he declares himself through signs, and when he is most wrathful, through comets, so that they might have recourse to expiatory sacrifice in order that he might be placated and change his mind. And I confidently predict that there will be great discord and calamity on earth. Indeed, you remember how the earth was shaken recently, how it was rocked, over and over again, from its deepest foundations![4] Great evils of some kind are apparently portended for mortals, and the mind is anxious and wary. Therefore, if you agree (for we are on holiday and our colleague Rhadamanthus can manage today's duty), let us withdraw to the river bank and sit for a while under the pleasant shade of the cypresses until someone comes to us from earth.[5] Either the gentle course of the stream can entice us or the fact that it is important for us to know what people are doing, so that we can prepare judgments for their actions.

Aeacus. An excellent and suitable idea, Minos; for I have a premonition that some dreadful danger is threatening mortals, and you yourself recall that when you were pronouncing sentence against those priests the other day, they complained in distress that Italy was afflicted with political unrest and that great armies were being called up there. Therefore, let us go down into this meadow, if you like.

Minos. Let us go down, and if you agree, let us invite Charon to join us. For he is at leisure, too.

Aeacus. So he is, and his speech is well informed and thoughtful.

Charon, Minos, Aeacus

3 *Char.* Equidem vel ex hoc conditionem hominum infelicem iudico, quod sperato omnes victitant; quid enim eorum est spe inanius?

Min. Quaenam sunt ista, Charon?

Char. Cuia ea est oratio? Quos ego procul video? O aequissimi animarum iudices, salvete multum, et, per Stygem, unde vobis tantum est ocii a foro ac iudiciis?

Min. Eadem nostri huius ocii causa est quae et tui. Scis enim quam hoc triduum nihil ad nos animarum traieceris.

Char. Istud ipsum mecum admirabar atque adeo indignabar, ita spe deceptum me mea, ut in Plutonis aerarium ne collybum quidem triduo hoc toto contulerim. Itaque quae vita esse potest mortalibus inter tot ac tam varias necessitudines, quos spes tam assidue frustretur ac ludat? Eorumque vel maximum[1] hunc errorem esse duco, quod inter deas spem numerant, quae humanae fortunae ancilla est, varia, inconstans, fallax pellacissimaque et bonorum et malorum omnium. Quod modo tyrannus declaravit, qui, dum regnum animo concipit, spe sua lusus, vix tandem ad ripam huc pervenit, nudus, plorabundus, claudus, senili gressu, fallentibus vestigiis, ex tot tantisque male partis divitiis vix annulum secum ferens.

4 *Aeac.* Doctiorem te factum, portitor, gaudemus; et, per Herebum, egregie philosopharis!

Char. Quid ni philosopher, qui tot annos doctissimos homines, qui trans ripam inhumati errant, disserentes audiam? Eorum ego disputationibus mirifice delector, et, ubi vacat, etiam audi-

Charon, Minos, Aeacus

Charon. For my part, I consider the human condition unhappy if 3
only from this—that they all live on hope. For what is more futile than their hope?

Minos. What are you talking about, Charon?

Charon. Whose speech is this? Whom do I see in the distance? Best greetings, O most just judges of souls! And—by the Styx!—how did you get so much time off from the court and its judgments?

Minos. For the same reason you yourself are at leisure. You know you haven't ferried a single soul to us for the last three days.

Charon. I've been wondering about this very thing myself, and in fact I've been complaining in my disappointment that I haven't brought so much as a penny of commission into Pluto's treasury this whole three days. Well anyway, what kind of life can mortals have among so many and such manifold constraints, since hope so constantly frustrates and deludes them? I consider this to be their absolutely greatest error, that they count hope among the goddesses—Hope, that handmaid of human fortune, changeable, inconstant, deceptive, and the greatest seductress of everyone, good and wicked alike! A tyrant just now proved my point: he aspired to a kingdom but was deluded of his hope and at last barely made it here to the shore, naked, weeping, limping, walking like an old man with doddering footsteps, and bringing with him hardly even a ring from so many ill-gotten riches.

Aeacus. We rejoice, ferryman, that you have grown wise. By Ere- 4
bus! You philosophize admirably.

Charon. Why shouldn't I philosophize, since for so many years I have heard the discussions of the most learned men as they wander unburied on the other bank? I am delighted by their disputations, and when I have time, I even become a pupil and

tor fio magnamque ex eorum dictis voluptatem huberemque fructum capio. Quosdam tamen ut ridiculos aegre fero et stomachor; sunt enim partim nimis captiosi et fallaces, partim inanes et lubrici; qualis Parisius sophistes, qui nuper congressus est mecum, et, per Plutonem, quam audacissime, 'Morieris, Charon!' vociferabatur. Ego me, qui de mortalium non essem numero, moriturum negabam; at ille: 'Morieris!' inclamabat. 'Quinam hoc fiet?' inquam. Tum ille distortis superciliis: 'Charo, inquit, es, omnis autem charo[2] morti est obnoxia, morieris igitur; et cum diutius vixeris, brevi morieris.' Tum ego, ut qui eius amentiam non ferrem, vix continui quin eum in fluvium deturbarim. Quid alter? quam pene risu me confecit! 'Remus, inquit, Romuli frater fuit; plures istic remos habes, plures ergo fratres tecum sunt Romuli.' Hoc audito, Aeace, ita sum risu commotus, ut dirumpi timuerim. Sed et tertius, cum me solventem videret: 'Audi, inquit, Charon, et disce.' 'Recte, inquam, hospes, admones, nunquam enim satis quisquam didicit.' 'Disce, inquit ille, novum est hoc: Palus, inquam, est quam navigas; palus autem lignum est; lignum ergo, non aquam navigas.' Vix hic finierat, cum quartus quoque aegre ferens priorem illum argumentatum, 'Et me, inquit, audi: Tribus, portitor, manibus, uteris; etenim palma manus cum sit et tribus ipse palmis remiges, tribus profecto manibus uteris.'

5 Atque ferenda haec fortasse videantur in pueris, dum ingenium acuunt. Senes vero tam insigniter delirantes, et eos praesertim qui de natura ac deo disserunt, quis ferat? Nuper superstitiosulus quidam, cum ex eo quaererem nunquid e terris novi afferret, plures qui diem obierant revixisse; quocirca scire e vobis vehementer cupio, qui animarum omnium tenetis nume-

take great pleasure and rich profit from their words. Yet I become annoyed and disgusted at some of the ridiculous ones; some are too captious and tricky, others empty-headed and slick—like the Parisian sophist who recently came up to me, and—by Pluto!—shouted in the boldest possible way, "You will die, Charon!" I said that I would not die because I did not belong to the number of mortals, but he cried, "You will die!" "How can this be?" says I. Then he furrows his brow and says, "You are Charo; all flesh [*caro*] is subject to death; therefore, you will die.[6] And since you have lived a long time, you will die soon." At that point I could scarcely keep from throwing him into the river, so unbearable was his lunacy. As for the second one—he almost finished me off with laughter! "Remus," says he, "was the brother of Romulus; you have several oars [*remos*] over there; therefore, you have with you several of Romulus' brothers." When I heard this one, Aeacus, I was so convulsed with laughter that I was afraid I'd burst. But when the third one saw me casting off, he said, "Listen, Charon, and learn." "Good advice, friend," says I, "for no one has ever learned enough. "Learn this, then," he says, "It's a new one. What you're sailing on, I say, is the Styx, but sticks are wood; therefore you are sailing on wood, not water."[7] This one had scarcely finished when also a fourth, annoyed at the previous disputant, said, "Hear me, too. You employ three hands, ferryman. For since an oar blade is called a *palma* ("hand") and you row with three palms [*palmis*], you're definitely using three hands."[8]

Perhaps such stuff might seem bearable in boys when they 5
are sharpening their wits. But who would put up with old men raving so outlandishly, especially ones discoursing on nature and god? Recently one superstitious fellow,[9] when I asked him if he brought any news from earth, claimed that many of the dead had come back to life. So I'm anxious to know from the two of you, who keep track of all souls, whether some of them

rum, an earum aliquae aut ipsae aufugerint aut furto subreptae vobis fuerint; ego certe scio neminem unam retro a me revectam.

Aeac. Et priora illa, Charon, omnino contemnenda non sunt, pertinent enim ad quaerendam veritatem, et posteriora haec nequaquam improbanda, quippe cum relligionem augeant. Quaedam etiam suapte natura nobis sunt incognita.

6 *Char.* Sint ista ut dicis, quando nihil ad nos attinent; quamobrem missa nunc faciamus. Sed quod nunc mihi in mentem venit et admirari nunquam ipse satis possum. Si per leges vestras licet nosse, id ex te velim: cur postquam de tyranni capite sententiam tulistis, non inter sontes eum et scelerosos, verum trans ripam illam, ubi solus agit, relegastis?

Aeac. Honestum sane est scire quod postulas; aequius tamen erit id te ex Minoe quaerere, cuius illud fuit iudicium.

Char. Nimirum, ut alia Minois omnia, sic et hoc est cognitu dignissimum. Quamobrem, optime Minos, ut cuius iudicium admiramur, eius quoque teneamus consilium, ne gravere palam illud nobis facere.

Min. Et facile est docere quod postulas et ego libenter hoc fecero; pertinet enim ad sapientiam, cuius te studiosum esse factum magnopere laetor ac laudo. Quamobrem, ut consilium illud de relegando tyranno iuxta mecum teneas, sic habeto: praeterquam quod varius, perfidus, immanis, et supra quam dici possit rapax fuerit, seditiosissimus omnium mortalium et fuit et ipse confessus est, nullis adhibitis tormentis. Itaque dies noctesque nihil unquam aut cogitavit aliud aut egit quam quomodo lites serere, tumultus excitare, bella movere aut augere mota posset, pacis ac quietis inimicus. Eum ego, cui aliena documento essent peri-

have either escaped by themselves or been spirited away from you on the sly. I'm sure that not a one has been ferried back by me.

Aeacus. The former type of discourse, Charon, should not be completely despised, for it pertains to the search for truth, while the latter is by no means to be condemned, since it increases religious awe.[10] There are even some things that by their very nature are unknown to us.

Charon. Whatever you say—such matters don't concern me, so 6
let's put them aside for now. But something now comes to mind that always astonishes me. If your laws allow one to know, I'd like you to tell me this: after you passed a capital sentence on the tyrant, why didn't you place him among the guilty and criminal, but instead banish him to the opposite shore, to spend his time in solitude?

Aeacus. It is certainly proper to answer your question, but it will be more appropriate for you to ask Minos, whose verdict it was.

Charon. Of course, like everything else to do with Minos, this too is very much worth knowing. Therefore, excellent Minos, so that we too might understand the purpose of the one whose judgment we admire, don't refuse to reveal it to us.

Minos. It is easy to answer your question and I will be glad to do so, since it pertains to wisdom, of which you have become a student. (I'm delighted and praise you for it.) To understand my reasoning in relegating the tyrant, think of it this way. Besides being untrustworthy, treacherous, brutal, and unspeakably rapacious, he was both the most seditious of all mortals and admitted it himself, without even being tortured. And so, day and night, all he thought about, everything he did, was aimed at sowing strife in any way he could, stirring up disorder, starting wars, or expanding those already started—a foe of peace and tranquility. I was instructed by the dangers incurred by

cula, ne inter Manes seditionem aliquando faceret, e republica esse duxi eiectum, urbe nostra omnique quod Lethe cingitur solo trans ripam illam inter errantes umbras exterminare; quin et legem statuere placuit, ne cui adire illum neve inspectare liceret a centesimo lapide.

7 *Char.* Et iuste et prudenter factum, Minos; sed quid quod septimo quoque die in rubetam versus, ubi diem totum concrepuit, vesperi ab hydro depastus interit maneque in umbram reviviscit?

Min. Quod fecit patitur: vorare alios suetus, ipse nunc devoratur.

Char. Quam iure, quam merito! Atque utinam mortalibus nota supplicia haec essent! moderantiores illos sperarem fore minusque ambitiosos, nec tam alieni appetentes.

Min. An, obsecro, Pythagorae oblitus es? Et meminisse certe debes; venit enim ad nos torrida facie, ustilato capillo, adesis naribus. Nam dum inter mortales haec praedicat, dum suppliciorum eos horum ammonet, igne ab nefariis adolescentibus aedibus iniecto occiditur.

Char. O bone Pluton, quaenam haec est tanta ingratitudo atque immanitas? hoccine docendi atque instituendi praemium?

Min. Ingratissimum est genus hominum atque incontinentissimum. Omitto poetas, qui primi de inferis vera prodiderunt, quam nunc omnes contemnunt! Socratem veneno petierunt, virum sane optimum ac sapientissimum; et profecto quae in Christum egerint nosti. Nam et lateris et pedum eius vulnera attrectavimus, vix credentes tantum homines facinus admittere ausos.

Char. Et quidem ille veritatem docebat.

others. So, to keep him from ever stirring up rebellion among the dead, I decided to cast him out of the state and to banish him from our city and all the land bounded by Lethe, sending him to its far bank among the wandering shades. Why, I even decided to make it a law that no one was permitted to approach or look at him within a hundred miles.

Charon. Both justly and intelligently done, Minos. But what about 7
the fact that every seventh day he turns into a poisonous toad, and when he has croaked all day long, in the evening he dies, gobbled up by a hydra, and in the morning comes back to life as a shade?

Minos. He is getting a taste of his own medicine. He used to eat up others; now he himself is devoured.

Charon. How just! How well deserved! And if only these punishments were known to mortals! I would expect them to be more moderate and less ambitious, and not so greedy for other people's property.

Minos. But tell me, have you forgotten Pythagoras? You certainly ought to remember him, since he came to us with his face burned, his hair singed, his nostrils eaten away. For while he was preaching moderation and restraint to mortals, while he was warning them of these punishments, he was killed when wicked youths set fire to his house.[11]

Charon. O good Pluto, can any ingratitude and cruelty be as great as this? Is this the reward for teaching and instructing?

Minos. The race of men is most ungrateful and intemperate. I do not mention the poets, who were the first to record the truth about the underworld—now how everyone despises them! Men went after Socrates with poison, surely the best and wisest of men; and of course you know what they did to Christ. For we have felt the wounds of his side and feet, scarcely believing that human beings would dare commit such a terrible deed.

Charon. And yet he was teaching the truth.

Min. O Charon, Charon, ignorare videris veritatem semper odio fuisse mortalibus; eam ex hominum coetu eiectam atque in exilio agentem dum restituere Christus nititur, quae passus est nosti.

8 *Char.* Unde haec hominibus improbitas, Minos? Nam et homo ipse fuisti et diu Cretensibus imperasti, res eorum moderatus.

Min. Quam mox istud. Nunc illud inspice et considera, quod unum tibi cum primis eorum declarare possit improbitatem.

Char. Expecto quodnam hoc sit.

Min. Audi et detestare. Nam et ipsis nunc mortalibus detestabilissimum videri satis scio quod Christus ab iis hominibus quos docuisset, quibuscum tot annos innocentissime conflictatus esset, crudelissime occisus sit, a nobis vero et turbis his, quibus esset incognitus, ubi primum visus, statim cultusque et adoratus fuerit.

Char. Quod quidem facinus imprimis abominor et causam nunquam admirari satis possum.

9 *Min.* Admirari desinas si mentem ad philosophiam revocaveris; etenim oportet memorem esse philosophantem. Et profecto dies ille memorabilis apud Manes fuit quo vocatus est in iudicium Stagirites ille qui se Peripateticum agnominabat, quod de praeceptore suo partim perperam sensisset, partim ingratus in eum fuisset. Hunc itaque die dicta, cum rerum a se commentarum rationem redderet, quasi ab initio dictionis disserere ita memini: duplicem esse hominis naturam, alteram rationalem, alteram carentem ratione; atque hoc ipsum quod ratione careret, duplex esse dicebat, alterum prorsus semotum a ratione, alterum vero solere ad rationem sese adiungere eique obtemperare. Cupiditates igitur appetitionesque vehementes atque in-

Minos. O Charon, Charon! You seem to be unaware that mortals have always hated Truth; while Christ was trying to restore her after she had been cast out from human society and was living in exile, you know what he suffered.

Charon. How did men get to be so wicked, Minos? You yourself, 8 after all, used to be a man, and you ruled over the Cretans for a long time, governing their affairs.

Minos. I will tell you in a minute. For now, consider and reflect on this, a single point that can best demonstrate their wickedness to you.

Charon. I'm waiting to hear what it is.

Minos. Hear it and loathe it. Indeed, I am well aware that even to mortals themselves it seems utterly detestable that Christ was most cruelly slain by the very men he had taught and with whom he had disputed in complete innocence for so many years; while by us and by these crowds to whom he was unknown, he was instantly worshipped and adored at first sight.[12]

Charon. I loathe this crime above all and I can never wonder enough at the reason.

Minos. You would cease to wonder if you were to turn your mind 9 back to philosophy; indeed, a person practicing philosophy needs to have a good memory. And without a doubt it was a memorable day among the dead when that well known Stagirite who called himself a Peripatetic was called into judgment, partly for having a faulty understanding of his teacher, partly for being ungrateful to him.[13] Accordingly, I remember that on the appointed day, when he was justifying the things he had lied about, he spoke as follows, almost from the beginning of his speech. He said that the nature of man was twofold, the one nature rational, the other lacking reason, and that the element lacking reason itself was double, one part altogether removed from reason, but the other accustomed to join itself to reason and obey it. Accordingly, desires and appetites, violent and dis-

compositas, nullis adhibitis frenis, solere partem illam quae rationis esset audiens ita deiicere de statu suo, ut nullum ea ad medium illud retinendum adiumentum afferre posset: hinc ortum ducere vitia seditionesque cieri et bella, coeteraque oriri mortalium mala; hinc veritatem molestam illis esse, ob eamque causam nec audire nec pati eos velle qui iusta honestaque praecipiant. Hoc itaque plane in ignem Pythagoram coniecit, hoc Socratem veneno extinxit, hoc ipsum item Christum cruci affixit. Caeca igitur mortalitas suisque victa libidinibus atque in furorem acta quem occidit nosse nec potuit nec voluit, nec, siqui bene illum norant, tutari potuere, quippe qui admodum essent pauci: rara est enim omnis bonitas. At Manes, quod corporibus non impedirentur, cognoverunt illum, et, qui corporis contagione mundi atque expurgati omnino erant, secuti etiam sunt.

Char. Et quanta cum frequentia et plausu! A corpore igitur omnis illa malorum origo et causa quam ab animo?

Min. Origo quidem tota est a corpore, verum et animus accusandus est, qui vinci se, cum imperare debeat, sinit. Felicem te igitur, Charon, qui corporis vinculis solutus ac liber semper fuisti, nec te aut titillantes illae voluptates, corporum dominae, commoverunt unquam aut cupiditates egerunt praecipitem, quae in hominibus infinitae quidem sunt atque insatiabiles. Sed nos fortasse longiores sumus munerique isti tuo, quod vacationem vix ullam patitur, impedimentum dicendo attulimus.

Char. An quod esse potest molestum tempus quod philosophiae impenditur? Atque utinam succisiva haec tempora saepius darentur! Sed tamen quantum munus hoc meum, cui deesse minimum, ut scitis, possum, patitur, id omne ad philosophiam

ordered if unrestrained, were accustomed to cast down from its seat the part obedient to reason so that it could bring no assistance to hold on to the mean.[14] From this, vices take their origin, and rebellions and wars are fomented, and the rest of human evils arise; from this, Truth is made a vexation to them, and for this reason they are willing neither to hear nor to endure those who propound what is just and honorable. And so this is clearly what hurled Pythagoras into the fire, this what destroyed Socrates with poison, this very thing likewise that nailed Christ to the cross. The race of mortals, therefore, blind and overcome by its own lusts and driven to madness, was neither able nor willing to know the man it killed, and even if some did know him, they could not protect him, since they were very few; for all moral excellence is rare. But the dead, because they were not hindered by bodies, recognized him, and those who were pure and completely cleansed of the pollution of the body followed him.

10 *Charon.* And with how great a multitude, with how much applause! So the whole origin and cause of evil, then, is from the body rather than from the rational soul?

Minos. The whole origin indeed is from the body, but the rational soul that allows itself to be conquered when it ought to be giving the orders is also blameworthy. And so you are fortunate, Charon. You have always been unfettered and free from the chains of the body, nor have titillating pleasures, the mistresses of the body, ever aroused you, or desires driven you headlong, which are boundless and insatiable in men. But perhaps we are going on too long and our talk is hindering your duty, which hardly allows any rest.

Charon. Can time spent on philosophy possibly be irksome? If only free times like the present were granted more often! But nevertheless, as much time as my duty allows — which I cannot neglect, as you know — I devote entirely to philosophy. It is the

confero; ea laborum meorum solatrix est et comes, ea solum esse me non sinit, atque a multitudine, quae me assidue circumsistit, longius etiam segregat.

11 *Aeac.* Aciem intende, Minos; nam cum Charonte sermonem istum dum habes, sub occidentem ipsum quasi nubem quandam eamque perquam tenuem videre visus sum, quae, ni me oculus fallit, cogi paulatim incipit.

Char. Quanam e coeli regione?

Aeac. Ab occidente, paulum ab leva tamen.

Char. An tenuissimus quidam fulgor eam praecedit?

Aeac. Praecedit.

Min. Bene habet. Mercurii agnosco talaria; quamobrem, portitor, illuc in ulteriorem ripam cymbam adige. Nos hic potius Mercurium maneamus.

Minos, Aeacus

12 *Min.* En, Aeace, consideras quanta sit vis institutionis? Quem nunc philosophum videmus, qui principio remex erat! Quid ociosus ageret, quid si a primis annis audisset philosophos?

Aeac. Nec animo volenti quicquam potest esse difficile, nec aetas ad discendum tarda est ulla. Nam, quanquam adolescentiae flores magnam prae se ferunt speciem, omnis tamen fructus est ingravescentis aetatis.

Min. Verissimum hoc quidem. Sed tamen, nescio quomodo, quod nobis pueris contingebat, vehementior quidam instinctus adolescentes impellit ad virtutem et laudem: in senibus tarda ac remissa sunt omnia.

Aeac. Maior est in illis impetus, ratio imperfectior. In his autem, quia ratio perfecta, vita etiam perfectior est. Adolescentulorum quoque studium omne cum sit propter laudem, senum gratuita virtus est.

consolation for my labors and my companion; it does not allow me to be alone, and yet also keeps me at a distance from the multitude that constantly surrounds me.

Aeacus. Look, Minos! While you were talking with Charon, toward the west I thought I saw something like a very thin cloud, which, unless my eye deceives me, is beginning to solidify bit by bit. 11

Charon. From what direction?

Aeacus. From the west, but a little to the left.

Charon. Is a very faint glow preceding it?

Aeacus. Yes, it is.

Minos. Excellent. I recognize Mercury's winged sandals. Therefore, ferryman, row your skiff over there to the farther bank. We would rather wait for Mercury here.

Minos, Aeacus

Minos. There, Aeacus, do you notice how great is the power of instruction? What a philosopher we now see in the one who started out as a rower! What would he accomplish if he had the time or if he had heard philosophers from his first years? 12

Aeacus. Nothing can be difficult for a willing mind, nor is any age too late for learning. For although the flowers of youth make a big show, the fruit all belongs to advancing age.

Minos. That is very true. But still, somehow or other, because it touched us as boys, a certain more powerful enthusiasm drove us in youth to seek virtue and praise. In old men everything is dilatory and easygoing.

Aeacus. There is greater energy in the young, but their reason is more undeveloped. In the old, because the reason has been developed, their life is more developed, too. For the very young, too, all application is for the sake of praise, but the virtue of the old is for its own sake.

Min. Ita natura comparatum est, quae ab initio curam hominis ac rationem habens, uti e floribus fruges, sic ex adolescentulorum teneritate atque inscitia senum voluit provenire sapientiam. Meministi quod pueris nobis studium esset, dum, nisi inviti in ludum atque ad grammaticum non ibamus, animus omnis erat in nucibus. Delitiae nostrae catellus, coturnix, monedula. Ex his tamen initiis vide quos uterque progressus fecerimus. Nam et tunc ferocissimis gentibus bene vivendi leges tulimus et nunc deum voluntate animis praesumus iudicandis. Itaque cum aetate simul crescit sapientia; cuius puer studiosus esse non potest, in quo maturum nihil sit. Et cum aetas omnis ad sapientiam properet, longissime ab ea distat pueritia, quae, tenerrima cum sit, paulatim est assuefacienda.

Aeac. Prudentissima in hoc quoque artifex natura fuit et fabricam suam admirabili artificio composuit; nimis tamen arctos illi terminos statuisse visa est satisque brevem vitam dedisse homini, quem ad tam multa ac magna genuisset. Ipsi scimus quosdam, dum rerum nobis suarum rationem reddunt, quantopere admirati fuerimus, quibus ad perfectam sapientiam praeter tempus nihil aliud visum sit defuisse.

13 *Min.* Vide quae loquaris, Aeace, et altius rem intuere. Quaecunque natura fabricata est, intra certos terminos compescuit. Haberent cupressus hae quo cacumen extenderent, sed et his suus est crescendi modus; habent terrae, habent maria fines suos; hominum quoque, uti corporibus, ita et cognitioni quidam fixus est limes; quin etiam naturae ipsius finita vis est. Atque ut octingentorum annorum hominis vita esset, nihilo tamen plus quam nunc saperet cum octogesimum agit annum; quod non

Minos. So it has been provided by Nature, which from the beginning had care and consideration for man, and—just as fruit comes forth from flowers—wanted the wisdom of the old to proceed from the immaturity and ignorance of the very young. You remember what we cared about as boys, when, even if we didn't go unwillingly to school and the schoolmaster, our whole mind was on trifles. Our delight was a puppy, quail, or jackdaw.[15] But from these beginnings see what progress both of us have made. For in the past we brought laws for living well to the most savage nations, and now by the will of the gods we preside over the judgment of souls. And so along with age grows wisdom, in which a boy cannot be interested, since there is nothing mature in him. And although every age hastens toward wisdom, farthest away from it is boyhood, which, since it is most immature, must be trained to it little by little.

Aeacus. In this too Nature was a most practical artisan, and she fashioned her work with admirable skill. Nevertheless, she seems to have established excessively close boundaries for it, and to have given a short enough life to man, although she had created him for so many and such great things. We ourselves know how much we admired some men while they were giving us an account of their affairs, because they seemed to lack nothing except time for perfected wisdom.

Minos. Watch what you say, Aeacus, and consider the matter 13
more deeply. Whatever Nature has fashioned, she has kept within fixed bounds. These cypresses might have the wherewithal to extend their tops, but even they have their own limit of growth. The lands and the seas have their boundaries; for men, too—both for their bodies and for their understanding—a boundary has been set. Why, even the power of Nature herself has a limit. And suppose that the life of a man was eight hundred years, he still would be no wiser than now when he is spending his eightieth year. The cause is not the space of days

dierum spatia, sed humani qualitas corporis efficit. Etenim octingenario illi in tanto longiore adolescentia non maior contigisset rerum cognitio quam octogenario huic in longe breviore. Nam et stirpes et animalia quae diutius vivunt tardius fructus ac foetus proferunt; citius quibus brevior data est vivendi meta; quodque ipsi saepe vidimus, qui pueri nimis cito sapiunt aut non multo post diem obeunt, aut, ubi viri evasere, multum de illo amittunt acumine et studio.

14 Sed cum sit genus hominum superbissimum, sua parum sorte contenti, vitae brevitatem accusant; nec intelligunt qui plures aetates vixisse memorantur, eos nec Solonem nec Catonem superasse virtute ac sapientia; quos ipsi causas suas dicentes cum audissemus, aegre tulimus tale illud collegarum par nobis a Plutone non dari. Quod autem defuisse illis tempus putes cognoscendo vero qui etiam coelum dimensi sunt stadiis quique parilisne an impar esset stellarum numerus scire tam laboraverunt? His et ocium et vita superabundasse mihi visa est. Nam quid de iis dicendum ducas qui, succis rerumque plurimarum temperamentis adhibitis et in unum coacervatis multoque igne conflatis, faciendo auro dies noctesque ac vitam totam conterunt? quod quidem abuti est et natura et tempore. Quid qui commenti sunt deos inter se bellum gerere, quorum cum vulnera tum casus alios describunt? Nonne qui nugis iis occupati fuere iure videntur de levitate sua quam de vitae brevitate debuisse queri?

15 *Aeac.* Rerum simul naturam et hominum expressisti vanitatem, ut vere, ut aperte! Et profecto ita res habet, ut qui nimio plus sapere studeant, ii demum praeter coeteros desipere inveniantur.

but the nature of the human body. An eight-hundred-year-old man in a correspondingly longer period of youth would have been granted no greater understanding of things than the present octogenarian in a far shorter one. Both plants and animals that live longer produce fruit and offspring more slowly; those granted a shorter span of life do so more quickly; and as we ourselves have often seen, boys who are too precocious intellectually either die young or in manhood lose much of that acuteness and zeal.

But since the race of men is arrogant and dissatisfied with their lot, they blame the brevity of life, and they do not understand that those reputed to have lived for several lifetimes excelled neither Solon nor Cato in virtue and wisdom. (When we had listened to these two pleading their cases, we regretted that Pluto had not granted a pair of colleagues like that to us.) Do you think that men who measured the sky in stades or exerted themselves to learn whether there was an even or odd number of stars needed more time to learn the truth?[16] I think myself that they had a good plenty of both leisure and life. Again, what do you think should be said of those who take potions and mixtures of many things and put them all together into one and melt them down with intense fire, wasting day and night and their whole life in making gold? This indeed is an abuse of both nature and time. What about those who claim falsely that the gods wage war among themselves and describe both their wounds and other misfortunes? Doesn't it seem just that people who have busied themselves with such trifles should be complaining of their own foolishness rather than of the shortness of life? 14

Aeacus. How truly, how frankly you have described the natural world and the vanity of mankind at the same time! And it is certainly the case that those who are eager to be excessively wise are in the end found to be more foolish than the rest. But we 15

Sed cohibenda est oratio considerandumque quid est quod Mercurius e tanta multitudine vix sese queat eximere.

Min. Recte mones et quidem ille frequenti circumsaeptus est turba. An, quod ex omni sint hominum colluvione, secernere umbras nititur et earum frontes inurere, quo et genus illarum et artes et disciplinae facilius cognosci a nobis valeant?

Mercurius, Pyrichalcus

16 *Merc.* Recede istinc tu cum venali hac plebecula. Pyrichalce, inure hos nota illa Iudaica.

Pyr. Genus agnosco, artem scire cupio.

Merc. Foeneratores hi omnes. At vos sinistram in ripam concedite; sequimini hunc. Laenones, properate; nosti qui sint et notis quibus inurendi.

Pyr. Artem novi, sed, ut video, gens non una est. Flandrius hic est, Germanus ille; manus ista partim Illyrica est, partim Italica. Hui! quantus Ispanorum numerus, quantus Graecorum! Et profecto e cuiusque nationis populis plurimos cum hic laenones videam, rarissimas necesse est in terris pudicas inveniri mulieres. Heus, ministri, candentem illam laminam deproperate.

Merc. Et hos statim ustilato: piratae sunt Sardi, Siculi, Celtiberi.

Pyr. Videlicet his omnibus urendae frontes naresque mutilandae?

Merc. Ferrum expedi; dextrorsum huc vos. Hi Galli sunt, fartores, caupones, coci, tibicines, aleones, ebriosi omnes ac stolidi.

Pyr. Si recte memini, guttur his compungendum, clavus cerebro figendus est.

must stop talking and see why Mercury is having difficulty escaping from that huge crowd.

Minos. Excellent advice, and indeed he is hemmed in by a dense throng. Can it be that, because they are from all the dregs of humanity, he is trying to sort the shades and brand their foreheads to help us identify their race and professions and schools?

Mercury, Pyrichalcus

Mercury. You! Get back from here with this venal mob. Pyrichal- 16
cus, brand these with the well-known mark of the Jew.

Pyrichalcus. I recognize the race, I want to know their profession.

Mercury. They're all usurers. But you, take yourselves to the left shore; follow him. Pimps, hurry up! You know who they are and what marks to brand them with.

Pyrichalcus. I know the profession, but as I see, they are not of a single nationality. This one is Flemish, that German; this lot is partly Illyrian,[17] partly Italian. Hah! Look how many Spaniards there are, how many Greeks! And, to be sure, since I see here a vast number of pimps from the peoples of every nation, there must be hardly a chaste woman to be found on earth. Here, servants, hurry up with that red-hot plate.

Mercury. And you must scorch these immediately. They are pirates—Sardinians, Sicilians, Celtiberians.[18]

Pyrichalcus. I suppose they all need their foreheads branded and their noses mutilated?

Mercury. Get the iron ready. You, get over here on the right. These are Gauls: poulterers, innkeepers, cooks, pipers, gamblers—all drunkards and fools.

Pyrichalcus. If I remember right, their throats should be punctured, and a nail stuck into their brains.

Merc. Atqui nullum est Gallis cerebrum, quocirca ventres potius figito. Coeteram illam multitudinem e cuiusque modi hominum genere secerni iubeto, faber, dum ego insignioris notae quosdam tanto in populo seligo. Ecquis hic est audacia tam perdita? Vultum agnosco. Et quidem sceleratissimus hic fuit, Petrus Bisuldunius Celtiber. At duo illi, post hunc qui latitant, velati puniceo galericulo, et hi perditissimi fuere sacerdotum omnium: alter Ludovicus, Aquilegiensis patriarcha, Samorensis cardinalis alter. Pyrichalce, aereum his galerum capiti imprimito, idque in primis videto, ut sit candens. Bisuldunio illi auriculas detondeto. Haec agito; Charon enim, ut video, hic me in portu manet manibusque et capite iam pridem innuit. Accedam ad eum, ut cur accersar ex eo cognitum habeam.

Charon, Mercurius

17 *Char.* Salvum te ac sospitem venisse, Mercuri, gaudeo.

Merc. Ubinam est, Charon, philosophia quam profiteris? Deum sospitem venisse gaudes, ac si nocere quippiam possit deo.

Char. Et deus male habitus ab hominibus fuit dum inter eos ageret, et coelum vereor ut securum sit, tot tam inter se dissentientibus diis; quorum alius sacrum immittere ignem dicitur, promittere sanitatem alius; hic bellis gaudet, pacem ille procurat; est qui caecitatem inferat, est qui lumen restituat. Multi feriunt, nonnulli medentur; quid hoc diversius? Iure igitur periculosam mihi deorum vitam arbitror, in tanta varietate ac discrepantia; praesertim cum e supremis coeli regionibus deiectus et quidem non unus, sed magnus etiam deorum numerus aliquando fuisse dicatur. Quamobrem non est quare salutationem hanc meam accuses; nam cum alia te pericula evasisse gaudeo, tum vel cum

Mercury. But the Gauls have no brain, so stick their bellies instead. Order the rest of that motley crowd of humanity to be sorted, workman, while I pick out some of a more distinguished stripe in the vast multitude. Can there be anyone here of such depraved presumption? I recognize the face. Yes, indeed, this was the atrocious criminal, the Celtiberian Pere de Besalú.[19] But as for the two with scarlet caps skulking behind him, these were the most depraved priests in the world: the one Lodovico, patriarch of Aquileia, the other the cardinal of Zamora.[20] Pyrichalcus, shove a bronze cap down on their heads, and above all, make sure that it's red-hot. As for Besalú, cut off his ears. Get on with it. Charon, I see, is waiting for me here at the landing, and he's been waving and nodding at me for some time. I'll go to him and find out what he wants.

Charon, Mercury

Charon. I'm glad you've arrived safe and sound, Mercury. 17

Mercury. Where in the world is the philosophy you profess, Charon? You are glad that a god has arrived safely, as if anything could harm a god!

Charon. And yet a god was maltreated by men while he lived among them, and I fear that heaven is not secure, with so many gods at odds with each other. One of them is said to let loose skin disease, another to promise health. This one delights in war, that one looks after peace. There is one who inflicts blindness, another who restores the light. Many kill, a few heal; what is more contrary than this? So I think I'm right to conclude that the life of gods is a dangerous one, given such great inconsistency and disagreement, especially since not one, but a great number of gods, is said to have been cast down at one time or another from the highest regions of heaven. So there is no reason to criticize this greeting of mine. I'm glad that you have

primis magnam mihi voluptatem affert quod mulierum evaseris veneficia, quae et Manes assidue vexant.

18 *Merc.* Nihil horum timendum nunc diis est, postquam desierunt puellas rapere.

Char. Consenueruntne coelestes, an spadones lex aliqua fieri eos iussit?

Merc. Fuerunt illa prioribus saeculis, dum Lacedaemonii nudas virgines luctari ad Eurotam una cum adolescentulis volebant, eorum ludorum coelites et ipsi spectatores cum adessent; ac nonnunquam ad coenas vocati merito exarsere in libidinem. Nunc vero mulieres, quod aut clausae tenentur aut multis circumsaeptae tunicis incedunt, deos non commovent. Lex quoque lata est, cui et dii omnes subscripsere, qua cautum est, ne quam mortalem cuiquam liceat immortali cognoscere.

Char. Quaenam causa ferendae legis?

Merc. Forte Iupiter in Tarentinam virginem commotus cum esset, versus ipse in adolescentulum, dum illius os nimis efflictim suaviatur, quod erat quam fucatissimum, labem inde contrahit, dentisque haud multo post de contactu illo amisit. Tum dii aegre ferentes regem suum esse edentulum promulgandae legis auctores fuere.

Char. An, quaeso, Iupiter nunc est sine dentibus?

Merc. Minime. Nam cum renasci nequirent deo tam annoso, elephantinos sibi faciundos curavit. Mulcta vero haec statuta est mulieribus, ut venire amplius in deorum complexus non liceat; permissum tamen est sacerdotibus, quod eorum sint ministri, ut in eum succedant locum.

19 *Char.* Hoc est, credo, quare delectat diu vivere, quod nova quotidie discantur. Verum ne congressus hi nostri utriusque simul munus impediant (etenim inter navigandum multa satis com-

escaped other dangers and I'm especially pleased that you have escaped the wiles of women, which constantly torment even the dead.

Mercury. Gods need have no fear of these things now that they have stopped ravishing girls. 18

Charon. Have the heaven dwellers grown old or has some law ordered them to become eunuchs?

Mercury. Those things belonged to previous ages, when the Spartans were willing for nude maidens to wrestle along with young men by the Eurotas, and when the heaven dwellers themselves attended as spectators of their games; and sometimes, when they were invited to their feasts, they burst into flames of lust with good cause. But now women, because they are either kept shut up or go out swathed in many garments, do not arouse the gods. Besides, a law has been passed—and all the gods have endorsed it, too—which stipulates that no immortal is allowed to have carnal knowledge of a mortal woman.

Charon. What was the reason for passing the law?

Mercury. As luck would have it, Jupiter was aroused by a girl of Taranto and turned himself into a young boy. While he was too passionately kissing her mouth, which was plastered with makeup, he contracted a disease from it and not long afterward lost his teeth from the infection. Then the gods, displeased that their king was toothless, supported promulgating the law.

Charon. Tell me, can it really be that Jupiter is now toothless?

Mercury. No indeed. For since the god could not grow new ones at his age, he had ivory ones made. But it was decreed as a punishment for women that they should no longer be allowed to come into the embraces of gods; but priests, as the gods' agents, were permitted to take their place.

Charon. This is why it is a pleasure to live a long time, I suppose, 19
because one learns new things every day.[21] But so that these exchanges don't get in the way of our duty (for we will get

mode transigemus), scias et quid est quod ego te velim, et quid tibi facto sit opus. Ambo te iudices, Minos, dico, et Aeacus, illic in ripa expectant, mirifice cupientes tecum colloqui, quando triduum iam e terris advenit nemo; multa enim verentur. Itaque aequum censeo ut, illorum praevertens imperiis, quam primum naviculam ascendas. Quod faciens, rem tum illis gratissimam, tum te ipso dignam feceris, et compungendis his tempus Pyrichalco dederis, quod te primum curare oportet; quis enim tantos greges noverit, ni notis quisque suis signati venerint?

Merc. Recte suades; mos eis gerendus est. Tu, si tibi videtur, velum explica; nam a tergo laenis exortus est flatus.

Char. Perquam libenter. Hac enim ratione citius provehemur in portum et remigandi mihi diminuetur labor.

Merc. Quam pleno velo ferimur!

Char. Auras sol citavit; aestivis diebus suscitari hac eadem hora quae solent.

Merc. Quinam venti diebus his vobis flavere? Nam in terris magnam vitibus, maiorem oleis citriisque boreas vastitatem intulit.

Char. Nobis acherontius ac solito clementior.

Merc. Charon, Charon, quid quod video? crudo pisce hominem vesci?

Char. Ne mirare. Cynicus hic Diogenes est.

Merc. Quid? quaeso, vivitne in flumine?

Char. Vivit. Nam ripae, ut vides, altissimae cum sint, nec ipse quicquam omnino habeat quo haurire aquam possit, maluit hic, ubi et pisces habeat et aquam paratissimam, quam in aliis Herebi locis vitam agere.

through many topics easily enough as we sail), you should know why I want you and what you need to do. Both judges—Minos, I mean, and Aeacus—are waiting for you there on the bank, very eager to talk to you, since no one has come here from earth for three days. In fact, they are very concerned. And so I think it would be good of you to anticipate their orders and get in the boat as soon as possible. In doing so you will accomplish something both most gratifying to them and worthy of yourself, and you will give Pyrichalcus time to tattoo these people, which ought to be your first concern. After all, who would be able to identify such great crowds unless they arrived each stamped with his own brand?

Mercury. You're right. One must defer to their wishes. Unfurl the sail, if you like, for a gentle following breeze has come up.

Charon. Gladly. This way, we'll sail faster into port and it will be less work for me to row.

Mercury. How quickly we are being carried along!

Charon. The sun stirs up the breezes, which usually pick up at this time on summer days.

Mercury. What winds have been blowing for you these days? On earth Boreas has inflicted great devastation on the vines, greater devastation on the olives and lemons.

Charon. For us the wind from Acheron has been milder than usual.

Mercury. Charon, Charon, what is this I see? A man eating raw fish?

Charon. Don't be surprised. It's Diogenes the Cynic.

Mercury. What? Tell me, does he live in the river?

Charon. Yes. For since the banks, as you see, are very high, and he has no means of drawing water, he has chosen to spend his life here, where he has fish and water easily at hand, rather than anywhere else in Erebus.

Merc. Valentissimo utitur stomacho. Quis, quaeso, fluvidus ille quem subinde videmus, perinde ac si mergus esset, nunc mergere nunc emergere, quod alias vidi nunquam?

Char. Nihil minus ignoras: Thebanus Crates est; aurum quaeritat quod olim proiecerat.

21 *Merc.* Recte teneo. Equidem memini, cum Athenis aliquando Panathenaeorum die essem, irrisum eum vehementer a Peripateticis; primum quod is rerum fines ignoraret, nec quarum rerum usus esset bonus, easdem quoque posse fieri bonas intelligeret—etenim pecunias usus comparari gratia, quae ut nec bonae per se sint nec malae, prudentem tamen atque honestum possessorem usu ipso bonas efficere—deinde quod male sensisset de philosophia; quem enim melius, honestius, sanctius, quam philosophum pecunia uti posse? Denique si honeri haberet divitias, cur non aliis potius ferendas atque utendas dedisset quas ipse imprudentissime in mare abiecisset, ubi nec hominibus nec piscibus usui esse possent?

Char. Et quidem iure irrisus. Sed, quaeso, Mercuri, quando in Athenarum mentionem incidimus, dicas cur non Atheniensis populus quas Plato tulisset leges acceperit, cuius et eloquentiam et doctrinam (plures enim dies mecum habui disserentem) magnopere sum admiratus.

22 *Merc.* Magna illos movit ratio. Nam cum de illius legibus Kalendis Graecis cum populo esset actum, ita plebs scivit:

> 'Quando respublica quam Plato institueret apud Germanos esset, accederet Plato ad barbaros. Esse apud illos Ubiorum civitatem, quae leges eas servaret; populum

Mercury. He enjoys a very strong stomach. Who, pray, is the one streaming with water whom we see from time to time just as if he were a gull, now diving, now coming up to the surface?[22] I've never seen that before.

Charon. Of course you know him: It's Crates the Theban; he keeps looking for the gold that he once threw away.[23]

Mercury. I remember it well. In fact, I recall that when I was once 21
in Athens on the day of the Panathenaea, he was laughed to scorn by the Peripatetics—first, because he did not know the limits of things, or understand that the things whose use was good could also become good, that money is acquired for the sake of use, and since it is neither good nor bad in itself, a sensible and honorable possessor makes it good by his very use of it; then, because he had the wrong idea about philosophy, for who can use money better, more honorably, more virtuously, than a philosopher? Finally, if he considered his riches a burden, why hadn't he given them to others to be carried away and used instead of throwing them so foolishly into the sea where they could be of use to neither men nor fish?

Charon. He was laughed at with good reason. But, I ask you, Mercury, since we have mentioned Athens, to explain why the Athenian people did not accept the laws that Plato passed. I greatly admired both his eloquence and learning (for I had him discoursing with me for several days).

Mercury. They had a compelling reason. When the people had 22
been addressed concerning his laws on the Greek Calends,[24] the populace came to this conclusion:

> Since the state that Plato instituted was in existence among the Germans, Plato should go to the barbarians. There was among them the state of the Ubii, which ob-

Atheniensem sineret his legibus vivere quas a maioribus, sapientissimis viris, latas accepisset.'

Senatus quoque consultum in haec scriptum est verba:

> 'Quando Graeci pro recipienda Helena viroque restituenda universi coniurassent, bellum Troianis intulissent, sumptus tantos fecissent, Graeciam omni pene nobilitate exhausissent, tot clades passi essent, non licere Platonis leges accipi, quae mulieres communes, uxorem nemini certam esse pudicitiamque, quae una aut certe maxima mulierum virtus esset, nullam in civitate esse vellent.'

Hoc ego senatus consultum et Athenis et in plerisque aliis Graeciae conventibus recitatum memini. Discipulus quoque eius Aristoteles multum de illius auctoritate detraxit. Fuit enim magistro argutior, nec tam recessit a civili consuetudine.

Char. Et magnae et honestae causae fuerunt. Eius igitur libri a multis condemnantur, discipuli vero leguntur?

Merc. Quidni? Et magno in honore habentur, etiam apud barbaros.

Char. Eram ipse fortasse, ut quidem eram, de labore fessus, et mens aliis occupata; sed tamen visus est Aristoteles nimis obscurus et cautus cum hac eadem in cymba quaedam ex eo quaererem. Quin etiam licet, mecum dum loqueretur, corporis vinculis solutus viveret, nihil tamen certi adhuc de immortalitate animae respondebat. Post tot igitur saecula scriptor tam argutus et subtilis non usque adeo est, ut arbitror, intellectu facilis.

> served these laws; he should let the Athenian people live by the laws passed and handed down by their ancestors, the wisest of men.

The decree of the senate was written in these words:

> Since the Greeks had taken an oath en masse to recover Helen and restore her to her husband, had made war on the Trojans, spent so much money, deprived Greece of almost its entire aristocracy, and suffered so many disasters, it was not permitted for Plato's laws to be accepted, which stipulated that women should be held in common, that no one should have a fixed wife, and that chastity, which is the only, or at least the chief virtue of women, should not exist in the state.

I remember this decree of the senate being read out both in Athens and in most of the other assemblies of Greece. Besides, Plato's pupil Aristotle greatly diminished his authority. In fact, he was a more adroit speaker than his master, and he did not depart so much from the customs of his fellow citizens.

Charon. These were great and honorable reasons [not to accept Plato's laws]. And so his books are condemned by many, but those of his disciple are read?

Mercury. Of course. And they are held in great honor, even among the barbarians.

Charon. Perhaps I was exhausted by toil—as indeed I was!—and my mind was occupied with other things; but still Aristotle seemed too obscure and circumspect when I was asking him certain questions in this very boat. In fact, even though he was living freed from the chains of the body when he was talking to me, he still gave no definite answer about the immortality of the soul. After so many ages, then, such a clever and subtle writer is still, as I believe, not so easy to understand.

23 *Merc.* Vix risum teneas, Charon, si tibi ipse retulero quam facete rhetor argutulum quendam philosophum nuper irriserit. Nam cum ille nimis intorquere Aristotelis sensa vellet: 'Auditores,' rhetor inquit, 'scitote non cum philosopho mihi, verum cum sutore contentionem esse: quod enim sutoris est proprium, dentibus alutam producere, hoc noster hic in Aristotelis dilatandis dictis facit. Quocirca videndum est tibi, philosophe, ne genuinos relinquas in corio.' Hinc factum est, Charon, tritum illud iam, 'bene dentatum esse theologum oportere.'

Char. Festivissime rhetor is, sed obscuritas utrunque fortasse et philosophum excusaverit et theologum.

Merc. Nequaquam in obscuritate omnia; verum, ut mihi videtur, duplex rei huius est causa: altera, quod qui nunc philosophantur ignorant bonas litteras, quarum Aristoteles gravis etiam auctor fuit; altera, quod dialectica corrupta fuerit a Germanis primum et Gallis, deinde et a nostris, in eaque maximam nunc quoque ruinam faciunt.

Char. His nuper artibus me adortus est sophistes.

Merc. Videlicet ex horum erat numero et fortassis ex illorum ordine qui fratres dicuntur.

Char. Recte. Nam praenomen ei frater erat.

Merc. Cautissimum itaque oportet esse te ac versutissimum quotiens in eorum aliquem incideris. Nihil est enim quod argumentando non consequantur, immo quod non extorqueant, et scin quomodo? ut velis nolis assentiendum sit eorum dictis; facileque hoc pacto efficiare e Charonte asinus.

Char. Nimis ridiculus es qui id arbitrere; in asinum mene illos captiunculis suis versuros quasi Apuleium amatorio poculo,

Mercury. You would hardly keep from laughing, Charon, if I tell you how wittily a rhetorician recently mocked a certain loquacious little philosopher. For when that fellow was trying to distort Aristotle's doctrines, the rhetorician said: "Audience, I must inform you that my dispute is not with a philosopher, but with a shoemaker: for it is characteristic of a shoemaker to soften leather with his teeth; this is what our friend here does in expounding on the words of Aristotle. Therefore, philosopher, you must take care not to leave your molars in the skin." This, Charon, is the origin of that now well-worn saying: "A theologian needs good teeth." 23

Charon. The rhetorician was extremely witty, but perhaps Aristotle's obscurity might excuse both the philosopher and the theologian.

Mercury. It's not all a question of obscurity; but, as it seems to me, the cause of this thing is twofold: first, that today's philosophers are ignorant of literature, of which Aristotle was in fact an important author;[25] second, that dialectic has been corrupted first by Germans and Gauls, then also by our own people, and they are now making a hash of it, too.

Charon. A sophist recently attacked me with these arts.

Mercury. Of course, he was one of these and perhaps of the order of those who are called brothers.[26]

Charon. Correct. For his title was "brother."

Mercury. You need to be very cautious and cunning whenever you come across one of these. There is nothing they would not pursue with argumentation—indeed, nothing they would not twist to pieces, and do you know how? So that, willy nilly, you must agree with their pronouncements, and in this way you might easily be changed from Charon into an ass.

Charon. It is very amusing of you to think so. Do you imagine that they might transform me with their snares, like Apuleius changed by the love potion, whom I hardly recognized when he

quem ego vix agnovi cum hac iter faceret? Nam auriculas ac supercilia adhuc retinebat asini. Egregie tamen philosophabatur et iucundus in disserendo erat. Eum ego cum in aliis multis ridebam, tum in hoc, quod hordeaceum panem siligineo praeferret. Etenim vestigia quaedam in eo reliqua erant asinini gustus et pene subrudebat. Verum, ut ad sophistas redeam, non est cur illos magnopere timeam, quippe qui, cognitis recte principiis, dum bene partiar, dum vere definiam, capi ab illis nullo modo possim. Sed dic, Mercuri, obsecro, quod nunc genus hominum in terris laetius ac liberius vivit?

24 *Merc.* Sacerdotes laetius, quos etiam in funeribus cantantis audias, liberius medici, ut quibus permissum sit hominem impune occidere.

Char. An non capitale apud illos est parricidium?

Merc. Etiam; medicos tamen lex non modo absolvit, verum mercedem quoque eis statuit.

Char. Quam inique comparatum!

Merc. Quinimo iure eos lex absolvit, siquidem medicus non occidit, verum qui medici utitur consilio et opera, quam quidem vel magno conducunt precio.

Char. Igitur civiles hoc leges considerant?

Merc. Considerant; prudentissimi enim mortalium fuere qui primi eas tulere maximamque habuere rationem civilium actionum omnium et publicarum et privatarum, quippe qui nullam nec vitae nec artis, nec facultatis cuiuspiam partem contempsere; nulliusque unquam patrisfamilias tam exacta fuit domesticae rei diligentia et cura quam horum ipsorum humanae societatis. Verum qui eas nunc interpretantur, prudentiam in malitiam vertentes, iura venditant, leges contaminant, fas nefasque solo

came this way? He still kept the ears and brow of an ass. Nevertheless, he philosophized admirably and was pleasant in discussion. I found him amusing in many other respects, but especially in liking his bread made with barley rather than wheat. In fact, certain traces of asinine taste remained in him and he almost brayed a little.[27] But, to get back to the sophists, there is no reason for me to fear them very much, since because I have mastered the principles, as long as I divide well, as long as I define truly, I cannot be caught out by them in any way. But tell me, Mercury, please, what sort of men on earth now lives more happily and freely?

Mercury. The priests live more happily, since you hear them singing even in funerals, and the doctors more freely, since they are allowed to kill a person with impunity. 24

Charon. But isn't murder a capital offense among them?

Mercury. Yes; yet the law not only absolves doctors but even sets a fee for them.

Charon. What an unjust arrangement!

Mercury. On the contrary. The law justly absolves them, since it isn't the doctor who does the killing, but the one who uses the doctor's advice and services, which people hire, even at great price.

Charon. Do civil laws, then, take this into account?

Mercury. They do; in fact, those who first proposed them were the most sagacious of mortals and had the greatest concern for all civil actions both public and private, since they disregarded no aspect of life or of occupation or of any skill whatever; and no father of a family ever had such scrupulous devotion and concern for his household as these men had for human society. But those who now interpret them, turning sagacity into a vice, sell justice, defile the laws, distinguish right and wrong by price

discernunt precio, ut nulla homini in vita maior sit pestis quam ubi eorum indiget patrocinio. Quocirca factum proverbium est 'litis comitem miseriam esse.'

25 *Char.* Hoc illud est, quod nuper praeco, dum eos ad praetores citaret, 'forensis Harpyas!' increpitabat. Sed iam, Mercuri, colligendorum rudentum tempus nos admonet horaque descensionis appetit. Itaque quanquam orationis nunquam me satietas capere potest tuae, quippe cum idem ipse sis et eloquentissimus et humanarum divinarumque rerum prudentissimus, videndum tamen est ne nostrum hoc quaerendi studium ab agendis nos rebus avocet, neve summum magistratum, qui de adventu tam solicitus est tuo, spe ducamus longiore.

Merc. Hoc est quod mecum adeo ipse laetor, tam secundo flatu cursum nos hunc confecisse. Et vero me ipsum expedio, ac, si tibi videtur, illic ubi minime caenosum est vadum descendamus. Inde pedibus ad praetores iter faciemus per amoenissima illa prata et secundum rivulum illum qui tam laeniter immurmurat; atque hoc non tam mea causa (ipse enim talaribus ubi opus est utor, et in quotidianis fere sum tum itineribus tum deambulationibus) quam tua, cui quandonam toto anno contingit[3] cymbam semel egredi et brevi saltem deambulatiuncula uti?

Char. Ut recte dicis, ut rem mihi gratam facis! Illam ipsam igitur maxime virentem ripam teneamus; et, per Plutonem, quam fons ille limpidum scaturit! Ramum illum, Mercuri, quam raptim comprehende.

Merc. Comprehendi, bene habet; continens iam nostra est.

Char. Licet igitur descendas, tantisper me in haerba manens, dum paxillo illi naviculam illigo.

alone, so that a man has no greater curse in life than when he requires their protection. Hence the proverb: "the companion of a lawsuit is misery."

Charon. This is the reason that the herald just now, when he was 25
summoning them to the magistrates, called out, "Harpies of the courtroom!" But time is already prompting us to pull up the ropes, Mercury, and the moment to disembark draws near. And so, although I can never get too much of your conversation, since you are both extremely eloquent and well versed in human and divine affairs, nevertheless we must not let this enthusiasm of ours for inquiry distract us from duty or keep the highest magistrate, who is so eager for your arrival, waiting too long.

Mercury. This is why I am so glad that we completed this voyage with such a favoring breeze. I'm certainly ready, and, if you approve, let us disembark over there where the shoal is not so muddy. From there we shall make our way on foot to the magistrates through these delightful meadows and along that little stream that murmurs so gently—not so much for my sake (for I use my winged sandals when necessary, and almost every day I am on the go and walking around) as for yours—for when in a whole year do you happen to get out of your bark even once and have so much as a brief stroll[28]?

Charon. How right you are! What a favor you do me! Let us then head for that bank, the greenest one; and by Pluto, how clear that spring gushes forth! Grasp that branch, Mercury, as fast as you can.

Mercury. I've got it. It's all right. We've reached the mainland now.

Charon. You may get off then, and wait for me on the grass a minute while I tie up the boat to this stake.

Charon, Mercurius ambulantes

26 *Char.* Et inter graves occupationes cessatio grata est omnis et, si qua interim voluptas offertur, ea quam est suavis! Equidem ego ita semper duxi, voluptatem raram esse debere, ac tum maxime delectare cum sit quam honestissima. Ocium vero nunquam ipse probavi, nisi quod cum reficiendis corporibus tum levandis animis concedatur. Ne biennio toto maiorem hac coepi voluptatem: ut blande rivus hic sussilit! Vide quam perspicuus est, quam etiam nitido fluit alveo!

Merc. Talis Clitunnus per Umbros fertur, et quanquam multarum ille est aquarum dives, hic tamen, quod gurgites nullos efficit, sed continuo et laeni currit tractu, ripas habet amoeniores et magis delectat. Sed qualia tibi prata videntur haec, Charon?

Char. Quam grata florum amoenitas et quanta copia! Ut halatiles hae sunt ferrugineae!

Merc. Violas eas mortales vocant, ex his sibi coronas faciunt multoque miscent ligustro.

Char. Quod est, obsecro, ligustrum?

Merc. Quod in margine illo tam candido et frequenti flore nitet.

Char. Albicantium nostri vocant. Quam me limes ille delectat!

Merc. Et quanto in precio flos is habetur apud superos! Rosam vocant.

Char. Videlicet roratilem dicis.

Merc. Eam ipsam roratilem. Verum age, illuc respice; an quicquam totis his pratis illo tibi videatur hiacyntho pulchrius?

Charon and Mercury as they walk

Charon. During heavy tasks any respite is welcome, and if some 26
pleasure is offered for a while, how delightful it is! For my part, I have always considered that pleasure should be rare, and that it is most delightful at the moment when it is most virtuous. But I have never approved of leisure beyond what is allowed to restore the body and refresh the mind. Not for a whole two years have I had more pleasure than this. How delightfully this stream springs up. See how clear it is, how it even gleams as it flows in its channel!

Mercury. So the Clitumnus flows through Umbria;[29] and although that stream is rich in waters, this one, because it creates no whirlpools but runs in a steady and gentle course, has prettier banks and is more pleasing. But what do you think of these meadows, Charon?

Charon. How pleasing is the beauty of the flowers, and how many there are! How fragrant these dark ones are!

Mercury. Mortals call them violets. They make themselves garlands out of them, mingling them with much ligustrum.

Charon. Please tell me, what is ligustrum?

Mercury. It's on that bank, the shrub that's blooming with so many white flowers.

Charon. Our people call it "albicantium." How that strip of land delights me!

Mercury. And how much this flower is prized among those above! They call it "rose."

Charon. You must mean "roratilis."[30]

Mercury. Indeed, this very roratilis. But come, look over there; does anything in this whole meadowland seem more beautiful to you than that hyacinth?

Char. Atqui, ut scias, Mercuri, flos ille lacrimulas mane mittit; hinc moerentiolum holitores nominant.

Merc. Et apud mortales quasdam habere notas doloris dicitur.

Char. Itineris laborem non sensimus in tanta hac florum varietate; cuius quod paulum admodum nescio quod reliquum videtur, eo magis properandum censeo.

Merc. Hoc ipsum considerantis est viri, in ipsa quoque voluptate tempus non labi frustra sinere.

Char. Atqui labor in voluptate non sentitur, et actio etiam omnis in ipso agendi cursu est periucunda. Sed pratis iam praeteritis, umbras subimus, ac, ni me oculus fallit, sub procera illa et annosa cupresso iudices praestolantur. Quocirca, in nemore ne oberremus, defixa in cupressum acie ad eos contendamus.

Minos, Aeacus

27 *Min.* Quam iuvit utrunque nostrum facilis ista deambulatio! et sessio haec quam postea suavis fuit, procul a iudiciis, procul a forensi solicitudine, ut dies hic (qui Cretensium ac meus maxime mos fuit) albo sit lapillo numerandus! Et tamen cessatio ipsa nec deses fuit nec languida.

Aeac. Imprimis me silentium beavit et concentus ille avium tam diversarum, qui coeteris ab rebus omnibus sic avertit animum, ut nulla interim de re alia aut soliciti fuerimus aut locuti. Quid umbrae amoenitas, quid arbuscularum tam ordinata dispositio rivulique interlabentes tam laeto, tam florido ac frondenti margine? Accessit Mercurii adventus, qui omnem expectationis nostrae solicitudinem levavit, ac navigatio tam secunda, et, ni

Charon. And yet, as you may know, Mercury, that flower sheds little teardrops in the morning; and for that reason the gardeners call it the mourning flower.[31]

Mercury. Among mortals too it is said to bear certain marks of grief.[32]

Charon. Amidst all this variety of flowers we have not noticed the effort of the journey; but since we seem to have only a little way to go now, I think we should hurry all the more.

Mercury. This is the mark of a thoughtful man, not to let time slip away unnecessarily even in the midst of pleasure.

Charon. And yet effort is not felt during pleasure, and every action is delightful in the very course of activity. But we have already passed the meadows and are entering the shadowy regions; and unless my eye deceives me, the judges are waiting under that tall old cypress. Therefore, so as not to get lost in the woods, let us keep our eye on the cypress and head toward them.

Minos, Aeacus

Minos. That easy walk you suggested did both of us so much 27
good! And this sitting down afterward—how pleasant it has been! Away from the courts, away from forensic responsibility—this day will have to be recorded with a white stone (which was a custom of the Cretans and my own especially).[33] And yet this respite was neither idle nor lazy.

Aeacus. I particularly enjoyed the silence and the song of the different birds, which so turned our attention from all other matters that, for a while, we neither cared nor spoke about anything else. What about the pleasant shade, the ordered arrangement of the bushes, and the little brooks gliding between, with the bank so fertile, so flowering and green! And now the arrival of Mercury, which has relieved all our anxious waiting, and such a favorable voyage, and unless my ears deceive me, I

me fallunt aures, utriusque pedum Charontis atque Mercurii strepitum subaudire inter virgulta visus sum, et, per Plutonem, eccos! Humilior eos excepit iuniper; iam apparent.

Min. Ut libenter eos video, ut Mercurii adventum gaudeo! atque adeo nihil nostrae huic voluptati defuisse videtur, quin omni e parte numeros impleverit suos. Sed quid quod Mercurius solito incedit lentior?

Aeac. Ne vereare, expectandi Charontis it tardior gratia. Is enim tardiusculus est, quando qui exercentur in navi brachiis quam pedibus magis valent.

Minos, Aeacus, Mercurius, Charon

28 *Min.* Expectatus venis atque adeo desideratus, mihique et collegae huic deus sapientissimus, nuntius diligentissimus.

Aeac. Solidissimam nobis affers adveniens voluptatem, facturus eam oratione tua longe solidiorem.

Merc. Quod adventus vobis voluptatem attulerit meus gaudeo; idque est mihi quam iucundissimum, et, si quid est quod ego ipse vel dicendo vel respondendo delectare possim amplius, id in voluntate situm est vestra. Dicam ubi iusseritis, aut, si interrogare malueritis, respondebo. Imperia enim vestra utpote aequissimorum praesidum fore quam aequissima satis scio. Quid enim uterque vestrum nisi honestissimum exigere, praesertim a Mercurio potest? Etenim, iudices, quod dicere hic liceat, nimis quam male de me est meritum humanum genus! Furtis me praeficiunt ac praestigiis, qui sim vel acerrimus furum ulctor praestigiasque usque adeo oderim ut quotidie insecter magis. Sed cum in plerisque aliis tum in hoc maxime peccant homines, quod scelerum suorum deos tum auctores faciunt tum magis-

think I catch the sound of both Charon's and Mercury's feet in the shrubbery, and—by Pluto—here they are! The low-lying juniper hid them; now they are coming into sight.

Minos. How glad I am to see them, how I rejoice in Mercury's arrival! And in fact, our pleasure seems to lack nothing to keep it from being perfect in every respect. But why is it that Mercury is moving with more deliberation than usual?

Aeacus. Don't worry. He is going more slowly in order to wait for Charon. He's a little slow, since men who work on ships have more strength in their arms than in their feet.

Minos, Aeacus, Mercury, Charon

Minos. You come looked for and longed for, and to both me and 28
my colleague you are the wisest of gods and the most diligent of messengers.

Aeacus. You bring us the most perfect pleasure with your arrival; you will make it far more perfect with your speech.

Mercury. I am glad that my arrival has brought you pleasure. This is the most agreeable thing in the world to me, and if there is any further enjoyment I can provide in speaking or answering, it is dependent on your will. I will speak when you order, or if you would rather question me, I will reply. Indeed, I know well that commands from you, the most just of governors, will be supremely just. For what can either of you require except what is most honorable, especially from Mercury? Indeed, judges, as I may say in this place, the fact is that the human race has treated me very badly! They make me the patron of thefts and trickery, although I am the most relentless punisher of thieves, and I dislike trickery so much that I attack it more every day. But both in many other cases and especially in this one, men are at fault because they represent the gods as the authors and teachers of their own crimes. For the other gods and me there

tros. Mihi et diis coeteris nulla maior est quam honesti cura. Atque adeo turpitudinem omnem detestatam habemus, ut precibus hominum, quanquam honestis, tamen, si turpem aliquem finem respectent, aures praebeamus occlusas. Quod autem, Minos, deum me appellas ac sapientissimum dicis, facis pro tua illa veteri in me, dum inter homines ageres, observantia et cultu; tamen sic habeto, deum esse me et e coelestium numero ubi in coelis aut terris vagor; hic vero apud inferos tum apparitoris, tum lictoris fungi, non dei officio. Sapientissimum vero nec me, nec deorum quenquam dixeris; neque enim tali dii indigent nomine, quippe qui labi, errare, decipi, ignorare nequeant. At apud mortales, qui tanta offusi sunt caligine et nube, nomen ipsum sapientis inventum est, ut ab ignorante et stulto is qui saperet discerneretur; quanquam vere sapiens apud illos adhuc inventus est nemo. Lictor igitur atque apparitor ad vos venio, vestris imperiis pariturus.

29 *Min.* Et deum te, Mercuri, ut par est, veneramur et sapientissimum appellamus, quando quo te honestiori exornemus nomine non habemus, ac tametsi lictoris fungare muneribus, nonne ipse scis etiam inter mortales maximorum regum lictores in maximis quibusque magistratibus ius ditionemque exercere? Quamobrem et nobis ut imperes iusque fasque est. Nostra vero interest tibi ut obediamus studeamusque doctiores a te fieri, quando et doctrinae inventor fuisti et rerum occultissimarum interpres.

Aeac. Quod pace tua, Minos, dixerim, neque cum Mercurio contendendum est tibi, qui primus et prudentiae et eloquentiae praecepta tradiderit, neque expectatio nostra longiorem fert cunctationem; aequius igitur magisque ex usu fuerit quam pri-

is no greater concern than righteous conduct. And in fact we loathe all turpitude, so that we keep our ears closed to the prayers of men, however decorous they are, if they look to some base end. Indeed, in calling me a god and saying that I am most wise, Minos, you are acting in accordance with your old reverence and veneration toward me while you were among men; nevertheless, know this: that I am a god and one of the heaven dwellers when I move around in the heavens or on earth; but here among the inhabitants of the underworld I perform the duty of a functionary or a lictor,[34] not of a god. But do not call me, or any of the gods, "wisest"; the gods require no such designation, since they cannot slip, err, be deceived, or be ignorant. But among mortals, who are immersed in great mists and clouds, the title of wise man has been invented so that a person with some sense may be distinguished from the ignorant and stupid, even though no one truly wise has yet been found among them. I come to you then as a lictor and functionary, to obey your commands.

Minos. We both venerate you as a god, Mercury, as is just, and we 29
call you wisest, since we have no more honorable title with which to adorn you. Although you perform the duties of a lictor, do you not know yourself that, among mortals too, lictors of the greatest kings exercise authority and power in all the highest offices? Therefore, it is both just and right that you should command us. Indeed, it is important to us to obey you and to strive to be made more learned by you, since you were both the inventor of learning and the interpreter of the most arcane lore.

Aeacus. This is what I would say, Minos, with your permission. You ought not to disagree with Mercury, since he was the first to impart the precepts of sagacity and eloquence; and our waiting does not brook further delay. Therefore it will be better, and

mum ei causas explicare, cur hic eum iam dudum praestolemur.

Merc. Et dei est, cui cogitationes quoque hominum notae sunt, id non expectare dum explicetis, et Charon certiorem me solicitudinis fecit vestrae. Principio Italia, unde ipse nunc venio, magnis quassata est terrarum motibus permultaque oppida prostrata solo iacent. Fontes plurimi partim mutarunt iter, partim exaruere. Videas editissimos montes illic subsedisse, hic iuga maiore quadam vi suis avulsa radicibus longius perlata magnosque hiatus factos, maiores paludos.

Min. Patiare, quaeso, Mercuri, (avidiores enim sumus) inter explicandum sciscitari quaedam nos et causas ex te quaerere.

Merc. Oppido quam libenter.

Min. Dicas igitur numquod saltem remedium, ne cunctae domus corruant, inventum atque adhibitum in tanta hac calamitate sit ab hominibus.

Merc. Non usquequaque firmum, sed tamen salubre pro tempore. Tignis procerioribus parietes vinciunt eaque concatenant, cum quibus quanto salubrius actum esset si affectus suos vincirent ratione nec cogitationes tam evagari sinerent! Quod singulis vix saeculis semel accidit, in eo avertendo magnopere occupati sunt omnes; quae vero pericula ac mala singulis pene momentis suae ipsorum nefariae cupiditates afferunt, ad ea volentes laetique feruntur. Nocte una post aliquot etiam saecula quod ad viginti hominum millia sub tectis oppressa sunt, omnes hoc horrent incusantque, ac damnant naturam, quae vix scio quamobrem amplius illos ferat. At bella, quae unius horae momento et fere quotannis multa hominum millia exhauriunt, interdum regna

more to the purpose, to explain to him as soon as possible why for some time now we have been waiting for him here.

Mercury. It is not for a god, to whom even the thoughts of men are known, to wait while you explain it; and Charon has also informed me of your worry. First, Italy, from which I am coming just now, has been shaken by great earthquakes, and many towns lie flattened on the ground in ruins.[35] Numerous streams have either changed their courses or dried up altogether. In one place you may see high mountains fallen down; in another, ridges torn by some great force from their roots and carried some distance away; and great chasms created and even greater pools of floodwater.

Minos. Please, Mercury (for we are very eager to hear), allow us to 30
question you in the course of your account and ask about the circumstances.

Mercury. Of course, gladly.

Minos. Tell us, then, whether men have discovered and put into effect some remedy, at least, to keep all the houses from falling down in this terrible disaster.

Mercury. One not completely secure, but still beneficial under the circumstances. They bind the walls with tall timbers and chain them together—although how much more beneficial their action would be if they bound their emotions with reason and did not let their thoughts run wild! They all are greatly occupied in avoiding something that happens scarcely once in a hundred years, but they go willing and happy to the dangers and ills that their own wicked desires present to them at almost every single moment. Because in a single night, after several centuries, around twenty thousand people have been crushed under their houses, they are all horrified and blame and condemn Nature. Why she still puts up with them I scarcely understand. But is there any art they don't use to bring about wars, which in the space of a single hour, almost every year, wipe out many thou-

tota populosissimasque extinguunt nationes, qua non arte quaerunt? In his sese exercent; hic illis ludus, hae delitiae sunt; summum habetur decus caput hostis affixum hastae referre.

31 *Aeac.* Nihil profecto video eos mutasse in melius ex quo ipsi homines esse desiimus.

Merc. Vix unum.

Aeac. Quodnam illud?

Merc. Imperitantibus vobis, viri uxores adulteras repudiabant, at nunc ferro enecant.

Min. Quid Mercurium ea quaerendo fatigas quae tute probe noveris? An non compertum satis habemus deteriores illos quotidie atque in dies fieri?

Merc. Exequamur igitur alia. Exortus est cometes, qui, cum gravissima bella tum regnorum portendere eversiones soleat, omnium mentes atque animos concussit etiam futurorum metu malorum; aequissimeque cum illis agit deorum omnium maximus, qui non praesentibus solum malis eos cruciat, sed futurorum metu solicitat atque hanc praecipue poenam illis statuit, qui quae futura sint scire nimis quam laborant.

Min. Cur, oro, Mercuri, rerum eventa nescire hominem deus voluit, quorum cognoscendorum tam sunt studiosi omnes?

Merc. Quod inutilem sciret futurorum scientiam mortalium generi.

Min. Quonam pacto inutile esse potest quod eventurum sit nosse, siquidem mala vel evitari penitus, vel ex parte saltem aliqua minui cognita possent, bona vero, ante quam evenirent, ipsa etiam spe atque expectatione mirum in modum delectarent animum?

32 *Merc.* Omnis quaestio quae de consiliis habetur ac decretis magni dei profana est minimeque nobis diis permissum est ea in vul-

sands of men, and sometimes obliterate whole kingdoms and populous nations? It is with wars that they busy themselves; this is their sport, this their delight; it is considered the greatest honor to bring back the head of an enemy impaled on a spear.

Aeacus. I see that they have certainly changed not a bit for the bet- 31
ter since the time when we ceased to be human.

Mercury. Barely in one detail.

Aeacus. What's that?

Mercury. When you were ruling, men used to divorce adulterous wives, but now they kill them with the sword.

Minos. Why do you wear out Mercury by asking things that you know perfectly well? Haven't we learned for a fact that they are growing worse with each passing day?

Mercury. Let us pursue other topics then. A comet has arisen,[36] which, since it generally portends both terrible wars and the overthrow of kingdoms, has struck the hearts and minds of all with fear of future ills; and the greatest of all gods is treating them with perfect fairness, since he not only torments them with present evils, but also disturbs them with fear of future ones and decrees this punishment especially for those who strive too hard to know the future.

Minos. Why, Mercury, I ask you, did god wish man not to know the outcomes of events—which all of them are so eager to discover?

Mercury. Because he knew that knowledge of the future was useless for the race of mortals.

Minos. How can it be useless to know what is going to happen, since evils could be either avoided altogether or at least diminished to some extent if they were known, while good things, even before they happened, would wonderfully delight the mind with hope and expectation?

Mercury. Any question asked about the counsels and decrees of 32
the great god is impious, and it is not allowed to us gods to

gum depromere. Tamen sic habetote: quaecumque eveniunt, ea aut fortuito contingere, aut fato evenire, idest divino consilio et ordine. Si fortuito, stultum est velle homines id assequi ratione cuius ratio nulla sit; sin fato, quanquam insita est homini scientiae cupiditas, parum tamen capacem eum natura fecit cognoscendi futuri, cuius cognitio captum hominis excedat. Etenim ut eius divinus sit animus, moles tamen corporis, cuius quasi vinculis et carcere tenetur compeditus, minus illum habilem atque idoneum reddit, cui ipsa sese divinitas pandat; cumque eventa ipsa bona sint aut mala, mala prius intellecta miseram afferunt solicitudinem, nonnunquam et desperationem. Deus autem non eo consilio hominem genuit, ut miserabiliorem quam suapte natura sit efficere illum velit futurorum cognitione malorum, quae sciat evitare illum minime posse. Bona vero, tametsi vitam iucundiorem expectando facerent, tamen qui scierit ea sibi necessario eventura, is deses ignavusque efficietur, quippe cum certum habeat eventura etiam dormienti.

33 At deus hominem ad agendum comparandamque agendo virtutem creavit; aegre patiens illum quiescere, nisi tantum quantum animorum levationi aut reficiendis corporibus necessario detur. Qui ne desidiosus efficeretur atque ignavus, egestatem illi rerum omnium comitem dedit laborareque in incerto eum voluit, dum semper eius certus labor esset. Sed his parum ipsi fortasse contenti, media quaedam esse dixeritis quae suapte natura ac simpliciter nec bona sint nec mala. Media quoque haec, sive ea casu ferantur sive fati contineantur necessitate, quod dubia appareant, satis fuerit, cum eveniunt, providere

disclose these things to common folk. Nevertheless, know this: everything that comes to pass either occurs by chance or comes about by fate, that is, by divine counsel and arrangement. If by chance, it is foolish for men to want to grasp by reason what has no reason; but if by fate, although a desire for knowledge is ingrained in man, Nature has made him incapable of learning about the future, since comprehending it exceeds human capacity. For even though his soul is divine, nevertheless the bulk of his body, by which he is held fettered as if by chains and a prison, makes him too unfit and unsuitable for divinity to reveal itself to him. And since events themselves are either good or bad, recognizing the bad ones ahead of time brings unhappy anxiety, sometimes even desperation. God, indeed, has not brought man into being with the intention of making him more unhappy, through the comprehension of future evils, than he is by his own nature, since he knows man cannot possibly escape those evils. As for good things, on the other hand, even though they might make life more pleasant with anticipation, nevertheless the person who knows that they will inevitably come to pass for him will be made slothful and lazy, since he is sure that they will happen to him even if he is asleep.

On the other hand, god has created man to act and to ac- 33
quire virtue through action, not liking him to be idle except to the extent required for refreshing the mind and restoring the body. To keep him from becoming slothful and lazy he has given him poverty as the companion of every circumstance, and he has desired him to toil in uncertainty, with the proviso that his toil should always be certain. But perhaps, not content with this explanation, you may say that there are some intermediate things that by their own nature and without complication are neither good nor bad. These intermediate things, whether they are set in motion by chance or are controlled by the necessity of fate, because they appear ambiguous, it will be sufficient for

homines ut in suam quisque utilitatem, quoad possit, vel convertat ea, vel, si minus id assequi valet, saltem hoc assequatur, ne rebus damno sint familiaribus, et, si ne hoc quidem, ut, quam fieri possit, minimum incommodent. Igitur casus atque fortuna, ut dixi, cum ab omni procul ratione seiuncta, incerta, inconstansque feratur, quonam modo quod natura sua incertum sit, certum id efficere, et quod inconstans firmum reddere ratio poterit? et cuius certitudo nulla est, qua id ratione futurum mortalis quispiam possit assequi? Quae si nec sciri nec comprehendi ratione antequam eveniunt possunt, evitari quonam pacto poterunt? ubi igitur ista utilitas futurorum cognitionis erit hominum generi? Fatum vero vitari multo minus poterit, quippe cum non secus necessarium sit quod fato eventurum est ut eveniat, ac illud idem, postquam evenit, necessarium est evenisse.

34 At liberae sunt hominum voluntates: sint, dum volendi libertas ista vel cum primis efficiat nihil esse utile mortalibus futuras res nosse. Quarum cognitio quid habere potest utile, si ubi quid evenerit, velint necne id homines, aut prehendere aut labi sinere in sua ipsorum voluntate sit positum? Et profecto quae tam certa futuris de rebus longe prius secernendi voluntas esse potest homini, quem sat scimus in praesentibus haesitare adeo ut momento eodem nunc hanc nunc illam et quidem contrariam itentidem probet damnetque sententiam, persaepeque, antequam quid constituat certum habeat, occasio ipsa praetereat? Verum de fato atque fortuna, Minos, hactenus. Utinam ne in scholas qui philosophi vocantur haec ipsa introduxissent magisque sese institutos vellent ad ea, ubi evenissent, ferenda quam quaerendo illa tempus frustra terere supraque vires intendere Quid enim aut stultius quam hominem officium hominis nolle

men to provide for when they happen, so that each one may turn them to his advantage as far as he can; or if he cannot manage that, at least make sure that they are of no harm to his domestic affairs; and if not even this, that they cause as little trouble as possible. Therefore, since chance and fortune, as I have said, crop up separated from all reason, uncertain, inconstant, how can reason make certain what is by nature uncertain and render what is inconstant stable? And with what exercise of reason could any mortal grasp a future of which there is no certainty? And if things cannot be known or grasped by reason before they come to pass, how will it be possible to avoid them? Where, then, will be your advantage to the human race of acquiring knowledge of future events? But still less can fate be avoided, since it is no less inevitable that what is going to happen by fate *should* happen than it is inevitable for that same thing, after it has happened, to *have* happened.

But men have free will. Granted—provided that this free 34
will ensures above all that it is not useful for mortals to know the future. What use can the capacity for understanding the future have, if whenever something happens (whether people wish it or not), it is placed in their will either to grasp it or let it slip away? And finally, what wish can man have to make such firm distinctions about the future long in advance? We know full well that he dithers so much in the present that over and over again, in the same moment, he will approve and condemn now this view, now that one—the very opposite one in fact—and very often, before he is sure what to decide, the opportunity is past. But enough about fate and fortune, Minos. If only those who are called philosophers had not introduced these matters into schools, and if only they preferred to be trained to endure things when they have happened rather than to waste time inquiring about them and to aim beyond their powers! For what is more foolish than for a man to be unwilling to see to

curare, aut magis temerarium quam hunc eundem hominem suis neglectis muneribus velle futurorum scientiam (quae unius est dei possessio) invadere?

Quamobrem redeamus ad crinitam. Hanc obstupefacti mortales utinam tam noscerent quam admirantur! Quam cum omnes metuant, omnes tamen male ominantur regibus, quasi non privata quoque regum mala in publicam cedant pernitiem. Equidem olim ludis Megalensibus Romae cum essem recitarenturque in theatro Graecorum ac Troianorum res, exclamare inter recitandum e doctioribus quendam memini nobileque hoc fudisse hexametrum:

Quicquid delirant reges, plectuntur Achivi.

Et vero ita comparatum est ut regum peccata populi plerumque luant.

Aeac. Ipsi haec olim magis experti sumus quam nunc audita referimus, et causam requirentes inveniebamus reges idem in populis ius habere quod in corpore animus, atque ut animorum perturbationes corpus inficerent, ita et regum vitia subiectos populos. Quoniam autem in regum mentionem incidimus, dicas velim, prudentissime Mercuri: quae nunc eorum qui civitates moderantur vita est, qui mores, quae studia, quale imperium, quam quietus eorum status? Nam quos paucis ante diebus pro tribunali causam dicentes audivimus non satis dignam nobis spem dedere successorum suorum.

Merc. Praetereunda nunc haec arbitror; nam et illic apud mortales de iis loqui satis tutum non est et hic apud vos parum nunc quidem necessarium esse duco; satque hoc sit nosse, quod eorum alii partim male habent populos suos, partim ipsi male habentur a populis. Tertium quoque portentum nimis graviter

the duty of a man, or more rash than for this same man to neglect his obligations and wish to usurp knowledge of the future (which is the possession of god alone)?

And so let us get back to the comet. If only the astounded 35
mortals understood it as much as they marvel at it! Although they all fear it, nevertheless they all see it as a bad omen for kings, as if even the private ills of kings did not result in public ruin. In fact, when I was once in Rome at the Megalensian games and the deeds of the Greeks and Trojans were being recited in the theater, I remember that one of the more learned men cried out during the recital and poured forth this famous hexameter:

> When kings go mad, the Achaeans are punished for it.[37]

And it certainly works out that that the sins of kings are generally paid for by their peoples.

Aeacus. This is a matter of past personal experience for us more than of present hearsay. And when we asked the reason, we discovered that kings have the same right over their peoples that the mind does over the body, and that just as disturbances of mind infect the body, so the vices of kings infect their subjects. But since we happen to have mentioned kings, I'd like you to tell me, most sagacious Mercury, what is the way of life now of those who govern states: what are their habits and their interests, what is the nature of their rule, how peaceful is their government? For those we heard pleading their cases before the tribunal a few days ago gave us a poor expectation of their successors.

Mercury. I think we should skip over these questions now. For there among mortals it is not safe to speak about them, and here now with you I consider it quite unnecessary. It is enough to know this: that some of them treat their peoples badly, others are badly treated by their peoples. A third portent also dis-

eos vexat: complures enim dies sol radios nullos misit aerque omnis ceruleus visus est, quae res hominum animos ad superstitionem vertit.

36 *Char.* Obsecro, aequissimi iudices, aequis animis patiamini quaedam et me e Mercurio quaerere.

Min. Iusque fasque est, atque (ut pro collega etiam pollicear) operae precium fuerit te tantum philosophum audire quaerentem.

Char. Et habetur nunc a me vobis et referetur olim gratia. Quamobrem, Mercuri, si placet, quando et his gratissimum fore ipse nosti, explices oro quam vobis diis grata sit ista superstitio.

Merc. Nihil ea molestius.

Char. Qui, quaeso?

Merc. Quia ridicula cum sit superstitio, qui ea in deos utitur illos quoque ridiculos facit.

Char. Mirum quod superstitionem ridiculam dicas!

Merc. Atqui nedum ridicula, infelix etiam est; quae cuius animum occupavit, nihil est eo homine miserius; cuius quaenam vita esse potest, dum omnia pavet, cuncta formidat, quodque infelicissimum est, dies ac noctes terit deos obtundendo, quos non multus sermo trepidaeque mussitationes aut excitae frigidissimis persaepe causis lacrimae, sed honestae gravesque actiones ac rectae voluntates moveant? An, Charon, eos esse deos iudicas qui hominum gaudeant lacrimis? Et bonos et iustos et continentes, non lacrimosos deus diligit. Etenim quid inde aut utilitatis deo aut honoris, ubi nudis quis pedibus templa adit? Medicis utile fortasse. At deus cur gaudeat hominum morbis, qui tot haerbarum genera, quae salubres illis essent, genuerit? Atque ut verum noscatis, nullum gravius malum homines invasit superstitione et studio ac metu isto in deos tam inani et fri-

tresses them very deeply: for several days the sun has not sent forth its rays and the whole sky has looked dark—a matter that has turned men's minds to superstition.[38]

Charon. Most equitable judges, please have patience and permit 36
me to ask Mercury some questions.

Minos. It is just and right, and—to speak for my colleague as well—it will be worth our while to hear a great philosopher like yourself putting questions.

Charon. I'm grateful to you now, and one day I'll repay you. So, Mercury, if you don't mind, since you know it will be most welcome to these others as well, please explain how well you gods like that superstition you've mentioned.

Mercury. Nothing is a bigger nuisance.

Charon. How do you mean, please?

Mercury. It's because superstition is ridiculous, so that those who practice it toward the gods make them ridiculous, too.

Charon. It's amazing that you should call superstition ridiculous!

Mercury. Not only ridiculous: it is also disastrous. There is nothing more wretched than the man whose mind it possesses. What life can such a man have, as long as he fears everything, dreads all things, and—what is most disastrous of all—day and night belabors the ears of the gods, who are moved, not by much talk and anxious mutterings or tears called up, often for the most feeble reasons, but by honorable and thoughtful actions and appropriate wishes? Surely, Charon, you do not consider those who would rejoice in human tears to be gods? God loves the good and just and continent, not the tearful. What use or benefit is it to god when someone approaches the temples barefoot? Perhaps it is useful to the doctors. But why should god rejoice in the diseases of men, after he has created so many kinds of health-giving herbs for them? If you want to learn the truth, no worse evil has befallen men than superstition and the terrified devotion toward the gods you refer to, so

gido, nec tam vera religio diis est grata quam molesta superstitio; quae quam sit detestabilis hinc tute iudicato, quod, tanquam caede saginemur ac sanguine, hominem homo nobis mactat, quin et proprium fundit sanguinem.

Char. Facinus quam nefandissimum! An, obsecro, sceleribus his sacerdotes ac pontifices non eunt ipsi obviam? quanquam ex omni hominum numero atque ordine quos ipse quotidie transveho fedioribus compunctum notis video neminem.

37 *Merc.* Nulli de vera religione sunt minus soliciti, quippe quorum studium est ampliare rem familiarem, congerere pecuniam atque in saginandis corporibus occupari; et cum nimis improbe avari sint omnes, nemo coenat lautius, nemo vestit elegantius. Dudum sacerdos cardinalis obsonatorem suum, quod in emendo lupo pisce pecuniae pepercisset (erat autem precium aurei sexaginta), quibus non maledictis est insectatus? parumque abfuit quin illi domo interdixerit, ut vitae suae parum studioso. Ac ne erres, Charon, vitam nunc quae olim gula dicebatur vocant. Alter quoque sacerdos eiusdem collegii moriens exoleto legavit aureum triginta millia.

Char. Utinam quibus haec audio carerem auribus! tantumne facinus impunitum abire coeteri mortales sustinent?

Merc. Superstitione tenentur.

Char. Iam assentior nihil esse infelicius superstitione.

Merc. Quantula sunt haec! Sacrum quoque sanguinem veneno tingunt!

38 *Char.* Utinam nescirem philosophiam dispudeatque talibus nunc deum ministris uti! Quamobrem, sapientissime Mercuri, relic-

empty and feeble. The gods are more troubled by superstition than they are gratified by true religious awe. Judge from this how detestable superstition is: as if we were being fattened up with blood and gore, man slaughters man for us, and even sheds his own blood.

Charon. What an unspeakable crime! Tell me, how can it be that even priests and pontiffs do not oppose this wickedness? And yet from every class and rank of men whom I ferry every day, I see no one tattooed with more loathsome marks of disgrace than they are.

Mercury. No men are less concerned about true religion, since 37
their aim is to increase their property, pile up money and keep busy fattening up their bodies; and although they are all terrible misers, no one dines more sumptuously or dresses with greater elegance. Not long ago a cardinal priest attacked his caterer with every kind of verbal abuse because he had been parsimonious in buying a pike (the price was sixty gold pieces), and he almost threw him out of the house for not being attentive enough to his style of life. And make no mistake, Charon, "life-style" is what they now call what once was termed the gullet. Another priest of the same college died and left thirty thousand gold pieces to a male prostitute.

Charon. If only I lacked ears to hear these things! Do other mortals allow so great a crime to go unpunished?

Mercury. They are held back by superstition.

Charon. Now I agree that nothing is more disastrous than superstition!

Mercury. These are small matters! They even taint the sacred blood with poison!

Charon. I wish I knew nothing of philosophy, and that, in light of 38
this, god might be ashamed to employ such servants! Therefore, wisest Mercury, leaving aside the priests, keep talking

tis sacerdotibus, perge de superstitione dicere, quae mortalis omnes tam infeliciter vinctos atque oppressos teneat.

Merc. Primum ea in mulierculis invenitur quam maxima. Illae ut picturam nactae sunt aliquam, ibi eam consulunt, et, ut coeteras res taceam, si anserculum vel gallinulam pituita occuparit, quibus tum precibus ac lacrimis illam obsecrant; pueros puellasque vix septuennes[4] nugis his imbuunt. Sed quid de aniculis et puellis loquor, qui sciam deos solicitari quotidie a principibus viris, ubi falco longius evolaverit, ubi equus pedem contorserit, quasi aucupes dii sint, qui accipitrum curam habeant, aut tanquam fabri ferrarii equorum contusa et morbos curent atque ex hoc quaestu rem familiarem augeant? Videas in templis affixos accipitres etiam argenteos et equos et aves loquaculas.

Char. Iam ut praedicas, nihil est homine inanius.

Merc. Inaniora his audies: non pedes modo et manus e cera aut metallo suspendunt tholis, sed et oscenas corporis partes, et quod medico erubescunt ostendere, id ante deorum effigies collocare non pudet. Atque ut vana illorum ingenia magis ac magis rideas, rem supra quam dici possit inanem ac despicabilem accipe: Martinum Galli, Ispani, Germani, Itali sic colunt, ut turpe sit eius festo die ebrium ac madentem non esse. Itaque nihil est in terris eo die vinosius, nihil petulantius. In quodam Germaniae oppido, ubi Martini dies illuxit, statuam eius per publica oppidani loca efferunt; qui si clarus serenusque fuerit, operae precium est quis suaviori possit vino Martinum inspergere. Omnes viae plenae sunt vasculis, nullus est qui non Martinum comitetur lagenatus atque hac ratione per vias, porticus, templa

about superstition, which keeps all mortals so disastrously bound and oppressed.

Mercury. In the first place, the greatest possible superstition is found among foolish women. When they get a painted picture, they consult it on the spot, and, to pass over the rest, if a gosling or chick has the pip, with what prayers and tears they entreat the image! They instruct boys and girls barely seven years old in this nonsense. But why do I talk of old women and young girls, when I know that the gods are pestered every day by princes whenever their falcon has flown too far or their horse has come up lame, as if the gods were fowlers to look after hawks or farriers to take care of the bruises and diseases of horses and made their living from this occupation. In the temples you may see votive hawks hung up—even silver ones—and horses and talking birds.

Charon. Just as you say, nothing is more foolish than man.

Mercury. You'll hear more foolish stuff than this. They suspend from the domes of their temples not only feet and hands of wax or metal, but also the obscene body parts, and what they blush to show to a doctor, they are not ashamed to put before the effigies of the gods. And to let you laugh all the more at their folly, hear something indescribably foolish and contemptible. The French, Spaniards, Germans, and Italians have a custom of venerating St. Martin, according to which it is a disgrace not to be drunk and drenched in liquor on his feast day.[39] As a consequence, nothing on earth is more drunken and wanton than that day. In one town in Germany, on the dawn of Martin's Day, the townsfolk carry his statue through the public places; and if the day is clear and fine, there is a contest to see who can spatter Martin with sweeter wine. All the streets are full of flagons; no one accompanies Martin without being drunk as a lord,[40] and in this way he is carried dripping with wine through the streets, porticoes, and temples. But if it rains, there is noth-

vino ille madens fertur. At si pluerit, nihil est Martino contemptius. Luto totus conspergitur viaeque et cloacae in eum eluuntur. Neapoli, Campanorum urbe celebri, Maio mense sacerdotes per urbem coronati incedunt, quasi amantes adolescentuli. Sed hoc quidem levius fuerit. Rem nosce dignam tamen quae a sapientibus viris clausis auribus audiatur. Ubi omnis populus in templo convenit, de trabibus summi tecti resti deligata porcella demittitur ac multo sapone circunlita. Adsunt agrestes ad ludum vocati. Ibi oritur magna contentio, agrestibus ut ea potiantur annitentibus, qui vero appensam illam tenent agrestium manus arte ludentibus ac nunc subtrahentibus funem nunc in diversa laxantibus. Dum haec geruntur, turba ludo intenta et nunc his nunc illis plaudente, ibi quasi himber magna vis aquarum, maior iuris atque urinae e tecto compluribus simul locis diffunditur; agitur etiam humanis excrementis, nec prius cessatur quam agrestes porcella vi potiti sint.[5] Quid igitur tibi videtur, Charon?

39 *Char.* Quod pace dixerim tua, Mercuri, non video cur haec sint condemnanda.

Merc. Iocaris fortasse.

Char. Imo serio dico. Nam et illi officium suum adversus Martinum faciunt, utpote qui ebrii cum sint, a vini ac gentis natura minime recedunt. Et hi qui porcellam lusitant palam faciunt aeque ac sues luto humanum omne genus superstitionis coeno sordibusque volutari.

Merc. Fateor me rationibus istis victum.

Char. Hoc est philosophari; sed nescis, Mercuri, paulo ante quam mihi animum pupugeris, ubi Campanos nominasti; nimis enim sum veritus ne de campanis dicturus esses aliquid, quarum non modo sonitum, verum etiam nomen ipsum odi. Nam qui pati

ing more contemptible than Martin. He is all spattered with mud, and the gutters and sewers are emptied on him. In Naples, a populous city in Campania, in the month of May priests go in procession through the city wearing garlands like young lovers.[41] But this is nothing. Learn a thing that deserves to be heard by the wise with their ears shut. When the whole population has assembled in the church, a female piglet is let down from the beams of the rooftop, bound with a rope and smeared with soap. The country folk are there, called to the sport. Then a great contest ensues, as the yokels strive to grasp the pig while those holding her suspended artfully evade the hands of the yokels and now pull the rope away, now let it loose in different directions. While this is going on, with the crowd intent on the game and cheering now one side, now the other, then, like a heavy rain, a great quantity of water, and a greater one of sewage and urine is poured from the roof in several places at the same time. Even human excrement is involved, and it doesn't stop until the peasants have taken control of the pig by force. What do you think of this, Charon?

Charon. Please excuse me for saying so, Mercury, but I don't see 39
any reason to condemn these things.

Mercury. Perhaps you're joking.

Charon. No, I'm serious. For the former are doing their duty to Martin, since by being drunk they are deviating not in the least from the nature of wine and their nation. And those who sport with the piglet clearly show that, just like pigs in the mud, the whole human race wallows in the slime and filth of superstition.

Mercury. I confess that I am won over by your reasoning.

Charon. It's called philosophizing. But you don't know, Mercury, how you pierced my heart a minute ago when you mentioned the Campanians, for I was very much afraid that you would say something about campaniles,[42] whose sound and very name I

eas homines possint sane quam miror, cum me interdum hic optundant, quarum fragor ad arborem illam usque quae ad septem millia passuum a nobis hinc abest perveniat. Noscis quam dicam arborem, Timonis ficum; Timon enim, quod iudices hi recordantur, cum in se dicta esset sententia, petiit dari sibi ficum eam et restim in loco illo solitario; habere enim odio frequentiam hominum ac velle ibi quaestum facere carnificinum; daturam eam ficum quotannis magnum Plutoni portorium, lege dicta ne cui ante cognitam causam nisi ex ea se arbore liceret suspendere.

Merc. Noli, obsecro, irridere homines, quod campanas tam saepe pulsitent.

Char. Desipere me vis.

Merc. Imo sapere magis quam sapis, quanquam multum ipse sapis; omnes homines, Charon, quanquam ventris multum, capitis certe minimum habent, atque hoc, quantuluncunque est, habere nollent. Quocirca diu quaeritantes quanam ratione facilius illud perderent, campanas adinvenerunt.

40 *Char.* Bellissime, par pari retulisti. Verum ego, dum quaerendi sum studiosior, vereor ne praetoribus, prudentissimis viris, quibus nullum frustra tempus praeterit, oratio mea, si non molestior, certe longior visa fuerit. Quamobrem dicendi finem faciam, si hoc a vobis impetravero, iudices, ut quod unum scire vehementer cupio, id ex Mercurio intelligam; non quod mea intersit aliquid — quid enim Charonti cum hominum levitate, nisi quod sapientiores illos vellem?

Min. Tuum hoc studium, sapientia nostra est, et, per Stygem, sermo hic qui de superstitione est a deo habitus rerum naturae maxime convenit. Sed tamen, nescio quomodo, dum homines ipsi essemus gentibusque imperaremus, gubernandis populis ea necessaria visa est; adeo videtur male agi cum iis civitatibus in quibus superstitio nulla est! Unde namque tantum boni in ho-

detest. I really wonder how men can stand them, since they sometimes assail my ears here, and their din reaches all the way to that famous tree seven miles away. You know what tree I mean, Timon's fig.[43] For Timon, as these judges recall, when the sentence against him had been pronounced, asked to be given the fig tree and a rope in that solitary spot, for he hated crowds and wanted to follow the profession of hangman there. He claimed that this fig would give Pluto a great toll every year, if a law was proclaimed that no one should be allowed to hang himself before his case was heard except from that tree.

Mercury. Please don't make fun of men because they sound the bells so often.

Charon. You want me to be foolish?

Mercury. No, to understand more than you do—though you understand a great deal. All men, Charon, although they have a lot of belly, certainly have very little head, and, this, however little it is, they don't want. Therefore, searching long and hard for an easy way to lose it, they invented bells.

Charon. Well done! You have given me tit for tat. But while I'm interested in asking questions, I'm afraid that the magistrates, most sagacious men, who let no time be wasted, might find my speech, if not too annoying, at least too long. And so I will stop talking, judges, if you grant me my request to understand from Mercury the one thing I am extremely eager to know—not that it would make any difference to me—for what has Charon to do with the folly of men except wanting them to be wiser?

Minos. This interest of yours is our wisdom, and, by the Styx, this discussion of superstition by a god is well suited to the natural order of things. But still, when we were men ourselves and ruling over nations, somehow superstition seemed necessary for governing communities. States where there is no superstition seem to fare so badly! Besides, what source would provide enough good in the life of men that true religion could be

minum vita, ut multitudini nota esse possit vera religio? Sed perge, Charon, nihil te impedimus.

Char. Utar permisso, brevi tamen dicendi vobis possessionem restituturus. Ne te igitur pigeat, deus, et mihi et his declarare: inter tot hominum genera, si te sors aliqua hominem fieri et inter mortales versari ut mortalem cogeret, quem te esse hominem malles?

Merc. Absit a deo quaecunque necessitas. Ex hoc enim ipso, quod deorum sum nuntius et hominum res disquiro, satis superque detestari possum humanam conditionem. Novi hominum labores, novi miserias; quibus quid esse potest erumnosius? Iure igitur, nedum recusem hominis subire velle affectus, perturbationes, aegritudines, nec animi minus quam corporis, humanam vitam miseror, ut quam omni e parte infelicissimam iudicem; sicque habeto, Charon, quae bona huic generi natura tribuerit, ea omnino esse quam paucissima, atque ea, quantulacunque sunt (sunt autem minutissima) dum vincuntur homines cupiditatibus, dum perperam agunt atque eligunt, ita sane corrumpunt, ut quae natura sunt bona, nequiter illis utentes in perniciem suam vertant. Verum inter tot ac tam varias hominum species quosdam nimis quam odi atque execror.

41 *Char.* Quinam sunt isti?

Merc. Iudeorum nomen quam infensissime insector.

Char. Scilicet recutiri times ac foenerare.

Merc. Nequaquam, siquidem commune est illud Turcis, Mauris, Syris, hoc omnibus; verum ne superstitio prorsus me miserrimum faceret.

Char. Nihil habent ergo Iudei quod ipse probes?

Merc. Vix unum.

known to the multitude? But go on, Charon; we aren't stopping you.

Charon. I will take advantage of your permission, but I'll soon give you back the floor. May it not displease you then, o god, to tell both me and these judges the following: if some destiny forced you to become a man and to move among mortals as a mortal, among so many sorts of men, what man would you choose to be?

Mercury. Necessity of any kind should be far from a god. Thanks to my role as messenger of the gods and my inquiries into the affairs of men, I am able to detest the human condition more than enough. I know the hardships of men; I know their afflictions. Can anything be more wretched than these? To say nothing of refusing to take on myself a man's emotions, anxieties, and sorrows of mind and body, I pity human life, and with good reason, since I judge it to be most miserable in every respect. And so consider this, Charon, how very few good things nature has given this race, and that—as long as men are overcome by greed, as long as they behave and choose badly—these good things, as small as they are (in fact they are infinitesimal) men so thoroughly corrupt that by using wickedly things that were naturally good, they turn them to their own destruction. But among all these numerous and varied kinds of men there are some that I exceedingly loathe and abhor.

Charon. Which ones? 41

Mercury. I pursue the race of the Jews with relentless anger.

Charon. I suppose you're afraid of getting circumcised and lending at interest.

Mercury. Not at all, since the former practice is shared by Turks, Moors, and Syrians, the latter by all. I fear that their superstition would make me utterly miserable.

Charon. Do the Jews have nothing that you approve of?

Mercury. Only one thing.

Char. Quodnam est illud?

Merc. Quod nihil de sepultura curant; in pratis ac sub divo humantur. At Christianus de sepulcro quam de domo solicitus magis est. Quid quod, perinde ac si cum mortuis bellum gerant, qui nunc vivunt quae mortui aut ipsi sibi dum viverent sepulcra posuerunt aut testamento faciunda caverunt, eiectis inde cadaveribus, ea sibi per vim occupant, ut nec vivis nec mortuis Christianis ulla sit requies aut locus ullus suus?

Char. Satis cognitum habeo nihil nec Christianis nec coeteris hominibus diu suum esse. Itaque recte plane facere eos iudico qui mortuis invideant. Sed iam tempus est me hinc abire, tu vero his ut reddare. Utinam et me sermonibus adesse his liceret! Verum muneri concedendum est; plurimos enim expectare in portu video, nec committendum ut, dum sciendi voluptate capimur, ab agendis rebus, quae quidem necessitas est, avocemur.

Charon, Diogenes, Crates

42 *Char.* Salve, Diogenes, ut recte?

Diog. Heroice ac magis etiam quam heroice. Heroes enim quanquam male assa, bubula tamen vescebantur, ego vero pisce, et quidem crudo; quae res effecit ut magna me e parte in piscis naturam induerim. Nam quod hominis proprium est, ambulare, id omnino dedidici; tantum natito.

Char. Rem igitur mihi gratissimam feceris, si dum illuc in portum revehor, natitans mecum serio aliquid loquere, quo laborem hunc meum dicendo leves.

Diog. Dum ne me canem appelles.

Charon. What's that?

Mercury. That they care nothing for their burial place; they are buried in fields and under the open sky. But a Christian worries more about his tomb than his house. And what do you think of this: just as if they were waging war on the dead, the living throw bodies out of tombs either erected by the dead in their lifetimes or provided for in their wills, and take possession of them by force, so that Christians neither living nor dead have any rest or place of their own?

Charon. I know very well that neither Christians nor other men have anything that is their own for long. And so I think that those who are jealous of the dead are behaving quite correctly. But now it is time for me to leave so that you might be returned to Minos and Aeacus. I wish I could be present at these discussions! But I must submit to duty, for I see many waiting in the harbor, and I must not be guilty, while I am captivated by the pleasure of learning, of being distracted from the performance of my duties—that indeed *is* a necessity.

Charon, Diogenes, Crates

Charon. Hail, Diogenes. How goes it? 42

Diogenes. Heroically, and even better than heroically. For although it was badly roasted, the heroes still used to eat beef, but fish is what I eat, and raw fish at that, which has made me take on a predominantly fishy nature. In fact I have completely forgotten how to walk (which is the special characteristic of man). I only swim.

Charon. Then you will do me a great favor if you keep swimming while I sail back into the harbor over there, and talk seriously about something with me to lighten my toil with conversation.

Diogenes. As long as you don't call me a dog.[44]

Char. Quid si piscicanem?

Diog. Perplacet.

Char. Dicas igitur, obsecro, piscicanis, an eorum quae in vita egeris alicuius te nunc delectet memoria.

Diog. Multorum atque unius maxime.

Char. Nam cuius, obsecro?

Diog. Dicam: cum aliquando et esurirem et algerem una nec haberem unde commodius, e deo quodam ligneo igniculum mihi paravi et coenulam eo coxi.

Char. Num non deus ille telum in te aliquod torsit seque est ulctus?

Diog. Fumulum statim in oculos immisit, quem ego buccis pilleoloque confestim pepuli.

Char. Gladiatoris hoc fuit magis quam philosophi.

Diog. Quid mirum? Gladiatoriam didiceram. Nam cum Athenis olim agerem Platonique in schola docenti bipedem pennatam obtulissem, tum ille: 'Amice Diogenes, inquit, qui tam robustos lacertos habeas, noli, obsecro, ante a nobis discedere, quam te gladiatorio in ludo dies aliquot exercueris.' Tum ego didici gladium agere ac caesim ferire et punctim.

Char. Qui adversus deum arte hac pugnaveris, leges quam statuunt poenam in eos qui sacras res violant arte qua declinasti?

Diog. Facile id quidem fuit. Nam cum frequenti populo contra me ageretur, tum ego: 'Praetor, inquam, tute scis me canem esse, quod et ipse confiteor; leges autem hominem, non canem puniunt; lege igitur mecum agere nihil tibi omnino licet.' Quo dicto cum qui aderant assensissent, illico me praetor absolvit.

43 *Char.* Quam bellissime! Cuiusnam alterius secundo tibi loco iucunda est recordatio?

Charon. How about dogfish?[45]

Diogenes. That's fine.

Charon. Tell me then, please, dogfish, whether you take pleasure in the memory of anything you did in life.

Diogenes. Of many things, and one in particular.

Charon. Which one, please?

Diogenes. I'll tell you. Once when I was hungry and cold at the same time and had nothing better suited to the purpose, I made myself a little fire out of a wooden god and cooked my supper on it.

Charon. Didn't the god hurl a spear at you and avenge himself?

Diogenes. He immediately sent a little smoke into my eyes, which I dispersed right away by blowing on it and waving my little cap.

Charon. That was the work of a gladiator more than a philosopher.

Diogenes. Are you surprised? I had learned the gladiatorial art. Once when I was in Athens and had presented a feathered female biped to Plato while he was teaching in his school, he said, "Friend Diogenes, since you have such strong arms, please don't leave us before you have trained for a few days in the gladiatorial school."[46] Then I learned how to wield a sword and to strike with the blade and the point.

Charon. Since you fought against a god with this art, with what art did you dodge the penalty established by law against those violating sacred things?

Diogenes. It was easy. When the case was being brought against me in the full assembly, I said, "Magistrate, you know that I am a dog, and I admit it myself. But the laws punish a man, not a dog. Therefore, you have no right at all to take me to court." Since those present agreed with this statement, the magistrate acquitted me on the spot.

Charon. Well done! What is your second-favorite memory? 43

Diog. Huius quae me beat. Cum venisset ad me Alexander egoque in dolio intus conquiescerem vererer que ne discedente illo milites quos secum comites adduxerat (erant autem quam importunissimi) per clivum me illum devolverent, consilium coepi hoc, quod eventus ipse comprobavit optimum: vesperi coenitaveram polentulam cauliculosque cum coepa et rapum tostulum. Vires igitur omnes ventris coegi et crepitum quantum potui ieci maximum, quo perculsi occlusis naribus statim versi sunt in fugam.

Char. Igitur qui vires orientis fregere, eos tu commento isto vicisti tam facile?

Diog. Ne mirare, siquidem ex meo hoc invento commenti nunc sunt bombardas, quibus muros urbium et, quod maius est, arces diruant.

Char. Igitur qui regem liberalissimum contempsisti, pauper, credo, decesseris.

Diog. Nemo philosophorum omnium amplius legavit testamento, ut qui aliquot ante quam morerer diebus arcessierim maximum ad me canum omnis generis numerum, eisque legaverim domos nobilitatis ac principum omnium, caverimque ut ne per ocium voluptatibus fruerentur, die illos venatibus exercerent, noctu ne quietos somnos agerent, latrando ululandoque interturbarent eos. Sed, obsecro, philosophe Charon, nolis mihi impedimento esse, mullum video quem expiscatum volo in coenam, et iam advesperascit. Vale igitur.

44 *Char.* Homo hic et vivus et mortuus contemptui omnes habet. Sed bene habet; Craten video, eum congrediar. Et bene valeas, Crates, et fortuna meliore utare.

Crat. Nec valere recte potest cui quotidie stultitia lugenda ac luenda sit sua, nec fortuna secunda uti qui per temeritatem illam sibi adversam facit.

Char. Ecquae inveniendae pecuniae relicta est spes?

Diogenes. This one makes me happy. When Alexander had come to me and I was resting inside the tub and feared that at his departure the soldiers he had brought with him might roll me down the hill (they were very awkward customers), I hit on an idea that turned out very well. In the evening I had eaten a little polenta and some cabbage sprouts with cheese and a lightly toasted turnip. So I compressed the full force of my belly and let loose the biggest fart that I could. When it hit them they held their noses and at once turned to flight.[47]

Charon. So those who broke the might of the Orient were that easily routed by your strategy?

Diogenes. Don't be surprised, since this discovery of mine was the inspiration for cannons, by which city walls and even citadels are turned into rubble.

Charon. And thus, having scorned the most generous of kings, you died a poor man, I believe.

Diogenes. No one of all the philosophers left more in his will, since a few days before I died I rounded up a great number of dogs of every kind and bequeathed to them the houses of the nobility and all the princes, with the stipulation that by day they should keep them busy with hunting to keep them from enjoying their pleasures in idleness, and that by night they should disturb them with barking and howling to keep them from sleeping in peace. But please, philosopher Charon, don't get in my way. I see a mullet I want to catch for supper, and twilight is already coming on. So goodbye.

Charon. This fellow, both alive and dead, holds everyone in con- 44
tempt. But that's all right, I see Crates; I'll go to up to him.[48] May you be well, Crates, and may you enjoy better fortune.[49]

Crates. No one can really fare well if he has to lament and pay for his stupidity day after day, and no one can enjoy favorable Fortune if he has rashly turned her against him.

Charon. Is there any hope left of finding your money?

Crat. Nihil hucusque indicii habeo.

Char. Cessa paulum a labore et mecum hos invise, qui maesti lamentantesque in portu manent.

Crat. Satis habeo de meo quod lugeam, ne quaeram aliunde. Sed parce, obsecro, Charon; loculos quosdam procul video super aquas ferri; magnum hoc indicium est.

Char. Infelix hic miseria sua facile et alios miseros faceret. Quocirca et huius et infelicium omnium fugienda est consuetudo atque familiaritas, qui cum ipsi nec levationem ullam nec rationem accipiant, nescio quomodo aliorum infixam animis doloris notam quandam relinquunt. Abeat igitur sua cum miseria; me satius erit remo incumbere, quando ventus nihil iam velum promovet.

Minos, Mercurius, Aeacus

45 *Min.* Quid autem portenta sibi ista volunt?

Merc. Pestem significant et bellum.

Min. Bellumne? a quibus?

Merc. A sacerdotibus.

Min. Ab iis igitur inferetur bellum quos maxime deceret pacis auctores esse?

Merc. Verbis pacem, coeterum rebus bellum petunt.

Min. Inferendi belli quaenam causa?

Merc. Ampliandi regni cupiditas.

Min. Horum igitur malorum causa est avaritia?

Merc. Ea ipsa; quae in hoc hominum genere quanta sit dici vix potest.

Min. Videlicet obliti sunt iustitiae.

Merc. Quae, obsecro, haberi potest iustitiae ratio ubi regnat avaritia?

Crates. So far I don't have any sign of it.

Charon. Cease awhile from your labor, and come with me to visit those who wait sad and wailing in the harbor.

Crates. I have enough of my own to grieve over without looking somewhere else. But let me alone, Charon, I beg you. A little way off I see some cash boxes floating on the water. This is a great sign.

Charon. That unhappy man would easily make others miserable too with his misery. Therefore, his company and acquaintance are to be avoided, and so are those of all unhappy people who accept no relief or reason themselves and somehow leave a brand of pain stamped in the minds of others. Let him be off with his misery. It will be better for me to lean on my oar, since the wind is not moving the sail at all now.

Minos, Mercury, Aeacus

Minos. What is the meaning of these portents? 45

Mercury. They signify pestilence and war.

Minos. War? By whom?

Mercury. The priests.

Minos. Then war will be made by those under the greatest obligation to be advocates of peace?

Mercury. They seek peace with their words, but war with their deeds.

Minos. What is their reason for waging war?

Mercury. Desire to increase their kingdom.

Minos. Then avarice is the cause of these evils?

Mercury. Exactly. The degree of avarice that exists in this type of man is almost indescribable.

Minos. Evidently they have forgotten justice.

Mercury. Tell me, what attention can be paid to justice where avarice rules?

Min. Quid? quae in Italia urbes florent, eae nonne pro tuenda libertate conspirant?

Merc. Earum nomine quidem libertas est, re autem tyrannis mera; quodque alius alio magis rapere de publico studet, cives quotidie proscribuntur, nec ratione in illis vivitur nec consilio, verum cupiditate ac partium studio.

Min. O libertatem cito perituram! Quid reguli?

Merc. Mirifice dissentiunt, et, quod praesentibus solum voluptatibus intenti sunt, nihil sunt de futuro soliciti, nec vident haud multo post seque suasque urbes in aliorum potestate futuras. Vana sunt eorum ingenia, corrupti mores animique, qui nihil principibus, nihil Italicis hominibus dignum concipiant.

Min. Interiit Romana virtus! Et vero, Mercuri, quamvis Graecus ipse fui, dum considero nullos populos, gentem nullam nec fortiores habuisse nec iustiores cives, qui etiam bene vivendi formulas nationibus tradiderunt, mirum in modum commoveor tantopere non Romam modo, verum Italiam omnem ingeniis destitutam esse ac viris.

46 *Merc.* Caret plerunque successoribus virtus, et cum bonis aliis caveri testamento possit, virtus in hereditatis appellationem minime concedit. Regnorum ut principium sic etiam finis est; perinde enim ut dies ortus atque occasus habent. Multum in hominum ingeniis tempus valet, plurimum institutio. Coeterum coelestis ordo mundique conversiones moventque et agunt cuncta. Quas, Aeace, Graecia illa tua olim tam clara et nobilis, quas inquam, passa est calamitates et urbium et ingeniorum! Quid? dixi passam, quae nulla iam est. Conversus sum ad te, Aeace, quem video iam dudum ingemiscere ac vix tenere posse

Minos. What? Are not the prosperous cities of Italy acting together to protect liberty?

Mercury. Indeed, they have liberty in name, but in reality there is out-and-out tyranny; and because one man is eager to outdo another in seizing public funds, citizens are proscribed every day, and life among them is not governed by reason and counsel but by greed and factionalism.

Minos. O to think that liberty will soon perish! What are the princes doing?

Mercury. They are at odds with each other to an astounding degree; and because they are intent only on present pleasure, they are not worried at all about the future, nor do they see that soon they and their cities will be in the power of others. Their talents are useless, their minds and characters corrupt, since they have no conception of the conduct worthy of princes or of Italians.

Minos. Roman virtue is dead! And truly, Mercury, although I myself was a Greek, when I consider that no peoples, no race had citizens either braver or more just than the Romans — a people who even handed down their rules for virtuous living to the nations — I am exceedingly distressed that not only Rome but all Italy is so destitute of able men.

Mercury. Virtue usually lacks successors, and although provision 46
for other goods can be made in a will, virtue does not assent to the designation "inheritance." Of kingdoms there is both a beginning and an end, just as days have their risings and settings. Time has much influence on men's natures, custom the greatest influence. But the arrangement of the heavens and the cycles of the firmament move and drive all things. What catastrophes of cities and talents, Aeacus — what catastrophes, I say — that Greece of yours, once so celebrated and noble, endured![50] What? I said "endured," since it exists no more. I have turned to you, Aeacus, and I see that you have been groaning

lacrimas. Ubi genus illud tuum? ubi successio tam illustris? Sed vetera sint ista nimis; ubi Musae illae Atticae? Quid Musas requiro, cum Athenae ipsae vix ullum teneant nunc vestigium, ut pene cum omni Graecia in somnos abierint? Victor barbarus omnia possidet atque utinam possideret tantum! Verum excisae urbes sunt, deleta nobilitas, artes disciplinaeque extinctae, et illa ipsa libertas triste nunc atque infelix est servitium. Quae causa est, ut arbitror, cur paulo ante Minos ferret tam graviter Italiam quassari bello, ne Graecarum disciplinarum memoria, quae illic quasi reliquiae quaedam servatur, funditus sublata intereat.

47 *Aeac.* Et internitione generis et patriae excidio si non movear, inique fecerim. Moveor certe. Nam quanquam nihil illa post mortem ad nos attinent, tamen, nescio quomodo, sicut recte actorum conscientia, ita naturalis illius amoris vis quaedam remanet generoso cuique post mortem, quae de rebus eorum quos amavimus qui vivi sunt, habeat nos solicitos. Sed consolatur me vel quod nihil coepit unquam quod non idem finiat, nec ortum prorsus quicquam est quod non idem occidat (omnia enim sub hac necessitate, quae naturae quidem lex, dei vero voluntas est, laborant), vel quod haud multis post saeculis futurum auguror ut Italia, cuius intestina te odia male habent, Minos, in unius redacta ditionem resumat imperii maiestatem.

Min. Haec ipsa me spes vehementer delectaret, ni deterrerent ea quae deus hic paulo ante de rebus Italicis nobis retulit.

Merc. Et alia quoque multa deterrere te iure possunt; parum etenim considerare videris quam brevis sit e Macedonia Epiroque in Apuliam Calabriamque traiectus, quam etiam facilis in

for a long time and can scarcely hold back your tears. Where is your nation? Where is your illustrious posterity? But these sorrows are too far in the past. Where are the Attic Muses? Why do I seek the Muses, when there is hardly any vestige of Athens itself now, so that it has sunk into sleep with almost all of Greece? The barbarian victor possesses everything, and I wish he merely possessed it! But the cities have been razed, the nobility wiped out, the arts and disciplines obliterated, and that famous liberty itself is now grim and unhappy servitude. And this is the reason, I think, for Minos' great distress just now that Italy was being battered by war: he feared that the memory of the Greek disciplines, preserved like sacred relics there, might be utterly destroyed and perish.

Aeacus. It would be wrong for me to be unmoved by the massacre 47
of my race and the destruction of my country. Of course I am moved. For although events after our death have nothing to do with us, still somehow, just like the consciousness of right actions, so a certain force of natural affection remains after death to each noble-hearted person, keeping us concerned about the affairs of the living whom we loved. But it consoles me that nothing ever began that did not come to an end, and that absolutely nothing has risen that has not fallen (for all things labor under this necessity, which is the law of nature to be sure, but at the same time the will of god). It consoles me too when I foresee that, after not many generations, Italy, whose internal hostilities distress you, Minos, will be brought under the dominion of a single man and regain the majesty of empire.

Minos. This hope would delight me very much, if it were not for the terrifying report about Italian affairs that this god brought us a little earlier.

Mercury. And many other things, too, can rightly terrify you; for you seem not to have thought enough about how short the crossing is from Macedonia and Epiros to Apulia and Calabria,

Venetiam e Dalmatia transitus, cum paucis ante diebus magnam in Liburniae finibus Turcae impressionem fecerint.

Aeac. Quanquam timenda haec sunt, tamen, si vetera respicimus, non ab Asia aut Graecia, verum a Gallis Germanisque timendum Italiae semper fuit.

Merc. Multa fert dies, ac tametsi ubique sibi fatum constet, eius tamen explicatio decipere hominum mentes consuevit, dum rerum conversiones easdem censent.

48 *Aeac.* Nos, o Minos, et Graeciae calamitates et Italiae casum satis diu flevimus ac temperandum est nobis considerandumque quid est quod magistratum deceat; et cum sciamus dei prudentia mundum regi omnem, quid opus est de rebus humanis tam esse solicitos, quas deus ipse moderetur?

Min. Sapientissime dicis; quamobrem, si tibi videtur, quando Charon iam e portu solvit, ad collegam properemus, cui, ut scimus, solitudo semper fuit molestissima.

Aeac. Est et alia causa quae properandum esse multo magis cogat. Nam si, ut deus iam docuit, pestis Italiae portenditur, nostra interest providere ne imparati offendamur in tanta ac tam diversa morientium multitudine.

Merc. Equidem et ego id vobis censeo faciendum, quando quae cupiebatis ex me iam intellexistis. Atque adeo ut haec certius sciatis, maximam hominum internitionem cum coeli inerrantiumque stellarum cursus futuram significant, tum multa partim ex aquis, partim e terra atque aere signa portendunt quae hoc ipsum significare consuevere.

Min. Nos igitur praeimus, te ipsum cum multitudine pro tribunali praestolaturi.

Merc. Vos praecedite; ego hic interim Charontem moror.

how easy the passage to Venice from Dalmatia, seeing that a few days ago the Turks made a great assault on the territory of Liburnia.[51]

Aeacus. Although this is frightening, still, if we consider the past, Italy has always had to fear danger, not from Asia or Greece, but from Gauls and Germans.

Mercury. Time brings many things, and although fate is consistent in all circumstances, nevertheless its explanation generally escapes human understanding, since people imagine that history repeats itself.

Aeacus. We have wept long enough, Minos, for both the calami- 48
ties of Greece and the fate of Italy, and we must pull ourselves together and consider our official duty. Since we know that the whole world is governed by divine providence, what need is there to be so worried about human affairs, which god himself directs?

Minos. Wisely spoken. Therefore, if you agree, since Charon is now casting off from the harbor, let us hasten to our colleague,[52] who has always hated being alone, as we know.

Aeacus. We have another, even more cogent reason for haste. For if pestilence is predicted for Italy as the god has already explained, it is important for us to avoid being caught unprepared in the case of such a large and diverse multitude of the dying.

Mercury. I also think you should make haste, since you have already learned what you wanted from me. And besides, to inform you more fully, the heavens and the courses of the fixed stars indicate a very great destruction of mankind, and many signs — some from water, some from earth and air — show portents that ordinarily indicate this same thing.

Minos. We will lead the way, then, and wait for you with the crowd before the tribunal.

Mercury. Go ahead; in the meantime I will wait here for Charon.

Mercurius, Pedanus et Theanus et Menicellus, grammatici

49 *Merc.* Phaselus ille nimis gravis est vectoribus remoque vix agi potest; hoc est quod mortales usurpant, 'qui nimis properet, sero eum pervenire.' Sed quaenam haec est umbra, quae tam sola volitat? heus, tu, cuius istud est simulacrum?

Ped. Pedani grammatici.

Merc. Quid tibi vis tam solus?

Ped. Te ipsum quaerebam, Maia genite.

Merc. Quanam gratia?

Ped. Oratum venio, quaedam meo nomine ut discipulis referas; quod te vehementer confido facturum, cum litterarum auctor atque excultor fueris.

Merc. Facile hoc fuerit; quamobrem explica quid est quod referam velis.

Ped. Virgilium nuper a me conventum dicito, quaerentique ex eo mihi quot vini cados decedenti e Sicilia Aeneae Acestes dedisset, errasse se respondisse; neque enim cados fuisse, sed amphoras; ea enim tempestate cadorum usum in Sicilia nullum fuisse; partitum autem amphoras septem in singulas triremes accessisseque aceti sextariolum, idque se compertum habere ex Oenosio, Aeneae vinario. Ex Hipparcho autem mathematico intellexisse Acesten ipsum vixisse annos centum viginti quatuor, menses undecim, dies undetriginta, horas tris, momenta duo ac semiatomum.

Merc. Idem ego memini me ex Aceste ipso audire.

Ped. Errasse item se quod Caietam Aeneae nutricem dixisset, quae fuisset tubicinis Miseni mater, nec dedisse illam loco nomen quod ibi fuisset sepulta, sed quod cum in terram descendisset legendorum holerum gratia, fuisset illic a Silvano vim passa. Anchisae quoque nutricem fuisse a Palamede raptam,

Mercury and the grammarians: Pedanus, Theanus, and Menicellus

Mercury. That bark is overloaded with passengers[53] and the oar can scarcely move it. As mortals say, "More haste, less speed." But what shade is this, flying all by itself? You there, whose image are you? 49

Pedanus. The image of Pedanus the grammarian.

Mercury. What do you want, all by yourself?

Pedanus. I was actually looking for you, son of Maia.[54]

Mercury. What for?

Pedanus. I come to beg you to report certain things to my students in my name, and I have every confidence that you will do so, since you were the founder and cultivator of letters.

Mercury. This will be easily done. So explain what you want me to report.

Pedanus. You shall say that I recently met Vergil, and when I asked him how many jars of wine Acestes had given Aeneas on his departure from Sicily, he said he had made a mistake; they were not jars, but amphorae, for at that time jars were not in use in Sicily.[55] Moreover, Acestes had apportioned seven amphorae to each trireme, and a pint of vinegar in addition, and he had found this out from Oenosios, Aeneas' wine merchant.[56] Besides, from the astrologer Hipparchus[57] he had learned that Acestes had lived for one hundred and twenty-four years, eleven months, twenty-nine days, three hours, two moments and half an instant.

Mercury. I recall hearing the same thing from Acestes himself.

Pedanus. He also said that he had erred in making Caieta the nurse of Aeneas, since she was the mother of the trumpeter Misenus, and that she had not given her name to the place because she was buried there, but because she had been raped by Silvanus there when she had disembarked to pick greens.[58] Also, the nurse of Anchises was ravished by Palamedes when

cum is agrum Troianum popularetur, excedereque tum illam annos centum et viginti fuisseque ei nomen *Psi;* quae quod notam haberet quandam in fronte, hinc Palamedem litteram Ψ et formasse et nominasse.

Merc. Magna sunt haec, litterator, cognituque dignissima.

Ped. Maiora ac multo digniora his audies.

Merc. Solis videlicet litteratoribus tantum sciendi studium est post mortem?

Ped. His nimirum solis; equidem et illud percunctari volui, dextrone an sinistro priore pede e navi descendens Aeneas terram Italiam attigisset; ad quod poeta ipse respondit satis se compertum habere neutro priore pede terram attigisse, sed sublatum humeris a remige, cui nomen esset Naucis, atque in litore expositum iunctis simul pedibus in arenas insiliisse; idque ex ipso remige habere se cognitum.

Merc. O diligentiam singularem!

50 *Ped.* Illud quoque, Atlantiade, quod cum gratia fiat tua, vel cum primis auditores meos qui sunt in Campania doctos facito, Horatium fuisse abstemium, quod ex eo sum sciscitatus; vinum autem tantopere ab illo laudatum in praeconis patris honorem, qui cum voce non posset, potando certe vino omnes sui temporis praecones superasset. Unum vero me ne ex ipso quidem Caesare scire potuisse, cum Galliam describeret in *tris*ne an *tres* partes divisam scriptum reliquisset.

Merc. Demiror, cum tam ipse accuratus atque humanus fuerit.

Ped. Iram id effecisse arbitror, in quam ob accusationem exarserat Theani litteratoris, qui eum reprehendere esset ausus quod *car-*

he was plundering the Trojan countryside, and at that time she was more than one hundred and twenty years old, and her name was Psi. Because she had a certain mark on her forehead, Palamedes both modeled the letter Ψ on it and gave it her name.[59]

Mercury. This is great stuff, schoolmaster, and well worth knowing.

Pedanus. You will hear greater and much worthier things.

Mercury. I suppose that it is only schoolmasters who have such zeal for knowledge after death?

Pedanus. The only ones, without a doubt. I also wanted to find out whether Aeneas first touched Italian soil with his right foot or his left when he disembarked from his ship. To this, the poet himself replied that he had established it to his satisfaction that he had not touched the ground with either foot first, but that a rower named Naucis[60] carried him on his shoulders and that when he was set down on the shore he jumped onto the sand with his feet together at the same time; and he had learned this fact from the rower himself.

Mercury. What extraordinary diligence!

Pedanus. And if you will be so kind, descendant of Atlas, do this 50
as well.[61] Please inform my students in Campania, first of all, that Horace was a teetotaler, as I found out by asking him: he praised wine so much in honor of his father, the auctioneer, because, although he was not able to outshout all the auctioneers of his time, he could at least outdrink them. But one thing I could not learn even from Caesar himself—whether, when he was describing Gaul as "divided into three parts," he left "three" written as *tres* or *tris*.[62]

Mercury. I am amazed, since he was such a meticulous and cultured man.

Pedanus. I think it was because he had already flown into a rage at the accusation of the schoolmaster Theanus, who had dared to

ros non *currus* dixerit. At a Tibullo Albio comiter fuisse exceptum, cumque Pedanum me vocari dicerem, gaudio eum exiliisse, arbitratum Pedo, in cuius agro rus habuisset, oriundum esse; atque huius rei gratia docuisse me nomen *senex* apud vetustissimos Latinos communis fuisse generis proptereaque dixisse se cum de anicula loqueretur *merito tot mala ferre senem.*

Merc. O rem nobili dignam grammatico!

Ped. Lucretium quoque nimis mihi familiariter deblanditum, quod diceret grammaticos debere a se amari propter morbi similitudinem; omnis enim dementia quadam agi; propterea docuisse me nomen illud *potis* apud maiores suos etiam neutri generis vim habuisse, quorum exemplo dixisset:

Nec potis est cerni quod cassum lumine fertur.

At Iuvenalem nimis me graviter obiurgasse, quod dicerem *oleagina virga* pueros a me verberari solitos; oportuisse enim *ferula* illos percuti. Quocirca, Arcas deus, monitos facias verbis meis grammaticos omnes ferula ut utantur.

Merc. Faciam libenter, o Arcadice magister. Sed quis[6] est qui tam te irridet a tergo? illum respice.

51 *Thean.* Ego sum Theanus grammatista.

Ped. Errasti: *grammaticum* te, non *grammatistam* debuisti dicere. Addisce igitur.

Thean. Peccasti: *disce*[7] enim nondum quisquam dixit. Itaque *disce*, non *addisce* dixisse oportuit.

Ped. Rursum peccasti, *dicere* enim, non *dixisse* oportebat dici.

criticize him for calling conveyances *carros,* not *curros.*[63] But do say that I was courteously received by Albius Tibullus, and when I said I was called Pedanus, he jumped up with delight, thinking that I came from Pedum, in whose territory he had had a country estate,[64] and because of this, he explained to me that among the most ancient Latins the word *senex* ("old") was of common gender and that was why, in speaking of a poor old woman, he had used *senem:* "deservedly the old woman endures so many evils."[65]

Mercury. O subject worthy of a famous grammarian!

Pedanus. Lucretius also flattered me in an exceedingly friendly way when he said he had to love grammarians because their disease resembled his own: they were all driven by a kind of madness.[66] For that reason, he explained to me that the word *potis,* "possible," among his ancestors also had the force of the neuter gender, and gave an example:

> Nor is it possible for a thing that moves without light to be seen.[67]

But Juvenal berated me very severely because I said I used to beat boys with an olive switch; they ought to have been struck with a rod.[68] Therefore, Arcadian god, on my behalf, advise all grammarians to use the rod.

Mercury. I will be happy to, O Arcadian schoolmaster.[69] But who is that laughing at you so hard behind your back? Turn around and look at him.

Theanus. I am Theanus the grammatist.[70] 51

Ped. Wrong. You ought to have said, "grammarian," not "grammatist." So you need to learn this in addition.

Theanus. You've misspoken, for no one has said "learn" yet. And so you needed to have said "learn," not "learn in addition."

Pedanus. You have misspoken right back, for "to say," not "to have said." was needing to be said.

Thean. Et tu rursum item peccasti, nam non *oportebat,* sed *oportuit* dicendum erat.

Ped. Prisciano caput fregisti, neque enim *erat,* sed *fuit* dicere debueras.

Thean. Prisciano pedes fregisti; *debuisti* enim, non *debueras.*

Ped. Immo *debueras,* non *debuisti.*

Thean. Immo *debuisti,* non *debueras.*

Ped. Immo hoc.

Thean. Immo illud.

Ped. Immo ego.

Thean. Immo tu.

Ped. Immo bene.

Thean. Immo male.

Ped. Hei mihi!

Thean. Hei tibi!

52 *Merc.* Reverentius, grammatici! verbis enim non manibus contendendum vobis est, deo praesertim arbitro. Quamobrem bonis et honestis posthac verbis de litteratura contendite. Sed bene habet, tertius, ut video, adest sive iudex sive litigator.

Men. Ego diutius, grammaticunculi, ineptiolas ferre vestras nequeo.

Thean. At ego insolentiam tuam laturus hodie nullo sum modo. Quamobrem qui tibi tantum tribuas, Menicelle, dicas velim cur *lapidem* hunc, *petram* vero hanc dicimus.

Men. Videlicet quod *lapis* agendi vim habeat, laedit enim pedem, at *petra,* quod pede teratur, ad patiendi genus transiit.

Merc. Nihil est grammatico insulsius; vide quam hi desipiant, cum *petra* Graeca sit dictio, *lapis* vero fuerit a *labando* dictus,

Theanus. You also have misspoken right back. For not "was needing," but "needed" was to be said.

Pedanus. You have broken the skull of Priscian.[71] For you had had to say not "was" but "had."

Theanus. You have broken Priscian's feet: "you had," not "you had had."

Pedanus. On the contrary, "you had had," not "you had."

Theanus. On the contrary, "you had," not "you had had."

Pedanus. On the contrary, the latter.

Theanus. No, the former.

Pedanus. No, I.

Theanus. No, you.

Pedanus. No, well.

Thean. No, badly.

Pedanus. Woe is me!

Theanus. Woe is you!

Mercury. More respectfully, grammarians! You must dispute with words, not fists, especially when a god is looking on. Therefore, from now on, dispute about philology with kind and decorous words. But it's all right, I see a third party here, either an arbitrator or a disputant 52

Menicellus. I can no longer put up with your silliness, foolish little grammarians![72]

Theanus. But I will put up with your insolence not at all. Therefore, Menicellus, since you give yourself so much credit, I would like you to say why we call "stone" (*lapis*) masculine but "rock" (*petra*) feminine.

Menicellus. Obviously because *lapis* is active in meaning, for it hurts a foot, but *petra,* since it is ground by a foot, has passed into the category of being passive.[73]

Mercury. Nothing is more obtuse than a grammarian. See how foolish they are, since *petra* is a Greek word, but *lapis* gets its

tertia immutata littera, quod labent ex eo ambulantium vestigia.

Thean. Qui de lapide petraque hoc sentias, de *manu* quid mihi respondes?

Men. An non manus faciendo operi occupata aliquid semper patitur?

Thean. At nunc agit cum te verbero; hem tibi!

Men. Heu me miserum!

Thean. Quid te miserum? rationem afferas oportet cur *manus* cum in pugnum coit, cum verberat, dici hic non debuerit.

53 *Men.* Nihil mihi tecum erit amplius. Quamobrem oratum te, Mercuri, volo, ut cum primum Neapolim in Opicos perveneris, in eo conventu qui ociosis fieri diebus ad Arcum solet, Iovianum Pontanum convenias verbisque commonefacias meis, posthac ut sit cautior atque ut *curso* a verbo quod est *curro* deducat, non *cursito*. Panhormitam quoque Antonium acriter increpitato, quod *epistolutiam* in diminutione protulerit.

Merc. At ego, Menicelle, pro Antonio hoc tibi respondeo: Italicam linguam non modo novas diminutiones fecisse, verum etiam augentium vocum formas quasdam invenisse detractionis ac ignominiae gratia. Quocirca Antonii nomine te tantum *grammaticonem* valere iubeo. Tu vero, Pedane, an quid habes praeter coetera eruditione dignum tua?

Ped. Unum hoc: *Boetium* non a *Boetia,* in qua ipse natus non fuerit, dictum, sed agnomentum hoc illi fuisse a vescenda boum carne, quod ipsius me Boetii cocus docuit.

Merc. Per Iovem mira agnominatio! tu quid ad haec, Theane?

Thean. Eiiciendos hereditate Pedani liberos, eius bona publice vendenda redibendamque auditoribus quam Pedanus ab illis acceperit pecuniam.

name from *labare* ("to slip"), with the third letter changed, because the soles of walkers slip on it.

Theanus. Since you have this idea about *lapis* and *petra*, what can you tell me about *manus* ("hand")?

Menicellus. Isn't a hand busy doing a job always passive?[74]

Theanus. But it's active when I beat you. Take that!

Menicellus. Alas! Woe is me!

Theanus. Why "woe is you"? You ought to give a reason why it shouldn't be called "marriage" (*manus*) on this occasion, when it couples into a fist and beats you.[75]

Menicellus. I'll have nothing more to do with you. Therefore, I 53
want to beseech you, Mercury, as soon as you arrive in Naples among the Oscans, to approach Gioviano Pontano in the gathering that usually takes place on free days at the Arch and remind him on my behalf to be more careful after this and to derive *curso* from the verb *curro*, not *cursito*.[76] Also, you are to berate Antonio Panormita severely for coining the diminutive *epistolutiam* ("a short note").[77]

Mercury. But I will give you this answer on Antonio's behalf, Menicellus. The Italian language has not only created new diminutives, but also invented certain patterns of accreting syllables in order to express scorn and opprobrium. Therefore, in Antonio's name I bid you farewell as a great, big "grammaticone."[78] As for you, Pedanus, do you have anything else to say befitting your erudition?

Pedanus. Only this. Boethius was not named from Boeotia (where he was not born), but he got the appellation from eating beef, as the cook of Boethius himself informed me.

Mercury. By Jove, what an amazing way to derive a nickname! What do you say to this, Theanus?

Theanus. I say that Pedanus' children should be deprived of their inheritance, his goods should be publicly sold, and the money that Pedanus took from his pupils should be refunded.

Merc. Atqui ego tuis vel maxime liberis cavendum praeiudicium hoc censeo.

Charon, umbrae diversae

54 *Char.* Ascendite, infelices umbrae; quid, miserae, ante diem fletis? quasi parum sit tum dolere cum malum venerit. Tu vero, tam culta et procax umbra, quaenam es?

Umbr. Cypria meretrix.

Char. Ubi gentium quaestum fecisti?

Umbr. Romae.

Char. Quis iste comes?

Umbr. Sacerdos cardinalis, qui me amavit.

Char. Miror quomodo senem puella, meretriculam sacerdos in delitiis habuerit.

Umbr. Mea illum forma, illius me aurum coepit.

Char. Plus igitur apud eum forma quam religio, apud te precium quam aut senectus aut illius os valuit.

Umbr. Aurum mihi suavissimum fuit, quo ille et oris deformitatem et senectutem saepissime redemit suam. Ad haec, quanquam senex, salacissimus tamen fuit,[8] utinamque sola illi fuissem satis!

Char. Mirum homo tam senex quod tam esset libidinosus!

Umbr. Ego ubi primum ad eum sum arcessita, putavi me cum adolescentulo coituram. At ubi aetatem vidi et os distortum, coepi queri meque deceptam esse ab laenone inclamitare. Tum ille; 'Ne, inquit, querare, animula, nam cuius nunc tortum os fugis haud multo post rectum nervum experiere.' Quod fuit: nihil enim illo tentius passa sum unquam.

55 *Char.* Ite, infelices, in ignem coiturae aevumque illic miserrimum acturae. Quis tu cucullatus?

Mercury. And I think that this sentence should be pronounced on your own children most of all.

Charon and various shades

Charon. Come aboard, unhappy shades. Why are you weeping too 54
soon, wretched ones—as if it would be not enough to grieve when the evil comes? You there, shade all dolled up and bold, who are you?

Shade. A Cyprian harlot.[79]

Charon. Where in the world did you ply your trade?

Shade. Rome.

Charon. Who's your friend?

Shade. The cardinal priest who loved me.

Charon. I wonder how a girl had an old man as a favorite, and a priest a harlot.

Shade. He liked my looks; I liked his gold.

Charon. Then with him beauty counted more than religion, and with you payment more than either his old age or his looks.

Shade. I thought the gold was very nice, and he very often used it to compensate for his twisted face and old age. Besides, although he was old, he was very randy—if only I alone had been enough for him!

Charon. It is amazing that such an old man was so lustful!

Shade. The first time I was summoned to him, I thought I was going to couple with a fine young fellow. But when I saw his age and twisted face, I started to complain and shout that I had been deceived by my pimp. Then says he, "Don't fuss, sweetheart, for the man whose crooked face you now flee has a nice straight member that you will soon try out." And so it was: I never submitted to anything harder than that.

Charon. Go, unhappy ones, into the fire to couple, and there to 55
spend a wretched eternity. Who are you in the monk's cowl?

Umbr. Frater.

Char. Ordo qui?

Umbr. Non semel ex ordine in ordinem transii.

Char. Quae causa?

Umbr. Facilius ut deciperem. Die mulieres audiebam peccata confitentes, noctu graecabar in ganeis.

Char. Unde tibi suppetebat ad id pecunia?

Umbr. E fraude et furto; decipiebam mulierculas, surripiebam sacra.

Char. Et fraudem et sacrilegium flammis lues. At tu tam nitida cute atque anatino gressu, quemnam profiteris?

Umbr. Episcopum.

Char. Mirum qui tam sis ventricosus!

Umbr. Minime mirum, quippe cum huic soli studuerim in eumque congesserim omnem ecclesiae censum meae. Quin etiam foeneravi.

Char. Satis igitur tibi non erat quod ex ecclesia quotannis rediret?

Umbr. Illud ventri satis erat, at foenus serviebat peni; complures enim concubinas alebam et corrumpebam libenter auro maritas mulieres.

Char. Infelix, cui tantus sit venter ferendus pedibus adeo imbecillis, infelicior, cui animus honeri, at venter penisque dii fuerint, infelicissimus, qui te ipsum cum minime noveris, deum, cui ministrabas, multo minus cognoscere potueris! Abi igitur, infelicissime; sera enim poenitentia est tua. Tu vero quaenam demissa facie atque ore tam pudenti?

56 *Umbr.* Infelix puella.

Char. Quae tam acerbi luctus est causa?

Umbr. Utinam carerem memoria!

Shade. A brother.

Charon. Which order?

Shade. I passed several times from one order to another.

Charon. For what reason?

Shade. To deceive more easily. By day I heard women confessing their sins; by night I behaved like a Greek in low dives.

Charon. Where did you get the money for it?

Shade. From fraud and theft. I deceived foolish women; I stole sacred objects.

Charon. You will pay for fraud and sacrilege with flames. But you, with the sleek skin and waddling like a duck, who do you claim to be?

Shade. A bishop.

Charon. My, what a big belly you have!

Shade. It's not surprising, since it was all I was concerned about, and I stuffed into it all the wealth of my church. Why, I even practiced usury.

Charon. Wasn't the annual income from the church enough for you?

Shade. It was enough for my belly, but the interest was at the service of my penis. I kept several concubines, and I liked seducing married women with gold.

Charon. Unhappy one, since your huge belly has to be borne on such weak feet; unhappier, since your reason was a burden to you, but your belly and penis were gods; unhappiest of all since you knew yourself not at all, and could know still less the God whom you served! Go away, then, most unhappy one. Your penitence is too late. But who are you with downcast face and bashful countenance?

Shade. An unhappy girl. 56

Charon. What is the cause of such bitter grief?

Shade. If only I could not remember!

Char. Noli, amabo, spem ponere; nam si coacta quippiam peccasti, leviore poena afficiere.

Umbr. Miseram me! decepta fui.

Char. Quidnam per fraudem amisisti?

Umbr. Virginitatem, infelix!

Char. Quis te decepit?

Umbr. Senex sacerdos.

Char. Arte qua?

Umbr. Adibam saepe templa deum orans ut nuptiae faciles, vir mihi foret e sententia. Ibi tum antistes me collaudare, spem bonam polliceri seque mihi facilem offerre. Igitur ubi saepius me confitentem audit et simplicitatem agnoscit meam: 'Desine, inquit, filiola, virum a deo petere, qui te innuptam esse iubeat.' Tum ego: 'Quia et tu id, pater, mones et velle deum dicis, deo virginitatem meam do dedicoque.' Tum ille me collaudata: 'Quod deo dedisti, filia, id alicui necesse est ecclesiae ut dices.' Tum ego: 'Cuinam, pater, ecclesiae prius eam dicem quam tuae?' 'Atqui,' inquit ille, 'quoniam oblatiunculae istius ecclesiae meae nomine capi a me possessionem oportet, quo deo sit acceptior, abi, filiola, mane ad me reditura. Etenim nocte hac deum orabo ut ratam istam rectamque velit esse dicationem. Tu postquam laveris, novo induta supparo ad me redi. Nihil enim nisi mundum fas est nos attrectare, hocque in primis effice, sola ac sine teste ut venias. In iis enim quae deus manu capit nulli adhibendi sunt testes.'

57 Mane itaque ad eum ubi veni, tum ille me in cellam induxit, in qua summi dei posita est statua, quam circa magna cereorum vis erat accensa. Ubi ambo oravimus: 'Filiola, inquit, et tunicam

Charon. Please do not give up hope. If you committed any sin under coercion, you will be visited with a lighter punishment.

Shade. Woe is me! I was deceived.

Charon. What did you lose through trickery?

Shade. My virginity, alas!

Charon. Who deceived you?

Shade. An old priest.

Charon. How?

Shade. I used to go often to church, beseeching God that I might find a ready marriage and a husband to my liking.[80] There a priest commended me, promised me good hope, and made himself agreeable to me. Accordingly, when he heard my confession a few times and realized my ignorance, he said, "Cease, little daughter, to ask God for a husband, since he commands you to be unwed." Then I said, "Because this is your instruction, father, and you say God wills it, I give and dedicate my virginity to God." Then, commending me, he said, "What you have given to God, daughter, you must dedicate to some church." Then I: "To what church, father, should I dedicate it rather than yours?" "By all means," says he, "since it is right for me to take possession of your little offering in the name of my church, in order that it might be more acceptable to God, depart, little daughter, and come back to me in the morning. Tonight I will beseech God to be willing for your dedication to be valid and right. After you have washed, put on a new dress and come back to me. For it is right for us to handle nothing except what is clean; and make sure above all to come alone and without a witness. In the matters God takes in hand, no witnesses can be present."

And so when I came to him in the morning, he took me into 57
his cell in which was placed a statue of the highest God, around which a great number of wax candles had been lit. When we both prayed, he said, "Little daughter, take off your tunic and

et supparum exue, deus enim et coelestes omnes nudi cum sint, nuda sibi offerri volunt.' Ubi ego nuda astitissem, tum ille papillas has pertractans: 'Hae, inquit, ecclesiae meae sunt.' Tum mentum manu demulcens: 'Et hoc ecclesiae est meae.' Hinc genas summis delibans digitis: 'Filia, inquit, oris possessio non nisi ore capiunda est,' meque ter osculatus cum fuisset, 'et labia haec meae sunt ecclesiae.' Sic pectus, sic ventrem ecclesiae suae esse cum dixisset, ut iacerem iussit. Iacui infelix; tum ille genu innixus femoraque contrectans: 'Deus, ait, qui tumidula haec femora castigatulumque ventrem cum brachiolis his teretibus tam venuste molliterque formasti, aspice virgunculam tuam et ista possessione laetare.' Ter haec cecinit; ibi, ut omnia transigeret, id respexit quo mulieres sumus. 'Et illud, inquit, filia, manu capiendum est. Verum ut oris capta est ore possessio, sic tui quoque illius meo hoc est capienda.' Utinamque tunc expirassem, misera!

Char. Quomodo deceptam te postea sensisti?

Umbr. Dum ille studiosius fundum colit suum, gravida facta sum, tandemque e partu mortua.

Char. Nunquid non ille te absolvit morientem?

Umbr. Absolvit.

58 *Char.* Laeta esto. Nam iudices et ipsi absolvent. Sed heus, tu, quid, miser, rides? crede mihi, non est nunc ridendi locus.

Umbr. Nulla mihi est quam tibi *credam* pecunia.

Char. Talisne tu es qui ludere Charontem velis?

dress, for since God and all those in heaven are naked, they want naked offerings to be made to them." Then, after I stood waiting, naked, he fondled my breasts and said: "These are for my church." Then, caressing my chin with his hand: "This, too, is for my church." Then, lightly pinching my cheeks with his finger tips, he said: "Daughter, one can take possession of the mouth only with the mouth," and after he had kissed me three times: "and these lips are for my church." When he had said in this way that my chest, and in the same way that my belly was for his church, he bade me lie down. I did so, unhappy girl that I was. Then he got on his knees, and fingering my thighs he said: "God, who formed these plump little thighs and taut little belly[81] along with these smooth little arms so delicately and delightfully, look on your little maiden and rejoice in your possession." He chanted this three times; thereupon, in order to complete the whole business, he turned his attention to the place where we are women. "This, too, daughter," he said, "must be taken in hand. But just as possession of your mouth was taken with a mouth, so possession of this part of you must be taken with this part of me." If only I had died on the spot, wretched girl that I am!

Charon. How did you realize afterward that you had been deceived?

Shade. While he was diligently tilling his farm,[82] I became pregnant, and I finally died in childbirth.

Charon. Didn't he give you absolution when you were dying?

Shade. He did.

Charon. Be joyful. For the judges themselves will also absolve you. 58
But you there, wretch, why are you laughing? Now is not the place for laughter, trust me.

Shade. I have no money to trust you with.

Charon. Are you the sort [*talis*] who wants to play games with Charon?

Umbr. Atqui nec *talis* ipse unquam lusi nec tesseris.

Char. Hic homo cavillatur et in moerore etiam iocari cupit. Dico ego tibi: alium paulo post sermonem seres, ubi ad forum veneris.

Umbr. Vendi in foro *halium,* non *seri* solet.

Char. Suavissimus hic est, ut video. Dic, quaeso, quam artem exercuisti?

Umbr. *Martem* ipse non exercui, sed male me Mars habuit.

Char. Tu me, facetissime homo, tuis istis dictis vel in risum rapis.

Umbr. Ego, amice, *rapis* nunquam sum usus, magis me delectavit coepa et porrum.

Char. Videlicet suae cuique sunt voluptates.

Umbr. Nullam ego e *sue* voluptatem coepi unquam: egone bestiolam tam immundam in delitiis haberem? parce, oro, Charon, delicatior ego fui quam reris; principes viros in iocis habui, non bestiolas, illos mihi ludos faciebam.

Char. Tum tu istrio fuisti?

Umbr. Etruria mihi patria fuit, non *Istria,* cui nihil aliud curae fuit unquam quam ut nunquam dolerem, nunquam irascerer. Ut quis uxorem ducebat, ridebam; efferebat quis filium, ridebam; insanibat amore alius, ridebam. Ridebam ubi quis nimis sumptuose vestiret, nimis magnifice aedificaret, ubi praedia nimis ampla emeret. Ridebam demum omnia. Semel autem in omni me flere vita memini, quod matre mortua, ubi illam sepellirem terra mihi emenda in sancto fuit; tum nimis graviter hominum conditionem flevi ac de religione sum questus. Sed tamen haud multo post dolorem hunc compressi atque ad naturam redii meque ipsum ridere coepi, qui non et id quoque risissem.

59 *Char.* Sub huius risu latet sapientia.

Shade. But I've never played games with either knucklebones [*talis*] or dice.

Charon. This fellow banters, and even in sorrow he wants to jest. I tell you: you'll soon sow another [*alium*] speech, when you come to the forum.

Shade. In the forum allium is generally sold, not sown.

Charon. This fellow is most agreeable, as I see. Tell me, I ask, what profession [*quam artem*] did you practice [*exercuisti*]?

Shade. I didn't trouble Mars [*exercui Martem*]; it was Mars who treated me badly.

Charon. You ravish [*rapis*] me right into laughter with your words, facetious fellow.

Shade. I have never enjoyed rape, friend; onion and leek please me better.

Charon. Of course. Each has his own [*suae*] pleasures.

Shade. I have never taken any pleasure from a sow [*sue*]. Should I have such a filthy creature as a pet? Spare me, please, Charon. I am more fastidious than you think. I had princes in my jests, not animals; I made *them* my sport

Charon. You were a performer [*istrio*] then?

Shade. Etruria was my homeland, not Istria, and I never cared for anything except never to be sad or angry. When someone took a wife, I laughed; when someone buried a son, I laughed; when another went mad with love, I laughed. I laughed when someone dressed too finely, built too grandly, when he bought too large a property. In short, I laughed at everything. I remember weeping once in my whole life, because when my mother died I had to buy land in holy ground to bury her in; then I very bitterly bewept the condition of mankind and grumbled about religion. Nevertheless, soon afterward I stifled my grief and returned to my nature and began to laugh at myself, since I had not also laughed at this.

Charon. Wisdom is hidden under the laughter of this man.[83] 59

Umbr. Quid tute tecum loqueris? audacter dic quod velis, non te ludo amplius.

Char. Rem mihi gratissimam feceris si vitae tuae genus ordine explicaveris.

Umbr. Quod ipsum vehementer iuvat; quid enim iuvare magis aut potest aut debet quam ubi vitae suae cursum quis repetens nihil invenit cuius poenitere iure debeat? Principio cum viderem nostram rempublicam ab improbis ac seditiosis civibus administrari, publicis muneribus abstinui meque ad privatam vitam contuli, nulli rei praeterquam agro colendo intentus; siquidem exercere mercaturam nolui, ne aut foenerandum esset aut fortuna continue timenda; nec servilem quaestum probavi aliquem. In suburbano mihi vita fuit. Raro in urbem accedebam atque eo cum venissem, decretum erat mihi nemini molestiae esse, nocere nulli nihilque molesti ex aliorum aut dictis aut factis capere. Ridens ingrediebar urbem, ridens exibam; ubi quem amicum aut notum videbam, salutabam illum curabamque congressus nostri ut essent quam iucundissimi. Si quam vel de nostra vel de Italiae republica facere mentionem coepisset, statim valere eum iubebam. Templa castus mane adibam neque cum sacerdotibus arctiorem habere familiaritatem volui; ubi rem divinam fecissent, abibam illico. Doctos quosdam amabam, qui non tam acuto essent ingenio quam recto iudicio; eorum disputationes libenter audiebam. Si quis e notis aut familiaribus, quos habere haudquaquam multos volui, adversi aliquid accepisset, consolabar illum meique ut similis esset rogabam. Nam et fortunae ludos ridendos esse et naturae necessitatem nullo pacto dolendam

His actis, referebam me in suburbanum; ibi partim legendo, partim deambulando aut aliquid in agro agendo dies conficiebam; noctu, nisi quantum quieti dandum esset, coeterum tem-

Shade. Why are you talking to yourself? State your meaning boldly. I'm not teasing you any more.

Charon. You will do me a very great favor if you give a systematic account of your way of life.

Shade. That is a great pleasure; for what either can be more pleasing or ought to be, than when a man, in retracing the course of his life, finds nothing that he has cause to regret? To begin with, when I saw that our commonwealth was being governed by wicked and factious citizens, I refrained from public office and went over to private life, intent on nothing except cultivating my land. I did not want to go into trade for fear that I would have to practice usury or continuously dread bad fortune, and I disapproved of any servile pursuit. I spent my life on my estate. I came seldom into the city, and when I did, I vowed to bother no one, to harm no one, and to take no offense at the words or acts of others. I went into the city laughing; laughing I left it; when I saw any friend or acquaintance, I greeted him and took care that our meeting should be as pleasant as possible. If he started to talk about either our state or that of Italy, I immediately said goodbye. I went chaste in the morning to church, and wanted to have no closer contact with the priests; when they had completed the service, I went away at once. I liked certain learned men, less for their keen intellect than their correct judgment; I enjoyed listening to their discussions. If any one of my acquaintances or friends (I chose to have very few) had some misfortune, I consoled him and encouraged him to follow my example. For one should laugh at the tricks of fortune and not grieve a bit at the inevitability of nature.

After that I would go back to my estate; there I spent my 60
days, partly reading, partly going for walks or doing something on the farm. At night I passed the time in study, except for what I needed to devote to sleep. Sometimes I went down to

pus lucubrando transigebam. Exibam interdum in quadrivia, atque ubi festi essent dies, ibi villicos de pronosticis temporum, de natura terrae, de insitione, de seminibus, de irrigatione deque aliis rusticae rei ministeriis disserentes audiebam fierique studebam eorum sermone prudentior. Et quoniam cognoscerem res hominum tam diversis ac variis periculis esse expositas, si quid vel in agro vel in domo adversi accidisset, ubi conditionem risissem humanam, curabam arte id industriaque corrigere. Ab litibus semper abhorrui et foro, convivia fugiebam; tenuissimus mihi victus erat, non ut naturam defraudarem, sed ne multum indigerem medico; ac ne te multis morer, ita me semper gessi ut qui non humanis me rebus, sed illas mihi subiectas vellem.

Char. Igitur qui omnia ridebas, de morte solicitus nunquam fuisti?

Umbr. Semel in omni vita de morte cogitavi, licet eam quotidie ante oculos haberem, reputansque et quid illa vellet sibi et quod ego adversus eam comparare possem praesidium; unum tandem hoc mihi in animo sedit, ut honeste tranquilleque aetatem ducendo viverem.

Char. Quod adversus paupertatem invenisti remedium?

Umbr. Ut iudicarem pauperem esse nequaquam posse qui secundum naturam viveret.

Char. Quod adversus honores atque ambitionem?

Umbr. Quod gravissimi casus non nisi ex alto essent loco.

Char. Quod adversus falsos rumores?

Umbr. Rectam conscientiam.

Char. Unquamne te movit superstitio?

Umbr. Deum ubi perspexissem, sacerdotum mendaciis aures occludebam.

Char. Quomodo cum invidia?

the square, and there on feast days I would listen to estate managers talking about weather signs, the condition of the soil, grafting, seeds, irrigation and other farming tasks, and I was eager to become more knowledgeable from their conversation. And since I knew that human affairs were exposed to such diverse and varied perils, if anything went wrong in either the field or the house, after I had finished laughing at the human condition, I took care to correct it with skill and diligence. I always shrank from quarrels and the law court, I avoided banquets, I ate most sparingly, not to cheat nature, but so that I would have little need of a doctor. And, to make a long story short, I always conducted myself in this way because I did not want to be subject to human concerns, but to have them be subject to me.

Charon. So then, you who laughed at everything—were you never worried about death?

Shade. In my whole life I thought about death just once, although I had it daily before my eyes, considering both what it meant and what protection I could provide against it. At length one thought became fixed in my mind: to spend my time in life honorably and in tranquillity.

Charon. What remedy did you find for poverty?

Shade. Deciding that a man could not be poor if he lived in accordance with nature.

Charon. What remedy against honors and ambition?

Shade. That the worst falls were from a high place.

Charon. What remedy against false rumors?

Shade. A good conscience.

Charon. Were you ever moved by superstition?

Shade. When I had thoroughly studied God, I shut my ears to the lies of priests.

Charon. How did you deal with envy?

Umbr. Qui doluerim nunquam, riderem omnia, quo pacto inviderem?

Char. Ecquandone iratus fuisti?

Umbr. Semel in omni vita, neque mea causa, sed quod viderem innocentem hominem iniuste plecti; maledixi concivibus, quod non de iniusto iudicio provocarent; quos ubi vidi mussitare ac tyrannorum vim timere, statim me repressi atque ad risum redii.

61 *Char.* In militiamne aliquando profectus?

Umbr. Semel lituum audii.

Char. Quid? regesne aut regulum quempiam secutus?

Umbr. Minime, mihi enim ipsi me, non regulis natum esse volui.

Char. Liberosne suscepisti?

Umbr. Quos statim extuli et quod bene actum cum illis iudicarem, deo gratias egi.

Char. Igitur et uxorem duxisti?

Umbr. Non tam mea, quam parentum gratia; ea cum triennium mecum exegisset, morte diem obiit; ex eo caelebs vixi.

Char. Cur non alteram duxisti?

Umbr. Quia scirem temeritatem non semper felicem esse et quod bene in illa successisset, veritus sum in secunda periculum facere, meque asserere in libertatem volui.

Char. Quam saepe cum illa litigabas?

Umbr. Nunquam, nam et illa virguncula ac suavis erat et ego ridere assueram domi, non minus quam foris.

Char. Quid de hominum rebus sentiebas?

Umbr. Vanitatem ac stultitiam esse omnia.

Char. Felicem te qui ista noveris.

Umbr. Nec felicem quenquam nec sapientem dixeris; nulli enim tot affuere unquam bona, ut non ei plura defuerint; nec quisquam tam sapiens habitus est usquam, ut non et illi ad veram

Shade. Since I never grieved, but laughed at everything, how should I be envious?

Charon. Were you ever angry?

Shade. Once in my whole life, and not for my own sake, but because I saw an innocent man being beaten unjustly. I abused my fellow citizens because they did not appeal the unjust decision; and when I saw them muttering and fearing the violence of tyrants, at once I restrained myself and went back to laughing.

Charon. Did you ever go to war? 61

Shade. Once I listened to the trumpet.

Charon. What? Did you follow a king or a prince?

Shade. Not at all. I maintained that I was born for myself, not for princes.

Charon. Did you have children?

Shade. Those I bore to the grave immediately, and because I judged that they were well off, I gave thanks to God.

Charon. And so you also took a wife?

Shade. Not so much for my sake as for my parents'. When she had spent three years with me, she died. After that I lived without a wife.

Charon. Why didn't you marry again?

Shade. Because I knew that rashness did not always prosper and since it had turned out well in her case, I was afraid to take a chance on a second wife, and I wanted to claim my freedom.

Charon. How often did you quarrel with her?

Shade. Never, for she was a pleasant young woman, and I was in the habit of laughing at home, no less than outside.

Charon. What was your opinion of human concerns?

Shade. That all was vanity and folly.

Charon. You are a happy man to know these things.

Shade. You should call no one happy or wise, for no one has ever had so many goods that he did not lack for more, nor was anyone ever considered so wise that he did not fall far short of true

perfectamque sapientiam defuerit multum. Nam cum humanae res imperfectae sint omnes, quid earum possit esse perfectum? cumque nihil sit in eis constans, felix quinam esse potest cui momento interdum adversa plurima succedant?

Char. Non dixi te felicem, hospes, sed felicem qui ista noveris.

Umbr. Non ex bonorum cognitione humana existit felicitas, verum ex eorum possessione et usu.

62 *Char.* At ego te et felicem ex hoc iudicaverim, quod cum intelligeres neminem esse posse felicem, ita tamen ipse vixeris, et sapientem, quod in tanta hominum vanitate atque ignorantia sapientem te non minus videri nolueris quam posse esse iudicaveris. Sed quis hic est tam molestus et impudens?

Umbr. Noli, quaeso, ei irasci, amicissimus hic mihi fuit.

Char. Miror qui inter duos tam dissimilibus moribus ulla potuerit esse familiaritas.

Umbr. Si amici proprium est prodesse amico, hic quam in amicum plura in me contulit. Nam tribulis meus cum esset et quotidie litigaret cum uxore, primum docuit cavendas esse secundas nuptias, deinde cum nulla non in re et mihi et vicinis coeteris esset molestus, patientissimum me reddidit mortalium omnium. An quod maius in amicum conferri ab amico beneficium potest quam ut recte ab illo instituatur? Iure igitur hunc amavi et mihi amicum esse duxi.

Char. Ex omni parte sapientia se ostendit tua. Tu vero, molestissime homo, quid tibi volebas istis moribus?

Umbr. Quod ipse sum consecutus.

Char. Quodnam illud?

Umbr. Quod ut eram musca, sic habebar ab omnibus.

and perfect wisdom. For since all human affairs are imperfect, which of them could be bought to perfection? And since there is nothing constant in them, can anyone be happy if sometimes, in a moment, the greatest adversities might overtake him?

Charon. I did not say that you were happy, guest, but happy in knowing the things you do.

Shade. Human happiness does not arise from understanding of good things, but from their possession and use.

Charon. But I would deem you happy also from the fact that 62
although you understood that no one can be happy, you still lived that way, and wise because, amid the great vanity and ignorance of mankind, you did not wish to seem less wise than you deemed it was possible to be. But who is this fellow, so difficult and impudent?[84]

Shade. Please don't be angry with him. This man was my closest friend.

Charon. I wonder how there could be any friendship between two men of such dissimilar characters.

Shade. If it is the property of a friend to be of use to a friend, this man has bestowed more on me than on a friend. For since he was a kinsman of mine and he quarreled with his wife every day, first, he taught me to avoid second marriages, then, since he was troublesome in everything to me and his other neighbors, he made me the most patient of all mortals. Is it possible for any greater benefit to be bestowed on one friend by another than being correctly instructed by him? Rightly, therefore, I loved him and considered him my friend.

Charon. Your wisdom reveals itself in every way. But, you difficult fellow, what did you want to achieve with these habits?

Shade. What I did achieve.

Charon. What was that?

Shade. That as I was a fly,[85] so I was considered by everyone.

Char. Unum illud puto tibi vehementer doluit, aculeis quod careres.

Umbr. At verba mihi erant aculei, quibus ego vel vincebam culices.

Char. Digna tibi pro factis istis et a culicibus et a crabronibus infligetur poena. Verum age, hospes Etrusce, quando percunctari singulos agendo remo nimis magno est impedimento et iudices iam abisse e ripa video, edoce in tanta multitudine si quos ipse noveris.

63 *Umbr.* Geretur tibi mos: hic qui se primum offert mendacissimus fuit omnium quos unquam viderim. Illud autem maximum iudicat mendaciorum quibus usus est unquam, quod cum uxore (ut ex eo aliquando audivi) nunquam se litigasse asseveraverit. Is qui eum sequitur adolescens in maximis vixit divitiis, senex in summam inopiam redactus est, quippe cuius studium fuerit ex aere fumum, e fumo metallum facere. Nam dum aurum ex fornace quaerit, sua omnia in ignem coniecit. Tertius ille non modo libidinosissimus, verum etiam immanis fuit, qui nec brutis abstinuerit. Duo illi, alter pernitiosissimus assentator fuit, laeno alter pellacissimus, quibus artibus primos sibi et ad Caesares et ad pontifices aditus fecere. At ille alius accusando maximas comparavit divitias; cui cum praeter insimulationem ac maledicentiam nihil dulce esset, arte hac primum apud principes locum tenuit; quae ego magis scio quod mihi relata essent a tribulibus quam quod nosse ea studerem. At illum tam severa et tristi fronte et novi et suspexi utpote omnium quos ipse viderim integerrimum et certe natum ad recte informandos animos; qui cum et verbis philosopharetur et moribus, quae ipse dissereret, ea re atque exemplo comprobabat; cuius operae precium fuerit audire orationem.

Charon. The one thing that pains you terribly, I suppose, is that you lack stings.

Shade. But words were my stings, and with them I outdid even gnats.

Charon. A worthy punishment for these actions will be inflicted on you by gnats and wasps. But come now, Etruscan guest, since it slows me down too much to interrogate individuals as I am plying my oar, and I see that the judges have already gone from the bank, tell me if you know any in this great multitude.

Shade. I will oblige you. The one who first presents himself is the 63
greatest liar I ever saw. But he considers the biggest lie he ever told to be his claim that he never quarreled with his wife (as I sometimes heard him say). The one who follows him enjoyed great wealth as a youth, but as an old man was reduced to extreme poverty, since it was his passion to make smoke out of bronze, and metal out of smoke. While he was seeking gold from the furnace, he threw everything he had into the fire.[86] The third was not only incredibly lustful but even monstrous, since he did not refrain even from dumb animals. As for those two, the one was the most pernicious flatterer, the other the most seductive pimp, and with these arts they gained themselves prime access to emperors and popes. But that other one gained great riches by making accusations; since nothing delighted him except allegation and slander, with this art he held first place among princes. I know these things more because I was told by kinsmen than because I was eager to have the information. But I knew that one personally—the one with such an austere and solemn countenance—and I esteemed him as the most honorable man I ever saw, born to educate minds with rectitude. Since he practiced philosophy in both words and behavior, he confirmed his teachings with fact and example. It will be worthwhile to hear what he has to say.

Char. Nihil est quod magis cupiam; sed quaenam illi patria?

Umbr. Ab Umbris ducebat originem.

64 *Char.* Hospes Umber, adventum ad Manes tuum gratulor, tum quod liberatus sis omnino curis iis quae mortales habeant tam male, tum quod audire te vehementer cupio. Novi enim quantus sis philosophus; quamobrem unde tibi maxime videtur exordiens, perge de virtute dicere, dum illuc in portum deferimur.

Umbr. Nec ingratum est quod postulas nec difficile. Et quoniam de virtute ut dicam exigis, nescio quid audire ipse malis quam quae vis sit eius et qui capiantur inde fructus. Etenim cum inter deos atque homines tantum intersit quantum norunt omnes, nec solum spatio, sed natura, nonne admirabilis virtutis vis haec est, quod et deos hominibus conciliat in vita et post mortem illorum coetui eos adiungit? Nam cum virtus medium quoddam sit extrema quae videantur in agendo fugiens, quae maxima illius laus est, haec certe summa est vis eius, quod eadem haec ipsa virtus inter deum et hominem medium tenet. Quo quidem dempto medio, nullus est ad deum accessus, nulla quae ad illum perducat via, quae et ipsa principio deum cognoverit et qui secundum se vixissent inter divos retulerit. Coetera cum fluxa et fragilia sint, auferri temporis momento possunt, at virtus firmum et stabile bonum est. Quae cum nullius sit externae rei indigens, alia tamen omnia absque illa manca sunt, hucque atque illuc incerta feruntur. Felicem igitur qui bene agendo recteque intelligendo perfectam fuerit virtutem assecutus, qui cupiditates compescens et quasi extra pericula positus, liber ac securus vixerit, cumque sibi ipse lex esset, leges nequaquam timuerit, et tanquam omnia sub pedibus subiecta haberet, tutus

Charon. There is nothing I would like better; but what is his homeland?

Shade. He traced his descent from Umbrians.

Charon. Umbrian guest, I congratulate you on your arrival among the dead, both because you have been entirely freed of mortal afflictions and because I greatly desire to hear you. I am aware of how great a philosopher you are. Therefore, starting from whatever point you like, go on to speak about virtue while we sail from here into port. 64

Shade. What you ask is neither disagreeable nor difficult. And although you require me to speak of virtue, I do not know what you want to hear about other than its power and its benefits. Indeed, since everyone knows how great a distance there is between gods and men, not only in space, but also in nature, is this not the admirable power of virtue, that it both makes gods well disposed to men in life and brings men into their company after death? Since virtue is a mean that shuns apparent extremes in action, its greatest praise is certainly its highest power: for this same virtue also occupies the middle ground between god and man. Indeed, if this mean is taken away, there is no access to god, no way that leads to him, since virtue both was acquainted with god in the beginning and has brought back among the saints those who have lived in accordance with it. Since other things are transitory and perishable, they can be carried away in a moment; but virtue is a strong and lasting good. Although it has need of no external thing, all other things are defective without it and are carried uncertainly this way and that. Happy the man who has achieved perfect virtue by right action and correct understanding; who, suppressing immoderate desires and placed beyond the reach of danger, has lived free and untroubled; who, being a law unto himself, has had no fear of laws; and who, as if he had all things cast beneath his feet, has proceeded safely in the face of the clamor of

incesserit contra populi rumores, contra tyrannorum libidines, atque adversus fortunam ita steterit, ut ingruentem eam a se repulerit, neque manum porrexerit blandienti!

Char. Quam vere et supra quam dici potest magnifice de virtute locutus es! Ac, per Plutonem, oratio ista hominum expressit felicitatem; quam parum tamen animo cernentes caecitate sua in pernitiem magis volentes eunt quam coacti trahuntur. Quotus enim ex his quos innumerabiles quotidie transveho, non se ipsum incusat? non stultitiam, quanquam sero, queritur suam! Quo magis, optimi hospites, vestrum utrique gratulor, qui et in agendo et in perspiciendo veritatem sic secuti atque adepti fueritis, ut quam a vulgi ignorantia longissime recessistis, tam ad felicitatem proxime accessisse videamini. Sed iam, ut videtis, cursum hunc confecimus, et me traiiciendis aliis opus est regredi, vos ut descendatis, Ite igitur felices, et quo animo vitam traduxistis mortem etiam feratis, per quam iam estis immortalitatis viam ingressi.

Tu vero, sapientissime Mercuri, gregem hunc coge, et ubi videbitur, ad iudices propera.

Merc. Ego vero propero, vos sequimini.

[Metrum I]

Grex Umbrarum Nocentium

Pergamus miseros visere Manes.
Flendo in lucis prodimus auras.
Flendo transigimus tempora vitae.
Tristem flendo navimus amnem.

Et quod restat iter hoc quoque flendo
Infelices conficiamus.

the multitude, in the face of the caprice of tyrants, and has taken a stand against Fortune in such a way as to repel its onslaught and resist its flattery.[87]

Charon. How truly and with what inexpressible eloquence you have discoursed on virtue! And, by Pluto, this discourse of yours has perfectly described human happiness. Yet not perceiving it because of their own blindness, men go to destruction willingly rather than being dragged by force. How few of those I carry across every day in countless numbers do not accuse themselves, do not blame their own stupidity, however belatedly! All the more, excellent guests, do I congratulate both of you, since in action and understanding you have so followed and achieved the truth that, to the degree that you have moved away from the ignorance of the crowd, you seem to have come closest to happiness. But now, as you see, we have completed this voyage, and it is necessary for me to go back to ferry others and for you to disembark. Go then in blessedness, and with the same spirit that you lived your life, may you bear also your death, through which you have already entered onto the path of immortality. 65

But you, wisest Mercury, round up this crowd and, when it seems best, hasten to the judges.

Mercury. I'm hastening. You there, follow along.

[Poem I][88]

Flock of Guilty Shades

Forward we march to view the pitiful dead.
Weeping we came forth to the breezes of light.
Weeping we passed the space of our lives.
Weeping we crossed the sorrowful stream.

And weeping too for the rest of the way
We must finish our journey in woe.

Minois miseris ora ferenda
Et formidata Aeacus umbra,

Spectandusque truci cum Rhadamantho.
Nos latranti Cerberus ore,
Nos et multiplici gutture serpens
Pascetque atro trux leo rictu.

[Metrum II]

Grex Umbrarum Innocentium

Nos favoni laenis aura
Et virenti prata flore,
Nos beatis rura campis
Perpetuique manent tempora veris.

Mella nobis sponte manent,
Vina largo fonte sudent
Ac liquenti lacte rivi,
Grataque decutiant balsama rami.

IOANNIS IOVIANI PONTANI
DIALOGUS QUI INSCRIBITUR CHARON
FINIT FELICITER

Pitiful, Minos' looks we must bear,
Gaze on Aeacus too, that hideous shade,

Rhadamanthus as well, coldblooded and harsh.
Cerberus will shepherd us, his baying mouth wide,
And the snake, bending and twisting its throat,
And the cruel lion, his maw black with blood.

[Poem II][89]

Flock of Innocent Shades

The soft breeze of the zephyr awaits us,
And meadows with flowers in bloom,
The fields of the blessed await us,
And seasons of eternal spring.

Let honey pour out for us freely,
Let vines drip with bounteous flow,
Let rivers run with milk, and trees
Cast sweet balsam from their boughs.

THE DIALOGUE ENTITLED *CHARON*
BY GIOVANNI GIOVIANO PONTANO
SUCCESSFULLY ENDS

ANTONIUS

Hospes Siculus, Compater Neapolitanus

1 *Hosp*. Quaenam, quaeso, bone civis, Antoniana est Porticus?

Comp. Antoniumne, hospes, requiris, an eam quae ab illo Porticus Antoniana dicitur?

Hosp. Et porticum ipsam nosse et Antonium videre cupio; audio enim pomeridianis horis illic conventum haberi litteratorum hominum; ipsum autem Antonium, quanquam multa dicit, plura tamen sciscitari quam docere solitum, nec tam probare quae dicantur quam Socratico quodam more irridere disserentes; auditores vero ipsos magis voluptatis cuiusdam eorum quae a se dicantur plenos domum dimittere quam certos rerum earum quae in quaestione versentur.

2 *Comp*. Haec illa est porticus, sane dignus tali conventu locus, in qua desiderare nunc quidem Antonium possumus, videre amplius non possumus. Etenim solitudo ipsa meusque hic ornatus plane tibi declarare possunt amisisse nos Antonium; neque enim unquam dicam mortuum quem putem vivere, quod et ipsum paucos ante quam decederet dies acerrime disserentem audivimus, neque eius me mors angit, quae vita est bonis, sed quod iucundissima eius consuetudine sapientissimisque colloquiis est carendum. Quid enim erat laetis in rebus Antonio iucundius? Quid rursus in turbatis atque asperis gratius?

3 Incredibilis quaedam in eius oratione vis inerat res humanas contemnendi ferendique fortuitos casus aequo animo, quippe cum omnia referret ad Deum diceretque latere nos et bonorum

ANTONIUS

Sicilian Visitor and Compater[1] of Naples

Visitor. Tell me, please, good citizen, which is the portico of Antonio?[2] 1

Compater. Are you looking for Antonio, visitor, or the portico that is named Antoniana after him?

Visitor. I want both to get acquainted with the portico itself and to see Antonio. For I hear that a gathering of literary men meets there in the afternoons and also that Antonio himself, although he speaks a great deal, generally offers more questions than answers and is less likely to approve of what is said than to mock the speakers in a sort of Socratic manner, and that in fact he sends his listeners home more filled with a certain pleasure in what he says than confident about the questions under discussion.

Compater. This is the portico, a worthy spot for such a gathering, 2
where now we can long for Antonio to be sure, but see him no more. As its emptiness and this garb of mine bear witness, we have lost Antonio — for I would never call anyone dead whom I consider to be living. We heard him discussing this point himself most vigorously a few days before he departed; and it is not his death that distresses me (for the good, death is life), but being deprived of his most delightful companionship and eminently wise conversation. Indeed, in happy times what was more delightful than Antonio? What more welcome in turbulent and adverse ones?

In his speech there was a certain extraordinary power to rise 3
above human concerns and to respond with equanimity to chance misfortunes, inasmuch as he ascribed all events to God and said that the causes of both goods and ills are hidden from

et malorum causas. Pleraque autem videri quae non essent mala, ut quae obiecta nobis essent a Deo, quo humana in iis constantia fortitudoque enitesceret. Quotum enim fortem inveniri, si quieta et secura omnia nobis forent? natos esse homines ad comparandam virtutem, ad excolendos animos; neminem autem sine laboribus plurimis posse hoc assequi, sed decipi opinione nimisque demisse ac molliter nobiscum nos ipsos agere; quae fluant aquas salubriores esse magisque probari, quae vero restagnent noxias ac pestilentes esse. Nullum fortem agricolam cui non incalluerint manus, nec medicum bonum qui non plurimis ac maxime gravibus morbis curandis versatus sit ipse diutius; milites ab assuetudine perpetiendorum laborum exanclatisque periculis laudari; nullos denique artifices claros evadere, praeterquam quos assiduus labor longaque exercitatio docuisset. Optimo itaque et fortissimo cuique labores ac molestias offerri a Deo eamque veluti materiam praeberi in qua sese exerceat, cum excellentia hominum coeterorum, tum imperatores ipsi quos praecipue ament et quorum virtus est perspectior,[1] iis gravissima et periculosissima quaeque demandent, atque hanc quidem ipsam, non quae praedam quaeritaret, maxime illustrem militiam esse. Et vero ignavi esse, imbecilli, desidis odisse labores, fugitare molestias velleque in ocio ac sub umbra marcescere.

4 Sed cum Antonio optime iam actum fuerit. Ad te, hospes, potius revertar. Haec, inquam, illa est porticus in qua sedere solebat ille senum omnium festivissimus. Conveniebant autem docti viri nobilesque item homines sane multi. Ipse, quod in proximo habitaret, primus hic conspici interim, dum Senatus, ut ipse usurpabat, cogeretur, aut iocans cum praetereuntibus aut secum aliquid succinens, quo animum oblectaret; ut nuper, paucos antequam morbo aggravaretur dies, recitare eum me-

us. And he said that many things seemed evil that were not, since they had been put in our way by God so that human fortitude and constancy could shine forth in them. For how many people would be found to be courageous if all our affairs were peaceful and secure? Human beings were born to achieve virtue, to cultivate the mind. No one can attain this goal without many struggles; but we entertain illusions and treat ourselves too indulgently and leniently. Flowing water is more healthful and more highly recommended, but standing water is harmful and full of disease. There is no respectable farmer with uncallused hands, no good doctor who has not been long engaged in curing numerous and grave diseases; soldiers are praised for being used to enduring hardships and for the steadfast endurance of danger. Finally, no artists achieve renown except those taught by constant effort and long practice. And so to all the best and the strongest persons God presents struggles and difficulties, and this is provided for them as material to practice on, so to speak. All preeminent men, and generals in particular, entrust all the most onerous and dangerous tasks to the men whom they especially love and whose courage is well tested. (This indeed is the most honorable form of military service, not hunting for booty.) Moreover, it is the mark of a coward, a weakling, a slacker to detest struggle, to flee difficulty, to be willing to go soft in idleness and in the shade.

But it has already worked out for the best for Antonio. I will 4
turn back to you instead, visitor. This, I say, is the portico in which that most companionable of all old men used to sit. Learned men and nobles as well gathered in considerable numbers. He himself, because he lived nearby,[3] was the first to be seen here in the interval while the "Senate," as he liked to call it, was assembling, either jesting with passersby or chanting something to himself for his own amusement. I remember that he recited recently in this way, just a few days before he was

mini, cum ego adessem una et Herricus iste Pudericus, quem hic vides. Est autem carmen, quo uti oppidatim dicebat Apulos, ad sanandum rabidae canis morsum; insomnes enim novies sabbato lustrare oppidum, Vithum nescio quem e divorum numero implorantes; idque tribus sabbatis noctu cum peregissent, tolli rabiem omnem venenumque extingui. Quod carmen quia memoria teneo, referam illud, si placet.

Hosp. Atqui pergratum feceris.

[Metrum I]

Comp.

Alme Vithe pellicane,
Oram qui tenes Apulam
Litusque Polignanicum,
Qui morsus rabidos levas
Irasque canum mitigas,
Tu, sancte, rabiem asperam
Rictusque canis luridos,
Tu saevam prohibe luem.
I procul hinc, rabies, procul hinc furor omnis abesto.

5 *Hosp.* Sane luculentum carmen et perquam facilem Apulis ipsis deum!

Comp. Felicissimos omnium eos mortalium dictitare solebat Antonius.

Hosp. Qui regionem incolerent tam intemperatam?

Comp. Etenim coeteros quidem homines cum nulli non stulti essent, vix stultitiae suae ullam satis honestam afferre causam posse, Apulos vero solos paratissimam habere insaniae excusandae rationem: araneum illum scilicet, quam tarantulam nominant, e cuius ammorsu insaniant homines; idque esse quam fe-

overcome by illness, when I was present along with Enrico Poderico, whom you see here.[4] It is a charm he said the Apulians used in the towns to cure the bite of a rabid dog. Unsleepingly, they would go around the town nine times on the Sabbath, calling on some saint or other called Vitus[5]; and when they had done this by night on three Sabbaths, all the rabies and poison were eliminated. Since I remember this song, I will repeat it if you like.

Visitor. I would like that very much.

[Poem I][6]

Compater.

Gentle Vitus, dog averter,[7]
you guard the coast of Puglia
and the shore of Polignano;[8]
you relieve their rabid bites
and tame the wrath of dogs.
Keep off cruel rabies, holy one,
and the dog with ghastly jaws;
keep off the savage scourge.
Get thee hence, O rabies, go; let all madness be far away.

Visitor. A very fine song, and a divinity exceedingly accommodating to the Apulians! 5

Compater. Antonio used to claim that they were the happiest of all mortals.

Visitor. People who lived in such an extreme climate?

Compater. He said that although there were no people who were not stupid, the rest could offer scarcely any decent reason for their stupidity, but the Apulians alone had a ready excuse for their insanity: to wit, the spider they call the tarantula, whose bite drives people crazy; and that this was the most fortunate thing in the world because anyone might decently avail himself

licissimum, quod, ubi quis vellet, insaniae quem suae fructum cuperet etiam honeste caperet. Esse autem multiplicis veneni araneos atque in iis etiam qui ad libidinem commoverent, eosque concubinarios[2] vocari; ab hoc araneo ammorderi quam saepissime solere mulieres licereque tum illas fasque esse libere atque impune viros petere, quod id venenum alia extingui ratione nequeat, ut quod aliis flagitium, mulieribus id Apulis remedium esset. An non summa haec tibi quaedam felicitas videatur?

Hosp. Per Priapum, summa!

Comp. Parce, hospes, oscenis, obsecro.

Hosp. Atqui putabam mihi in Osca regione uti oscenis licere, cum populariter audiam iurari per deorum ventres perque iecinora atque per eam partem cuius ipsos etiam Cynicos perpuderet.

6 *Comp.* An ignoras pessimum morum auctorem populum esse? Quid enim habet quod maximo etiam iure non improbes? Atque hanc quidem iurandi impuritatem mare attulit, utinamque hoc solum a Catalanis didicisset noster populus! Sicam ab iis accepimus, nec est quod Neapoli quam hominis vita minoris vendatur; quod nisi vester Blancas, Aesculapius alter, curator accessisset, maiorem civium partem excisis auribus, labiis, aut naso mutilo videres. Scortari quoque sine pudore didicimus atque in propatulo habere pudicitiam. Iuventus nostra lustris dedita quod locandis noctibus a meretricula quaeritur ipsa die ligurit; ideoque innocentissimus olim populus, dum a Catalonia reliquaque Ispania comportandis gaudet mercibus, dum gentis eius mores ammiratur ac probat, factus est inquinatissimus. Sed quando accusari haec possunt magis quam corrigi nec satis est

of the desired profit from his insanity, whenever he liked. There were spiders with different poisons, and among them even some, called concubinary spiders, that stirred people to lust. Women liked to get bitten by this spider as often as possible, and then it was permissible and lawful for them to seek men freely and with impunity, because the poison could be eliminated by no other means; as a result, what was a disgrace for other women was a cure for those of Apulia. Wouldn't this seem to you the highest form of happiness?

Visitor. The highest, by Priapus!

Compater. No obscenities, visitor! I obsecrate you.

Visitor. But I thought I was allowed to use obscenities in Oscan territory,[9] since I hear that in common parlance people swear by the bellies of the saints and their livers and by the part that made even the Cynics blush.

Compater. Don't you know that the masses are the worst authority 6
on behavior? For what attribute do they have that you might not most justly condemn? And indeed the sea has brought this foul way of swearing—and I wish this was the only thing our people had learned from the Catalans! From them we have acquired the dagger, nor is anything in Naples sold more cheaply than a man's life, and if your Branca,[10] a second Asclepius, had not arrived to heal them, you would see the majority of the citizens with their ears and lips cut off, or with their nose mutilated. We have also learned to consort shamelessly with prostitutes and to put chastity on sale. Our young men, given over to dens of iniquity, sponge in the daytime on what a little tart asks to hire out her nights; and so what was once the most innocent populace, while it was delighting in amassing goods from Catalonia and the rest of Spain, while it was marveling at and assenting to the customs of that nation, became the most debased. But since these things can be blamed more than they can be corrected, and since it is not really safe, let's stop talk-

tutum, dicere de populi moribus desinamus. Quod autem ad iusiurandum attinet, Scythas maxime laudare solebat Antonius, quibus non per deorum capita aut corda, ut his ipsis Ispanis, non per corpora, ut nostris, sed per convictum iurare mos esset; at Poenos maxime irridere, qui per triplex iurarent uxoris repudium, quippe quam ubi ter quis repudiasset, revocare amplius in domum fas non esset. Sed qui praeterit percunctandus est, ut Antonium iam agamus.

Compater Neapolitanus, Peregrinus, Hospes Siculus, collocutores

7 *Comp.* Heus, viator.

Per. Sessores, salvete.

Comp. Tu, ut video, de sole aestuas.

Per. At vos, ut sentio, de umbra frigetis.

Comp. Hic homo sitit, ni fallor.

Per. Hi madescunt, quod satis scio.

Comp. Heus, hospes, dic, quaeso.

Per. Heus, cives, tacete, obsecro.

Comp. At nos scire ex te quaedam volumus.

Per. At ego sciscitari pauca.

Comp. Sciscitator; vacat, atque etiam, si placet, sedeto.

Per. Ad regem propero; ad regiam utra ducit via?

Comp. Utraque; sed quaenam salutandi regis causa? hoc enim ipsum scire cupimus, itaque vicem redde.

Per. Nimis quam timeo nostrae reipublicae, ne paucis post annis occidione occidant populi.

ing about the behavior of the populace. But as for swearing, Antonio used to praise the Scythians most highly, since it was their custom to swear, not by the heads or hearts of divine beings, like these Spaniards, nor by their bodies, like our own people, but by their banqueting; yet he used to laugh most at the North Africans because they swore by the triple rejection of their wives, since when anyone had rejected a woman three times it was unlawful to call her back any more into the house. But we must question the one who is passing by, so that we can play the part of Antonio.

Compater of Naples, Traveler, and Sicilian Visitor as interlocutors

Compater. Hey, traveler! 7

Traveler. Hello, seated ones.

Compater. You, I see, are overheated by the sun.

Traveler. But you, I sense, are growing cold in the shade.

Compater. This man is thirsty, if I'm not mistaken.

Traveler. These people are drunk, I'm quite sure.

Compater. Well then, stranger, speak, I ask you.

Traveler. Well then, citizens, be quiet, I beseech you.

Compater. But we want to know some things from you.

Traveler. But I want to ask a few questions.

Compater. Ask away; there is time, and take a seat, too, if you like.

Traveler. I am hastening to the king. Which way leads to the palace?

Compater. Both ways. But what is your reason for greeting the king? We are eager to know this, so return the favor.

Traveler. I am in great fear for our state, that within a few years the people will be destroyed in wholesale destruction.

Comp. Ab gladione, an a pestilentia, an a diluvione timendum est nobis? Equidem et te siderum progressiones observasse reor, quando astrologorum est has clades praedicere.

Per. Certiora affero: Maxima in singulis non modo oppidis, sed pene domibus vis est gallorum septennium; eos satis compertum est anno septimo parere enascique basiliscos serpentes, quorum obtutu homines infecti pereant. Quod nisi a rege probe prospectum fuerit, actum est de regni Neapolitani populis; opus autem esse ut singulis in oppidis singuli deligantur cauti et solertes viri, qui haec mala gallorum caede procurent videantque ne quid respublica detrimenti capiat. Ego hac de causa atque ut reipublicae prosim meae, ad regem eo, vos valete.

8 *Comp.* Abi, bone civis deque patria bene merite. Dii boni, quam multiplex est hominum stultitia! quam inanes cogitationes! quid vanitatis in vita! quanta inanissimarum etiam rerum solicitudo! An est, hospes, quod irridere hoc homine magis possis? si ridenda quam miseranda potius stultitia est nostra.

Hosp. Quid, obsecro, ad haec Antonius?

Comp. Fabellam hic aliquam subtexuisset, qua declarare amplius posset hominum levitatem. Calletiam olim mulierculam victum quaeritasse Caietae; hanc coetera vitae munera obiisse satis laboriose atque industrie. Cum autem Alfonsus rex Caietae diversaretur aliquando videretque Calletia tum viros tum matronas, omnes denique id agere, quo maxime modo regem honorificentissime exciperent, eam, pannis supra pudenda convolutis, proficiscentem ad rem divinam regem et praecedere in pompa nu-

Compater. Is it the sword or pestilence or flood that we should be afraid of? I suppose that you have also observed the movements of the stars, since predicting these catastrophes is the sort of thing astrologers do.

Traveler. My news is more reliable. Not only in every single town, but almost within every household there is a great number of seven-year-old cocks; it is well known that in the seventh year they give birth and basilisk serpents are hatched, and that by looking at them people are poisoned and die. Unless the king takes care of this properly, the peoples of the Kingdom of Naples are done for. It is necessary that skilled and careful individuals in each town be chosen to avert these evils by a slaughter of the cocks and to see to it that the republic takes no harm.[11] For this reason, and to be of service to my state, I go to the king. Farewell.

Compater. Depart, excellent citizen; you have served your country 8
well. Good gods, how manifold is the stupidity of mankind! How foolish their ideas! What vanity there is in life! How much anxiety there is about even the most futile matters! Is there anything, visitor, you could find more laughable than this man? That is, if our stupidity is to be laughed at rather than pitied.

Visitor. What, I ask you, would Antonio have said to these things?

Compater. At this point he would have added some anecdote to demonstrate more fully the folly of mankind. Once upon a time a silly woman called Callezia made her living in Gaeta; she had met all the other obligations of life with plenty of hard work and diligence. But one time when King Alfonso was staying in Gaeta, and Callezia saw both men and women—everyone in fact—talking about how to receive the king with the greatest possible honor, she rolled up her skirts above her private parts and made it a habit both to precede the king in procession with

dato femore et recedentem in regiam eodem habitu reducere solitam, nullisque abduci potuisse rationibus, quin hoc honoris genere, sic enim dicebat, regem prosequeretur. Quocirca explicandis fabellis Antonius vel improbare quippiam solebat vel laudare.

9 *Hosp.* Bellissimum hominem! Sed praeconem hunc audiamus qui tantam sibi facit in populo audientiam: regium videlicet edictum; nunquam vidi turgidiores buccas. Puto ego hominem fermento vesci; quos clamores, dii boni!

Praeco. Licere fasque esse Iovianum Pontanum, qui habitat in proximo, tuto egredi domo, tuto per urbem incedere, tuto etiam de rebus Latinis Latinum hominem disserere; istos vero Graecissantis homines atque Italo-graecos nihil ei maledicere, nihil incessere; non oculis, non barba, non superciliis, non denique ulla Graeca arte illudere. Hoc regem ipsum edicere. Si quis secus fecerit, barbam ei evellere impune licere, pilleum auferre, crepidulas eripere. Quod edictum sanctum esse omnes sciunto idque tuba hac testor.

Hosp. Quid? Obsecro, Ioviano huic Graecine tam sunt infesti?

Comp. Quin ipse Graecorum est studiosissimus eorumque veneratur disciplinas ac suspicit ingenia, nec est quod Graecos timeat. Esse autem nostratis quosdam adolescentes eosque nuper e Graecia rediisse, qui cum nec Graece sciant nec Latine, esse tamen gloriosissimos; quibus si barbam pilleolumque ademeris, nihil omnino Graecum habeant. Eos, ait, et Graecae et Latinae orationis inculcatores esse; ubi cum Graecis fuerint, mussitare, cum Latinis autem mirum esse quam Graece omnia; hinc illos

her thighs bare as he set out for divine service and to escort him in the same fashion on his return to the palace; and no arguments could dissuade her from attending the king with this sort of honor, as she called it. Thus, by telling stories Antonio was accustomed either to criticize or to praise something.

Visitor. An exceedingly fine fellow! But let us listen to this herald who is getting such a hearing in the crowd. It must be a royal edict. I have never seen more puffed-out cheeks. I think the fellow feeds on yeast. Good gods, what a noise! 9

Herald. It is permitted and lawful for Gioviano Pontano, who lives in the neighborhood,[12] safely to leave his house, safely to proceed through the city, also safely to discourse as a Latin man about Latin matters. But those Grecizing fellows and Italo-Greeks are not to slander or attack him; they are not to mock with their eyes, nor with their beard, nor with their eyebrows, nor, in short, with any Greek art. The king himself publishes this decree. If anyone does otherwise, it is permissible to pull out his beard with impunity, to take off his felt hat, to snatch off his sandals. Let all men know that this edict is inviolable, and I testify to it with this trumpet.

Visitor. What? I ask you, are the Greeks so hostile to this Gioviano?

Compater. In fact, he himself is most devoted to the Greeks and venerates their teachings and admires their abilities, nor is there any reason for him to fear Greeks. But there are certain young men of our country, recently returned from Greece, who, although they know neither Greek nor Latin, are nevertheless very full of themselves; if you took away their beard and felt hat, they would possess nothing Greek at all. These, he says, are crammers of Greek and Latin speech; when they are with Greeks they keep quiet; when with Latins it is amazing how Greek everything is. That is why they are enraged and almost

irasci et pene furere, horum timeri audaciam cervicesque insolentissimas.

Hosp. Quid? ipse didicitne Graecas litteras?

Comp. Eas adolescens attigit, sed in Italia; nam in Graecia magis nunc Turcaicum discas quam Graecum; quicquid enim doctorum habent Graecae disciplinae in Italia nobiscum victitat.

10 *Hosp.* Satis haec novi; sed observemus pilleatulum hunc.

Comp. Recte mones.

Hosp. Quidnam is succinit? At vide quam sibi placet, atque utinam praeteriens salutaret!

Per. Ἄριστον μὲν ὕδωρ.

Hosp.[3] Quid sibi haec volunt verba?

Comp. Rem optimam ait esse aquam.

Hosp. An hic nos accusat ut parum sobrios? ego tam insignem iniuriam non feram.

Comp. Parce, hospes, Pindarica est sententia, etiam ab Aristotele laudata.

Per. ὁ δὲ
χρυσὸς αἰθόμενον πῦρ
ἅτε διαπρέπει νυ-
κτὶ μεγάνορος ἔξοχα πλούτου.

Hosp. An pergit maledicere?

Comp. Desine commoveri, aurum laudat.

Hosp. Heus, tu, Graecanice homo, quid malam in rem non te hinc proripis? Iudeis aurum et foeneratoribus laudato.

11 *Comp.* Iram ponito, abiit. Hos ventris crepitibus similes dicebat Antonius; nares tantum offendere, coetera ventum esse, siquidem ventosos esse ac putidos. Sed quando suffarcinatulus iste iam abiit, nos ab Antoniana consuetudine aut quaerendi aliquid

in a fury; their insolence and overbearing arrogance are terrifying.

Visitor. Really? Has he himself learned Greek?

Compater. He took it up as a young man, but in Italy; for in Greece now you might learn Turkish more easily than Greek. All the learned men Greek studies possess make their living in Italy with us.

Visitor. I know that well enough; but let us keep our eyes on this 10
little fellow in the felt hat.[13]

Compater. Good advice.

Visitor. What is he reciting? Just see how pleased with himself he is! I wish he would greet us as he passes!

Passerby.[14] *Ariston men hydor.*[15]

Visitor. What do those words mean?

Compater. He says that the best thing is water.

Visitor. Is he accusing us of being drunk? I won't put up with such an egregious insult.

Compater. Hold on, visitor. The sentiment is Pindar's, praised even by Aristotle.

Passerby. *ho de*
chrysos aithomenon pyr
hate diaprepei nu-
kti meganoros exocha ploutou.[16]

Visitor. Is he still uttering slanders?

Compater. Stop worrying. He's praising gold.

Visitor. Hey, you, Greekish fellow, why don't you go to hell? Praise gold to the Jews and the moneylenders.

Compater. Give your anger a rest. He's gone. Antonio used to say 11
that these people are like rumblings in the belly: they only displease the nose; the rest is wind. It's because they are full of hot air and stink. But since that puffed-up fellow[17] is gone now, let's stick with Antonio's habit of inquiring or speaking on

aut dicendi ne recedamus. Et iam dudum video Herricum hunc dicere aliquid velle; quamobrem dicentem audiamus.

Herricus Pudericus, adolescens, senex, hospes

12 *Herr.* Ammonuere me qui nuper praeteriere adolescentuli Neapolitanae nobilitatis, quae prope iam interiit. Etenim cum considero iuventutem nostram praeter maiorum instituta domi ac sub porticibus desidere, eos vero qui rempublicam amministrent publicorum oblitos morum nihil nisi suas tantum res agere atque in privatum consulere, non possum non deplorare nostrae nobilitatis interitum. Dii boni, Ladislao rege quae nostrorum civium domi forisque erat industria! quam honesta de omni virtute contentio! Certamen erat, domine senes aequitate atque consilio an foris iuventus fortitudine ac fide maiore rempublicam gererent. Itaque videres seniores praesidere provintiis, moderari populos, iuvenes in maximis rebus ac periculis regi adesse, certare quis fortiorem navare posset operam; adolescentulos mirum in modum a primis annis meditari patrium decus equitando, iaculando, semper aliquid agendo, quo ipsorum apparere posset industria. Nunc placet ocium atque mollities: sequimur scorta, desidemus in ganeis, alea in manibus est atque fritillus, turpissima quaeque habentur in precio. Contentio est cuius uxor, soror, filia, pluris veneat nullumque inter ignavos fortisque discrimen, nisi quod fortitudo odio est atque contemptui; ignavissimus quisque maxime carus acceptusque multitudini; iura, pietas, decus, demum omnia venalia. Sed me ipsum compescam revertarque ad Antonium atque hunc qui praeterit

some topic. In fact, for some time now I've noticed that Enrico wanted to say something; so let's hear him speak.

Enrico Poderico, Young Man, Old Man, Visitor

Enrico. The young men who went past just now reminded me of the Neapolitan nobility, which now has nearly disappeared. When I consider that our young men, contrary to the customs of their ancestors, lounge about at home and under porticoes, and moreover that those who govern the state, forgetful of public morals, transact nothing but their own business and take counsel for their personal interest, I cannot help lamenting the dissolution of our nobility. Good gods, when Ladislas was king,[18] what industry there was among our citizens at home and abroad! How honorable the competition for every virtue! It was a point of contention whether greater service was performed for the state by the old men at home with equity and counsel or by the young ones abroad with courage and loyalty. And so you might see older men presiding over provinces, governing peoples, the young serving the king in the most important matters and greatest dangers — competing to see who could show the more vigorous effort. In a remarkable manner boys from their first years kept in mind the glory of their fatherland — riding, throwing the javelin, always doing something to demonstrate their industry. Now idleness and luxury are in favor; we follow whores, we sit around in dives, dice and dice box in hand, all the most disgraceful things are held in high regard. It is a competition to see whose wife, sister, daughter can bring a higher price, and there is no distinction between the cowardly and the brave except that bravery is hated and despised, while the greatest coward is beloved and popular with the multitude. Justice, piety, glory — everything, in short — is for sale. But I will restrain myself and turn back to Antonio and question this 12

potius adolescentem percunctabor. Amabo, unde tantum hilaritudinis tecum affers, bone adolescens?

13 *Adol.* Meo ab antistite.

Herr. Obsecro, nisi praeproperas, hilaritudinis tantae nobis rationem explica.

Adol. Laborabat ex intestini plenioris morbo[4] meus antistes, de cuius salute medici cum desperassent, unus Panuntius, archiater, solam hanc salutis relictam spem docuit, si disploso intestino animam inclusam expederet. Eum igitur, cum diem totum deos orans contrivisset nec aliquid exploderet, reversus Panuntius monuit uti, corporis salute desperata, pro animae salute deos fatigaret. Tum ille in deos deasque conversus, integram fere noctem in gemitu lamentationibusque exegit, dum peccatorum condonationem ac vitae coelestis tranquillitatem coelites ipsos orat. Aderat familiaris ingenio non adeo superstitioso, qui antistitis questus precesque non satis aequo ferens animo: 'Ecquaenam tandem, inquit, pater, dementia ista est, putare deos coeli tibi particulam donaturos, qui ne levissimi quidem pediti liberales esse voluerint?' Hac urbanitate captus antistes, cum in risum solveretur, intestinum exolvit, quo de risu in crepitum exoluto, statim morbo liberatus est. Haec laetitiae meae causa, haec voluptas est, qui herum salvum factum tantopere gaudeam. Is igitur post aliquot dies confirmatis ac refectis viribus, cum ludere quantillum cupiat, Frontonillam arcessit, quam intellexit non multos ante dies facere quaestum coepisse; me, qui scortillum nossem, rogatum mittit, uti cum laverit leveritque, ad coenam eat. Dixi quae cupiebatis; abeo, vos valete.

young man going by instead. Please, good youth, what makes you so merry?

Young Man. My bishop. 13

Enrico. Please, unless you are in a terrible hurry, tell us the reason for your high good humor.

Young Man. My bishop was suffering from too full a belly, and when the doctors had despaired of saving him, one Panuntius, the court physician, explained that his only remaining hope of salvation was to explode his gut and release the gas trapped inside. Accordingly, when he had prayed all day long and worn out the saints and expelled nothing, Panuntius returned and instructed him, since there was no hope for the salvation of his body, to importune the saints for the salvation of his soul. Then turning to the saints both male and female, he spent nearly the whole night in groaning and lamentations while he prayed to the heaven dwellers for the remission of his sins and the tranquility of life in heaven. At hand was a servant, not very superstitious by nature. Tiring of the moans and prayers of the bishop, he said: "What is this madness of yours, father, to think that the saints will give you a piece of heaven, when they begrudge you even the slightest fart?" Taken with this witticism, the bishop burst out laughing and let loose his gut; and when it had been loosed into a thunderous crash from laughter, he was at once freed of his ailment. This is the cause of my delight, this is my pleasure, since I am so happy that my master has been saved. And so several days later, now that his vigor has been built up and restored, being eager for a little sport, he sends for Frontonilla, having learned that she began to ply her trade just a few days ago. He has sent me, since I'm acquainted with her, to ask the little whore to come to dinner when she has washed and perfumed herself. I have told you what you wanted to know; I'm going now; farewell.

14 *Herr.* O saecula, o mores! fuit, fuit olim in sacerdotibus christianis continentia et castitas, dum innocentia in honore, dum paupertas in precio fuit. Nunc, proh pudor! quae non sentina mundior sacerdotio est? Ecce autem qui levare dolorem hunc queas; senex praeterit, octogenarius, cantitans, amore insaniens; e media scilicet Valentia delatum hoc est. Audiamus si placet.

[Metrum II]

Sen. Ne rugas, Mariana, meas neu despice canos.
De sene nam iuvenem, dia, referre potes.

Herr. Bellissimum senem! Videtis quam blande salutat fenestellas? quam larga etiam manu rosam spargit? quid hoc sene delirius?

Sen. Digna Iovis thalamis, o et Iove digna marito,
Quid mirum si me, candida nympha, fugis?

Herr. Etiam lacrimatur!

Sen. Delitiae, Mariana, meae, si diggeris annos,
Iuppiter hac fiet iam ratione senex.

Herr. Lepidissimam argumentationem!

Sen. Et cani flores, orientia sidera cana;
Canaque quae torquet spicula blandus amor.

15 *Herr.* Canitiem sane iuvenilem! sed compellemus hominem. Amantissime adolescens, per eum quem colis amorem perque viridem atque florentem aetatem tuam eamque quam deperis virginem rogatus et nos de amoribus solicitos nostris adi atque alloquere. Equidem vel ex te uno iudicari plane potest, recte sensisse illos qui Venerem elegantiarum deam fecere; quid enim

Enrico. What an age we live in! What morals![19] Once, once, conti- 14
nence and chastity existed in Christian priests, while innocence was honored and poverty esteemed. Now—for shame!—what sewer is not cleaner than the priesthood? But look! Here's a way you can lighten this woe: an old man is going by, eighty years old, singing, crazy with love. Clearly this has been brought from the heart of Valencia! Let's listen if you like.

[Poem II][20]

Old Man. Despise not my wrinkles, Mariana, nor yet my white hair.
O goddess, you can turn an old man into a boy,

Enrico. A very fine old man! Do you see how ingratiatingly he salutes her little windows? With what a generous hand he scatters roses? Is anything more deranged than this old man?

Old Man. O worthy of Jove's bed, and worthy of Jove as a husband,
What wonder, fair nymph, if you flee me?

Enrico. He's even weeping!

Old Man. If you add up the years, Mariana, my darling,
Jupiter by this count will already be old.

Enrico. A most charming line of argument!

Old Man. White, too, are flowers, white the stars in their rising,
And white the darts sent spinning by sweet love.[21]

Enrico. His white hairs are certainly youthful! But let's speak to 15
the fellow. Most enamored young man, I entreat you by the love you cherish and your green and flowering youth and the maiden you love to distraction: approach us, since we are concerned for our own loves, and speak. It's plain to see, just judging from you, that those who have made Venus the goddess of

te, qui in Veneris contubernio vivis, elegantius? Age, amabo, quam tibi cum amoribus tuis blande? quam e sententia?

Sen. Suavissime, quippe cum decreverim, quaecunque in amore hoc mihi accidant, iucundam in partem accipere; irascitur, aversatur, contemnit, fugit, ad voluptatem refero, gravissimeque obiurgandos censeo qui regnum Amoris accusant, bellissimi pueri, laenissimi heri, indulgentissimi dei. Hic munditias, nitorem, ornatum, leporem, comptum, ludos, iocum, carmen, elegantiam, delitias, omnem denique vitae suavitatem invenit; me, qui senex sum, aetatis huius molestiarum oblitum, non tantum non invitum, sed volentem quoque ad suavissima quaeque secum trahit. Sequor convivia, cantus, hymeneos, choreas, pompas, festos dies, theatra. Sed iam asserenascit: illam ego ad fenestram video quae me immortalium vitam agere inter mortales facit. O fulgentissimum iubar ac rerum specimen!

16 *Herr.* O inane et lubricum caput! Ne autem delirantem hunc senem, hospes, mirere, civitas nostra tota delirium est, utinamque non tam vere urbem hanc solam liberam esse usurpasset Antonius, in qua una cuique quod libitum esset liceret! Sed comprimenda est oratio: Euphorbia transit. Assurgamus mulieri atque offam hanc Cerbero obiiciamus. Et iam praeteriit, abiit; bene habet, salva sunt omnia. Memor es, hospes, beluae illius quam dux Poenorum Annibal vidit in somnis, silvas, agros, villas, oppida quaque incederet cuncta vastantem? Haec illa est belua, nequaquam tamen ut illa somnium, sed historia et vera quidem belua. Cives quidem coeteri aut horologium aut galli cantum secuti e somno cubilibusque excitantur, at viciniam nostram

elegance had the right idea; for what is more elegant than you, who live in the fellowship of Venus? Come, please, how pleasantly are things going with your love? To your satisfaction?

Old Man. Most delightfully, since I am determined to put an agreeable construction on whatever happens to me in this love. She is angry, she turns away, she despises, she runs off—I enter it in the pleasure column; and I consider deserving of the harshest censure those who find fault with the rule of Amor—the most beautiful boy, the gentlest master, the most indulgent god. He has devised elegance, style, fine dress, charm, adornment, sport, jest, song, refinement, delight, in short, every pleasant thing in life; he takes me, an old man, forgetting all the troubles of my time of life, not only not against my will, but even with my eager consent, to all the sweetest pleasures with him. I frequent dinner parties, music, weddings, dances, processions, holidays, theatre. But now evening is near;[22] at the window I see the one who makes me live among mortals the life of the immortals. O most gleaming radiance and ideal of the world!

Enrico. O vain and unsteady character! In case you are surprised 16
at this raving old man, visitor, our whole state is a madhouse. If only Antonio had not spoken so truly when he used to say that this city alone was free, since here alone everyone could do as he pleased! But we must stop talking. Euphorbia is going by. Let us stand up for the woman and toss this sop to Cerberus.[23] And now she has passed. She is gone. That's good; all is safe. Do you recall, visitor, the beast that Hannibal, the Carthaginian general, saw in his sleep laying everything waste—forests, fields, farms, towns—wherever it went?[24] She is that beast, but definitely not a dream like the other, but a reality and an actual beast. Other citizens are roused from sleep and their beds in response to a clock or cockcrow, but Euphorbia's shouting doesn't let our neighborhood get even a wink of sleep at

Euphorbiae clamores ne videre quidem somnum noctibus patiuntur, quasi dies agere quietos valeamus. Clamat, inclamat, frendit, dentitonat, hinnifremit, rixatur, furit; veru, pelves, patinas iaculatur, titionatur, candelabratur: novis enim vocibus novus beluae huius furor exprimendus est, atque utinam exprimi plane posset! ancillas alias delumbat fustibus, alias mutilat gladio, has unguibus excaecat, illas pugnis exossat; quid multis opus est? pestis quidem ipsa Euphorbia pestilentior non est. Ferunt Germanos olim praedicare solitos se a Dite patre ortos; ego vel deierare ausim tris illas Furias, Herebum quoque ipsum Euphorbia prognatos esse.

17 *Hosp.* Dii, talem pestem avertite! Quid, obsecro, de hac Antonius?

Herr. Optime consultum iri Romano pontifici si Euphorbia haec in summo Alpium iugo constitueretur, cuius vociferationibus momento eodem Germaniae, Galliae, Britanniae ad concilium arcessiri possent: orbis enim terrarum campanam Euphorbiam esse.

Hosp. O salsum atque urbanum hominem! Sed quinam hi sunt quos composito admodum gradu vultuque adeo gravi concedentes ad nos video?

Herr. Iunior ille Elisius Gallutius, suavi vir ingenio, Andreas alter Contrarius, facundus ac praestans rhetor, gravissimi uterque viri nostroque ex ordine, quibus advenientibus de more collegii huius assurgendum est.

Andreas Contrarius, Compater, Herricus, Elisius

18 *Andr.* Salutem vobis multam atque opulentam dicunt Elisii Camenae.

night—as if we were able to spend our days in peace. She shouts, she reviles, she howls, she makes noises with her teeth, she whinnies, she quarrels, she rages; she throws a skewer, basins, pans; she brandishes pokers, hurls candlesticks: the novel madness of this beast needs new words to describe it, and if only it could be clearly described![25] Some of her maids she cripples with cudgels, others she maims with the sword; she scratches out the eyes of these with her claws, beats those to a pulp with her fists. Need I say more? Not even the pestilence itself, in short, is more pestilential than Euphorbia. They say the Germans once used to claim that they were the offspring of Father Dis;[26] I would even venture to take an oath that the three Furies and Erebus itself were the offspring of Euphorbia.

Visitor. Gods, avert such a pestilence! What, please, did Antonio have to say about her? 17

Enrico. That it would be in the best interest of the pope in Rome for Euphorbia to be set upon the highest peak of the Alps, so that at the same moment the peoples of Germany, Gaul, and Britain could be summoned to a council by her shrieking; for Euphorbia was the bell of the world.

Visitor. What a witty and amusing man he was! But who are these men I see walking toward us with measured step and such a serious expression?

Enrico. The younger is Elisio Calenzio, a pleasant-natured man; the other is Andrea Contrario, an eloquent and distinguished speaker.[27] Both are extremely eminent men of our class, at whose coming we must rise in accordance with the custom of this college.[28]

Andrea Contrario, Compater, Enrico, Elisio

Andrea. The Roman Muses of Elisio wish you great and opulent good health. 18

Comp. At nos et Elisium havere et Andream opulenter salvum esse iubemus, neque enim grammaticos adeo veremur ut opulentiam cum salute coniungere timeamus.

Andr. O minime superstitiosum hominem! Sed ut hoc facilius condonetur a nobis tibi, tamen ne in grammaticorum iram incidas etiam atque etiam vide.

Comp. An oblitus es Antonii catellorum (hoc enim verbo utebatur) eos persimiles dicentis qui de ossibus deque frustillis ac miculis, si quae forte sub mensam decidant, rixentur ? Odi ego cimicum genus stomachorque agrestem acerbitatem ac putidas insectationes; sed, amabo, quinam inter vos sermones erant ?

19 *Andr.* Hoc ipsum agebamus, aut potius indignabamur, ab rabiosa eorum garrulitate tuti nihil esse, sive versiculum edideris sive epistolam scripseris; quorum ipsorum scriptis oculum si admoris, nihil inertius, nihil inconcinnius, nihil oscitatius videas, quippe cum nihil supra grammaticum habeant. Et tamen operae precium est videre, neglecto aut potius abiecto Cicerone, quantam prae se ferant dicendi artem atque scientiam. Invasere rhetorum materiam, quorum etiam agros depopulati, quod videant acutiora quaedam, ut ipsi putant, a Quintiliano tradi, in Ciceronem sublatis signis agmineque instructo procedunt; nec intelligunt Ciceronem sic a Quintiliano laudari, ut hunc suspiciendum, hunc imitandum esse moneat, *dono quodam providentiae genitum, in quem totas virtutes suas eloquentia experiretur,* id denique non immerito consecutum, ut *Cicero iam non hominis nomen, sed eloquentiae habeatur.* Quodsi loqui vera volumus, illa vel summa Quintiliani laus est, quod divinae Ciceronis eloquentiae diligentissimus observator atque inspector fuerit. Quid enim quamvis acute ab eo in dicendi arte praecipitur quod non

Compater. But we both greet Elisio and bid Andrea to be opulently healthy, nor are we so much in awe of the grammarians that we are afraid to join wealth with health.[29]

Andrea. You are the least superstitious man in the world! But although we readily pardon you for it, still you must always take care not to incur the wrath of grammarians.

Compater. Have you forgotten Antonio's saying, that they were just like whelps (for that was the word he used) fighting over any bones and bits and crumbs that happen to fall under the table? I can't stand bedbugs like that, and boorish strictness and offensive criticisms make me angry. But, please, what were you talking about?

Andrea. We were discussing this very thing, or rather we were 19
complaining that you can't put out a line of verse or write a letter that is safe from their rabid jabbering; but if you should cast an eye on their own writings, you would see nothing flatter, nothing more graceless, nothing more yawn-making,[30] since grammar is all they have to offer. And yet it is worth the effort to see how much skill and knowledge of language they pride themselves on, despite their neglect, or rather rejection, of Cicero. They have invaded the material of the orators. After plundering their fields, because they see that certain more sagacious ideas, as they think, are handed down by Quintilian, they pick up their standards, draw up their battle lines, and march against Cicero; and they do not understand that Quintilian so praises Cicero that he advises us to look up to him and imitate him, saying that "by some gift of providence he was born in order for eloquence to try out her full powers on him" and that with good reason "Cicero is now considered not the name of a man, but of eloquence itself."[31] But to tell the truth, the highest praise of Quintilian is that he was the most attentive observer and examiner of the divine eloquence of Cicero. For what instruction in the art of speaking does he present, however saga-

e Ciceronis fonte haustum sit? quid tam rarum aut sepositum ostenditur quod non Ciceronis orationum exemplis testimoniisque doceamur illum orantem egisse quae post a Quintiliano rhetoribusque aliis considerata atque animadversa scriptis observanda tradantur?

20 Arguitur Ciceronis de oratoris fine sententia, quod non sit *dicere apposite ad persuasionem,* sed sit solum *bene dicere* oratoris finis; nec vident acutissimi homines duplicem in oratore finem considerandum esse. Quod Boetius quidem vidit, si non tam acutus grammaticus, at certe rerum naturae peritissimus ac definiendi magnus artifex. Ait enim quod inter dialecticam atque rhetoricam interest, id in materia non cerni, quippe cum utraque thesim atque hypothesim subiectam habeat, sed in usu, cum altera interrogatione, altera perpetua oratione utatur, ac dialectica integris syllogismis, rhetorica enthymematibus gaudeat; item in fine, quod dialectica quae vult extorquere ab adversario conatur, rhetorica iudici persuadere; siquidem dialecticus dialecticum tantum habet adversum se constitutum, orator vero habet etiam iudicem, qui inter se atque adversarium sententiam ferat. Quocirca oratoris finem duplici ratione considerandum esse censet; alterum quidem in oratore ipso, in iudice vero alterum; in ipso quidem *bene dicere* (quod quid est aliud quam *dicere apposite ad persuasionem?*) in iudice vero persuadere. Neque enim si qua impediant oratorem quominus persuadeat, dum officium suum fecerit, iccirco finem consecutus non est; siquidem, qui officio suo cognatus est finis, eum facto officio consequitur; ac tametsi eum qui extra positus est finem non semper attingit, fine tamen suo contentus esse potest, sentiens

ciously, that was not drawn from Cicero's well? What revelations so rare or choice does he make that do not show us — from the examples and evidence of Cicero's own speeches — how it was Cicero's oratorical practice that Quintilian and other rhetorical teachers later examined, evaluated, and handed down to be followed in their writings?

20 They blame Cicero for his opinion about the aim of the orator on the grounds that the end of the orator is not "to speak in a manner suited to persuasion,"[32] but only "to speak well"; but these sagacious fellows do not see that one needs to bear in mind a twofold end in the orator. This Boethius certainly saw — if he was not so sagacious a grammarian, he was surely most knowledgeable about the natural order and a great master of the definition. For he says that the difference between dialectic and rhetoric is not discerned in their matter, since each has a thesis and a subordinate hypothesis, but in their practice, since the one employs question and answer, the other continuous discourse, and dialectic delights in whole syllogisms, rhetoric in enthymemes. They likewise differ in their end because dialectic attempts to wrest what it wants from an adversary, rhetoric to persuade the judge, inasmuch as the dialectician has only a dialectician to face, but the orator has also the judge, who decides between him and his opponent.[33] For this reason he believes that the end of the orator should be examined on a double basis, the one end lying in the orator himself, but the other in the judge. That lying in the orator himself, to be sure, is to speak well (and what is that except "to speak in a manner suited to persuasion"?); but that lying in the judge is to persuade. Indeed, if something should keep the orator from persuading, as long as he has performed his duty, he has not failed to accomplish his end; for he accomplishes the end associated with his duty when his duty has been done, and although he does not always attain the external end, he can still be con-

artem ipsam qui suus est fine non fraudari. Etenim medici opera cum in sanitatem intenta sit, imperatoris in victoriam, licet neuter finem, qui extra constitutus est, nonnunquam adipiscatur, uterque tamen suum assequitur si alter aegrotum recte curaverit, alter exercitum ac rem bellicam bene administraverit.

21 Duplex igitur oratoris finis est: bene dicere ac persuadere; quod utrunque Cicero complexus est, et cum ait oratoris officium esse *dicere apposite ad persuasionem* (nam qui apposite dicit bene quidem dicit, id quod Quintiliani sententiae convenit iudicantis rhetoricae finem ac summum esse *bene dicere*), et cum post subdit oratoris finem esse *persuadere dictione* (quia oratoris dictio apud iudicem est, complectitur qui sit pro suscepta causa bene dicendi finis).

22 Quodsi orator dicendo persuadet, neque enim temere a Cicerone dictum est *persuadere dictione,* nec Quintiliano nec oblatratoribus his dicere opus est, quod pecunia etiam persuadet, quod forma, quod alia etiam multa; nam nec pecunia dicendo persuadet, nec forma; trahit enim animos hominum pecunia rerum utilium cupiditate ac gratia, forma voluptatis. Ostendere autem cicatrices inde susceptum est, quod insitus est homini naturaliter misericordiae affectus, qui tum videndo, tum audiendo movetur, idque consilii prudentiaeque est agere. Quo orator cum utitur, non quidem dicendo, sed agendo persuadere conatur, licet huiusmodi actiones oratoris propriae sint, unde agere dicitur, quibus etiam verba gestumque idoneum accommodat. Et cicatricum quidem ostentatio non multum habitura est virium si oratio defuerit, quae lacrimas ac misericordiam excitet. Nam

tented with his own end, recognizing that his skill is not cheated of the end which is his own.[34] For although the effort of a doctor is directed to healing, that of a general to victory, even if sometimes neither accomplishes the end that is determined externally, nevertheless each does achieve his own end if the one has correctly treated the sick person, and the other has well managed his army and the activity of war.

Thus the end of the orator is twofold: to speak well and to 21
persuade. Cicero includes both—both when he says that the duty of the orator is "to speak in a manner suited to persuasion" (for the one who speaks suitably certainly speaks well, a point that harmonizes with Quintilian's conclusion that the end, in fact the highest end, of the art of oratory is "to speak well"[35]), and when he adds afterward that the end of the orator is "to persuade with speech"[36] (because the orator speaks before a judge, he includes the purpose of speaking well on behalf of the case one has taken on.)

But if the orator persuades by speaking—for Cicero said 22
"to persuade with speech" not without good reason—there is no need either for Quintilian or for these present yappers to say that money also persuades, as do beauty and many other things.[37] Indeed, money does not persuade by speaking, nor does beauty, for money influences people's minds by the desire and attraction of useful things, beauty with the desire and attraction of pleasure. Then they take up the showing of scars, because man is naturally imbued with the emotion of pity, which is moved both by seeing and hearing; and achieving this is a matter of strategy and skill. When the orator uses it he attempts to persuade not by speaking but by acting, although actions of this kind are proper to the orator (that is why he is said "to act" in a case); and he also accommodates his words and the appropriate gesture to them. In fact, showing scars is not likely to have much effect in the absence of an oration of a

auctoritas, dignitas, aspectus, si mutus fuerit, quomodo persuadeat aut quid persuadeat? Quod vero ad meritorum recordationem attinet, an parum tibi loqui merita ipsa videntur, quae beneficiorum in rempublicam, quae rerum fortiter gestarum memoriam revocent, quae gratitudinis ammoneant? Etenim eorum qui diem obiere, sive amici sive inimici fuerint, cum recordatio nos subit, quod ab iis recte aut male facta, quae in mentem veniunt, loquendi vim quandam habeant, vel excitatur in nobis desiderium vel odium renovatur. Quocirca loquuntur haec quodammodo per se, ac nihilominus, ut iudices, ut auditores moveant, dicente indigent, qui, quo fuerit eloquentior, eo magis commovebit.

23 Ac mihi quidem videtur Cicero tum addendo *apposite ad persuasionem* tum dicendo *persuadere dictione* avertisse a se id quod Quintilianus, pace eius dixerim, non modo non avertit, sed ne quidem vidit.[5] Si quis enim, quod declamatores faciunt, nullo dato iudice causam domi fingat et utriusque, id est suas et adversarii partes agat, hinc accusando, illinc defendendo, huius nimirum erit finis tantum *bene dicere*. Quid enim aliud in causa domi composita, nullo vero adversario, nullo iudice, quaeretur nisi solum *bene dicere?* Quo fit ut in causa ficta idem sit finis qui est in vera, *bene dicere,* neque inter fingere et apud iudicem vere agere aliquid intererit. Quo quid magis absonum? quid magis absurdum? Hoc videns Cicero declamatorem sic ab oratore seiunxit, ut quod unum intererat, id officium ac finem oratoris ostendendo exciperet cavillamque averteret; inter officium autem et finem parum interesse Cicero ipse ostendit, cum docet *in officio quid fieri, in fine quid officio conveniat considerari.* Videtis quam

kind to arouse tears and pity. If authority, dignity, or appearance is mute, how or of what might it persuade us? But as for the evocation of meritorious actions, do you think that the merits themselves speak too little to recall the memory of benefactions to the state and of heroic deeds that would inspire gratitude? When we recall those who have died, whether they were friends or enemies, because their excellent or wicked actions that come to mind have a certain power of speech, either longing is aroused in us or dislike renewed. So these things somehow speak for themselves, and yet still need a speaker in order to move judges and hearers; and the more eloquent a speaker is, the more he will move them.

Indeed, I think that Cicero, both by adding "in a manner suited to persuasion" and by saying "to persuade with speech," 23
avoided what Quintilian (speaking with all due respect) not only did not avoid, but did not even see. For if anyone, as the declaimers do, should make up a case at home without a judge and argue both sides (that is, his own and his opponent's), accusing from this side and defending from that, of course his end will be only "to speak well." Indeed, in a case concocted at home, with no real adversary and no judge, what else will be sought except just "to speak well"? And so the end in a fictitious case is the same as that in a real one, "to speak well," nor will there be any difference between make-believe and really pleading before a judge. What could be more incongruous than that? What more ridiculous? Seeing this, Cicero separated the declaimer from the orator in such a way that, by pointing out the duty and end of the orator, he picked out the single difference and avoided petty criticism. On the other hand, Cicero himself demonstrates that there is little difference between one's duty and one's end when he explains that "with regard to duty one considers what should be done, with regard to the end what is suitable to the duty."[38] Do you see how clearly through duty he

plane per officium expresserit finem qui in oratore consideratur, cum *quid fieri conveniat* ait? Porro quid facere oratorem convenit aut quae eius officii partes sunt, nisi *bene dicere?* Quod quibus artibus et quae faciendo assequi possit ipse iam tenet; per finem vero ostenderit id quod bene dicendo quaeritur, persuadere.

24 Nam cum ipsae hominum actiones ob finem aliquem suscipiantur ac finis alius alium respectare videatur, finis ille quem in oratore ipso constitutum diximus, hoc est *bene dicere,* in alium illum finem intendit qui extra positus est, sicuti recte curandi finis aegroti sanitatem ac rei bellicae bene administrandae de hoste victoriam respicit; ab illis enim ad has est via. Etenim cum finis in rebus humanis sit, ut opinor, ad quem cuncta referantur et cuius gratia fiunt coetera omnia, nimirum ut sit finis oratoris *bene dicere,* bene dicendi ipsius finis est persuadere. Itaque si oratorem considerare volumus ut dicentem tantum, finis eius erit *bene dicere;* sin ut agentem in foro ac iudicis animum quibus potest artibus in sententiam suam atque in causam quam agendam suscepit trahere contendentem, Ciceronis de fine sententia erit absoluta, Quintiliani vero manca atque imperfecta.

25 Non considerari autem forum forensisque actionis finem ab eo qui dicit oratoris finem esse *bene dicere,* quamvis paucis, manifesto tamen ostendemus. Quintiliani ipsius, cum de rhetoricae nomine latine interpretando loquitur, verba haec sunt: *Nam oratoria sic efferetur ut elocutoria, oratrix ut elocutrix; illa autem de qua loquimur rhetorice, talis est qualis eloquentia.* Igitur si rhetorica eloquentia est, et orator erit eloquens. Eloqui autem aliud non est quam bene dicere; qui enim eloquitur bene dicit, et eloquen-

has expressed the end to be considered in the orator when he says, "what should be done"? Furthermore, what is appropriate for the orator to do, or what is the role of his duty except "to speak well"? He himself grasps the arts and actions by which he can achieve this; but through the end he will demonstrate that the object of speaking well is to persuade.

Since people's actions are undertaken for some end, and one end seems to look to another, the end that we have said is located in the orator himself, that is, to speak well, aims at another end which is placed outside him, just as the purpose of correct treatment looks to the health of the sick person and that of good management of military matters looks to victory over the enemy; the road leads from the former to the latter. For since there is an end in human affairs, as I believe, to which all things are referred and for the sake of which everything else is done,[39] clearly even supposing that the end of the orator is "to speak well," the end of speaking well is to persuade. And so if we want to think about the orator only as a speaker, his end will be "to speak well"; but if we think of him pleading in the forum and striving with the skills at his command to draw the mind of the judge to his own view and to the cause he has undertaken to plead, Cicero's opinion on the orator's end will be complete, Quintilian's defective and unfinished. 24

Moreover, we will demonstrate clearly but briefly that anyone saying that the orator's end is "to speak well" is not taking into account the forum and the end of forensic action. Here are Quintilian's own words when he talks about translating the Greek word *rhetorice* into Latin: "For *oratoria* will be formed like *elocutoria, oratrix* like *elocutrix,* but the *rhetorice* that we are talking about is equivalent to *eloquentia.*"[40] Thus, if rhetoric is eloquence (*eloquentia*), the orator likewise will be eloquent. But to be eloquent is the same thing as to speak well, for the person who is eloquent speaks well, and eloquence will be the ability or 25

tia erit bene dicendi sive facultas sive ars sive scientia. Quare dicere *oratoris finem esse bene dicere* eius est qui nec susceptae in foro dictionis finem considerat, ut si quis aratoris finem dixerit bene arare, cum bene arandi finis sit serere, nec clientem respicit, non secus ac si quis dixerit medici finem esse bene curare, quae definitio aegroti ipsius, qui medicum sibi adhibuit, nullam videtur habere rationem. At qui dicit oratoris finem esse *dicere apposite ad persuasionem* et eius qui dicit et eius pro quo dictio suscepta est rationem complectitur. Quae finitio perfecta quidem est, cum et officium eius qui dictionem suscepit ostendat et causam, idest finem cur officium susceptum sit, declaret.

26 Qua tamen in re pertinaciores non erimus, ut qui honus hoc defendendi Ciceronis adversus Quintilianum non susceperimus, quippe qui non oblatrando, sed quaerendo modestissime oratoris finem investigare nititur; quem quodam in loco dicentem audiamus:

> *Nam illud genus ostentationi compositum solam petit audientium voluptatem ideoque omnes dicendi artes aperit ornatumque orationis exponit, ut quod*[6] *non insidietur nec ad victoriam, sed ad solum finem laudis et gloriae tendat. Quare quicquid erit sententiis populare, verbis nitidum, figuris iucundum, translationibus magnificum, compositione elaboratum, velut institor quidam eloquentiae, intuendum et pene pertractandum dabit; nam eventus ad ipsum, non ad causam refertur. At ubi res agitur et vera dimicatio est, ultimus sit famae locus.*

the skill or the science of speaking well. Therefore, the statement that "the end of the orator is to speak well" is that of one who neither takes into consideration the end of speech undertaken in the forum, as if someone were to say that the purpose of a plowman is to plow well, when the purpose of plowing well is to sow, nor has any regard for the client, just as if someone were to say that the end of the doctor is to treat correctly, a definition that seems to take no account of the sick man who has called in the doctor. But someone who says that the end of the orator is "to speak in a manner suited to persuasion" includes a consideration of both the one who speaks and the one on whose account speaking has been undertaken. This definition is complete since it both demonstrates the duty of the one who has undertaken to speak and declares the reason—that is, the end for which the duty was undertaken.

Yet we will not be too pertinacious in this matter since 26
we have not undertaken the task of defending Cicero against Quintilian, who is endeavoring to examine the end of the orator not by yapping, but by modest inquiry. In one place we hear him saying:

> For the oratory composed for display seeks only the pleasure of the audience, and accordingly it demonstrates all the arts of speaking and puts on show stylistic embellishment since it is not laying traps and striving for victory, but for the single end of praise and glory. For that reason, the orator, like a peddler of eloquence, will lay out for inspection and almost for handling whatever is popular in sentiment, elegant in language, charming in rhetorical figures, rich in metaphors, and highly finished in composition. Indeed, success is ascribed to him, not to his case. But when a case is being tried and there is a real contest, fame should be the last consideration.[41]

Videtis ut his verbis victoriam quaeri, non bene dicendi laudem et gloriam ostendit? Sentitis quid dicit, cum eventum non ad ipsum, sed ad causam referri dicit? Et quod hoc fortasse minus apertum esset, subdit: *ubi res agitur et dimicatio vera est, ultimus sit famae locus,* docens in victoriam totis viribus incumbendum, quae quidem nisi persuaso iudice ac bene dicendi arte viribusque eloquentiae expugnato comparari nequeat.

27 Verum adversus grammaticos, istos inquam grammaticos, haec dicenda suscepimus, quorum dentibus ut nihil mordacius sic morsibus venenosius nihil est, errasseque non parum videri potest Antonius, qui catellorum eos persimiles ac non canes, immo rabidas canes aut venenosas potius aspides diceret. Operae precium est etiam videre quibus latratibus quoque impetu in Ciceronianam *status* definitionem ferantur. Sed nolo vobis, hospiti praesertim huic, esse molestior.

28 *Comp.* Et hospiti huic et coeteris qui assumus rem gratissimam feceris, quod declarare nostrum omnium tibi abunde perspectum in Ciceronem studium potest et hospitis tanta in te audiendo attentio. Sed de Antonio aliter tibi persuadeas velim; narrare enim solebat grammaticorum rationem nullam esse praetoribus, quippe qui furentium in numero haberentur; cumque furoris atque amentiae genera licet diversa, comprehensa tamen a physicis essent, solam grammaticorum vesaniam non modo incomprehensam, verum etiam incomprehensibilem esse, quam novo quodam ficto nomine *labirynthiplexiam* vocabat. Referebat enim Sibyllam, nutricem suam, quotiens grammatico cuidam qui per id tempus Panhormi docebat, obviam fieret, carmine usam quo Siculi adversum canes rabidas uterentur;

Do you see how with these words he demonstrates that victory is the goal, not the praise and glory of speaking well? Do you understand what he means when he says that success is ascribed, not to the speaker himself, but to the case? But because it might perhaps seem unclear, he adds: "when a case is being tried and there is a real contest, fame should be the last consideration," explaining that one must bend all one's energies to victory, which cannot be attained unless the judge has been persuaded and overpowered by the art of speaking well and the powers of eloquence.

But we have undertaken to say these things against the 27
grammarians — against the grammarians, I say — whose teeth are the most likely to bite, and whose bites are the most poisonous thing in the world. I think Antonio erred not a little in comparing them to whelps and not calling them dogs, in fact rabid dogs, or rather poisonous asps. It is also worthwhile to see the barking assault they make on Cicero's definition of *status*.[42] But I don't want to bore any of you, especially this visitor.

Compater. You will do a great favor both to this visitor and to the 28
rest of us here. The enthusiasm you know we all have for Cicero can testify to the fact, and so can our visitor's great attentiveness in listening to you. But I would like to change your mind about Antonio. In fact, he used to say that magistrates paid no attention to the grammarians since they were counted among the mad, and that although the types of madness and insanity, however various, were comprehended by physicians, the frenzy of grammarians alone was not only not comprehended, but not even comprehensible; and he made up a name for it: "labyrinthiplexia."[43] He used to say that his nurse Sibylla, whenever she met a certain grammarian who was teaching at that time in Palermo, had recourse to the charm the Sicilians used against rabid dogs; and that only the souls of grammarians

solas etiam grammaticorum animas post mortem non expurgari; quodque infernus eas expiandas non caperet, statim redire in corpora ac propterea contingere ut in dies atque in saecula grammatici dementiores essent; Platonemque hoc ipsum latuisse, item Virgilium Dantiumque, qui de rebus infernis ultimus scripsit. Haec habui quae pro Antonio excusando dicerem. Tu perge, Andrea, et Ciceroniani status defensionem adversus Antonianos catellos vel tuas potius aspides aggredere.

29 *Andr.* Faciam eo libentius quod Herricum nostrum video ex oratione hac, quae adversum grammaticos habita est, mirificam voluptatem coepisse.

Herr. Dici vix potest quam me sermo iste delectet, praesertim cum in memoriam veniat inter duos olim grammaticos gladiis actam rem esse, dum alter alteri vitio daret quod verbo *impleo* generandi casum adiunxisset ac neuter memor esset Livii hoc ipso casu utentis libro quarto: *Ne ita omnia tribuni potestatis suae implerent ut nullum publicum consilium sinerent esse.* Item quinto libro: *Ipse multitudinem quoque, quae semper ferme regenti est similis, religionis iustae implevit.* Sexto etiam casu utitur, cum ait: *Carcerem impleveritis principibus.* Adeo promiscue veteres verbum hoc et secundo et sexto casui iunxere, quod docti illi et acuti grammatici dum ignorant, dum alter alterius sinum atque os despuit, res ad gladios venit tandemque a grammaticis ad chirurgos. Sed quae mihi multa generis huius in mentem veniunt referre desinam, ne tibi sim impedimento; quare quod coepisti perge exequi ac voluptate hac nos exple.

30 *Andr.* Primo loco Ciceronem videamus: *Constitutio est prima conflictio causarum ex depulsione intentionis profecta, hoc modo: fecisti,*

were not purified after death, and that, because the lower world did not accept them for expiation, they returned at once into their bodies, and that was why it was that, day by day and century by century, grammarians became more demented. He said this fact had escaped Plato, and likewise Vergil and Dante, who has written most recently about the affairs of the underworld. This is what I had to say in justification of Antonio. But go on, Andrea, and begin your defense of *status* in Cicero against Antonio's whelps, or rather your asps.

Andrea. I am all the happier to do so because I see that our friend 29
Enrico wonderfully enjoyed your speech against grammarians.

Enrico. I can scarcely express how much that discourse of yours delighted me, especially when I recall how a dispute between two grammarians was once settled by swordplay. One of them charged the other with a fault for constructing *impleo* ["fill"] with the genitive case, and neither one recalled Livy's use of this case in book four:[44] "The tribunes should not so fill everything with their own power that they preclude the possibility of public deliberation." Likewise in book five: "He also filled the masses (which for the most part always follow their ruler's example) with a correct feeling of religious awe."[45] He also uses the ablative case when he says: "You will have filled the prison with the foremost citizens."[46] In fact, the ancients joined this word with the genitive and the ablative case indiscriminately, and since those learned and keen-witted grammarians were ignorant of the fact, when one spat in the lap and the face of the other, the matter came to swords, and finally passed from grammarians to surgeons. But I will refrain from telling the many incidents of this kind that come to mind since I don't want to hold you up. So go on: finish what you started and fill us with this pleasure.[47]

Andrea. First let us look at Cicero: "The *constitutio* [point at issue] 30
is the first clash of pleas that proceeds from the rebuttal of a

non feci, aut iure feci. Deinde Quintiliani status qui sit ex ipsius verbis intelligamus: *Statum quidam dixerunt primam causarum conflictionem; quos recte sensisse, parum elocutos puto. Non enim est status prima conflictio, fecisti, non feci; sed quod ex prima conflictione nascitur.* Et paulo post: *Si enim dicat quis: sonus est duorum inter se corporum conflictio, erret, opinor; non enim sonus est conflictio, sed ex conflictione.* Haec uterque de status constitutionisque definitione.

31 Nos quid definitio ipsa sit primum videamus; quae, ut doctissimis viris placet, *oratio est explicans quid sit id de quo est quaestio.* Quocirca proprium definitionis esse videtur explicare, hoc est distincte atque expresse demonstrare rei quae definitur substantiam, seu quid illud ipsum de quo quaeritur sit. Hoc enim intellecto, ipsa res ut intelligatur oportet, siquidem id quod ante definitionem erat, ut ita dixerim, confusum et complicatum, ubi definitio accessit, distinctum atque explicatum cernitur. Etenim cum hoc ipsum nomen *homo* parum expresse quid homo ipse sit indicet, ubi dixeris 'hominem esse animal rationale mortale,' quod erat involutum nec satis patebat fit expressum et clarum; ipsaque substantiae explicatio fit quotiens genus quo quid continetur et species illae quae differentiae vocantur definitionem ipsam abunde simul constituunt; qua hunc in modum constituta, quae confusa erant diffusius tractata cernuntur. Ex quibus efficitur ut, genere differentiisque monstratis, substantia ipsa appareat.

32 His sic explicatis, videamus harum utra definitionum rem quae definitur melius clariusque ostendat, cum videamus de re

charge, in this fashion: 'you did it; I did not, or I did it justly.'"[48] Then let us understand from his own words what Quintilian means by *status*: "Some have defined *status* as the first clash of pleas, and I think that they have judged rightly but not expressed themselves fully enough. In fact, *status* is not the first clash ('you did it; I did not'), but what arises from the first clash."[49] And a little later: "For if someone should say: 'sound is the clash of two bodies against each other,' he would err, I believe: for the sound is not the clash, but the result of the clash."[50] This is what each says about the definition of *status* and *constitutio*.

First let us see what a definition itself is. According to very learned men it is "a statement explaining what it is that the inquiry is about." Therefore, the task of a definition seems to be to explain, that is, to show precisely and clearly the substance of the thing being defined or what the thing is that is under investigation. For once this is understood, of necessity the thing itself is understood, since what was jumbled together and tangled up, so to speak, before the definition, is seen divided into categories and put in order when the definition has been applied. For example, although the word "man" by itself does not clearly show what a man actually is, when you say that a man is a rational mortal animal,[51] what was obscure and not at all obvious becomes unambiguous and clear. And the substance is explained whenever the genus in which something is included and what is called the specific difference together fully establish the definition. When the definition is established in this way, things previously treated in a confused and diffuse fashion are distinguished from each other. As a result, when the genus and differentiae have been pointed out, the substance itself is obvious. 31

Having explained this, let us see which of these definitions reveals the thing being defined better and more clearly—al- 32

ipsa quaestionem non esse, siquidem Quintilianus ipse qui hac definitione usi essent *recte quidem sensisse, parum tamen elocutos* putat. Ciceroniana, ni fallor, definitio, quod genus et differentias explicat, substantiam profecto ipsam explicat. Nam *conflictio* generis locum obtinet; omnis enim status conflictio est, non contra; siquidem non soli oratores confligunt, perinde ut non solum homo est animal, sed athletae, sed milites, sed exercitus etiam confligunt. *Prima* vero cum dicitur, species ac differentia indicatur, siquidem plures quaestionum status esse eadem in causa possunt, quod ipse quoque Quintilianus ostendit. *Prima* igitur *conflictio* species quaedam conflictionis est, sicuti rationale species quaedam animalis. Deinde additur *ex depulsione intentionis profecta*. Quo addito plane declaratur conflictionem hinc ex intentione, illinc ex depulsione nasci, ut intelligatur, quemadmodum non omne rationale animal, ut Plato putat, mortale est, sic non omnem conflictionem ex telorum missiliumque iaculatione ac manuum consertione, cuiusmodi militaris conflictus est, existere. Videtis ut his in definitione simul positis, res ipsa non implicata et in abdito posita, sed explicata atque in lucem cernatur exposita?

33 Contra Quintiliani definitio non solum rem ipsam in lucem non educit, sed audientem statim turbat et cogitationem eius ad plura ac diversa trahit. In lucem autem non exponi rem ex Quintiliani definitione hinc probatur, quod genus ipsum nimis remoto e loco apparet, cum sit *res*, sive, ut hodie dicunt, *ens*; dicitur enim: *id quod ex prima conflictione nascitur*, idest *res* quae inde nascitur; ac tametsi verum est quod conflictio causarum sit *res*, sit *ens*, tamen hoc ipsum *ens* maxime generale est, siquidem et lapis et lignum et lana et corpus et color et vox et forma et statura et coelum et animal et quodcunque in naturalibus est

though we see that the dispute is not about the thing itself, since Quintilian himself thinks that those using this definition "have judged correctly, but not expressed themselves fully enough." Cicero's definition, if I'm not mistaken, because it explains the genus and differentiae, assuredly explains the substance itself. For the word "clash" takes the part of genus; for every point at issue (*status*) is a clash or conflict, not the reverse—since not only orators clash—just as not only man is an animal—but athletes, soldiers, and armies also clash. But when one says "first," the species and differentia are indicated, for there can be several points at issue in the same case, as Quintilian himself also points out. Therefore, the "first clash" is a species of clash, just as "rational" is a species of animal. Then one adds, "proceeding from the rebuttal of a charge." This addition makes it clear that the clash arises from a charge on one side and a rebuttal on the other, so that it may be understood that, just as not every rational animal, as Plato says, is mortal, so not every clash comes into existence from the hurling of spears and missiles and hand to hand fighting like a military conflict. Do you see how, when these points are included in the definition, the thing itself is perceived as something not implicit and shadowy, but rather explicit and brought to light?

Quintilian's definition, on the other hand, not only does not 33
bring the thing itself to light, but confuses the listener from the start and pulls his thoughts in several different directions. That the thing is not brought to light from Quintilian's definition is demonstrated by the fact that the genus itself is too remote, although it is the thing, or the entity, as they say today. For it is called "what arises from the first clash," that is, the thing that arises from it; and although it is true that the clash of pleas is a thing, an entity, nevertheless this entity itself is exceedingly general, since also stone and wood and wool and body and color and voice and shape and stature and sky and animal and what-

ens ac *res* est. Itaque genus hoc confundit magis quam explicat, dum auditoris mentem in tam multa ac diversa rapit.

Illud deinde *quod ex prima conflictione nascitur* magis ac magis et turbat et confundit et quasdam quasi tenebras illorum qui audiunt mentibus offundit, ut cum dicimus 'homo est id quod ex corpore et anima constat'; quod ipsum non modo de bove, crocodile, ape, serpente, pisce, accipitre, sed de arbore, haerba fruticeque dici potest, nec aliud est dicere quam 'quod animans est,' quod genus plurima diversaque complectitur; siquidem et arbores et haerbae et frutices animantes sunt; anima enim constant et corpore. Quod si dicere malueris: 'homo est id quod ex animali rationali mortali est,' hominis substantiam non solum non explicabis neque in apertum proferes, sed rem ipsam magis ac magis implicabis. Neque enim homo solum est ex animali rationali mortali, sed coniugium, sed familia, sed civitas, sed humani generis societas. At dicere: 'homo est animal rationale mortale' non solum mentem non confundit, sed rem ipsam plane ostendit, idque quod definitur et quod definit ita sibi invicem conveniunt ut mutuam conversionem alternatim faciant, siquidem et animal rationale mortale est homo; id quod non usu venit cum dicitur, 'homo est id quod ex corpore et anima est' et 'quod ex corpore et anima est homo est,' cum possit esse accipiter, piscis, equus, apes, ulmus, brasica, vitis, ligustrum, quae quod animantes sunt, e corpore et anima sunt.

34 Itaque cum dicimus, 'constitutio est prima conflictio causarum nata ex intentionis depulsione,' ita sibi quod definit definiturque invicem consentit, ut convertere liceat pari maximeque conveniente consensu; recte enim explicateque dicetur:[7] 'prima causarum conflictio ex intentionis depulsione nata constitutio est.' Contra confusa nimis definitio erit, nec cum eo quod fini-

ever exists in the natural world is an entity and a thing. And so this genus confuses rather than clarifies since it carries the hearer's mind off into so many different directions.

Then that phrase "what arises from the first clash" disturbs and confounds more and more, and pours a kind of darkness over the minds of those who hear it, as when we say, "man is that which consists of body and soul" — something one could say not only of an ox, crocodile, bee, snake, fish, hawk, but also of a tree, plant, and bush, and it is the same thing as saying, "what is alive," a genus that includes a vast number of different things; for even trees and plants and bushes are alive, since they consist of soul and body. But if you should prefer to say, "man is that which is from a rational mortal animal," you will not only not explain the substance of man or bring it out into the open, but you will complicate the thing itself more and more. For not only man arises from a rational mortal animal, but so do marriage, the family, the state, the society of the human race. But to say, "man is a rational mortal animal," not only does not confuse the mind, but also plainly reveals the thing itself; and what is being defined and the definition harmonize so reciprocally that they can be exchanged with each other in turn, since a rational mortal animal is a man.[52] This does not occur when one says, "man is that which consists of body and soul, and "what consists of body and soul is a man," since it could be a hawk, fish, horse, bee, elm, cabbage, vine, or privet, which, because they are alive, consist of body and soul.

And so, when we say, "*Constitutio* (the point at issue) is the 34
first clash of pleas arising from the rebuttal of a charge," the definition and what is defined agree so well with each other that one can exchange them with equal and perfect agreement, for one may say correctly and without ambiguity: "The first clash of pleas arising from the rebuttal of a charge is the *constitutio*." On the other hand, the definition will be too confused

tur pari modo consentiens si dixerimus, ut Quintiliano placet: 'status est id quod ex prima conflictione causarum nascitur, idque quod ex prima conflictione causarum[8] nascitur est status,' cum e prima conflictione, in qua causa consistit, plura nascantur quae ad statum et causam faciunt, ut cum signa ex quibus coniectura capitur afferuntur, cum testes in medium adducuntur, cum leges recitantur, cum de legibus pugnatur, et huiusmodi alia, quae non modo conflictionem sequuntur, sed absque iis conflictio esse nequeat.

35 Age, consideremus rem maxime similem, militarem conflictum, non sonum, ut Quintilianus. Si quis dixerit, 'militarem conflictum esse id quod existit ex militum certamine manibusque consertis,' primum nec rem ipsam distincte explicabit nec convertere alterum in alterum tam aequa reciprocatione poterit ut recte dicatur, 'id quod ex militum certamine manibusque consertis existit conflictus militaris est'; neque enim ex militum certamine manuumque consertione solus conflictus existit, sed caedes, mutilationes, percussiones, vulnera, fuga, victoria. Itaque cum haec audiuntur, quod quid potissimum intelligere habeatur incertum sit, distrahetur huc atque illuc animus rapieturque in plura atque diversa. At si dixero: 'conflictum militarem esse militum manum conserentium certamen,' statim genus apparebit, idest certamen; omnis enim conflictus certamen est. At non contra certamen omne conflictus est; nam et puellae certant de forma et reges de magnificentia. Cum addo 'manum conserentium,' speciem differentiamque sic exprimo ut nihil dubium, nihil in confuso relinquatur licebitque magno utrinque consensu convertere: 'militum manum conserentium certamen conflictum esse militarem ac militarem conflictum conserentium manum militum certamen esse.'

and not in equal harmony with what is being defined if we say with Quintilian, "*Status* (the point at issue) is what arises from the first clash of pleas, and that which arises from the first clash of pleas is *status*," since from the first clash, in which the plea consists, more things arise that meet the needs of the *status* and the plea, as when evidence is adduced from which a conclusion is grasped, when witnesses are produced before the public tribunal, when laws are read out, when there is a dispute over the laws, and other things of this sort, which not only follow the clash but are indispensable to it.

Come, let us consider the most similar case, a military con- 35
flict, not a sound, as Quintilian did. If someone should say that a military conflict is that which results from a contest of soldiers in close combat, first he will neither explain the thing itself clearly nor will he be able to change one into the other with such equal reciprocity that one could rightly say: "That which results from a contest of soldiers in close combat is a military conflict," for not conflict alone results from a contest of soldiers and hand to hand engagement, but also slaughter, mutilations, blows, wounds, flight, victory. And so when one hears this, because it is uncertain what exactly one is supposed to understand, the mind is pulled this way and that and carried off into several different directions. But if I say, "a military conflict is a contest of soldiers engaging in close combat," at once the genus is obvious (that is, a contest), for every conflict is a contest. On the other hand, however, not every contest is a conflict, for girls compete in beauty and kings in magnificence. When I add "engaging in close combat," I express the species and differentia in such a way that nothing is left doubtful, nothing in confusion, and one can turn it either way very harmoniously: "a contest of soldiers engaging in close combat is a military conflict," and "a military conflict is a contest of soldiers engaging in close combat."

36 Illud igitur inter Ciceronis Quintilianique definitionem interest quod inter has quas modo posui militaris conflictus definitiones; ac si loqui vera volumus, altera, idest Ciceroniana, est philosophi rem explicantis atque ante oculos ponentis, altera eius qui id potius quaerere videatur, ut qui audiunt caecutiant magis quam ut recte videant. Quoniam igitur Quintilianus ipse *recte quidem sensisse, parum tamen elocutos* putat qui sic statum definiere, videte, obsecro, uter ipsorum rem eloquatur. Mihi quidem Cicero eloqui rem et explicare, Quintilianus vero balbutire quodammodo (tanti viri pace dixerim) videtur. Poteram multa quae de ratione definiendi a doctis viris traduntur hunc in locum conferre, quae non duxi esse necessaria, contentus paucis his ostendisse Ciceronem bene, expresse, caute, plane statum definisse. Quam nostram defensionem tantum ab accusando Quintiliano abesse volumus, ut videri velimus non adversus Quintilianum causam suscepisse, sed ut qui potius Ciceronem a grammaticorum qui nunc vivunt rabidis morsibus liberare studeremus.

37 Tu vero, Herrice, vicem redde et quam adversus grammaticos bilem paulo ante conceperas meo etiam rogatu evome, aut, si te capitis fortasse gravat abscessus, Elisio nostro provintiam hanc delega.

Herr. Quin potius quando in Virgilium quoque dentes exacuere et me tussis male habet, maximi poetae studiosissimus poeticae Elisius patrocinium suscipiat. Quod te, Elisi suavissime, per Antonii nostri Manes, quando qua te maiore obtestatione cogam non habeo, oro atque obtestor.

38 *Elis.* Et poterat Andreas et sponte etiam debebat provintiam hanc pro Virgilio suo suscipere. Quis enim Andrea Virgilii studiosior ac dignitatis excellentiaeque carminis atque operis eius inspec-

And so the difference between Cicero's definition and Quintilian's is the same as that between the definitions of military conflict that I have just laid out; and to tell the truth, the one—that is, Cicero's—is the work of a philosopher explaining a matter and putting it before our eyes, the other of a man who apparently seeks to blind his hearers rather than illuminate them. Therefore, since Quintilian himself thinks that those who defined *status* this way "judged rightly but did not express themselves fully enough," please see which of the two fully expresses the thing. In my view, Cicero expresses and explains the matter, but Quintilian (I would speak with all due respect to such a great man) stammers a bit. I could have collected here many things that learned men have handed down about the method of definition, but I did not think it was necessary, being content to demonstrate with these few words that Cicero defined *status* well, precisely, carefully, and plainly. This defense of ours is not intended as an accusation of Quintilian—far from it. We don't mean to give the impression that we have taken the case to prosecute Quintilian, but rather because we were eager to free Cicero from the rabid bites of living grammarians. 36

But you, Enrico, return the favor and at my request spew out the bile against grammarians you had stored up a little earlier, or if your head is suffering from congestion, turn over the responsibility to our friend Elisio. 37

Enrico. That would be better. Since they have also sharpened their teeth on Vergil and I have a bad cough, let Elisio, a most expert devotee of the poetic art, undertake the defense of the greatest poet. Do this, dear Elisio; I beseech and entreat you by the spirit of our Antonio, since I can compel you with no greater appeal.

Elisio. Andrea could also take on this responsibility on behalf of his Vergil, and he should do it gladly. Indeed, who is more enthusiastic about Vergil than Andrea and a keener observer of 38

tor acutior? Sed me vel obtestatio ad hoc impellit tua, vel quod abunde multa memini quae de Virgilii laudibus dicere solebat Antonius, cuius memoriam hospiti huic ut Siculo, quem esse Siculum ornatus ipse indicat, arbitror quam gratissimam. Coeterum Andreas et quae a me referentur locupletare rationibus poterit et tanquam iudex adversus Virgiliocarpos sedere—qui magis enim dicere Virgiliomastigas liceat? Atque hinc potissimum incipiam, de quo me paulo ante Claudianus ammonuit; cuius versus sunt de monte Aetna:

Nunc movet indigenas nimbos piceaque gravatum
Fedat nube diem; nunc motibus astra lacessit
Terrificis damnisque suis incendia nutrit.

Virgilii sunt:

Portus ab accessu ventorum immotus et ingens
Ipse, sed horrificis iusta tonat Aetna ruinis;
Interdumque atram prorumpit ad aethera nubem
Turbine fumantem piceo et candente favilla
Attollitque globos flammarum et sidera lambit.
Interdum scopulos avulsaque viscera montis
Erigit eructans liquefactaque saxa sub auras
Cum gemitu glomerat fundoque exaestuat imo.

39 Hos[9] Favorinum philosophum dixisse aliquando Gellius scribit a Virgilio inchoatos magis quam factos, quod absolvi, quando mors praeverterat, nequiissent. Et Favorinus quidem ea

the value and excellence of his poetic work? But I am persuaded to do it, whether by your appeal or because I remember the great many things Antonio used to say in praise of Vergil. The mention of Antonio I consider most welcome to this visitor—a Sicilian, as he is shown by his dress.[53] But Andrea can both enrich my discussion with explanations and sit in judgment against the Vergil-shredders—for how might one better describe the Vergil-scourgers?[54] And so I will begin in particular with the following case, of which I was recently reminded by Claudian, who has these verses about Mt. Etna:

> Now it stirs up the smoke born within it
> And with pitch-black cloud befouls the leaden sky;
> now it assails the stars with awful tumult
> and feeds the flames with its own collapsing mass.[55]

Here are Vergil's lines:

> There is a harbor away from the attack of the winds, itself
> unmoved and vast, but Etna thunders close by with horrific crashes;
> and sometimes it throws out to the sky a black smoky cloud
> with a pitch-black whirlwind and glowing ash
> and sends up masses of flame and licks the stars.
> Sometimes it belches and spews out boulders and the ripped-out entrails
> of the mountain, and with a roar rolls masses of molten rock
> up to the sky and boils in its lowest depths.[56]

Gellius writes that the philosopher Favorinus once said that 39
Vergil had begun rather than finished these verses, since death had prevented him from giving them the finishing touch.[57] Of course, Favorinus seems to have adopted this respectful tone

verecundia usus videtur, ut excusasse magis quam incusasse Virgilium videri possit, quem Antonius non poterat de moderatione hac non laudare. Coeterum non omnium esse de liniamentis, inumbrationibus artificioque poetarum iudicium ferre, quae praeterquam a poetis ipsis vix cognoscerentur; quod in pictura quoque contingit, in qua multa sunt quae nisi summi etiam artifices non videant. Aetnae montis naturam id consilii non fuisse sibi Virgilius ipse prae se fert, ut vellet pro assumpta et quodammodo destinata materia describere, nec rei causas exquirit, ut Claudianus, nec spumantis materiae flumina ostendere vult, ut Pindarus; sed cum describere portum Aeneae ore coepisset dixissetque *ab accessu ventorum immotum et ingentem ipsum* quidem, subdidit rem maxime admirabilem adeoque monstrosam, cuius Aeneas ipse memor factus esset, ut a portus descriptione rei ipsius miraculo averteretur. *Ipse,* inquit, *portus ingens* quidem, hoc est navium plurimarum capax, sed visu, sed auditu mirabile est Aetnam montem terrificis iusta ruinis tonare; qua commotus ammiratione atque a portu aversus, in illa explicanda primum ab auditu coepit. Videtis artificiosi poetae prudens consilium, quod in ammirabili re enarranda tractum se ammiratione ipsa ab initio statim ostendit?

40 Audire est, inquit, cum nulli corporum videantur conflictus, e quibus soni fiunt, non sonitum modo, ac si parum esset *sonitum* dicere, sed tonitrum ex horrificis montis eius ruinis. Quae in aere maximo cum terrore fierent, ea dixit sub terris fieri; simul cum rei miraculo causam quoque leviter attingit. Nam neque decebat Aeneam causas incendii atque fragoris illius exactius quaerere aut aperire. Tantus autem fragor nisi e fractione esse non poterat, quam fractionem *ruinas* nominans ostendit. Cum etiam dicit *tonat,* montem confragosum innuit; nanque

to give the appearance of excusing rather than accusing Vergil, and Antonio could only praise him for this moderation. But he said that it was not for everyone to pass judgment on the contours, subtleties, and craft of poets, because these matters were scarcely understood except by poets themselves—just as also happens in painting, in which there are many things that only the greatest artists can see. Vergil makes it clear that it was not his intention to describe the nature of Mt. Etna as a borrowed and set theme, so to speak, and he does not seek out the causes of the thing, like Claudian, or try to show rivers of foaming matter, like Pindar. But when he had begun to describe the harbor in Aeneas' words and had said "away from the attack of the winds, itself unmoved and vast," he added a most astonishing and in fact portentous thing, which Aeneas himself had recalled, so that he was diverted from the description of the harbor by the marvel of the thing. To be sure, he says, "the harbor itself vast," that is, large enough for many ships; but it is astounding to see, to hear Mt. Etna thundering with terrifying crashes nearby. Seized by astonishment and diverted from the harbor, he describes it, beginning with the act of hearing. Do you see the clever plan of the skillful poet, that in describing an astonishing thing he shows himself gripped by astonishment right from the start?

One can hear, he says—although no clashes of bodies are 40
visible by which the sounds are made—not just a din, as if it were not enough to say "din," but thunder from the horrific collapse of the mountain. Things that would be terrifying if they happened in the open air he said were happening under the earth, lightly touching on the cause at the same time as the marvel of the thing. For it was not appropriate for Aeneas to seek out or explain too precisely the causes of the flames and explosive noise. There could be such noise only from something breaking apart, and he indicates this breaking with the word

conflictus illi et tanti sub terris fragores nisi in concavo et cavernoso fieri nequeunt, easque conflictiones ventorum atque ignium in cavernis esse dicit, ut confligentium nubium tonitrua imitentur. Singulis verbis rem auditu mirabilem facit: quod *iusta* quod *tonat,* quod *ruinis,* et quidem *horrificis,* cum horror absque membrorum concussione animique consternatione non contingat.

41 Dehinc cum auditui satisfecisset, transit ad visum, aliquanto longius in parte hac immoratus, ut per hunc sensum rem admirabiliorem redderet, quod videndo quam audiendo apparere plura soleant. Utque audientium animos magis ac magis rei miraculo afficeret, non secernit ea quae noctu quaeve interdiu viderentur, ut Pindarus. Dicit: *Interdum,* idest nunc hoc nunc illud, dum non vult diem a nocte secernere, *atram prorumpit ad aethera nubem.* Videtis ut a se non recedit: dixit *tonat,* dicit *nubem;* tonare enim et nubescere in aere contingit. Cernitis ut rem effert, cum non fumum, sed *nubem,* et quidem *atram,* et *prorumpit,* quod violentum verbum est, et *aethera* potius quam aerem, ut nimium impetum absolveret. *Fumantem* non ita quidem veritatem velat, ut non suis aliquando nominibus rem exprimat; fumi enim ex aspiratione ignea, non nubes exurgunt. *Turbine piceo* et impetum et colorem non sine quadam animi commotione designat; est enim turbo ventus et tortuosus et violentus, et fortasse respexit turbinis ipsius glomerationem; ad haec *piceus* color in nubibus terrificus est. Duo haec simul coniunxit, ut rei miraculum augeret. Nec non flammas, fumos, lucem, tenebras, favillas simul miscet et *turbinem piceum* et *favillam candentem.* Quid amplius? *Globos* etiam *flammarum attollit;* et quod satis hoc

"crashes." When he says "thunders," he suggests that the mountain is fissured, for those impacts and such great underground explosions could happen only in a hollow and cavernous space, and he says that these collisions of wind and fire take place in caverns so that they imitate the thunderclaps of clouds crashing together. He creates a wonderful auditory effect with individual words, like "close by," "thunders," "crashes," and even "horrific," since horror involves shaking limbs and mental alarm.

Then, when he had devoted enough attention to hearing, he 41
went on to sight, lingering a little longer on this part to make the thing more amazing through this sense, because generally more things are perceived by seeing than by hearing. To impress the minds of his listeners all the more with wonder at the thing, he did not separate the phenomena visible at night from those of the daytime, like Pindar. Not wanting to separate day from night, he says, "sometimes"—that is, now at one time, now at another—"it throws out to the sky a black cloud." You see how consistent he is: he said "thunders," and he says "cloud"; for thunder and cloud formations are produced in the air. You notice how he expresses the thing, since he says not "smoke" but "cloud," and "black" at that, and "throws out," which is a violent word, and "sky" rather than "air," to convey the excessive upward force. "Smoky" reveals the actual state of affairs, expressing it at last in its own terms, for smoke, not cloud, arises from a burst of flame. With "pitch-black whirlwind" he indicates force and color, along with mental agitation, for a whirlwind is a twisting and violent gale, and the phrase perhaps suggests the massing action of the wind; in addition, a "pitch-black" color in clouds inspires dread. He has joined the two ideas together to make the thing more awe inspiring. He also mingles flames, smoke, light, darkness, ashes all together, and "pitch-black whirlwind" and "glowing ash." What else? It "also sends up masses of flame,"

non videretur, *lambit* etiam *sidera*, ut quo ultra prodiret non haberet.

42 Non possum primo loco non magnopere Gellium admirari, vel potius ridere, qui Virgilium arguat quod dixerit *fumantem turbine piceo et favilla candente*, cum nec fumare soleant, ut ipse dicit, nec atra esse quae sunt candentia, nisi si pervulgate dixit et improprie *candente* pro *fervente*, non pro *ignea* et *relucenti*, quod *candens* est a *candore* dictum, non a *calore*. O bone Gelli, cum Noctis istas Atticas scriberes, non potuisti non aliquando dormitare; ignorabas an parum animadvertebas antiquissimum et latinissimum hunc loquendi morem Virgilio etiam familiarissimum? Neque enim dixit 'fumantem candente favilla,' sed *nubem candente favilla*, ut 'puella forma adeo venusta' et 'magno vir ingenio' et quod in loco maxime simili legitur:

Ipse Quirinali lituo parvaque sedebat
Succinctus trabea;

atque ut ibi non 'succinctus Quirinali lituo,' sed 'succinctus parva trabea,' Quirinalemque tenens seu gestans lituum, sic neque hic 'nubem fumantem favilla candente,' sed fumantem turbine piceo et emittentem seu spargentem atque efflantem simul candentem favillam. Expressit autem quod fieri saepissime in aere videmus, ut e nigerrimis nubibus post tonitrum erumpant fulgura et coruscationes, videaturque interdum coelum dehiscere flammasque evomere. Dici non potest quam sibi undique in eorum quae fiunt in aere similitudine constet.

43 Solebat irridere Antonius qui Virgilium dicerent voluisse montis Aetnae flagrantiam ad Pindari imitationem exequi eosque censebat et caecutire et delirare, nec Favorinum sed Fabari-

and because this did not seem enough, even "licks the stars," so that it could shoot out no further.

To begin with, I have to wonder at Gellius, or rather laugh at him, because he blames Vergil for having said "smoky with a pitch-black whirlwind and glowing ash," since (and I quote): "generally what glows does not smoke and is not black, unless he has spoken colloquially and incorrectly, using 'glowing' for 'red hot,' not for 'fiery and blazing,' because the word 'glowing' (*candens*) is related to 'whiteness' (*candor*), not 'heat' (*calor*)."[58] O good Gellius, when you were writing those *Attic Nights* of yours, you must have nodded off a time or two. Didn't you know or did you overlook this ancient and very Latin idiom, which was perfectly familiar to Vergil as well? He did *not* say "smoky with glowing ash," but "a cloud of glowing ash," like "a girl of such charming appearance," and "a man of great ability," and as one reads in a very similar passage: 42

He sat wrapped with his Quirinal staff
and a short cloak.[59]

And just as in that place one understands not "wrapped with a Quirinal staff," but "wrapped with a short cloak" and holding or wielding a staff, so here we have not "a cloud smoky with glowing ash" but smoky in a pitch-black whirlwind and emitting or scattering and giving off glowing ash at the same time. He has described something we see happening very often in the sky, that after thunder, lightning bolts and flashes break out of black clouds and sometimes the heavens seem to crack open and vomit flames. In his depiction of what happens in the sky he is inexpressibly consistent in every detail.

Antonio used to make fun of people who claimed that Vergil wanted to imitate Pindar in describing the heat of Mount Etna, and he deemed them blind and demented. He considered that not Favorinus but Fabarinus[60] was turning up his nose, since no 43

num naso suspendere, cum nemo tam aversi aut parvi esset ingenii qui non palam videret Virgilium se totum a Pindarica enarratione avertisse, ut nec verbis nec translatione, qua ille utitur parte aliqua, similis esse vellet. Etenim Pindarus ad fontium, fluminum, fluctuum similitudinem rem omnem exequitur, amnes in incendii enarratione imitatus; at noster nulla huiusmodi similitudine usus, rebus ipsis inhaerens, et quam potest et Aeneae narrantis dignitas patitur, verbis explicans, ab ipso igne et a nubibus et ab iis quae in aere fiunt non recedit. Et Pindarus quidem solum fluxum et scaturiginem habet quam in aquis imitetur; Virgilius omnia pro materia proque suscepta explicatione a rebus ipsis, non aliunde sibi dicenda atque ostendenda assumit. Viderique Virgilius potest parum hac in parte Pindarum probavisse, qui dum se totum ad amnes, ad fluctus, ad scaturiginem vertit, eructationem ipsam quaeque inter erumpendum eructandumque contingerent inexpresse leviterque attigerit, nec *monstrum* illud suum *tum auditu tum visu mirabile* plene absolverit. Referam Pindari verba a Gellio ipso conversa.

> *Sane eructantur inaccessi ignis purissimi ex imis fontes. Flumina vero interdiu quidem inundant fluctum ferventem fumi. At per noctes punicea proglomerata flamma ad profundum ponti fert solum; cum strepitu illa Vulcani fluenta serpentia emittit saevissima, monstrum profecto tum visu, tum auditu mirabile.*

44 At Virgilius et aures et oculos et animum admiratione implet, cum montem *tonare* ait et e terrae penetralibus *atras nubes prorumpere, fumare piceum turbinem, volitare candentem favillam, attolli globos flammarum;* quid amplius? *lambere* etiam *sidera,* et tamen a rei natura non recedit, siquidem eructatio illa talis est,

one was so perverse or foolish that he could not plainly see that Vergil had turned his back entirely on Pindar's account and had no desire to imitate either his language or a single one of his metaphors. Pindar compares everything to springs, rivers, and floods, representing flowing waters in his description of fire; but our poet uses no simile of this kind. Sticking to the things themselves and explaining in words—as far as he can and the dignity of the narrator Aeneas permits—he does not deviate from the fire and the clouds and the events in the sky. Pindar, moreover, has only the flow and rush of water to imitate. Vergil takes everything he wants to say or demonstrate to suit the material and the description he has undertaken from the things themselves, not from somewhere else. And it is evident that Vergil did not approve of Pindar's devoting himself entirely to rivers, floods, and gushing water, just touching vaguely on the eruption itself and the events of the outpouring and eruption, and not fully describing that "monstrous thing of his, remarkable both to hear and to see." I will report Pindar's words in Gellius' translation.[61]

> In fact, pure springs of unapproachable fire are thrown up from the lowest depths. By day its rivers roll out a boiling flood of smoke. But at night a mass of dark red flame sweeps down to the deep bottom of the sea. Roaring, it sends forth violent twisting streams of fire, A monstrous thing remarkable both to see and to hear.[62]

But Vergil fills our ears and eyes and our mind too with 44
amazement when he says the mountain "thunders" and that from the depths of the earth "black clouds burst forth, a pitch-black whirlwind smokes, glowing ash flies about, masses of flame rise up." And what else? Even "licks the stars." And yet he does not depart from the facts of nature since the eruption is just as he has described it, except for licking the stars. But this

praeterquam quod sidera non lambit. Sed haec exuberantia[10] poetarum est propria et haud scio an alibi magis quam hic deceat. Ac tanquam minora haec quae dicta sunt essent, quippe quae frequenter contingant, ea subdit quae ut maiora et rarius contingerent et longe monstrosiora essent. Itaque et *scopulos erigit* et *avulsa montis viscera eructat,* et *saxa sub auras glomerat* et quidem *liquefacta* et *cum gemitu.* Ac ne quid quod movere admirationem posset praetermitteret, quid ultimo loco ponit? *fundoque exaestuat imo:* quod cum oculis exponere non posset, animis existimandum permisit. Quid hoc Virgiliano monstro absolutius? et tamen docet glomeratus eos fieri non posse nisi vento igneque intus aestuante. Ac Pindaro quidem dare potest veniam lyricum carmen. At Virgilio implenda erat tuba illa heroica et magno personandum ore, neque ut illi succinendum qui a lyra sua non ita longe recessit. Quocirca noster heros tubam sic implet ut monstrum Pindaricum per *tonitrum, ruinas, turbinem, picem, candentem favillam, erectos scopulos, avulsa viscera, saxa liquefacta sub auras* ad sidera usque intonet et aures, oculos, animos admiratione simul atque horrore compleat.

Tonat Aetna ruinis: coepit Virgilius a tonitru, in quo Pindarus obmutescit; post etiam tempus nullum secernit, tum ut rem admirabiliorem faceret tum ut qualis res ipsa esset exprimeret; neque enim noctu solum flammarum illi globi cernuntur, sed etiam interdiu, quotiens et aer est nubilus et cacumen montis exhanelatis[11] incendii fumigationibus caligat atque offunditur. An non die medio, cum coelum maxime nubilum est, videntur coruscationes et mediis e nubibus ignes emissi? quod poeta noster sentiens, non ante dixit *candente favilla* quam praemisit

kind of hyperbole is characteristic of poets, and I can't think of another place where it would be more suitable. And as if the things he has already described were insufficient, since they are of frequent occurrence, he adds still greater events, of a kind that would both happen more rarely and be far more monstrous. And so it "spews out boulders and belches out the ripped-out entrails of the mountain and rolls masses of rock up to the sky"—"molten rock" at that, and "with a roar." And so as not to omit any detail that could arouse amazement, how does he end? "And it boils in its lowest depths." What he could not set before our eyes, he leaves to the imagination. What is more perfectly finished than this "monstrous thing" of Vergil's? And yet he shows that these masses of matter[63] could not be created without the wind and fire raging within. Of course, lyric poetry can give Pindar an excuse. But Vergil had to blow into the heroic trumpet and make it resound with a loud voice, and there was no need for him to sing along with one who kept close to his lyre. For that reason our hero so blows his trumpet that he makes Pindar's "monstrous thing" resound to the stars through "thunder, crashes, whirlwind, pitch, glowing ash, spewed-out boulders, ripped-out entrails, molten rock up to the sky," and fills ears, eyes, and minds with amazement and horror at the same time.

"Etna thunders with crashes." Vergil begins with the sound 45
of thunder, on which Pindar is silent. Afterward, he makes no distinction of time, both to make the thing more amazing and to convey the kind of thing it actually was: those balls of flame are seen not only at night, but also by day, whenever the air is cloudy and the peak of the mountain is dark and covered with smoky exhalations of fire. At midday, when the sky is very overcast, does one not see lightning flashes and flames shooting out of the middle of the clouds? Understanding this, our poet preceded the words "glowing ash" with "pitch-black whirlwind," so

turbine piceo, ne a rerum natura recederet. Ad haec non nisi post multos annos contingit amnes illos Pindaricos fluere, cum Virgiliana tonitrua fragoresque et fumi picei et prorumpentes in coelum nubes favillaeque frequentiores contingant, praesertim flante aut impendente austro. Ac nihilominus post *liquescere saxa* et *avelli montis viscera* ostendit, adeo nihil prorsus omittit.

46 Videturque noster Maro rem ipsam et loci situm contemplatus, siquidem cacumen montis, qua tanta fumigatio emittitur, hiatum habet profundissimum ac late amplum, quem dixerunt *craterem,* hodie plerique *os* vocant, exesis undique atque exustis rupibus. Quocirca non uti e fontibus fluere ignes possunt, sed materia ipsa vi ventorum incensa et diutius intra cavernas exagitata tandem evomitur magnoque in aerem impetu effertur, post in partem qua ventus inclinat decidens, igne liquefacta defluere incipit. Unde alibi ut rei huius peritus dixerat:

Vidimus undantem ruptis fornacibus Aetnam
Flammarumque globos liquefactaque volvere saxa.

Et hic vere ac naturaliter dicit:

Interdum scopulos avulsaque viscera montis
Erigit eructans liquefactaque saxa sub auras
Cum gemitu glomerat.

Prudentissime omnia: Nam *interdum,* quia non semper; et *cum gemitu,* quia tanta ebullitio et pugna illa intra cavernas ventorumque ac concepti ignis violentus ac praeceps exitus absque ingenti fragore fieri nequit; et *erigit eructans,* quia ruptis caminis

as not to depart from nature. Furthermore, those rivers Pindar talks of run only once in a great while, whereas Vergil's thunders and crashes and pitchy smoke and clouds of ash bursting into the sky are frequent occurrences, especially when the south wind is blowing or threatening. And all the same, afterward he shows "rock melting" and the "entrails of the mountain being ripped out." In fact, he leaves out not a single detail.

Evidently our Maro looked closely at the phenomenon and 46
the topography of the place, since the top of the mountain from which such clouds of smoke are emitted has a very deep and broad chasm—something they [the Romans] called a "crater" but which most people today call a mouth[64]—with the cliffs eaten and burned away all around. For that reason, fires cannot flow as from springs, but matter kindled by the violence of the winds and blown about for a long time within the caverns is at last thrown out and carried with great force into the air; falling down afterward where the wind blows it, it begins to flow down, melted by the fire. And so in another passage, as an expert on the matter, he had said:

> We have seen Etna seething, her furnace walls burst,
> rolling down balls of flame and molten rock.[65]

And here he says, with truth to nature:

> Sometimes it belches and spews out boulders and the ripped-out entrails
> of the mountain and with a roar rolls masses of molten rock
> up to the sky.

Everything is said most judiciously: "sometimes," because not always; and "with a roar," because such a spouting and the battle inside the caverns and the violent and headlong outrush of wind and kindled fire cannot take place without a terrific din; and "belches and spews," because when the furnaces have been

effractisque, ut ita dixerim, claustris, igne, vento, vaporibus, quaecunque obviam facta sunt in altum tolluntur; et cum dicit *glomerat,* ostendit pugnam confligentium corporum; et cum dicit *viscera,* et *liquefacta* et *avulsa,* designat tum ingentissimam vim ventorum, tum quod ignis est excoquere ac liquefacere lapides, tum quod materia ipsa monte continetur atque illic generatur.

47 Dicet aliquis: at fluere liquescentem illam materiam mare versus omisit. Primum nec mare versus semper fluit, nam et saepenumero in mediterranea elabitur; deinde quod cum dixisset *sub auras glomerat,* visum est poetae tam defecati iudicii quodcunque adderetur minus esse; et profecto minus mirum est fluere decidentem illam liquefactamque materiam quam ex imis terrae visceribus ad auras maiore quam exprimi possit impetu ferri. Itaque hoc omisso, imo despecto ac repudiato, concludit: *fundoque exaestuat imo,* relinquens in audientium animis quae non cernerentur cum admiratione cogitanda atque qui intus aestus, quae ruinae, quanta etiam certamina ex iis quae oculis obiicerentur existimanda.

48 Quin etiam ad fabulosum commentum ut mirificum, ut ad deos relatum transit; adeo nihil quod audientium animos admiratione impleat praetermittit.

Fama est Enceladi semustum fulmine corpus
Urgeri mole hac ingentemque insuper Aetnam
Impositam ruptis flammam expirare caminis;
Et fessum quotiens motet latus, intremere omnem
Murmure Trinacriam et coelum suttexere fumo.

split open and the bolts, so to speak, have been shattered by fire, wind, and steam, everything in the way is carried aloft; and when he says "rolls masses," he shows the clash of colliding matter; and when he says "entrails" and "molten" and "ripped-out," he indicates the terrific violence of the wind, that the fire can melt down and liquefy stone, and that the material itself is contained in the mountain and created there.

Someone will say: "But he has left out the fact that the mol- 47
ten matter flows toward the sea." In the first place, it does not always flow toward the sea, for very often it runs off into the interior; then, once he had said, "it rolls masses up to the sky," any addition seemed anticlimactic to a poet of such refined taste; and certainly it is less remarkable for the falling liquefied matter to flow than for it to be carried with inexpressible force from the deepest bowels of the earth to the skies. And so when he has omitted this detail—or rather scorned and rejected it—he concludes, "and it boils in its lowest depths," leaving the minds of his hearers to consider with amazement the things not seen and to reckon what turmoil, what crashes, what great clashes there must have been within from the things that did meet their eyes.

Indeed, he even passes on to a mythological fiction,[66] an 48
amazing tale having to do with the gods; to such an extent does he omit nothing that would fill his hearers' minds with wonder.

A story there is that Enceladus' body, scorched by
lightning,
is buried beneath this mass; that lofty Etna, piled
upon him, breathes out flame from its exploding forges;
and whenever he turns his weary side, all Sicily
shakes with a rumbling sound and veils the sky with
smoke.[67]

Quamobrem Pindarum non solum imitandum a se Virgilius non iudicavit, sed ab illo sic recessit ut non verba, non rei faciem, non ullam sit Pindaricae descriptionis adumbrationem secutus.

49 Nunc ostendat nobis Favorinus iste tam enucleati iudicii tamque teneri auditus philosophus, ut opimam[12] et pinguem Pindari (ut ipse cum Gellio fortasse non recte sentiebat) facundiam praetereamus, ostendat, inquam, ubinam Virgiliana insolentia? ubi tumor? Mihi quidem cum duobus maxime modis concipiatur tumor, re, idest sententiis, atque oratione, ubi sunt verba ista tumentia, ubi res insolentiam parientes?

50 At dixit *tonat Aetna* quia tonat aer et nubium conflictus tonitrum facit; *prorumpit ad aethera nubem atram:* nihil hic insolens, nihil tumidum; nam *prorumpo* verbum sic violentum est ut eo etiam historici utantur; et *nubes atra* ut nox atra; *turbine piceo:* an quo verbo vel impetum vel colorem expressius potuisset efferre? cum e pice densissimus, id est nigerrimus halet fumus; et turbo, cum impetuosus tum etiam tortuosus atque glomerosus sit; et favillae flammaeque seu coruscationes e nigerrimis nubibus erumpere sic soleant ut candere videantur. Nihil a natura recedit, et verba rebus accommodat; non dicet poeta *globos,* cum idem verbum ab historicis non reformidetur? non dicet *lambere* sidera? Atqui honestiori verbo uti non potuisset, ut levem ac fluitantem ignis, ut ita loquar, attactum significaret; nec cum dixit *candente favilla,* Pindari verba *fluxum fumi calidi* significantia, nec cum *globos flammarum, ignis fluenta,* crasse, duriter atque improprie interpretatus est, hoc est, *ῥόον καπνοῦ αἴθωνα* et *κρουνούς,* quippe qui ne interpretatus quidem sit, cum illum

For this reason Vergil not only decided that he should not imitate Pindar, but also departed from him so much that he copied neither the language, nor the spectacle, nor any hint of Pindar's description.

Now let Favorinus show us, your philosopher of such meticulous taste and delicate hearing, let him show us, I say—to pass over the luxuriant and rich eloquence of Pindar (as he and Gellius considered it, perhaps not correctly)—where is Vergil's extravagance? Where is his bombast?[68] Since bombast in my view is produced in two ways above all—by matter, that is, by substance, and by language—where are the inflated words, where the substance giving rise to extravagance? 49

But he said "Etna thunders" because the air resounds and the clashing of clouds sounds like thunder. "It throws out to the sky a black cloud"; there is nothing extravagant, nothing inflated in that, for the word "throw out" is so violent that even historians use it, and "black cloud" is like black night. "With a pitch-black whirlwind": what language could he use to express both force and color more clearly? Pitch gives off the thickest, that is, the blackest smoke, and a whirlwind is violent and twisting and rounded; and ashes and flames, or flashes, typically break out from the blackest clouds so that they seem to glow. He departs not at all from nature, and he suits the words to the situation. Shall the poet not say "masses," when historians do not fear the same word? Shall he not say "licks" the stars? And yet he could not have used a more appropriate word to signify what I might call the light and undulating touch of fire. And when he said "glowing ash" and "masses of flame," he was not inartistically, awkwardly, and incorrectly translating Pindar's words meaning "a discharge of hot smoke" and "rivers of fire"—that is, *rhoon kapnou aithona* and *kronous*.[69] Indeed, he was not even translating, since he not only did not want to imitate but even disapproved of Pindar's treatment in this section for the reasons we 50

non modo imitari nollet, verum etiam hac in parte non probaret propter eas quas attulimus rationes velletque rem ipsam ut admirabilem, ut horroris plenam verbis suis ante oculos ponere animisque infigere ac tubae suae canorem tenere. Nec cum dixit *scopulos et viscera avulsa,* et *liquefacta saxa* et *lambit sidera,* et *exaestuat imo fundo* verba et strepitum verborum conquirit, rem inquam, ipsam inquam rem, suis atque heroicis verbis enarrat. Ad haec quod non semper ignis fluant amnes, *interdum* hoc fieri dixit, atque ubi fit, non diffluere e cratere illo perinde ac e fonte aut e fornace massae illius rivos, sed iactari in sublime materiam per frustra, per saxa, per scopulos, quae post in terram decideret et in fecis ac liquescentis spumae modum coacta flueret.

51 Quocirca, bone Favorine, ad philosophiam tuam redi, de syllogismo deque bonorum finibus tantum sententiam laturus, quando nec mihi satis magnus physicus videris, qui montis Aetnae naturam ignores ac poetarum figuras lineamentaque; et quid carmini conveniat, quid materiam susceptam deceat, qua ratione humilis res tollatur, qua elata prematur iudicandum pensitandumque poetis ipsis relinque.

52 Vidimus in Aenaria insula factum quod Virgilius de Aetna scribit, cum e quadam eius parte ignis erupisset centum ante annis aut paulo amplius. Nam et ad mare et sparsim per agros praeter fluxum illum magna mole lapides iacent, et in ipso litore et paulum etiam intra mare grandes eminent scopuli adeo excocti exustique ut hodie quoque appareat spumosa illa liquefactio; quin etiam Pindarica fluenta lapidum sunt in spumam solutorum, non materiae continuae liquescentisque quale liquefactum fluere aes solet. Cur autem praeter naturam cuiquam videatur ab incluso sub Aetna igne torqueri lapides, cum videa-

have explained, and he wanted to put the event itself, remarkable and horrific as it was, before our eyes with his words and fix it in our minds and keep his trumpet sounding. And in saying "boulders and ripped-out entrails" and "molten rock" and "licks the stars" and "boils in its lowest depths," he is not chasing down words and verbal noise; he is describing the thing—the thing itself, I say—in his own heroic language. In addition, because rivers of fire do not always flow, he said that it "sometimes" happens; and when it does happen, he does not say that streams of matter flow away in all directions from the crater as from a spring or out of a furnace, but that material is hurled into the air in bits and pieces, in stones, in boulders, and falls to earth afterward and flows, congealed into the form of liquefying slag and foam.

Therefore, good Favorinus, go back to your philosophy and 51
make pronouncements only on the syllogism or the highest good, since I don't think you're much of a natural scientist, given your ignorance of the nature of Mount Etna and of the figures of speech and designs of poets; leave it to the poets themselves to judge and weigh what is appropriate to poetry, what is becoming to the subject undertaken, how a low thing may be exalted and a lofty one brought down to earth.

We have seen that what Vergil writes about Etna happened 52
on the island of Ischia when a fire erupted from one part of it a hundred years or so ago.[70] Both near the sea and scattered through the fields beyond the flow lie stones of vast size, and on the shore and even a little way into the sea rise up great boulders, so scorched and burned that even today the foamy liquefaction is visible. Indeed, even the streams Pindar talks of consist of stones dissolved into foam, not of continuous liquescent matter like the flow of melted bronze. Why would anyone think it contrary to nature for stones to be shot out by the fire trapped under Etna, when we see stone balls shot with such

mus aeneis e tormentis quae bombardae dicuntur tanto impetu pilas torqueri lapideas turbinesque illos piceos glomerari tanto etiam fragore ut ad sexaginta passuum millia exaudiantur? Hoc quod in Aenaria factum diximus legimus scriptum in monumentis Caroli Neapolitanorum regis, quo incendio etiam castellum haustum est.

53 *Andr.* Quanquam Aenariae exemplo potes esse contentus, tamen et Vesuvii montis ruina et ager squalore obsitus ad sextum ab Neapoli lapidem hoc ipsum quod de liquefactis igne saxis a Virgilio traditur docere abunde potest. Est enim passim videre hic exustorum lapidum erectos cumulos, illic excussa summo e monte mirae magnitudinis saxa impune sparsa, alibi profluentis rivi lapidosos decursus, nec uno in loco saxorum strues simul congestas, ut facile appareat materiam illam omnem e lapide constare, eiectam vi vaporum atque ignium longiusque agglomeratam, quae videre cuivis in promptu est. Sed redeas ad quod, Elisi, coeperas et Macrobium adversus Aeneam a Latinis moti belli causas tanquam leves ac pueriles ridentem ut rudem, grammaticorum omnium importunissimum, ferula sua feri atque intra cancellos grammaticae redire coge audentem se quoque viris conferre.

54 *Elis.* Recte mones. Hunc hominem Antonius cum nebulonem aliquando obiurgari sensisset: 'Nimis parce, inquit, praesumptonem potius, quando nemo unquam plura sibi praesumpsit aut permisit.' Quaeso, Macrobi, poetarum iudex tam sobrie, quaeso inquam, quae inter Latinos Troianosque belli causa excogitari accommodatior poterat? nam nec Latini per id tempus mercaturam navibus exercebant nec Aeneas piraticam, ut per causam praedocinii excitari bellum potuisset; nullae antecedebant inimicitiae et Aeneas eo consilio in Latinum litus descensionem fecerat, ut in terra fato debita sedes profugis statueret. Itaque

force from the bronze catapults called cannons and the pitch-black whirlwinds sent rolling with such a din that they are heard up to sixty Roman miles away? We have read what we said happened in Ischia in the records of Carlo, king of Naples.[71] Even his stronghold was burned by the fire.

Andrea. Although you can be content with the example of Ischia, both the ruined condition of Mount Vesuvius and the landscape, desolate up to the sixth milestone from Naples, can fully demonstrate what Vergil reports about stones liquefied by fire. In every direction one can see, in one place, heaped-up piles of burnt stones; in another, harmlessly scattered boulders of amazing magnitude that have been shaken from the mountain top; somewhere else, the stony course of a flowing stream; and in many places piled heaps of rocks, so that it is obvious that all that material consists of rock thrown out by the force of steam and fire and heaped up at a distance in full view for anyone to see. But return to what you had begun, Elisio, and beat Macrobius with his own rod as ignorant, the most misguided of grammarians, for mocking as trivial and childish the causes of the war stirred up against Aeneas by the Latins. Force him to go back within the confines of grammar, for daring to match himself against men.[72] 53

Elisio. Good advice. After Antonio had observed that this man was occasionally censured as a windbag, he said, "That's too mild. A great presumptuous fellow[73] rather, since no one ever presumed more or took more on himself." I ask you, Macrobius, such a sensible judge of poets, I ask you, I say, what more suitable reason for war between Latins and Trojans could be imagined? For the Latins at that time had no sea trade and Aeneas was not a pirate, so that a war could break out by reason of brigandage.[74] There was no antecedent hostility, and Aeneas had landed on the Latin coast with the intention of establishing a seat for the refugees in the land owed to them by 54

non belli, sed amicitiae potius causas quaerebat, ut qui conciliare sibi finitimorum animos studeret, missis etiam oratoribus cum muneribus. Vidit acutissimus auctor fortuitam causam, quam lippus caecutiensque grammaticus quomodo videret? Moris est classiariorum militum, ne piratarum tantum putes, saepius in continentem descendere, carnis, ut ipsi dicunt, faciendae gratia: nec solum ex hostico, sed ubi maior cogit inopia, etiam ex pacato pecora abigere. Quam ob causam, ut quotidie videmus, inter socios amicosque indigne multa committuntur. Hanc occasionem, et quidem fortuitam, cum Aeneas nihil minus quam bellum quaereret, nactus Virgilius, non armentalem aut aratorium bovem, sed regii villici cervum atque in deliciis habitum et agrestibus notum vulnerat, quo facilius multitudo cogniti cicuris gratia ad tumultum concurreret Troianosque non tantum ut abactores, sed qui regias res violare ausi essent armis ulciscerentur atque e finibus pellerent quos aegerrime ferrent illic considere perindeque ut exteram atque ignotam gentem odio persequerentur.

55 Quae oportunior excogitari occasio potuit, muliere praesertim agrestes excitante, quae vim passa videri posset, cum etiam Iunonem belli causas quaerentem introduxisset? Atque haec quidem tanquam scintilla furtim elapsa, quae paulatim serpens, mox vento exorto illapsa stipulis agros, silvas, obvia simul cuncta deflagrat. Quid aliud? Tanquam duos e diverso mundi cardine spiritus, qui accensum ignem excitent, exuscitat: alteram e coelo delapsam, deam Iunonem scilicet, alteram Furiarum maximam, Herebo excitam, cogentem buccina populos et duces vocantem in bella; proque stipula subiicitur Amata, mulier, mater, regina,

fate. Thus, he was seeking reasons, not for war, but for friendship, since he was eager to win over the minds of his neighbors, even sending ambassadors ahead with gifts. Did the sharp-eyed author see a chance cause of a kind that even a bleary-eyed and dim-sighted grammarian might see somehow? It is the way of marines (don't think it's only pirates that act this way) to descend on the mainland from time to time to get meat, as they say: they drive off flocks not only from enemy territory, but, when great need forces them, even from a friendly country. For this reason, as we see every day, many shameful deeds are committed among allies and friends. Making use of this circumstance—and a chance one, to be sure, since nothing was further from Aeneas' mind than war—Vergil wounded, not a bull from the herd or a plow ox, but the stag of the king's bailiff that was treated as a pet and known to the country folk, so that the populace might more easily rush to violence for the sake of the well-known pet, and so that they might punish the Trojans by force of arms, not just as cattle thieves, but as men who had dared to violate the king's property—driving from their territory those whom they did not want to settle there and pursuing them with hatred like a foreign and unknown race.

What more convenient opportunity could be imagined, es- 55
pecially with a woman—one who could appear to have suffered violence—stirring up the country folk, after he had also introduced Juno seeking reasons for war?[75] And indeed this was like a spark that escapes unnoticed and moves stealthily little by little, then, when the wind rises, falls on straw and at once burns to the ground fields, forests, everything in its path. What more? He rouses two spirits from opposite poles of the universe to stir up the fire that has been kindled: one gliding down from the sky—the goddess Juno, of course—the other the greatest of the Furies, roused from Erebus, marshaling the peoples with her trumpet and calling the leaders to war; and

importuna quidem mulier, mater indulgentissima, regina foeminarum choros solicitans; ad haec Latinus senio confectus ac vix sui iuris. Incensa igitur stipula, agri silvaeque exuruntur. Tela novat Atina, vomeres in enses excoquuntur, scribuntur exercitus, leguntur duces, primusque Mezentius bellum sic init ut ne mulieres quidem arma detractent. Videtis e parva fortuitaque favilla quantum incendium accenderit, ut subrigantur quidem legentium animi quotiens crines illi anguinei subriguntur! Quid hoc artificiosius, quid magis sepositum atque a vulgo abductum? Cognovit ammirabilissimam excogitatissimamque inventionem Iuvenalis cum dixit:

caderent omnes a crinibus hydri,
Surda nihil gemeret grave buccina.

56 Quam, si diis placet, cognoscet Macrobius, sordidae locutionis, ne dicam orationis grammaticus. Quid tu, peregrine homo, de maximi poetae admirabili artificio nobilissimisque inventis te iudicem statuis, qui ne latine quidem loqui scias? *Maluissem,* inquis, *Maronem et in hac parte apud auctorem suum vel apud quemlibet Graecorum alium quod sequeretur habuisse.* Scilicet non vis fingere Virgilium, non vis optimum artificem arte sua uti artificiose? At ego maluissem te, cum latine loqui vis, Ciceronem aut quem alium e doctissimis in loquendo sequi. An tu apud Ciceronem, Sallustium, Caesarem invenisti *in diggeriem concoquere, in memoriam atque in ingenium ire, in incrementum succrescere, tale praesens hoc opus volo, nativa Romani oris elegantia, noscendorum congeriem polliceri,* et mille his etiam absurdiora magisque barbara,

Amata is supplied as the straw, a woman, mother, queen—a woman truly misguided, an overindulgent mother, a queen inciting bands of wives—and in addition to all this, Latinus, exhausted by old age and barely his own master.[76] And so the straw is set alight, the fields and forests burnt down. Atina renews its arms, plows are melted into swords, armies are enrolled, leaders are chosen, and Mezentius is first to come to war, so that not even women refuse weapons.[77] You see what a conflagration he has kindled from a small, chance spark, so that the minds of readers are stirred indeed whenever those snaky locks are roused![78] What is more artful than this, what more choice and removed from the crowd? Juvenal recognized his most admirable and ingenious invention when he said:

> All the snakes would drop from her locks,
> her trumpet, mute, would sound no mournful note.[79]

If it pleases the gods, Macrobius will recognize it, too, a 56
grammarian whose speech—to say nothing of his language—is unrefined. Why do you, foreigner, set yourself up as the judge of the admirable art and noblest inventions of the greatest poet when you do not even know how to speak Latin? "I would have preferred," you say, "for Maro in this passage too to have had a model to follow in his own author or in any other Greek author you please."[80] May one suppose that you do not wish Vergil to create, that you do not wish the best artist to make artful use of his art? But I would have preferred for you, when you want to speak Latin, to follow Cicero or any other of the most learned authors in speaking. Or did you find in Cicero, Sallust, or Caesar [phrases like] "to process into digestion," "to go into the memory and intellect," "to grow into an increase," "I wish this present work such a thing," "native elegance of the Roman accent," "to promise a heap of things worth knowing," and a thousand things even more absurd and barbarous than these,

quibus tu, ineptissime, cum sis ipse ineptissimus, uteris? Atqui, audacissime grammatice, cum fateris te sub alio ortum coelo a linguae latinae vena non adiuvari, cur de maximo deque alieno poeta tanquam praetor iudicas? Unum tamen dare tibi veniam potest, quod conviva, quod satur, quod inter rorantia pocula, quod in Saturnalibus haec proferebas. O bellissimum hominem, qui convivam iudicem, qui mensam praetorium statuas!

57 Sed ad imitationem quam in Marone desideras redeamus. Ciceronem si legisses, non solum latine loqui, sed recte quoque de scriptorum ingeniis deque scriptis ipsis sententiam ferre didicisses. Ait et orator et philosophus eminentissimus nostros aut melius invenisse aut inventa a Graecis fecisse meliora. Quod si poetae cuiusquam fuit inventa ab aliis meliora facere, haec mihi laus Virgilii propria videtur.[13] Sed neque melius invenerint nostri, neque fecerint aliorum inventa meliora; non tamen caecutientis grammatici sententiae standum est. Quonam auctore usus est Homerus in fingendis tot monstris? quem imitatus est Orpheus in commentis adeo fabulosis? quem secutus est qui primus finxit Castorem Pollucemque ortos ovo? qui primus commentus est Plutonem in inferno regnare, hydram septicipitem esse, natos e serpentum dentibus armis instructos homines? Denique ab quo accepit Homerus auctore arma a Vulcano Achilli fabricata, vulneratam a Diomede Venerem, perlatum utribus Ulissem et mille talia? Atqui poetarum haec non modo licentia, sed pene ars est; quin etiam ab aliis enarratas fabulas in aliam atque aliam formam convertere permittitur, nedum fingere novas liceat.

which you use most ineptly since you yourself are most inept?[81] And yet, most audacious grammarian, since you confess that, "born under another sky," you are not nourished by the artery of Latin language,[82] why do you pronounce a verdict on the greatest poet (and one foreign to you) as if you were a judge? One can make allowances for you on one point, that you uttered these things as a banqueter, full of food, among the dripping wine cups, on the Saturnalia. O what a fine fellow, to make a banqueter a judge, a dinner table a bar of judgment!

But let us go back to the imitation you find lacking in Maro. 57
If you had read Cicero, you would have learned not only to speak Latin, but also to pass judgment correctly on the abilities of writers and on the writings themselves. This preeminent orator and philosopher says that we Romans either were better at thinking of ideas or else improved those thought of by the Greeks.[83] But if it was for any poet to improve the ideas thought of by others, in my view this praise belongs to Vergil. But suppose we Romans were neither better at thinking of ideas nor improved the ideas thought of by others; one should still not abide by the verdict of a dim-sighted grammarian. What source did Homer use in creating so many monsters? Whom did Orpheus imitate in such mythological fictions?[84] Who was the model for the person who first made up the story that Castor and Pollux were hatched from an egg? Who first invented the tale that Pluto reigns in the underworld, that the hydra has seven heads, that armed men were born from serpents' teeth? Finally, from what source did Homer get Achilles' arms fashioned by Vulcan, Venus wounded by Diomedes, Ulysses conveyed by bags of wind and a thousand things of that kind? And yet this is not only the privilege but almost the art of poets; indeed it is permissible to change the stories told by others into one form after another, to say nothing of its being legitimate to make up new ones.

58 Sed veniamus ad alium locum videamusque quam intempestivus canis huius latratus sit:

> *Parva metu primo, mox sese attollit in auras,*
> *Ingrediturque solo et caput intra nubila condit.*

> *Homerus,* inquit, *contentionem a parvo dixit incipere, postea ad coelum usque succrescere. Hoc idem Maro de fama, sed incongrue; neque enim aequa sunt famae contentionisque argumenta, quod contentio, etiamsi ad mutuas usque vastationes ac bella processerit, adhuc contentio est et manet ipsa quae crevit; fama vero cum in immensum prodiit, fama esse iam desinit et fit notio rei iam cognitae. Quis enim iam famam vocet cum res aliqua a terra in coelum nota sit? Deinde neque ipsam hyperbolen*[14] *potuit aequare: ille* coelum *dixit, hic* auras *et* nubila.

Atque, ut ab ultimo incipiamus, nesciebas, puto, grammatice, versus facere, qui non videris tribus tantum syllabis potuisse hyperbolen aequare et 'caput intra sidera condit' dicere. O crassum et supinum ingenium! Atqui noluit Virgilius 'intra sidera' dicere; nam cum intelligeret famam plura saepe quae certa non essent divulgare ac vera falsis miscere et facta atque infecta nuntiare, caput eius condit *intra nubila,* cum coeterum corpus videri dicat. Itaque et magnitudinem eius ostendit, cum attollit eam in auras et versari inter homines docet, cum ingredi eam solo facit, et quod multa secum ferret quae non statim cernerentur verane an falsa essent, intra nubila caput abscondit; etenim cum oculis nostris offusa nubes est, veras cernere rerum species nequimus.

But let us go to another passage and see how inappropriately that dog barks. 58

Small at first through fear, soon she rises up to the sky,
and walks on the earth and hides her head in the
clouds.[85]

Homer (says he) said that strife begins from a small thing and afterward grows up to the sky. Maro says the same of *fama* (rumor), but incongruously; for the subjects of *fama* and strife are not the same, because strife, even if it progresses to mutual destruction and war, is still strife and remains itself grown large; but *fama*, when it has advanced to an infinite extent, now ceases to be *fama* and becomes a conception of a thing already known. For who now would call it *fama* when something is known from earth to the sky? Then, he could not match even the hyperbole. Homer said "sky," Vergil "air" and "clouds."[86]

In fact, to begin with the last point, grammarian, you didn't know how to make verses, I think, since you didn't see that he could have matched the hyperbole with only three syllables and said "hides her head *in the stars*." O thick and lazy intellect! And yet Vergil did not want to say, "in the stars," for since he understood that *fama* often promulgates a number of things that are uncertain and mingles truth with falsehood and reports things done and not done alike, he hides her head in the clouds, while saying that the rest of her body is visible.[87] And so he demonstrates her size when he raises her into the sky and shows that she goes among men when he makes her walk on the earth; and since she brings with her many things whose truth or falsity cannot be immediately verified, he hides her head in the clouds, for when a cloud is spread before our eyes we cannot discern the true character of things. That is why he says in another pas-

Unde ipse alibi: *nubem quae mortales hebetaret sensus caligaretque, oculos circum eripit.*

59 Agnoscitis singularem Maronis prudentiam, grammaticis non modo non perspectam, sed ne quidem nisi[15] maximis poetis perspectabilem: *Non sunt,* inquit, *aequa famae contentionisque argumenta.* Detur ignorantiae hominis non esse paria; sed tu mihi videris, bone Macrobi, fama quid sit non intelligere, qui dicas eam postquam in immensum prodiit, famam esse desinere ac rei cognitae notionem esse. Quod si sit, passim Livium, Sallustium, Ciceronem et rerum scriptores alios errare inveniemus, nec permissum nobis erit dicere: *fama proelii ad Cannas facti adhuc manet,* nec *rerum a populo Romano gestarum fama perpetua erit,* nec *Atheniensium res gestae minores aliquando fuere quam fama feruntur,* nec *famae consulendum est.* Atqui scriptores famae potissimum student: et Caesar Alexanderque plura famae gratia fecisse videntur, nec temere Alexander dicebat *fama bella constare.*

60 Aliud est igitur fama quam quod tu, grammatice, putas, nec fama esse desinit cum in immensum crevit efficiturque rei cognitae notio, ut tu ipse garris. Nam et Ciceronem consulem plane fuisse scimus, tamen famam consulatus eius dicimus magnam adhuc esse; et Annibalem in Africa superatum fuisse a Scipione notissimum est, tamen famam victoriae eius extare dicimus. Caesarem maximas res gessisse etiam mulierculis cognitum est; num propterea minus dicimus rerum a Pompeio quam a Caesare gestarum famam maiorem esse, aut Alexandri famam nulla posse vetustate obliterari, licet eius facta sint cognitissima? Et quod ab occasu solis ad ortum usque Herculis

sage, "She snatched away the cloud around my eyes that dulls and darkens the senses of mortals."[88]

You recognize the remarkable sagacity of Vergil, which is not only not perceived by grammarians but also not even perceptible except to the greatest poets. Macrobius says, "The subjects of *fama* and strife are not the same." Let their not being the same be conceded to the fellow's ignorance; but I don't think you understand what *fama* is, good Macrobius, since you say that, after it has advanced to an infinite extent, it ceases to be *fama* and is a conception of a known thing.[89] If that is what it is, we will find everywhere that Livy, Sallust, Cicero, and other historians are in error, and we will not be allowed to say, "the *fama* (fame) of the battle of Cannae still remains," or "the *fama* of the deeds of the Roman people will be everlasting," or "the deeds of the Athenians were sometimes less than *fama* reports"[90] or "one must take *fama* into account."[91] And yet writers are very eager for *fama*; both Caesar and Alexander clearly did much for the sake of *fama*, and it was not for nothing that Alexander used to say, "Wars are based on *fama*."[92] 59

Fama is not what you think it is, grammarian, and it does not cease to be *fama* when it grows into something immeasurable and turns into the conception of a known thing, as you babble nonsensically. For we clearly know that Cicero was a consul, and nevertheless we say that the *fama* of his consulship is still great; and it is well known that Hannibal was defeated in Africa by Scipio, and still we say that the *fama* of that victory survives. The great accomplishments of Caesar are known even to foolish women; surely, we do not stop saying for that reason, do we, that the *fama* of Pompey's deeds is greater than that of Caesar's, or that no time can erase the *fama* of Alexander, although his deeds are well known? And because the labors of Hercules are known from the setting to the rising sun, will it be forbidden for that reason to speak of the *fama* of Hercules' 60

labores cogniti sint, famam propterea laborum Herculis dicere non licebit? Desine igitur oblatrare, catelle, et fama quid sit, quot etiam dícatur modis, disce; nam et vetustissimarum rerum celebritas fama dicitur et quae nunc a Turcarum geruntur rege fama per orbem terrarum feruntur. Et Theodorus Graecus, qui diem nuper obiit, magnam ingenii sui famam posteris reliquit; et qui nunc scribundis annalibus dant operam famae suae illorumque de quibus scribunt consulunt. Et fama est gentes quasdam vagantes atque incertis sedibus vitam agere, et nescio cur pecuniae magis quam famae serviendum sit, ac si quibus aliis modis fama inter loquendum scribendumque usu venit.

61 Damnatur etiam Virgilius ab oculatissimo hoc exploratore quod immodice sit usus exemplo illo Homerico de Diomedis armis; nam et de Turno ait:

Tremunt in vertice cristae
Sanguineae clypeoque micantia fulmina mittit;

et alibi de Aenea:

Ardet apex capiti cristisque ac vertice flamma
Funditur et vastos umbo vomit aureus ignes.

Hoc, inquit, *importune positum est, quod neque tum pugnaret Aeneas, sed tantum in navi veniens apparebat.* Imo magis oportune non potuisset, siquidem apex ille ardere visus et Troianis obsidione laborantibus ac tantum non expugnatis castris magnos addidit animos, unde viso clypeo clamorem tollunt ad sidera spesque

labors? So stop barking, whelp, and learn what *fama* is, in how many ways it is spoken of; for not only is the celebrity of very ancient things called *fama,* but also the present deeds of the king of the Turks are carried by *fama* (report) throughout the world. Theodore the Greek, who died just recently, left to posterity the great *fama* (reputation) of his intellect;[93] and those who are now hard at work writing historical annals are looking out for their own *fama* and that of the men they are writing about. And there is *fama* (report) that certain tribes are nomadic and lead their lives in unfixed locations, and for some reason one must be a slave to money more than to *fama* (reputation), as if *fama* is used in these different ways in the course of speaking and writing.

Vergil is also condemned by this eagle-eyed investigator for 61
inapposite use of the well-known Homeric model of Diomedes' armor.[94] For he says of Turnus, too:

> The bloodred plumes on the top of his helmet
> shake,
> and he hurls glittering thunderbolts with his shield.[95]

And elsewhere of Aeneas:

> The helmet on his head blazes, and flame pours from
> the plumes at the top,
> and the golden boss of his shield belches out
> tremendous fires.[96]

"This," says Macrobius, "is out of place, because Aeneas was not fighting at that point, but only making an appearance as he arrived on his ship."[97] On the contrary, it could not have been more appropriately placed, since the sight of the blazing helmet greatly heartened the Trojans suffering under siege and with their camp all but taken by assault. Consequently, when they saw the shield, they "raised a shout to the stars, and the addition of hope stirred their battle rage, and they hurled their

addita iras suscitat iaciuntque manu tela et Ausoniis ducibus nedum militibus is metus iniectus, ut soli Turno fiducia non cesserit. Quin etiam Aeneas ipse, ut qui sentiret quantum armis illis opis, quantum opinionis atque expectationis inesset, *celsa stans in puppi,* sinistra clypeum extulisse inducitur, cum primum in suorum atque hostium conspectum venit. Itaque non potuit magis oportunum tempus servari, cum suorum res tam in angusto, hostium tantus esset successus; et profecto armis illis coelo missis nec tempore magis necessario sese instruere Aeneas potuit, cum de summa rerum contendendum esset, et primus illorum aspectus necesse erat ut vim divinitus insitam et Troianis et Rutulis cum spe, metu, horrore, fiducia atque admiratione prae se ferret.

62 Damnatur etiam quod importune allatis recens armis Aeneas miratur

Terribilem cristis galeam flammasque vomentem.

An non divinum illud opus mirabitur? et cum illa manu tractaret versaretque inter brachia non conciperet magnam spem, praesertim in rebus tam asperis? non animos inde sumeret, videns quantum terrorem galea illa terribilis incussura esset hosti, quae tum ipsi quoque flammas vomere videretur? Quomodo igitur expleri laetitia non potuisset, nisi iam animadvertisset quantus illorum usus adversus hostem futurus esset in proeliis, quae etiam tum sub quaercu posita (neque enim temere sub quaercu posita dicit, cum corona quaerna civium liberatores donarentur) terribilia apparerent? Quocirca, ut dictum est, cum primum in hostium conspectum venit, illa statim extulit. Vide-

spears," and fear beset the Ausonian leaders, to say nothing of the soldiers, so that only "the confidence of Turnus did not fail."[98] And Aeneas himself, when he sensed how much power was in those arms, how much belief and expectation, "standing high on the stern," was led to raise his shield with his left hand as soon as he came into the sight of his own men and the enemy.[99] And so no more suitable time could have been looked for, when his men were in such desperate straits and the success of the enemy was so great; and undoubtedly there could have been no more critical time for Aeneas to equip himself with those arms sent down from heaven, when the decisive battle was to be fought and the first sight of them was necessary to announce the power divinely instilled in them to both Trojans and Rutulians with hope, fear, horror, confidence, and amazement.

Vergil is also criticized for Aeneas' inappropriate amazement 62
when the arms have just been brought to him:

> the helmet terrifying with its plumes and pouring out
> flames.[100]

But will he not marvel at that divine work? And when he was handling the weapons and turning them over in his arms,[101] would he not conceive great hope, especially in such a difficult situation? Would he not take heart from them, seeing what great terror that terrifying helmet would strike into the enemy, when he himself saw it pouring out flames? How could he not have been overjoyed, unless he had already noticed how effective they would be against the enemy in battle, since they seemed terrible even when they were placed under the oak (and Vergil does not say "placed under the oak"[102] for nothing, since those who freed their fellow citizens were presented with an oak-leaf garland)? And so, as has been stated, when he first came into the enemy's sight, he immediately raised them aloft.

tis quam sibi Virgilius constet, qui nihil inaniter dicat et singula exactissime pensitet?

63 Parum hoc visum est; condemnatur etiam quod de Turno dixit:

Cui triplici crinita iuba galea alta Chimeram
Sustinet Aetneos efflantem faucibus ignes;
Tam magis illa fremens et tristibus effera flammis,
Quam magis effuso crudescunt sanguine pugnae.

Turnum, hostium ducem, ad bellum missurus, sane illum qui tot malis Troianos sociosque affecturus esset, qui bellum tantis animis suscepisset, qui morte sua Aeneam esset nobilitaturus, non una e parte artificiosissimus poeta commendat:

Ipse inter primos praestanti corpore Turnus
Vertitur arma tenens et toto vertice supra est.

Facit enim versari inter primos, qua e re ad singulare animi robur corporis quoque vires adiungit; et cum dicit *Vertitur arma tenens*, corporis dexteritatem sub armis atque animi vigorem significat; et cum adiungit *toto vertice supra est*, corporis proceritate suis admirabilem, hostibus formidolosum apparere facit. Ad has corporis atque animi dotes addit armorum horrorem, ex triplici iuba atque e monstro flammas efflante, quippe cum quae Chimera aspectu ipso ante pugnam terrifica esset, fictoris artificio, ubi ad manus ventum esset, tum ea maxime et voce fremeret et flammas evomeret, ut de gemitu deque afflatu campi sanguine caesorum natarent. Atque ut nihil desit, post laevem atque extersum clypeum, siquidem qui de re militari scribunt ad praestringendos adversarii oculos armorum in primis fulgo-

Do you see how consistent Vergil is, since he says nothing in vain and weighs out every detail most precisely?

Evidently this was not enough; he is also censured for saying 63
of Turnus:

> His lofty helmet with its triple long-haired plume
> holds a Chimera breathing Etna's flames from its jaws;
> the greater its rage, the more savage its ominous flames,
> the more violent the battle, the more blood is spilled.[103]

Preparing to send Turnus, the enemy leader, to war—the very one who would afflict the Trojans and their allies with so many evils, who had entered on the war with such courage, who would ennoble Aeneas by his death—the artful poet commends him on more than one point:

> In the vanguard Turnus himself, preeminent in
> strength,
> went holding his weapons, taller by a head than the
> rest.[104]

He makes him move among the vanguard, joining physical might to his singular strength of mind; and when Vergil says, "He went holding his weapons," he indicates his physical dexterity under arms as well as his mental vigor; and when he adds, "taller by a head than the rest," with the height of his body he makes him inspire admiration in his men, terror in the enemy. To these gifts of body and mind he adds the dread caused by his arms from the triple plume and the flame-breathing monster, since, although through the artistry of its maker the very sight of the Chimera before the battle was terrifying, in hand-to-hand fighting it gave voice to a great roar and poured out flames, so that after its cry and its breath the battlefield swam with the blood of the slain. And that nothing might be lacking, after the smooth and polished shield—since for dazzling the eyes of the adversary military writers especially recom-

rem commendant, post altam galeam et ignes efflantem Chimeram addit nimbum peditum et totis castris agmina clypeata densat. An est quod aliud desiderari in extollendis adversarii sive ab insitis a natura corporis atque animi viribus sive ab externis possit rebus? Num igitur importune galea alta Chimeram sustinet, praesertim post tot enumeratos armisque decoratos duces?

64 Atque hoc quidem non tanti faciendum videatur, accusari aut potius damnari a grammatico eximium poetam, neque enim Indus elephas curat culicem; illud me vehementer movet, quod video doctos quosdam viros, dum grammaticis nimis tribuunt, et ipsos delirio eodem vexari, tum in iis locis quos posuimus, tum quod existimant parum prudenter a Virgilio inductum Iovem in primo, quarto et nono volumine, qui loqueretur sine tumultu et absque mundi obsequio, post vero

eo dicente deum domus alta quiescit,
Et tremefacta solo tellus, silet arduus aether,
Tum zephiri posuere, premit placida aequora pontus,

ac si non idem esset qui ante locutus fuerat. Imo idem erat, sed nec ante Venus Iunoque ad contentionem et iurgia Iove coram proruperant, qua e re vario assensu ob factionis studium coelicolae fremebant. Itaque ut ostenderetur concionantis Iovis ea maiestas fuisse ut mussitare ultra nullus auderet, oportunissime dicitur summaque cum prudentia, quod non solum eo dicente deum domus silentium tenuit, sed orbis totus summi dei super-

mend the gleam of arms—after the lofty helmet and the fire-breathing Chimera, he adds a storm-cloud of infantry and fills the whole camp with close-ranked warriors bearing shields.[105] Could anything else be desired in magnifying the physical and mental power of the adversary, imparted to him by both nature and external factors? Surely then it is not "inappropriate," is it, that "the lofty helmet bears a Chimera," especially after so many leaders have been listed and adorned with their arms?

To be sure, this does not seem worth making so much of— 64
that a preeminent poet is accused, or rather condemned, by a grammarian—nor indeed does an Indian elephant trouble himself with a gnat. But it greatly disturbs me when I see certain learned men paying too much attention to grammarians and getting afflicted with the same madness—first in the passages we have presented and then because they think that Vergil introduced Jupiter too carelessly in the first, fourth, and ninth book since he spoke without raising a tumult and without the respectful deference of the universe.[106] But later:

> As he spoke, the lofty house of the gods grew still,
> the earth trembled on its foundations, the high ether
> fell silent.
> Then the Zephyrs dropped, the deep sea made quiet
> its waves:[107]

"As if he were not the same one who had spoken before."[108] In fact, he was the same, but before, Venus and Juno had not burst into strife and invective in the presence of Jupiter, making the heaven dwellers clamor on different sides out of partisanship.[109] And so to demonstrate that the majesty of Jupiter as he addressed the assembly was such that no one dared utter another word, it is said most appropriately and skillfully that when he spoke, not only the house of the gods kept silence but the whole world respected the authority of the highest god. Indeed,

cilium veritus est. Etenim poeta ex verbis ipsis vult innuere Iovem supercilium obduxisse ob dearum iurgia et coelicolarum fremitum ac partium studia, ut qui speciem irati prae se ferret. Unde quodam cum supercilio ait: *Rex Iupiter omnibus idem,* iuratque *per pice torrentis ripas,* atque ut dictis pondus adderet, caput movet, *totumque nutu tremefacit Olympum.*

65 Sed nec mihi Iulius Hyginus aequior videri potest, qui Virgilium accuset quod litus Velinum ex ore Palinuri dixerit, cum Veliam Servio Tullio[16] regnante conditam fuisse tradat, sescentesimo post Aeneae adventum in Italiam anno, aut etiam amplius, ac si poetis permissum non sit quaedam etiam ad sua tempora in carmine referre, ut locorum, ut fluminum nomina, ut armorum genera. Dicat mihi velim Hyginus: cur non etiam accusat Virgilium quod Aeneam, qui Troianus esset, latine loquentem inducat? Facessat igitur diligentia tam arcessita et huiusmodi multa permittantur poetis, in quae etiam volentes incidunt non rerum ignorantia decepti. Idem reprehendit quod cum antea dixisset Virgilius Theseum superas evasisse ad auras, post dicat: *sedet aeternumque sedebit.* Atqui Theseus vivens Herculem ad inferos secutus, inde Herculis ipsius praesidio evasit, ut est in fabulis. Post mortem vero, cum anima eius ad inferos delata esset, nunquam ad viventis rediit, sed propter filium iniuste occisum sedet illic atque aeternum sedebit, iniquissimam Hyppoliti mortem infeliciter deplorans. Recteque et ante vivum rediisse ab inferis ait, unde argumentandi locum Aeneas coepit, et post inter eos qui mortui essent enumerat; neque enim haec sibi adversantur.

the poet wants to indicate from the language itself that since he showed an angry demeanor, Jupiter frowned on the bickering of the goddesses and the murmuring and partisanship of the heaven dwellers. Accordingly, he says with a certain sternness, "Jupiter the king is the same to all" and swears "by the banks hot with pitch" and — to add weight to his words — moves his head "and makes all Olympus tremble with his nod."[110]

Nor do I consider Iulius Hyginus more just, since he blames 65
Vergil for having Palinurus mention the shore of Velia, since he says that Velia was founded in the reign of Servius Tullius, six hundred years or even more after Aeneas' arrival in Italy[111] — as if poets were not allowed in a poem to refer some things even to their own times, like the names of places or rivers, or types of arms. I would like Hyginus to tell me: why does he not blame Vergil for having Aeneas speak Latin although he was a Trojan? Away then with such far-fetched pedantry! Let many liberties of this sort be permitted to poets; they fall into them on purpose and not because they are deceived by ignorance of the facts. The same man finds fault because, although Vergil had said earlier that Theseus had made his way to the upper air, he says later: "he sits [in Hades] and will sit for ever."[112] And yet the living Theseus followed Hercules to the underworld, from which he escaped with the help of Hercules, according to myth. But after death, when his spirit had been carried down to the underworld, he never returned to the living, but because of the unjust slaying of his son, he sits there and will sit for ever, unhappily lamenting the unjust death of Hippolytus. And Vergil is correct both to say first that he returned alive from the underworld, from which Aeneas took a point of his argument, and to list him afterward among the dead; and these passages do not contradict each other.

66 Errasse etiam dicit in his versibus:

Eruet ille Argos Agamennoniasque Micenas
Ipsumque Aeaciden, genus armipotentis Achilli,
Ulctus avos Troiae, templa et temerata Minervae,

quod et personas confundat et tempora, cum neque eodem tempore neque per eosdem duces cum Acheis Pyrrhoque pugnatum sit, siquidem Pyrrhus, quem Aeaciden dicit, ex Epiro in Italiam transgressus cum Romanis depugnavit adversus Curium, belli eius ducem; Argivum autem bellum id est Achaicum, multos post annos a L. Mumio imperatore gestum est; itaque censet medium versum eximi posse, qui quidem de Pyrrho importune immissus esset, quem Virgilius procul dubio fuisset exempturus. Non possum non admirari etiam ad risum usque tum Hyginum tum Gellium, qui studio quodam reprehendendi praecipites in maximos errores inciderint: primum quod de Pyrrho dictum, non de Persa rege putent; neque enim Pyrrhus a populo Romano victus est neque regnum Epirotarum Pyrrho vivente captum atque in provintiam redactum est, sed Perses, qui a Paulo ductus est ante triumphum, quo capto Macedoniaque spoliato, Aeacidarum imperium finivit; de quo etiam Propertius ait:

Et Persen proavi stimulantem pectus Achilli
Quique tuas proavus fregit, Achille, domos.

Hoc igitur superato regnoque Aeacidarum deleto, populus Romanus videri potuit Troiae ruinas ulctus fuisse. Deinde non animadvertere induci a Virgilio Anchisen nequaquam singulos

Hyginus also says that he erred in these verses: 66

That one will destroy Argos and Agamemnon's Mycene
and the descendant of Aeacus, of the line of mighty
Achilles,
avenging his Trojan ancestors and the violated temple
of Minerva,[113]

because "he confuses persons and times, because the wars with the Achaeans and with Pyrrhus were fought neither at the same time nor with the same generals, since Pyrrhus, whom he calls the descendant of Aeacus, crossed from Epirus into Italy and did battle with the Romans opposite Curius, the general of that war. But the Argive war (that is, the Achaean war) was waged many years afterward by the general Lucius Mummius; and so Hyginus thinks that the middle verse can be removed since it was inserted inappropriately about Pyrrhus, and that Vergil undoubtedly would have taken it out."[114] I have to be amazed almost to the point of laughter at both Hyginus and Gellius, who in their enthusiasm for criticizing have fallen headlong into major errors. First, they think Vergil was speaking of Pyrrhus, not King Perses. Of course, Pyrrhus was not conquered by the Roman people nor was the kingdom of the Epirotes captured and reduced to a province in Pyrrhus' lifetime; but Perses, who was led by Paulus at the head of his triumph after he had been captured and stripped of Macedonia, brought the rule of the Aeacids to an end. Propertius says of him:

And Perses, stirring the heart of his ancestor Achilles
and the ancestor who destroyed your house,
Achilles.[115]

Therefore, after this man had been conquered and the kingdom of the Aeacids abolished, the Roman people could be seen to have avenged the destruction of Troy. In the second place, they did not notice that Vergil presented Anchises, not as mention-

referentem qui ab Aenea originem ducturi essent, sed quosdam tantum, neque tempus ordinemve servari, quippe cum de Caesare atque Pompeio antequam de Fabio, Marcello, Scipionibus mentionem faciat; satis enim habebat Anchises, quibusdam nominatis, quibusdam a rebus gerendis significatis, spe atque gaudio futurae stirpis Aeneam implere.

67 Quare cum dicit:

Ille triumphata Capitolia ad alta Corintho
Victor aget currus, caesis insignis Achivis,

iure potest videri Mumium, qui Achaicus cognominatus est quique Corinthum sustulit, significare; post vero cum addat: *Eruet ille Argos Agamennoniasque Micenas,* alium profecto significat, et hic quidem Paulus est, qui Persen vicit regnumque Aeacidarum subvertit; quanquam autem Paulus neque Argos evertit neque Micenas, hoc tamen ut Aeneam soletur ab Anchisa dicitur, cuius ipsius posteri eversuri essent Argos, sive Achaicum, quae arx videbatur Acheorum, quorum principes adversus Troianos coniuraverant, sive Thessalicum, quando ducum Thessaliae virtus in eo bello plurimum enituerit, et Micenas, Agamemnonis patriam, qui fuit Graecorum ac belli dux. Quocirca dum Virgilium non minus imprudenter quam impudenter accusant, uterque, et Hyginus sententiae huius adversus Maronem auctor et suffragator eius Aulus in errorem maxima animadversione dignum incidere.

68 His tam iniquis calumniis cum indigne ferret Antonius eximium poetam affici ac venenosis grammaticorum morsibus laniari, quid mirum si catellorum persimiles dicebat, si doctos

ing every single person who would trace his lineage from Aeneas, but only particular ones, and without observing time or sequence, inasmuch as he speaks of Caesar and Pompey before Fabius, Marcellus, and the Scipios. Anchises was content to fill Aeneas with the hope and joy of his future line by mentioning a few descendants and by indicating a few of their future achievements.

Therefore, when he says: 67

That one will drive his chariot to the lofty Capitol in
triumph
a victor over Corinth, renowned for slaying
Achaeans,[116]

he can rightly be seen to be pointing to Mummius, who had the cognomen Achaicus and who destroyed Corinth; but afterward, when he adds: "That one will destroy Argos and Agamemnon's Mycene," he is undoubtedly pointing to someone else, and that is certainly Paulus, who conquered Perses and overturned the kingdom of the Aeacids. Moreover, although Paulus brought down neither Argos nor Mycene, Anchises says this to console Aeneas, whose own posterity would overturn Argos (whether it was Achaean, the citadel that seemed to belong to the Achaeans whose princes had taken an oath against the Trojans, or Thessalian, since the courage of the leaders of Thessaly was most conspicuous in that war), as well as Mycenae, the homeland of Agamemnon, who was the leader of the Greeks and the war. For that reason, while they find fault with Vergil no less imprudently than impudently, they each—both Hyginus, the source of this verdict against Maro, and his supporter Aulus—have fallen into an error worthy of the greatest censure.

Since Antonio was indignant that the preeminent poet should be criticized so unfairly and torn to pieces by the poisonous bites of grammarians, is it any wonder if he said they 68

quosdam ut deliros ridebat? Poteram etiam multa addere, quibus Antonii adversus grammaticos iram iustissimis e causis conceptam ostenderem, sed me ipse continui, quod videbam in Virgilii laudes prorumpendum esse, quibus explicandis cum sentiam me imparem, temperare malui.

Andr. Eadem et me ratio te dicente cohibuit, ne quae a te praeteriri videbam consilio ea ipse subiicerem, quippe cum laudabilior sit Maro quam ut a me praesertim laudari satis digne queat.

69 *Comp.* Et apposite quidem atque accumulate adversus grammaticos ex Antonii sententia disputavit Elisius et Andreas pro moderatione sua quae sedulo ab Elisio praeteriri videbat subiicere noluit, non tam, ut mihi persuadeo, viribus diffisus, si in Maronis laudes descendendum esset, quam quod locus hic explicandis summi poetae virtutibus satis idoneus non est. Verum, bone hospes, ut cupiditati tuae pro virili satisfacere et ipse studeam, referam quanto paucioribus quidem potero Antonii sermonem eum quem aliquando eodem hoc in loco habuit de recensendis ducibus qui aut Aeneam aut Turnum in expeditionem secuti sunt, sentiens condemnari Virgilium tum quod oppida urbesque non eo quo sitae sunt ordine referret, tum quod nonnulli pugnantes inducantur, qui non essent in belli apparatu numerati, cum Homerus eosdem illos quos retulisset in catalogo solos pugnantes dicat et Graeciae oppida locaque per ordinem referat.

70 Dicebat igitur similibus in rebus sive agendis sive scribendis non idem semper aut agenti aut scribenti consilium esse nec eundem ad finem eadem in re ubique contendi. Homerum quidem voluisse in enumerandis auxiliis Graeciae urbes locaque describere ordineque Graeciae situs catalogum exequi, quippe

were like whelps and if he mocked certain scholars as insane? I could also have mentioned many additional points to show that Antonio harbored his wrath against grammarians for good reason, but I restrained myself because I saw that I would have to rush into Vergil's praises, and since I felt that I was unequal to treating them, I have preferred to refrain.

Andrea. The same consideration prevented me from adding points during your discourse that I saw you were deliberately omitting, since Maro is too praiseworthy to be praised as much as he deserves, especially by me.

Compatre. Elisio has argued both appropriately and copiously 69
against the grammarians in accordance with Antonio's views, and Andrea with his usual moderation has been reluctant to add what he saw was being carefully omitted by Elisio. It was not, I'm sure, that Andrea lacked confidence in his own abilities if it came down to praising Vergil, but rather that the present occasion is not really suitable for setting out the merits of the greatest of poets. But, excellent visitor, so that I too may strive to satisfy your desire myself to the best of my ability, I will report as succinctly as I can what Antonio once had to say on this very spot about the catalogue of the leaders who followed either Aeneas or Turnus on campaign.[117] He understood that Vergil was censured both for recording towns and cities out of their proper order and for bringing in some warriors who had not been listed in the preparation for war, whereas Homer mentions only the same warriors he had reported in the catalogue and records the towns and places of Greece in order.[118]

He used to say, then, that in doing or writing similar things 70
a person acting or writing does not always have the same intention, nor does one in all circumstances strive toward the same end in the same matter. To be sure, Homer in listing the allies had wanted to describe the cities and places of Greece and to make a catalogue in the order of their position in Greece, since

cum universam Graeciam adversus Troianos coniurasse ostendat. At nostro poetae consilium non fuisse Italiam describendi; neque enim omnes Italiae populi aut pro Aenea aut contra Aeneam stetere, quando Etruscorum etiam multi belli se medios praebuere. Quinimo maiore e parte vetustissima oppida et ea maxime quae e memoria exciderant conquirit, ut qui restituere illa in lucem velit. Quodque historici etiam Latini servant in enumerandis auxiliis, regiones non describit ac satis habet duces ipsos et loca e quibus auxilia venerint nominare. Quo enim consilio aut Italiam aut Etruriam universam describeret qui neque Italiae neque Etruriae totius populos sciret aut pro hac aut pro illa parte arma coepisse? Iure itaque contentum fuisse illis tantum populis ac ducibus qui in expeditionem profecti sunt nominatis. In quibus referendis necesse non fuit situs ordinem tenere, cum universae regionis populi non enumerentur et Mantuam solam e tot trans Appenninum populis nominet, videlicet ut patriae assurgeret atque ut *avis divitem* laudaret *caputque populis* statueret.

71 Affirmabat praeterea Virgilium imaginem quandam secutum pugnarum atque oppugnationum quae in rebus in Gallia gestis a Caesare describuntur; fecisse etiam Ascanium nudato capite pugnare, quod de Caesare ipso legitur. Deflexisse quoque in quibusdam ab Homero de industria, ut qui Romanae militiae disciplinam potius sequi vellet eamque ob rem singulos duces pugnantes minime inducere, quos nisi cum necessitas vocaverit obiectare sese periculis aut manum conserere non deceat. Quodque plures inter pugnandum nominaret qui in enumeratione auxiliorum dicti prius non essent; in hoc quoque a Romanae historiae consuetudine non recedere, siquidem Romanarum

he was showing that the whole of Greece had formed an alliance against Troy. But it was not our poet's intention to describe Italy, nor did all the peoples of Italy take a stand either for Aeneas or against him, since many of the Etruscans acted as neutrals in the war. On the contrary, for the most part he seeks out the most ancient towns and especially those that had been forgotten, since he wants to bring them back to light. And in accordance with the system observed by the Latin historians in listing allies, he does not describe their regions and considers it sufficient to name the leaders themselves and the places from which the allies have come. Indeed, to what purpose would he describe either all of Italy or all of Etruria, since he knew that the peoples neither of all Italy nor of all Etruria had taken up arms for one side or the other? Rightly, then, he was content with naming only those peoples or leaders who set out on the campaign. In recording them it was not necessary to maintain the order of their location since the peoples of the whole region were not being enumerated. Of the many communities on the other side of the Apennines he names only Mantua, evidently to show respect to his homeland and praise it as "rich in ancestors" and establish it as "a capital for peoples."[119]

Besides, he asserted that Vergil used as a kind of model the 71
battles and sieges described by Caesar in his *Gallic Wars;* he even made Ascanius fight with his head uncovered, which one reads of Caesar himself.[120] In certain details he also intentionally deviated from Homer since he wanted to adhere to Roman military discipline instead; and for that reason he very seldom presents leaders fighting in single combat, since it is inappropriate for them to put themselves in peril or go hand-to-hand unless necessity demands it. And as to the fact that he named several in the fighting who had not been mentioned earlier in the catalogue of allies, here too he does not depart from Roman

scriptores rerum, nominatis consulibus praetoribusve, aut dictatore atque equitum magistro, alios in suscipiendis expeditionibus vix nominant; at cum pugnas describunt et qui in bello desiderati sunt recensent, tunc milites, centuriones, praefectique nominatim dicuntur, quorum in apparando exercitu nulla mentio facta est. Referuntur fortia tum peditum, tum equitum facta et navatae ab infimi etiam ordinis militibus operae, de quibus nihil ante dictum est. Hanc igitur fuisse rationem censebat cur Virgilius partim ad Homeri exemplum duces quosdam pugnantes induceret, ne ab illo, cuius maxime similis esse vellet omnino recederet, partim ad Romanae militiae disciplinam non omnes pugnantes faceret, sed militum potius qui sub illis militarent virtutem referret, cum invidia quaedam videri possit suis milites laudibus defraudare.

72 Ad haec, cum de Romanae militiae disciplina esset mitti supplementa, qui a Virgilio post nominantur perinde ac cum supplementis ad Aeneam Turnumve profectos intelligi vult; sic Oximum regem, sic alios quosdam ab eo post nominatos, ac si cum supplementis, postquam in expeditionem ab imperatoribus itum esset, in castra profecti sint. Plures quoque cognomines idest eiusdem nominis ab eo referri, quod Romanorum plurimi eodem nomine vocarentur indeque tot praenomina agnominaque inventa esse. Reges quoque sub imperatoribus militare et hoc quoque Romanum esse, cum reges multos socios haberent, quos sub imperatoribus consulibusque pugnasse satis compertum est, atque ad hoc ipsum, Homero nonnunquam relicto, voluisse Virgilium alludere.

73 Illud vero maxime nefandum esse et quovis animadvertendum supplicio praedicabat, quod essent nonnulli adeo improbi ut non alia se magis ratione doctos atque in litteris claros haberi posse persuasum habeant quam si Virgilio detrahant, si in poe-

historical practice, since the writers of Roman history will name consuls or praetors or a dictator and master of horse at the outset of campaigns while barely mentioning others; but when they describe battles and list those lost in battle, then they cite by name soldiers, centurions, and prefects of whom no mention was made in preparing the army. The brave acts of both foot soldiers and cavalry are recorded and energetic efforts by soldiers of even the lowest rank, of whom nothing was said before. This, then, he reckoned was Vergil's reasoning: in part, on Homer's example, he presented certain leaders fighting, so as not to depart entirely from the one he wished most to resemble; and in part to suit Roman military discipline, he did not have them all fight, but instead reported the courage of the soldiers serving under them, since it could seem an act of ill will to cheat the soldiers of their praise.

And in addition, since sending reinforcements was in accor- 72
dance with the Roman military system, he wants those named later by Vergil to be understood as having set out with the reinforcements to Aeneas or Turnus. Hence he named King Oximus[121] and several others later, as if they had come into the camp with the reinforcements after the generals had embarked on the campaign. He also mentions several men with the same name (that is, the same cognomen), because a great many Romans were called by the same name, which is why they invented so many forenames and nicknames. Kings also served under generals, and this too was Roman, since kings had many allies who are known to have fought under generals and consuls, and Vergil wanted to refer to this, sometimes abandoning Homer.

Antonio also used to declare that it was especially wicked, 73
punishable with any penalty you like, that some people were shameless enough to convince themselves that the best way to be considered learned and illustrious in literature was to disparage Vergil—to sharpen their fangs on the prince of poets.

tarum nostrorum principem dentes acuant. Qui si quando pro rei locique natura variantior et, ut ita dixerim, festivior est, hic Homeri simplicitatem magis probant; ubi simplicior atque castigatior, tum copiam illius et ornatum requirunt maiorem; nunc quod Homeri ipsius nimius sectator fuerit, nunc quod ab illius imitatione longius recesserit accusant; alias non probant tantum antiquitatis studium, alias quaedam sine ullo exemplo protulisse damnant; interdum supercilium eius, interdum iucunditatem insectantur; denique esse inventos qui dicerent scripta eius mera furta esse, qui censerent Ennium quanquam rudem et inconditum ei anteponendum, qui nullo demum ingenio, nulla inventione fuisse nugarentur. Hoc loco rei indignitate commotum exclamare Antonium memini improbos, facinorosos, detestabiles eos dicentem Iovemque ausos regnis detrudere, quippe qui Romanae poeticae principem et quasi deum quendam suo e regno, suo e solio pellere ac deturbare conarentur.

74 Sed nec meliore usum fortuna patrem ipsum poeticae omnis Homerum querebatur; laceratum, vexatum, discerptum etiam ab ignorantissimis fuisse, hocque de posteris meritum, quibus lumen accendisset, retulisse, ut etiam grammaticorum caecutienti ignorantiae obnoxius fuerit. Censebat igitur duos hos in duabus nobilissimis linguis Graeca Romanaque summum iure principatum tenere, et alterum Graecae, alterum Romanae poeticae regem esse; horum dicta inventaque locum, vim, auctoritatemque legum habere; hos venerandos, hos patres patriae publicis privatisque honoribus prosequendos, his ubique atque ab omnibus assurgendum. Qui contra sentirent rebellium atque hostium in numero habendos esse, atque uti subiectis populis popularibusque nullum ius, nulla iurisdictio esset in regibus

Whenever he is more variegated and lively, so to speak, to suit the character of the subject and the occasion, they put a higher value on the simplicity of Homer; when he is more unadorned and severe, they demand Homer's abundance and ornament; they blame him now for following Homer too closely, now because he has not imitated him closely enough; on one occasion they will disapprove his great zeal for antiquity; on another they will condemn him for not following precedent; sometimes they criticize his gravity, sometimes his charm. And finally, Antonio said that there were some people who said that his writings were mere thefts, who decreed that Ennius, although rude and barbarous, was preferable to him, who babbled foolishly that he was without talent or the power of invention. At this point I remember Antonio, moved by the outrageousness of the thing, shouting that they were shameless! criminal! detestable! — saying that they would dare to force Jupiter out of his kingdom, since they were trying to push and topple the prince of Roman poetry from his throne, like a god from his dominion.

But he also used to complain that Homer, the very father of 74
all poetry, had fared no better, that he had been shredded, attacked, pulled to pieces even by ignorant dolts, and that the reward he had from posterity for enlightening them was to be exposed to the blind ignorance even of grammarians. Thus he believed that these two men rightly held supreme leadership in the two noblest languages, Greek and Roman, and that the one was king of Greek poetry, the other of Roman; that their words and inventions had the standing, force, and authority of law; that they were to be venerated, celebrated as fathers of their country with honors public and private, and paid homage by all men everywhere. Those who took the opposing view should be numbered with rebels and enemies, and just as subject peoples and citizens had no right and no standing with the kings whose

quorum praescriptis, imperiis decretisque ab illis pareretur, sic a litteratis omnibus quae duo hi reges decernant iis ubique parendum esse. Qui aliter sentiret contrave auderet aqua et igni interdicendum atque in loca deserta exterminandum ferisve obiiciendum statuebat.

75 Haec, Sicule hospes, dicere Antonium in Virgilii causa memini; quae tibi propterea referenda duxi ut quod eius iudicium, quae etiam doctrina fuerit perspicere hinc possis; relaturus etiam quae aliquando in defendendo Cicerone copiose, acute magnificeque disseruit, ni Herricum hunc dicere nescio quid velle animadverterem.

76 *Herr.* Dii boni, videone ego Antonianum sapientem, estne ille Iuratius Suppatius? Certe ipse est. O diem iucundissimum! Per ego Ciceronem, perque divinam Ciceronis eloquentiam oro obtestorque uti, valere aliquantulum iussis grammaticis, Antonianum sapientem de sapientia disserentem placide audiatis; nihil est, mihi credite, homine hoc urbanius. Videbitis quod loquendi principium adveniens dabit.

Suppatius, Herricus

77 *Supp.* Et sapere vos et corde uti quam cordatissime iubeo.

Herr. At nos valentissimi capitis hominem, oppido valentem advenisse gaudemus.

Supp. Estne hic Pudericus meus? O desideratissimum mihi amicum, ut cordate?

Herr. Satis quidem cum corde recte, cum capite tamen parum sane; de abscessu enim vix utor oculis, amicissimum tamen ac sapientissimum hominem libentissime et video et alloquor.

Supp. Cui cum corde bene est huic valitudo nisi secunda esse non potest.

precepts, laws and decrees they obeyed, so it was incumbent on all men of letters to obey the decrees of these two kings in all circumstances. He laid down the law that whoever disagreed or dared to act otherwise should be forbidden water and fire and banished into desert regions or thrown to the beasts.

This, Sicilian visitor, is what I remember Antonio saying on Vergil's behalf, and I thought I should report it to you so that you could have an idea of his taste and learning. I would also report what he once argued abundantly, acutely, and splendidly in defense of Cicero if I did not see that Enrico here wants to say something. 75

Enrico. Good gods, do I see a wise devotee of Antonio? Is that Giurazio Suppazio? Yes, it is he. O happy day! By Cicero and by the divine eloquence of Cicero I beseech and call on you to say farewell for a time to the precepts of grammarians and listen quietly to the wise devotee of Antonio discoursing on wisdom. Believe me, there is nothing more charming than this fellow. You will see that he will begin speaking on his arrival. 76

Suppazio, Enrico

Suppazio. I bid you to be wise and to use your heart as heartily as possible.[122] 77

Enrico. But we rejoice that a man of such a strong head has come on so strong.

Suppazio. Is this my dear Poderico? O my most longed-for friend, how goes it with your heart?

Enrico. Well enough with my heart, all right, but my head is not so healthy. Thanks to an infection I scarcely have the use of my eyes; nevertheless, I'm delighted to see and address a very great friend and a very wise man.

Suppazio. If it is well with a man's heart, his health can only be good.

Herr. Unde, bone?

78 *Supp.* A sapientibus quaeritandis. Fui Senae studiorum fama ductus; ibi mirificum hoc vidi, in maximo populo, in urbe quam ipsi veterem agnominant vix unum atque alterum senem esse; qui autem rempublicam administrarent plerosque adolescentulos esse; adeo vetus Sena vix quicquam habet quod senile dicas. Fui Pisis, urbe tum antiqua, tum Graeca, ut volunt; ibi senes plurimos, omnes quidem corio, cordi deditum esse neminem; quem enim cordatum apud eos invenies, qui domesticas ob seditiones civiliaque odia tantam tam brevi rempublicam amisere? Hinc Lucam concessi, quorum hominum deum cum tam crasso capite animadvertissem, coniecturam coepi nihil nisi crasse sapere Lucensem populum posse. Pratum inde profectus, quo mortales multi convenerant (festus enim dies erat); cives, incolas, advenas ita in cingulum illud divae matris intentos vidi cunctos, uti confestim inde abierim; quae enim scabies superstitione scabiosior? Veni post Florentiam, in qua quod mulieres formae nimium studerent, quosdam ab iis aliquanto alieniores animadverti. Una mihi civitatis eius mirum in modum disciplina placuit, quod singulis in domibus singulas stateras videbam appensas; eos autem qui magistratus gererent duplici etiam statera uti, altera enim civitatis altera Italiae res expendunt. Hinc Bononiam cum venissem, vivum illic sapientem inveni neminem, mortuos vero multos eosque in catenis habitos. Galliae citerioris urbes vidi tantum; quae quod tyrannis servirent, quomodo sapientem in illis quaererem? Tamen animadverti pullulare aliquando apud eas sapientiam coepisse. Consuesse enim tyrannos a popularibus occidi, libertatem vero retinere diutius cives nescire. Volui videre Genuam, quam ubi vidi, dii boni, beluam illam multorum capitum vidi; annus ipse neque

Enrico. Where did you get that idea, my good friend?

Suppazio. From seeking out wise men. I was in Siena, drawn there 78
by the reputation of its schools. There I saw an amazing thing: in a very large population, in a city that that they themselves nickname "old," there are scarcely one or two old men; moreover, those who govern the state are mostly mere youths; thus old Siena has hardly a thing you might call old.[123] I was in Pisa, both an ancient city and a Greek one, as they say; there you will find a lot of old men all given over to their hide [*corio*] but none to the heart [*cordi*].[124] For what person of good heart can you find among those who have lost their republic in such a short time because of domestic rebellion and hatred among the citizens?[125] From there I went to Lucca; since I observed that the god of those people was so thickheaded, I supposed that the populace of Lucca could only be thick-witted.[126] Then on to Prato, where many mortals had gathered (it was a feast day). I saw citizens, inhabitants, strangers, all so intent on the famous girdle of the holy mother that I left there in a hurry; what itch itches more than superstition?[127] Afterward I went to Florence, where, because women pay too much attention to their looks, I noticed that certain men are somewhat estranged from them.[128] One system of this state wonderfully pleased me, that I saw scales hanging in every single house, and moreover, that the magistrates use a double scale: on one they weigh the affairs of the state, on the other the affairs of Italy.[129] When I came from there to Bologna, I found no living wise man, but many dead ones hanging in chains.[130] I just looked at the cities of northern Italy: how should I seek a wise man in places enslaved to tyrants? Nevertheless, I noticed that wisdom had occasionally started to sprout up in them. Indeed, tyrants had often been killed by the populace, but the citizens did not know how to hold onto liberty for long. I wanted to see Genoa, and when I saw it (good gods!) I saw a many-headed beast; indeed,

tam varius, neque adeo mutabilis quam Genuensium civium sunt ingenia. Unde secunda navigatione usus atque in Telamonis portum delatus, animadverti tertium quoddam illic hominum genus esse physicis ipsis ignotum. Nam cum hominum alii vivi, alii mortui dicantur, qui Telamone agunt eos nec vivis nec mortuis annumerandos censeo.

79 Fugi statim larvarum gregem, ac zephiro spirante Romam devectus, ibi biduum egi, tum monumentis veterum cognoscendis, tum sacris perscrutandis. Tertio die, dum sapientem quaero, venio ad Floram; praeter popinones, laenones, ganeones, vix illic video alios. Venio ad Pontem; omnia invenio plena foeneratorum. Eo Lateranum; soli ibi coqui, solae tabernae meritoriae. Perrecto diversa urbis loca, regiones, angiportus, compita, greges; cuiusque modi generis hominum incompositi passim obviam fiunt, omnes, ut mihi videbantur, ventri dediti. Dum sic per urbem vagor, duo maxime periculosa contigere: nam et meretricum manus vix evasi, pallio etiam timens, et sacerdotum mulabus pene subtritus sum. Quorum vitam, mores, instituta dum novisse curo, invenio ex his non paucos quos reliquis mortalibus ad omnem vitae partem optime agendam exemplum iure statuas, quosdam tamen quos vere dicas nihil nisi voluptatem quaerere eamque solam sequi.

80 Captus itaque fama unius atque alterius sacerdotis, dum eos quaerito, factus est mihi obviam litterator, qui me pugnis male habuit, cum inter loquendum excidisset ut dicerem *ocio illic marcescere homines*, quod huiusmodi verba *splendesco, tabesco, liquesco*, casum illum respuant; ac dum Ciceronem testem adduco: *nihil*

a year itself is not so varied, so changeable as the natures of the citizens of Genoa.[131] From there after a successful voyage I sailed into Porto di Talamone, where I observed a third race of men unknown to science. For although some men are called alive, others dead, I think those who live in Talamone must be classified as neither living nor dead.[132]

I immediately fled the flock of ghosts, and after sailing to 79
Rome on a freshening breeze, I spent two days there getting acquainted with the monuments of the ancients and investigating the churches. On the third day, while I was looking for a wise man, I came to Campo dei Fiori; there I saw scarcely anyone except drunks, pimps, and low characters. I came to Ponte Sant'Angelo; I found it all full of moneylenders. I went to the Lateran; there, only cooks, only cheap lodging houses. I made my way through the different parts of the city, districts, alleys, crossroads, crowds; everywhere I met motley characters of every sort — all, as it seemed to me, dedicated to their belly. While I was wandering through the city like this, two great perils befell me: I barely escaped the hands of prostitutes, even fearing for my cloak, and I was nearly trampled by the mules of the priests. While I was taking the trouble to learn about the priests' life, customs, and doctrine, I found quite a few of them whom you would rightly pronounce to be an example to the rest of mankind of the best conduct in every aspect of life, but some you would truly say sought nothing except pleasure and used it as their only guide.

I was taken with the reputation of a priest or two, and while 80
I was looking for them, I ran across a schoolmaster who pummeled me with his fists when while speaking I let fall the words, "there men grow feeble [*marcescere*] with idleness." This was because (as he thought) words of this sort, *splendesco* ("grow bright"), *tabesco* ("waste away"), *liquesco* ("melt"), are not constructed with the ablative. When I cited Cicero's phrase, "there

est quod non splendescat oratione, dum Virgilium: *cera liquescit/uno eodemque igni* et *molli paulatim flavescet campus arista,* dum Columellam: *multa sunt, ut dixi, quae negligentia exolescant,* dum etiam Plinium: *igne spissatur, humore fervescit,* ille in iram ac iurgia prorumpens, miseris me modis habuit. Ego satis habui incolumi pallio inde me proripere. Itaque dum Romae sapientem quaero, mercedem hanc accipio. Illud etiam quam incommodissime accidit, quod dum ab hoc litteratore vix me avello, in alterum incidi; cui percunctanti iniuriamne aliquam accepissem, quod videret male me fuisse acceptum, cum responderem insignem me a grammatico iniuriam passum, 'Quam rectissime,' inquit grammaticus ille. 'Quid, malum, non te pudet senem loqui latine nescire? ubi tu gentium reperisti *iniuriam patior?*' –'Atqui,' inquam, 'apud Ciceronem in Philippica tertia: *aequo animo belli patitur iniuriam, dummodo repellat periculum servitutis,* et in Laelio: *is in culpa sit qui faciat, non qui patiatur iniuriam.*' Hoc vix dicto, quod is iam pugnos stringeret, dedi me in pedes, ac Roma egressus, Velitras quam citatissimo gradu petii; ex eoque decretum est mihi valere sapientem sinere.

81 *Herr.* Cur, obsecro, trans Alpes non profectus?

Supp. Quod scirem Gallos maxime stolidos esse corpusque curare magis quam animum colere, regemque eorum quamvis splendidissimum, tam brevi tamen vestitu incedere ut pudenda non velet, ac si Cynicorum sectator sit institutorum.

is nothing that does not grow bright (*splendescat*) with oratory"; when I cited Vergil, "the wax melts (*liquescit*) with one and the same flame," and "little by little the plain will grow golden (*flavescet*) with tender grain"; Columella, "there are many things, as I have said, that deteriorate (*exolescant*) with neglect"; even Pliny, "it becomes dense with heat, becomes hot (*fervescit*) with moisture," he burst into angry invective and cruelly mistreated me.[133] I was just glad to get away from there with my cloak in one piece. And so this is the reward I got when looking for a wise man in Rome. I had just torn myself away from this schoolmaster, when I had the utter misfortune to fall into the hands of another. Because he saw that I had been badly used, he asked whether I had received unjust treatment. I replied that I had suffered an extraordinary injustice from a grammarian. "And quite right, too," said this grammarian. "Damn it! aren't you ashamed, old man that you are, not to know how to speak Latin? Where in the world did you find the expression, "I suffer an injustice?" "But," says I, "in Cicero: in the third *Philippic*, 'he suffers the injustice of war with equanimity, provided that he might fend off the danger of slavery'; and in *Laelius*, 'the man who commits an injustice is at fault, not the man who suffers one.'[134] When the words were barely out of my mouth, because he was already clenching his fists, I took to my heels. Leaving Rome, I sought Velletri as fast as I could; and after that I made up my mind to let the wise man go.

Enrico. Why didn't you set out across the Alps, if I may ask? 81

Suppazio. Because I knew that the French are dreadfully dull and take more care for their bodies than for their minds, and that their king, although he is most magnificent, nevertheless walks around in a garment too short to cover his private parts, as if he were a follower of the precepts of the Cynics.

Herr. Satis magna causa. Ispanias vero adire quae te ratio vetuit, ubi genus hominum acre atque ingeniosum?

Supp. Ne, dum sapientem quaero, in piratas inciderem remoque adiicerer; neque enim tam Sicilia tritici quam praedonum Ispania ferax est.

82 *Herr.* Venetias cur non visisti, quam sapientium urbem sunt qui dicere audeant?

Supp. Destinaveram animo ultimam hanc petere plusculumque illic temporis agere, dum mores civitatis, dum civium ingenia, leges, ritus, reipublicae temperationem noscerem, et fama quidem acceperam senes illic moderari. Nec me deterruit quod elatissimi mortalium dicuntur omnium, sed quod, ut dixi, decretum est mihi posthac meas tantum res agere nec me grammaticis credere, quos audio ibi regnare quosque malo meo fato genitos scio; neque enim Romae solum, sed Velitris, sed Terracinae pessime ab illis habitus atque acceptus sum. At videte, obsecro, quam ob causam: Adieram medicum, sciscitaturus an distillationi frictio esset utilis. Aderat forte grammaticus audacia tam importuna ut respondere medicum non passus, obiurgare me statím coeperit quod *fricatio* non *frictio* diceretur; nomina enim quae a primae coniugationis verbis deducerentur supinum habentibus in *itum* vel in *ctum* praeter coeterorum verborum legem exire in *atio*, non in *itio*, nec in *ctio*: itaque *fricatio*, non *frictio* dicendum esse. O bone, inquam, verbalia in *io* aut a supinis ipsis aut a genitivis participiorum praeteriti temporis fiunt, quae ab ipsis ducuntur supinis, ut *oratus, orati, oratio; audi-*

Enrico. A good enough reason. But what consideration kept you from visiting the Spains, where the race of men is energetic and clever?

Suppazio. I feared that, while seeking a wise man, I'd encounter pirates and be turned into a galley slave: Sicily is not less fertile in grain than Spain is in pirates.

Enrico. Why didn't you visit Venice, since some venture to say that 82
it is a city of wise men?[135]

Suppazio. I had decided to seek it out last and to spend a great deal of time there while I became acquainted with the customs of the state, the character, laws, and way of life of the citizens and the constitution of the republic; and I had learned by report that old men governed there. And I was not deterred by the fact that they are called the most arrogant people in the world, but because, as I've said, I determined after this to see only to my own affairs and not entrust myself to the grammarians who I hear reign there and who I know were born to my misfortune. For not only in Rome, but in Velletri and Terracina I was very badly treated and received by them. But do please observe the reason why. I had gone to a doctor to inquire whether massage [*frictio*] was helpful for catarrh. By chance a grammarian was there, and his impudence was so great that, without letting the doctor reply, he at once began to censure me because (as he thought) *fricatio*, not *frictio* was the right word for "massage," since nouns derived from verbs of the first conjugation having the supine in *-itum* or *-ctum*, contrary to the rule for other verbs, end in *-atio*, not in *-itio*, or in *-ctio*. For that reason one was supposed to say *fricatio*, not *frictio*.[136] "My good man," says I, "verbal nouns in *-io* are created either from the supines themselves or from genitives of the past participles derived from those supines — like *oratus, orati, oratio; auditus, auditi, auditio;*

tus, auditi, auditio; auctus, aucti, auctio; profectus, profecti, profectio; largitus, largiti, largitio. Quocirca nomina deducta a verbis supini positionem habentibus in *ctum,* cuiuscunque sint coniugationis, in *ctio* exeunt, non in *catio,* ut: *perfectum, perfectio,* non *perfecatio; distractum, distractio; lectum, lectio; actum, actio; sanctum, sanctio,* nec aliter; sic *frictum, frictio,* non *fricatio;* nam ex *internetio,* ut quidam volunt, *c* littera dempta est suavioris soni gratia. Simili modo *sectum, sectio,* non *secatio.* Sic Caesar, sic Quintilianus *sectionem,* non *secationem:* et Plinius Celsusque *frictionem* non *fricationem* dixere; nec te moveat *explicatio* et *vetatio,* quorum supina in *ctum* non exeunt; quare ne te librariorum imperitia decipiat vide. Dii boni! ac si non verba haec, sed verbera fuissent, ita in me irruit, ut nisi medicus quique cives aderant ab illius me unguibus eripuissent, actum de Suppatio tuo fuerit! Vide pallium conscissum et faciem dissectam vide: cum urso leoneve, non cum homine mihi esse rem putavi.

83 Grammatico ab alio tumidum supercilium fero ac bene mecum actum puto, quod non ex eo pugno oculum amiserim. At quam ob causam? quod affirmarem post negandi adverbium licere etiam copulationem ponere quae negationem ipsam redderet, exemplo Caesaris commentario septimo: *tanto accepto incommodo neque se in occultum abdiderat et conspectum multitudinis fugerat;* item: *quod in conspectu omnium res gerebatur neque tegi ac turpiter celari poterat.* Licere item dicere *e contrario,* auctoritate eiusdem Caesaris eodem commentario: *ut reliquorum imperatorum res adversae auctoritatem minuunt, sic huius e contrario dignitas incommodo accepto in dies augebatur.*

auctus, aucti, auctio; profectus, profecti, profectio; largitus, largiti, largitio. Therefore, nouns derived from verbs having the ending of the supine in *-ctum*, of whatever conjugation they may be, end in *-ctio*, not in *-catio;* thus, *perfectum, perfectio*, not *perfecatio; distractum, distractio; lectum, lectio; actum, actio; sanctum, sanctio*, and not otherwise; thus, *frictum, frictio*, not *fricatio;* for from *internetio*, as some people argue, the letter *c* has been taken away to produce a more pleasant sound.[137] In similar fashion, *sectum, sectio*, not *secatio*. Thus, Caesar, thus Quintilian said *sectio*, not *secatio;* and Pliny and Celsus said *frictio* not *fricatio*. And do not be influenced by *explicatio* and *vetatio*, whose supines do not end in *-ctum;* for that reason, be careful that the ignorance of scribes does not mislead you." Good gods! As if my remarks had been not words but blows,[138] he rushed on me in such a way that, if the doctor and some citizens who were there had not torn me from his claws, it would have been all over with your friend Suppazio! Look at my shredded cloak and look at my face cut to pieces; I thought I was dealing with a bear or a lion, not a man.[139]

I endured furious arrogance from another grammarian and 83
thought myself lucky not to lose an eye from his fist. But for what reason? Because I asserted that after an adverb of negation one could also place a connective that would repeat the negation, for example in the seventh book of Caesar's *Gallic Wars:* "Although he had received such a setback he had *not* hidden himself away *and* fled the sight of the multitude"; and again, "because the thing was being done in the sight of all it could *not* be covered up *and* basely concealed."[140] Likewise, I said that it was allowed to say *e contrario* ("by contrast") on the authority of the same Caesar in the same book: "while adverse circumstances diminish the authority of other generals, his standing, by contrast, increased daily, although he received a setback."[141]

84 Nec non verbis *significo, addo* et *peto* accusandi casus loco casum auferendi cum praepositione apponere auctoritate Caesaris eiusdem commentario eodem dicentis: *conclamare et significare de fuga Romanis coeperunt;* et quinto commentario: *addunt etiam de Sabini morte;* item: *de suis privatim rebus ab eo petere coeperunt.*

85 Quin etiam nomen *unus una unum* plurali numero licere etiam adiungere nominibus quae singularem numerum haberent, quod Caesar etiam faceret commentario primo: *animadvertit Caesar unos ex omnibus Sequanos nihil earum rerum facere quas coeteri facerent, sed tristes capite demisso terram intueri;* commentario quarto: *sese unis Suevis concedere, quibus ne dii quidem immortales pares esse possint;* commentario sexto: *erant Menapii propinqui Eburonum finibus, perpetuis paludibus silvisque muniti, qui uni e Gallia de pace ad Caesarem legatos nunquam miserant.* Cicero tertio *Rhetoricorum: duplices igitur similitudines esse debent, unae rerum, alterae verborum.*

86 Latine etiam dici quinam et quisque de duobus, non aliter quam uter et uterque, exemplo Caesaris, qui ait commentario quinto: *erant in ea legione fortissimi viri, centuriones, qui primis ordinibus appropinquarent, Titus Pullo et Lucius Vorenus. Hi perpetuas controversias inter se habebant quinam anteferretur.* Et commentario septimo, cum de controversia Convictolitavis et Coti Heduorum mentionem faciens inquit: *suas cuiusque eorum clientelas.* Quintilianus libro decimo: *nam Macer et Lucretius legendi quidem, sed*

I also said that with the verbs *significo* ("make known"), *addo* ("add"), and *peto* ("seek," "ask") one could use the ablative case with a preposition in place of the accusative, on the authority of the same Caesar speaking in the same book: "they began to shout and to make the flight known to the Romans"; and in the fifth book "they also add the death of Sabinus"; also "they began to ask him about their own affairs in private."[142] 84

Indeed, I even said that one could also attach the word *unus, una, unum* ("one," "alone") in the plural to nouns that indicate a singular number, as Caesar did in the first book: "Caesar noticed that alone (*unos*) of all the peoples the Sequani did none of the things the others did, but looked sadly at the ground with their heads bent"; in the fourth book: "that they were inferior to the Suevi alone (*unis*), whom not even the immortal gods could equal"; in the sixth book: "The Menapii were close to the territory of the Eburones, protected by an unbroken expanse of marshes and woods; they alone (*uni*) of Gaul had never sent ambassadors to Caesar concerning peace"; Cicero in the third book of the *Rhetorica*: "therefore, likenesses are inevitably of two sorts, one (*unae*) of subject matter, the other of words."[143] 85

I said that in Latin *quinam* ("which") and *quisque* ("each") are used of two entities—as well as *uter* ("which of the two") and *uterque* ("each of the two")—on the example of Caesar, who says in book five: "There were in that legion very brave men, centurions, who were getting close to the first ranks, Titus Pullo and Lucius Vorenus. These men wrangled continually as to which (*quinam*) ranked more highly."[144] And in book seven, when he mentions the dispute of the Aedui Convictolitavis and Cotus, he says, "each one (*cuiusque*) of them had his own adherents."[145] Quintilian in book ten: "for one should certainly read Macer and Lucretius, but not to form style—that is, the sub- 86

non ut phrasin, id est ut corpus eloquentiae faciant; elegantes in sua quisque materia, sed alter humilis, alter difficilis.

87 *Pristinum* quoque *diem* recte dici commentario quarto docet Caesar: *milites nostri pristini diei perfidia incitati in castra irruperunt.* Quin etiam *utraeque* et *utraque* numero plurali exemplo maiorum Romane dici de iis quae duo duaeve tantum essent aut singulari numero proferrentur; Sallustius in *Catilinario: agitabatur magis magisque in dies animus ferox inopia rei familiaris et conscientia scelerum, quae utraque his artibus auxerat quas supra memoravi;* Caesar commentario primo: *duae fuerunt Ariovisti uxores, una Sueva natione, quam domo secum duxerat, altera Norica, regis Boctionis soror, quam in Galliam duxerat a fratre missam, utraeque in ea pugna perierunt.*

88 Inique etiam accusari Lactantium, qui dixerit: *maxime tamen Erythrea, quae celebrior et nobilior inter coeteras habetur,* cum Caesar dicat commentario quarto: *ad alteram partem succedunt Ubii, quorum fuit civitas ampla et florens, uti est captus Germanorum, qui paulo sunt eiusdem generis etiam coeteris humaniores propterea quod Rhenum attingunt;* et Plinius ad Gallum: *terra malignior coeteris, hac non deterior* et ad Caninium: *quo in certamine puer quidam audentior coeteris in ulteriora tendebat;* itaque permissum esse uti comparatione etiam ad eos qui sunt complures eiusdem generis.

89 Falso etiam tradi quod *instruo puerum* aut *instruit magister discipulum* Latine non dicatur, cum libro primo Quintilianus dicat: *quae non eorum modo scientia, quibus quidam nomen artis dederunt,*

stance of eloquence; they are each (*quisque*) elegant in their own subject matter, but the one is slight, the other difficult."[146]

It is correct to say *pristinus dies* ("previous day"), too, as Caesar shows in book 4: "our soldiers, roused by the treachery of the previous day (*pristini diei*), burst into the camp."[147] Indeed, on the example of our ancestors, the plurals *utraeque* and *utraque* ("both") were also used in the language of the Romans of things which were only two or were presented in the singular. Sallust in *Catiline*: "day by day his fierce spirit was more and more disturbed by poverty and guilt for his crimes, both of which (*quae utraque*) he had increased in the ways I mentioned above."[148] Caesar in the first book: "Ariovistus had two wives, one of the Suevan tribe whom he had brought with him from home, the other Norican, the sister of king Boctio, whom he had brought into Gaul after she had been sent by her brother, and both (*utraeque*) perished in that battle."[149] 87

It is also unjust to censure Lactantius for saying, "especially the Erythraean Sibyl, who is considered more celebrated and famous among the rest (*inter coeteras*)," since Caesar says in the fourth book: "up on the other side came the Ubii, whose state was great and prosperous by German standards, and they were a little more civilized than the rest (*coeteris*) of the same nation because they bordered on the Rhine"; and Pliny writing to Gallus: "land more unfavorable than the rest (*coeteris*), but not worse than this"; and to Caninius: "in this contest one boy more daring than the rest (*coeteris*) was heading farther out."[150] And so it was allowed to use the comparative even for several things of the same kind. 88

It is also wrongly handed down that *instruo puerum* ("I instruct the boy") or *instruit magister discipulum* ("the teacher instructs the pupil") is not said in Latin, since Quintilian says in book one: "which not only might instruct students (*studiosos instruat*) in the knowledge of the things to which some have given 89

studiosos instruat et, ut sic dixerim, ius ipsum rhetorices interpretetur, sed alere facundiam, vires augere eloquentiae possit. Item libro secundo: *ita ipse quoque historiae atque etiam magis orationum lectione susceptos a se discipulos instruxerit.*

90 Non minus falso etiam praecipi quod substantivis gerundivum tantum, non infinitivum addendum sit, cum Caesar dicat commentario septimo: *priusquam munitiones ab Romanis perficiantur, consilium capit omnem a se equitatum noctu dimittere,* Cicero tertio *Rhetoricorum: tempus est ad coeteras partes rhetoricae orationis proficisci,* Sallustius in *Catilinario: non fuit mihi consilium secordia atque desidia bonum otium conterere.* Quin etiam ineptissime sentire eos qui negent Latine dici: *non habeo plus uno praedio,* cum dicat Quintilianus libro tertio: *simplex autem causa, etiamsi varie defenditur, non potest habere plus uno de quo pronuncietur; atque inde erit status causae.* Item: *ideoque in eo statum esse iudicabo quod dicerem, si mihi plus quam unum dicere non liceret.*

91 Quae quam moleste bonus hic grammaticus tulerit, meum hoc supercilium docet. An tibi videor grammaticorum furiis amplius obiectandus? Facessant posthac igitur sapientes, dum a grammaticis me in libertatem vendicem. Fundis Hytriisque fuere mihi res aliquanto quietiores, ubi nedum litteratores, nullos quidem litteratos invenio, quippe cum oppidani non urbanam colant, sed villaticam Palladem; omnes enim oleo dediti sunt. Post Caietam ingressus, obviam habui mulierculam, quae me blande appellatum deque via fessum ad umbram invitavit frigidamque qua me perluerem vitreo quam conspicatissimo

the name of art, and (so to speak) interpret the law of rhetoric itself, but could also nourish fluency and increase the power of eloquence."[151] Likewise in book 2: "thus he will have instructed the pupils (*discipulos instruxerit*) he has taken on in the reading of history and even more in the reading of oratory."[152]

No less wrongly is it advised that only a gerund, not an infinitive, is to be added to substantives, since Caesar says in book 7: "he made a plan to send away all the cavalry by night, before the fortifications were completed by the Romans."[153] Cicero in book 3 of the *Rhetorica*: "it is time to proceed to the other parts of rhetorical discourse."[154] Sallust in *Catiline*: "It was not my plan to waste my valuable leisure in laziness and sloth."[155] Indeed, those claiming that in Latin one cannot say, "I do not have more than one (*plus uno*) estate," have a very foolish opinion since Quintilian says in book 3: "a simple case, even if it is defended in various ways, cannot have more than one (*plus uno*) detail on which it is to be decided; and from that will arise the point at issue of the case."[156] Also: "and so I will determine the point at issue to lie in what I would say if I were not allowed to take more than one (*plus uno*) line of argument."[157] 90

My forehead shows how annoyed the worthy grammarian was at these remarks. Do you think I should expose myself any further to the frenzy of grammarians? Therefore, away with wise men after this, provided that I can free myself from grammarians. Things were somewhat more peaceful for me at Fondi and Itri, where I came across no literate men, much less men of letters, since the townsfolk cultivate not the urban but the rustic Minerva: they are all dedicated to olive oil. Entering Gaeta afterward, I ran into a little woman who called to me politely and invited me into the shade since I was weary from my journey, and produced cool water for me to wash with in a wonderfully clear[158] glass vessel. I was delighted by her friendliness and 91

protulit. Delectavit me familiaritas coepique de patria deque re familiari percunctari, cum statim puella non inhonesta facie nigricantem gallinam ac novem simul ova detulit, quae die Veneris nata esse diceret. Nec multo post venit ancillula cum anaticulo et albo filo. Abire ambas iussit, redituras accensis facibus, tertium eum lunae diem esse admonens, atque ad me conversa: 'Ex quo, inquit, virum amisi, cum mihi nihil moriens reliquisset, quaestum facere hunc coepi; et profecto Caietanae mulieres cum sint superstitiosulae, satis commode hinc victitarem, ni fratres quidam proventum interciperent, dum somnia coniiciunt, dum iras deorum venditant, dum viros nubilibus, mares gravidis, prolem sterilibus promittunt; quodque scelestissimum duco, quia Caietana plebecula piscatui pleraque dedita est, noctu ad plebeiorum uxores domum ventitant, quas interdiu per speciem religionis in templo audiunt. Ac ne decipiare, hospes, quam vidisti ancillulam, ea herae iussu, quae gravida e fraterculo est, ad me consulendam venit; quae prior venerat puella sponsum habebat, cuius forma captus bonus nescio quis Deoque percarus fraterculus suis artibus seductum induere cucullum suasit ac nunc secum habet in cellula.'—'Improbe, inquam, factum, sed tu velim ne fratres in te commoveas, quos videam in Italiae urbibus regnare.' Tum illa: 'Desine timere, obsecro; nam ex quo iuvencula eram, conventus custodem cognovi, ac, ni fallor, is est quem huc venientem conspicaris'; confestimque hoc dicto domum ingrediens me valere iussit.

92 Abeo inde ad mare; gregem illic piscatorum invenio ac dum singulos contemplor, optimos quosque pisces seligi ab eis video.

I was beginning to ask about her home and family circumstances, when all of a sudden a respectable-looking girl brought down a blackish hen along with nine eggs that she said had been laid on Friday, the day of Venus. Soon afterward a little maid came with a duckling and a white thread. The woman instructed both of them to go away and return with lighted torches, reminding them that it was the third day of the moon. And turning to me, she said, "Since I lost my husband, because he left me nothing at his death, I have begun to follow this occupation; and since the women of Gaeta are certainly gullible,[159] I would be making a pretty good living at it, if some monks were not horning in on my business, since they too interpret dreams, peddle curses, promise husbands to the marriageable, male children to the pregnant, offspring to the barren; and—what I consider particularly wicked—because the common people of Gaeta are mostly occupied with fishing, they like to come at night to the wives of the poor citizens in their houses, to the same women they listen to in the church in the daytime on the pretext of religion. And to tell you the truth, stranger, the little maid you saw came to consult me on the orders of her mistress, who is pregnant by a dear little monk; the girl who came first used to have a fiancé. Taken with his good looks, some fine little brother, very dear to God, seduced him with his wiles, persuaded him to put on a cowl and now keeps him in his cell." "A wicked act," says I, "but I wouldn't want you to get the monks stirred up against you, since I see that they rule in the cities of Italy." Then she: "Please stop worrying; from girlhood I have been on intimate terms with the warden of the monastery, and, unless I'm mistaken, he is the man you see coming this way." As soon as she had said this, she bade me farewell and went into the house.

Next I went to the seashore. There I found a crowd of fish- 92
ermen, and as I observed them one by one, I saw that they were

Quaero venalesne habeant; respondent asservari fraterculis seque Deo illos velle offerre. Tum ego mecum: 'Macti, inquam, pietate, adulteros tam delicate qui pascitis!' Eo hinc ad meritoriam cumque inter prandendum repente in proximo muliercularum pugillatus exortus esset, harpyarum vitare iras constitui meque propter Vitruvii sepulcrum Molam, quae in Formiano est litore, atque inde Suessam contuli. Ibi mane in foro spectantem me scitulas puellas cum biferarum quasillis mulier compellat eloquentia non vulgari, et quod palliatum videbat, postquam benigne salutavit, 'Amabo, inquit, quam tibi mores nostri placent? Credo admiraris scitulas has, credo Platonis legisti rempublicam, quam si cives nostri non omnino probant, vitam certe aliquanto liberiorem non improbant. Haec puellae partim nuptae, partim sponsae, quaedam etiam nondum viris collocatae sunt; licet tamen cum iis et iocari et liberius etiam ludere; ne te igitur delitiarum pudeat, blandulae sunt, virosque ad se holerum ac frugum gratia invitant, cupiunt vendere; sic se civitatis nostrae mores habent. Neque enim, vir bone, ignoras probum improbumque pro locis, populis, nationibus iudicari, neque tam naturam quam leges atque instituta sequi aliaque alibi laudari.'

93 Quid multis? coepit etiam de virtutibus deque Deo tandem disserere. Ego vix avellere me ab ea potui, tandemque digressus notumque mihi hominem percunctatus unde tantam mulier doctrinam hausisset, cum suspicerem tum rerum cognitionem tum dicendi copiam. 'Neque, inquit, nostra haec fabulosum illum Musarum fontem hausit, sed theologi linguam compluri-

picking out all the best fish. I asked if they were for sale; they replied that they were being saved for the dear monks and that they wanted to offer them to God. Then I said to myself, "Three cheers for your piety, you who feed adulterers so luxuriously!" From here I went to an inn, and when a fistfight of the tarts suddenly broke out nearby during my meal, I decided to avoid the harpies' wrath and betook myself to Mola di Gaeta near the sepulcher of Vitruvius on the shore of Formia, and from there to Sessa. In the morning there in the forum, as I was looking at the pretty girls with baskets of figs, a well-spoken woman accosted me; and because she saw me wearing a Greek cloak, after a courteous greeting she said, "Tell me, please, how do you like our customs? You are surprised at these pretty girls, I suppose; you have read Plato's *Republic,* I suppose; and if our citizens do not altogether approve of it, at least they do not disapprove of a somewhat freer way of life.[160] Some of these girls are married, some betrothed, some are also not yet assigned to husbands; yet one may jest and sport with them rather freely. So don't be embarrassed by their flirting, they are charming and they attract men for the sake of their vegetables and fruits; they are eager to sell. That is the custom of our state. Nor are you unaware, good man, that decency and indecency are judged in accordance with places, peoples, and nations, and that they are guided less by nature than by laws and institutions and that different things are praised in different places."

Why should I go on? She began to discourse on the virtues 93
and finally on God. I was hardly able to tear myself away from her; and getting away at last, I asked an acquaintance of mine where the woman had imbibed so much learning, since I admired both her knowledge and her fluency of speech. He said, "This woman of ours has not drunk from the legendary spring of the Muses, but for several years she has turned the tongue of

bus annis ore suo versavit, neque ut priscus ille Ennius in Parnaso somniavit, sed vigilans in toro atque in theologi complexibus cubuit. Ex huius ipsius lingua manat eloquentia tam suavis, ex ore theologi orat tam copiose atque inundanter; spiritum huic ille inspiravit roremque instillavit unde oratio eius spirat stillatque tam suave.'

94 An igitur posthac, Herrice, habes quod adversus institutionem edisseras? Vides quantum ars, quantum disciplina, quantum domestica consuetudo valeat? Intelligis quantum doctorum familiaritas possit? Quanta in omni genere institutionis vis sit assuetudinis? Mulierculam eloqui! femellam sapere! Hoc est profecto cur, contempta grammaticorum importunitate, libeat sapientem adhuc quaerere.

95 *Herr.* O gnave ac sapiens Suppati, scis quid de theologis his nostris sentiret Antonius, quando Suessanam istam tuam hausisse a theologo eloquentiam cum scientia dicis? Scis, inquam, quid de iis sentiret Antonius? Optime cum ipsis agi quod in claustris atque in solitudine vivant, quod plebecula vanas eorum disputationes non intelligit; fore enim, si in publico vitam agerent, si eorum dissertiones notae vulgo essent, uti sutores formulis, ferrarii malleolis, indusiarii forficibus insectarentur, primum quod minime castam agant vitam, deinde quod inanissimis de rebus ad insaniam disserunt; ac si qui sunt qui veterem probatamque theologiam sequuntur, contemptui eos habent. Verum, si placet, optime Suppati, relictis his, peregrinationem perficias oro, ac si quid Capuae, si quid Aversae videris, noveris, compereris, explica.

a theologian over in her mouth; and she has not dreamed on Parnassus like old Ennius, but lain awake in her bed in the arms of the theologian.[161] From his tongue drips such sweet eloquence; it is from the mouth of the theologian that she prays so abundantly and profusely; he has breathed his spirit into her and poured in, drop by drop, the dew of which her speech is redolent and which pours out so sweetly."

Well then, Enrico, after this, do you have any argument against education? Do you see the great efficacy of art, teaching, and personal intercourse? Do you understand how much close acquaintance with learned men can achieve, how great is the power of intimacy in every kind of instruction? To think that a mere woman is eloquent, a female creature intelligent! This is certainly why it is a pleasure to disregard the insolence of grammarians and to keep looking for a wise man. 94

Enrico. O diligent and wise Suppazio, since you say that your woman of Sessa drank in eloquence along with knowledge from a theologian, do you know what Antonio thought about these theologians of ours? Do you know, I say, what Antonio thought of them?—That it was just as well for them that they live in cloisters and solitude, because ordinary people do not understand their empty debates. If they spent their life in public, if their debates were commonly known, cobblers would go after them with their lasts, blacksmiths with their hammers, and tailors with their shears, first because they live not at all chastely, then because they go on about utterly inane matters to the point of insanity, and they hold in contempt any who follow the time-tested theology.[162] But please, excellent Suppazio, leave these matters and finish your pilgrimage, I beg you, and if you saw, learned, or found out anything at Capua or Aversa, give an account of it. 95

96 *Supp.* Capuam ingressus obvium habui qui, quod physicum profiteri me crederet, consuluit quid oculis maxime conferre ducerem. Respondi: 'Si causidicum advocatumque nunquam videris.'—'Quid auribus?'—'Si nullam domi mulierem habueris.'—'Quid stomacho?'—'Si nunquam in mensa cum sacerdote cardinale accubueris.' Consuluit quid item rei familiari multum prodesset.—'A Catalano mercatore mutuum non accipere.' Quid ad vitae tranquillitatem:—'Aulas dominantium nunquam ingredi.' Quod tempus minime esset utile:—'Quod audiendo fratri Francisco, cui Ispano cognomen est, impenderetur.' Hunc ego ubi video plura quoque paratum quaerere: 'Quando, inquam, faciendo itineri occupatus sum, quaeso, mutuum mihi redde et comitem quo Neapolim usque commodiore uti possim, edoce.' Tum ille: 'Agrum, inquit, hunc nostrum peragranti, si bene tibi consultum velis, lupum comitem adhibebis; neque enim comite alio, tot tantorumque molossorum rabiem evitaveris, atque utinam unus tibi satis sit lupus!'—'Atqui inquam, meus hic asellus uni lupo satis non est.'

97 Egressus igitur Capua, puerum, quod aliquantulum de via fessus esset, asino impositum praecedere cum iussissem, ipse post sequebar; nec multum viae progressus, audio irrideri me a viatoribus ac fatuum dici, quod senex ipse ac pannis involutus pedibus iter facerem, puerum firmis pedibus atque expeditum asino ante ducerem. Itaque haud multo post cum iussissem puerum descendere, ipse asino vehi coepi; nec ita multum itineris confeceram, ecce qui me accusare coepit, quod validis viribus puerum aetate tenera atque imbecilla ire pedibus paterer, ipse asello veherer. E quo statim, crimen ut averterem, descendi bestiolamque ducere capistro coepi; nec multum ab Aversa aberam; ibi miris me modis ab iis qui et ipsi oppidum petebant

Suppazio. When I entered Capua I met a man who thought I was 96
a physician and asked what I considered to be most beneficial to the eyes. I replied, "If you never see a lawyer or a barrister." "What for the ears?" If you have no woman in the house." "What for the stomach?" "If you never sit down to dinner with a cardinal priest." In the same way he asked me what was best for the pocketbook. "Not to take a loan from a Catalan merchant." What for a peaceful life? "Never to set foot in the courts of rulers." What time was the most wasted? "The time spent listening to Brother Francesco, surnamed the Spaniard."[163] When I saw that he was ready to ask even more questions, I said, "Since I am engaged in making a journey, please return the favor and let me know of a suitable companion I could use as far as Naples." Says he, "If you want to take good care of yourself when you're going through this territory of ours, take a wolf as a companion; for with no other companion will you escape the mad rage of so many huge Molossian hounds, and I hope you find one wolf enough!" "At least," says I, "this little ass of mine is not enough for one wolf."

Then I left Capua. I had bidden the boy to ride ahead on the 97
ass because he was a little worn out from the journey, so I followed behind.[164] And I hadn't gone far when I heard myself being mocked and called a fool by travelers because I, old and wrapped in rags, was making my way on foot and taking ahead of me on an ass an agile boy with sound feet. And so I told the boy to dismount and soon began to ride on the ass myself. I had not completed much of the journey like this, when suddenly a man began to criticize me because, although I was strong and healthy, I was riding on an ass myself and letting a boy of tender and delicate years go on foot. After that, to avert blame, I immediately dismounted and started to lead the little animal by the halter. I was not far from Aversa, and there I realized that those who were coming behind me, also on their

meque sequebantur condemnari atque, ut ita dixerim, excachinnari sentio, quod cum puero una ferri asello commodissime possem, vacuum tamen illum atque expeditum reste ductarem. Quibus ut satisfacerem, ascendi cum puero asellum; vix autem oppidum intraram, cum sublatis primo cachinnis, post etiam clamoribus, intelligo me a popularibus incessi: 'O senem delirum, o asellum miserrimum! Non corruit infelix sub tanta sarcina? non crepuit misellus? videtisne asinum asello vehi? sentitis quadrupedem beluam quam bipes belua est non adeo quidem beluam esse?' Denique pueri lapidibus me insectari coepere; quibus instigatus asinus currere cum coepisset, me cum puero una in lutum excussit; nec defuere qui pallio pedibus insultarent. Irrisus contemptusque, lutosam urbem luto collitus transeo, nec iam Suppatius ab iis quibus essem cognitus, sed Lutatius vocitabar. Atque hic quidem susceptae ob quaeritandum sapientem profectionis exitus ac finis fuit.

98 Habes, Herrice, bone ac vetus amice, peregrinationis meae rationem, quae utinam Antonio nostro cognita esse posset. Verum cum illo melius actum est, quod solutus humanis curis inter beatos nunc agit, nec de sapientia ulterius solicitus est, cuius me studium, ut intellexisti, ad asinum redegit, tibique persuadeas velim multos divites, non paucos doctos recte dici et quidem esse, sapientem autem neminem. Qua de re post etiam plura: nunc Pontanum nostrum ut visam eo, quem Capuanam ingressus dextrum crus fregisse accepi atque e dolore vehementer laborare.

way to the town, were blaming me and guffawing at me (so to speak)[165] to an amazing degree because, although I could ride very comfortably along with the boy on the ass, I had left it unburdened and frisky and was leading it along by a rope. To satisfy them I got on the ass with the boy; but scarcely had I entered the town, when first from a burst of laughter, then from an outcry, I realized that I was being reproached by the townsfolk. "You crazy old man, you poor little ass! Why hasn't the unhappy beast collapsed under such a load? Why didn't the poor little thing break in two? Look at the big ass riding on a little ass! Don't you see that the four-footed beast is not as much a beast as the two-footed one is?" Finally boys began to pelt me with stones. The ass was provoked by this and started to bolt, and he threw me along with the boy into the mud. Some people even trampled on my cloak with their feet. Mocked and despised, I went smeared with mud through the mud-filled city, and I was no longer called Suppazio by my acquaintances, but Lutazio ["Muddy"]. And so this was the outcome and finale of the journey I had undertaken in order to look for a wise man.

You have an account of my pilgrimage, Enrico, good old 98
friend, and I wish Antonio could have known of it. But he is better off because he has been freed of earthly cares and is now among the blessed, and he has no further interest in wisdom, enthusiasm for which, as you have understood, reduced me to an ass; and I would like you to be convinced that, although many are rightly called rich, and not a few learned, and are so in fact, no one is wise. On this subject more later. Now I am going to see our friend Pontano. When I came in the Capuan Gate,[166] I learned that he had broken his right leg and was suffering great pain.

Hospes, Compater, Lucius filius

99 *Hosp.* Multa quidem a Siculis meis audio de Pontano hoc praedicari, eiusque in primis facilitatem atque mansuetudinem laudant cuperemque illum nosse atque alloqui ac per familiarem aliquem aditum ad eum habere, sed laenito dolore, qui dum crudior est, non tam facile visitationem admittit. Interim contentus ero qua facie sit novisse.

Comp. Bona et recta statura, fronte lata, calvo capite, superciliis demissioribus, acuto naso, glaucis oculis, mento promissiori, macilentis malis, producta cervice, ore modico, colore rufo, adolescens tamen perpalluit, reliquo corpore quadrato. Unum nunc illi male contigit, nobis amicis non incommode, quod pede altero debilior cum sit factus, in deambulationibus remissior futurus est. Sed bene habet, eius filiolus domo egreditur, quem compellasse non iniucundum fuerit, cum sit bona et laeta indole, atque, ut video, ad nos venit. Luciole, quid agit pater?

100 *Luc.* Cum matre litigat. Accessit ad eum adolescentulus cum mandatis; putat illum mater missum a pellice; eam vociferantem quo magis ridet pater eo vehementius irritat. Ego e cubiculo me proripui atque eo libentius quod sacerdos ad eum ingressus est; vult enim mater sacerdoti se ut purget ac peccata nudet, rem sane importunam; sat enim scio matrem et sua et patris peccata nudiustertius sacerdoti ordine aperuisse. Nam cum ipse ad confitentis matris genua assedissem, maternam confessionem, aut rectius questum, attente aucupatus sum: 'Bone sacerdos, maritus meus amat ancillulas, si quas facie liberali vidit, sectatur ingenuas puellas. Anno superiore Tarenti cum esset, cognovit

Visitor, Compater, Pontano's son Lucio

Visitor. Certainly, I hear much said by my fellow Sicilians about this Pontano, and they especially praise his affability and gentle nature; I would like to be acquainted with him and talk to him and have an introduction to him through some friend, but after his pain has abated. While it is too acute, it does not so easily allow a visit. In the meantime, I will be content to know what he looks like. 99

Compatre. He has a fine and upright stature, with a broad forehead, a bald head, down-slanting eyebrows, a sharp nose, grey eyes, a prominent chin, thin cheeks, a long neck, a rather small mouth, ruddy coloring (although he was quite pale as a youth), and the rest of his body is squarely built. Now one thing has happened—badly for him, but not inconveniently for us, his friends—that since he has become lame in one foot, he will be less energetic on his walks. But we're in luck. His young son is coming out of the house, and it will be pleasant to talk to him since he is good-natured and cheerful. I see he is coming toward us. Luciolo, what's up with your father?[167]

Lucio. He's quarreling with my mother. A young boy came to him with a message. My mother thinks it was sent by his mistress, and the more my father laughs at her shouting, the more he enrages her. I rushed out of the room and was glad to do so because a priest has come in to him; my mother wants him to purify himself to the priest and bare his sins, which is clearly uncalled for. Indeed, I know very well that my mother duly confessed both her own sins *and* my father's to the priest day before yesterday. Since I was sitting at my mother's knee as she confessed, I listened attentively to the maternal confession, or rather complaint. "Good priest, my husband makes love to any decent looking maidservants he sees, and he runs after girls of good family. Last year when he was at Taranto, he carried on 100

non unam; anno ante in Etruria cum Gaditanula deprehensus fuit. Iocatur etiam domi cum Aethiopissis, nec pati possum eius intemperantiam. Ille ridet, ego dirumpor; perreptat[17] urbem ac principum aulas, ego domi inter pedissequas partior pensa. Nam quid ego illum cum sodalibus, quibus quam familiarissime dies ac noctes utitur, nisi de amoribus deque voluptate loqui atque agere putem, cum interim misera in cubiculo de re familiari solicita domesticis curis maceror? Dii me omnes aspexere quo die crus fregit; non licebit claudum totis diebus domo abesse, singulis horis prostibulas adire. Rideat nunc, urbem inambulet, frequentet sodalium domos, audiat via in media pellicum pueros; ego vel ex hoc deos aequissimos iudicaverim, quod tandem iusto eum supplicio affecere.' Quid igitur opus patrem errores iterato confiteri, quos mater tam aperte explicaverit? Nuper notus quidam et vetus, ut arbitror, familiaris patrem cum adiret, ubi eum vidit mater, exclamare[18] statim coepit: 'Scilicet ab Etruria? ab scortillis? Quid agunt Pisatiles meretriculae?' Prae ira non Pisanas, sed Pisatiles dixit. 'Ut valet Gaditana illa? ut memor est amorum hirquiculi[19] huius? detulistine ab ea litterulas, cum mandatis? ubi munuscula? ubi monumenta veterum deliciarum?' Ac tantum non manum iniiciebat; quod ille veritus retro ad ianuam mature concessit atque actutum abiit. Mihi pater, ut cederem innuit; ipse carmen decantare evomium coepit.

101 *Hosp*. Scitum puerum! Sed, obsecro, carmen evomium quod sit edoce.

with more than one girl; the year before in Etruria he was caught in the act with a little dancing girl from Cadiz. He even plays around at home with Ethiopian girls, and I cannot put up with his licentiousness. He laughs, I burst with rage; he trails through the city and the halls of princes, I supervise the maids at home. What else should I think he does with the cronies he associates with—and on the most familiar terms both day and night—except talk about and pursue love and pleasure, while I sit miserable in my chamber, anxious about our finances, harassed by domestic cares? All the saints took pity on me the day he broke his leg; lame, he won't be able to be away from home all day, or to go to the prostitutes every hour. Now let him laugh, now let him walk up and down the town, let him frequent the houses of his cronies, let him listen in the middle of the street to harlots' messenger boys. From this alone I would judge the saints most just, that they have visited him at last with the perfect punishment." What need then has my father to confess his errors a second time, since my mother has set them out so openly? Just now when an acquaintance—an old friend, I believe—visited my father,[168] my mother began to say loudly as soon as she saw him: "From Etruria, I suppose? From the little whores? How are the little harlots of Pisa? In her anger she said, not "Pisan" [*Pisanas*] but "of Pisa" [*Pisatiles*].[169] "How fares that girl from Cadiz? Does she remember her affair with this old goat? Have you brought a note from her? With instructions? Where are the trinkets? Where are the souvenirs of old pleasures?" And she all but laid hands on him, but fearing that, he retreated to the door in time and went off in a hurry. My father nodded at me to depart; and he himself began to sing the spewing[170] poem.

Visitor. Excellent boy! But please explain what the spewing 101
poem is.

Luc. Qui carmen dicit in mulierem furore percitam conversus ter despuit; illa statim bilem evomit ac rabie levatur. Ipsum autem carmen est:

[Metrum III]

Triceps est Cerberus, ter te ego despuo.
Triplex est Eumenis, ter te ego despuo.
Vomas, dico vomas, ter vome et improbam
Pectore purgato rabiem ad Phlegethonta remitte.

Hosp. Mirum huic carmini vim tantam inesse!

Luc. Ipsa res docet. Sed desine, obsecro, mater est in fenestra, cuius conspectum vereor. Valete bellissime.

Herricus, Suppatius, Lyricen, Hospes

102 *Herr.* Opinione citius redit ad nos Suppatius.

Supp. Hoc deerat ad quaeritandam sapientiam, mulierem irritatam adire. Ne id velit sapientiae ipsius pater Iupiter! Et disputant adhuc sapientes quidam de uxore ducenda! Non quidem si ipsa Sapientia ducenda sit uxor mihi ducenda videtur. Bonus tamen hic et constans Pontanus ridebat et vultu quidem quam maxime tranquillo; o confirmatissimi pectoris hominem! Mihi quidem, si haec vita est maritorum, ne ipsa quidem constantia videri virtus potest, quae vitae inquietudinem ac miseriam alat. Quid enim offirmatio tam constans ac perpetua, nisi continuae rixationis alimonia est? Valeat, valeat virtus ista coniugalis, litigiorum nutricula! Valeat maritalis vita! Ego me ad Herricum refero.

Herr. Quaeso, cur tam cito?

Lucio. The person who speaks the poem faces an enraged woman and spits three times. At once she spews out her bile and is relieved of her madness. Here is the song itself:

[Poem III] [171]

Cerberus has three heads, thrice spit I on thee.
Threefold is the Fury, thrice spit I on thee.
Spew, I say, spew, thrice spew. Get vile rage
off your chest and send it to Phlegethon.

Visitor. This poem has amazing power!

Lucio. The proof is in the pudding. But stop, please. My mother is at the window, and I'm afraid she'll see me. Fare very well.

Enrico, Suppazio, Lutenist, Visitor

Enrico. Suppazio has come back to us more quickly than we ex- 102
pected.

Suppazio. This was what was missing in my search for wisdom: to encounter an angry woman. May Jupiter, the father of wisdom itself, not desire it! And yet some wise men still debate about taking a wife![172] If Wisdom herself were to be the bride, I don't think *I* should marry. Nevertheless, our good and steadfast Pontano was laughing, and with the most tranquil expression in the world—O most stout-hearted man! In my opinion, if this is the life of married men, not even imperturbability itself can be a virtue, since it fosters turmoil and misery in life. What else is such steadfast and lasting self-possession but fuel for uninterrupted strife? Away, away with that conjugal virtue of yours, nurse of quarrels! Away with married life! I'm going back to Enrico.

Enrico. Tell me, why so soon?

Supp. Dormiscere aiebant atque a dolore paulum modo requiesse. Interea dum edormiscat, Antoniano munere, si placet, fungamur.

Herr. Placet, ac perquam oportune lyricen et quidem non malus sese offert. Ades, lepide homuntio, lyram tange, amabo, sepositumque aliquid succine.

Lyr. Perquam libenter:

[Metrum IV]

Ne faciem, Telesina, colas, neu finge capillum,
  Bella satis, soli si modo bella mihi.
Munditiae, Telesina, iuvant, fuge candida luxum,
  Munditiis capitur deliciosus amor.
Luxus obest formae, forma est contenta pudore,
  Ipse pudor veri iura decoris habet.
Simplicitas nam culta sat est. Tu, lux mea, cultum
  Effuge, bella quidem simplicitate tua es.

Herr. Accipe mercedulam, et carmen ipsum itera.

Lyr. Quin aliud potius?

[Metrum V]

Sirenes madidis canunt in antris,
Dum captas male subruunt carinas.
Sic mortalibus ipsa vita blande
Illudens canit ut dolosa Siren,
Donec vel gravis ingruit senecta
Aut mors occupat, estque nil quod ultra
Iam restet nisi fabula atque inane.

Herr. Lepidissime, atque utinam non tam vere; quae autem facilitas est tua, etiam aliquid quod novum sit.

Suppazio. They said he was falling asleep and had just now had a little relief from his pain. In the meantime, while he is sleeping it off, if you like, let us do as Antonio did.

Enrico. A fine idea. And at the right moment here comes a lutenist, and not a bad one at that.[173] Come here, charming little man, touch your lute, please, and sing something special.[174]

Lutenist. Gladly.

[Poem IV][175]

Don't paint your face, Telesina, or do up your hair;
you're pretty enough if you're pretty only for me.
I like taste, Telesina; don't overdo it, my fair;
delicious love is won by good taste.
An excess spoils beauty; beauty likes what is chaste;
authentic allure is in chastity's charge.
What's simple is dressed up enough. Don't dress up, dear.
Simplicity's the source of your charm.[176]

Enrico. Here's a little reward, and sing that song again.

Lutenist. Why not another one instead?

[Poem V][177]

The Sirens sing in their sea-drenched caves,
enthralling ships, and running them aground.
So too for mortals life sings so sweet,
deceiving like the crafty Siren
until harsh old age bears down
or death takes hold, and nothing more
is left except a tale and emptiness.

Enrico. Delightful, and I wish it were not so true. But if you can, yet again, sing something new.

Lyr. Quam libentissime, Suppatii praesertim gratia, senis tum iucundi, tum etiam musicae huius non imperiti:

[Metrum VI]

Dulce dum ludit Galatea in unda
Et movet nudos agilis lacertos,
Dum latus versat fluitantque nudae
   Aequore mammae,[20]

Surgit e vasto Poliphemus antro,
Linquit et solas volucer capellas;
Nec mora, et litus petit et sub altos
   Desilit aestus.

Impiger latis secat aequor ulnis,
Frangit attollens caput et per undas
Labitur, qualis viridi sub umbra
   Lubricus anguis.

Illa velocis movet acris artus
Dum peti sentit; simul et sequentem
Incitat labens, simul et deorum
   Numina clamat.

Illicet divum chorus hinc et illinc
Fert opem fessae. At Poliphemus ante
Non abit, lassus licet et deorum
   Voce repulsus,

Quam ferox nymphae tumidis papillis
Iniicit dextram,[21] roseoque ab ore
Osculum victor rapit. Illa moesto
   Delitet amne.

103 *Supp.* Habetur a me tibi non parva gratia; habebitur et abunde quidem magna, si ut in Herrici gratiam sic in meam quoque

Lutenist. Most gladly, especially to please Suppazio, who is both a pleasant old man and skilled in this music.

[Poem VI][178]

As Galatea frolics sweetly[179] in the waves
and nimbly moves her naked arms,
as she turns her side, and her naked breasts
  bob in the sea,

Polyphemus rises out of his dreary cave
and quickly leaves his she-goats all alone.
Without delay he seeks the shore and dives
  under the swell.

Eager, he cuts through the sea with strong arms,
breaks through, raises his head, and glides
through the waves, like a sinuous serpent
  under green shade.

She wildly moves her arms and legs—fast—
when she senses pursuit; and gliding, spurs on
the one who pursues her, and at the same time
  calls on the gods.

At once a chorus of gods on this side and that
brings help to the weary girl. But Polyphemus,
though weary—the gods' shouting driving him back—
  doesn't retreat

Before he boldly lays claim with his hand
to the nymph's swelling breasts, and, triumphant,
steals a kiss from her rosy-red mouth. The stream
  hides her in grief.[180]

Suppazio. I give you no small thanks, and indeed I will give you 103
very great thanks if, to please both Enrico and me, you also sing

adhuc aliquid dignum te, dignum hoc consessu, dignum etiam nova et rediviva ista disciplina.

Lyr. Geretur a me tibi mos. Utinam tamen is essem cuius ingenio musicae ipsi aliquid collatum esset! Ac ne ex eorum sim numero qui, ut ab Horatio iure irridentur, nunquam rogati cantare inducunt animum, etiam hoc accipe, in tuam atque Herrici ipsius, si tibi non displicet, gratiam:

[Metrum VII]

Ad quaercus, Amarilli, veni, dum retia servo,
Aere dum timidas funda detrudo palumbes,
Ipsa dolo errantem per devia falle sororem.
Ipsa ades, o Amarilli, recens tibi caseus et lac
Ad fontem pendetque gravis fiscella sub alno.
Te cucumis viridisque pepon, hortensia dona,
Te servata cavo iampridem subere mella
Expectant; bini lento de vimine quali
Servantur, quis labra niger flaventia claudit
Iuncus et intexto dependent cornua cervo;
Percurrit medius lacrimoso flore hyacinthus,
Et niger auratas suspendit gracculus ansas,
Gracculus, a dextra serpens latet et fugit ala.
Quid cessas, Amarilli? duos tibi pascimus agnos,
Hinnuleosque duos, quos matris ab hubere raptos

something else worthy of you, worthy of this gathering, and also worthy of this new and revived art of yours.[181]

Lutenist. I am at your service. If only I had the talent to make a contribution to music! And yet in order not to be one of those who (as Horace mocks justly) "never bring themselves to sing when they are asked,"[182] hear this as well, in your honor and Enrico's too, if it does not displease you.

[Poem VII][183]

Come to the oak grove, Amaryllis, while I watch the nets,
While I shoot timid doves from the air with my sling,
Slyly lose your sister as she wanders far out of the way.
Come here yourself, Amaryllis; for you there is fresh cheese and milk
By the spring, and the twig basket hangs heavy under the alder.
Gifts from the garden await you, cucumber and green melon,
Honey, too, kept a long time in the hollow cork tree;
I'm keeping two baskets of pliant wickerwork.
Their light yellow edges are closed with a black twig of rush,
And woven within is a deer with drooping horns;
Through the middle runs a hyacinth with tearful bloom
And a black jackdaw supports the golden handles—
A jackdaw; on the right lurks a serpent, and he flees on the wing.
Why are you slow, Amaryllis? I am feeding two lambs for you,
And two fawns, which I snatched from their mother's teats

Inter lactantes ipsi saturavimus hedos;
Nec dominum ignorant catuli veniuntque vocati.
Est mihi praeterea, thalami seposta supelex,
Supparus; hunc nevit Lyrineia, texuit Alcon,
Palladi dilectus Alcon, cui tortile collum
Nectit ebur, laevi stringit nova fibula buxo;
Brachia ceruleae decurrunt tenuia lanae,
Lanae, quis medius pavo nitet intertextus,
Filaque purpureus miscet variantia limbus.
Haec tibi servatur festis, Amarilli, diebus
Rara chlamis, rarum specimen, mirabile textum,
Vel tibi ut invideat Lalage, rumpatur ut Olcas,
Spectatum veniant ut munera ad ipsa Napeae,
Maeonis ut tantum decus admiretur Aragne.
Obvius ad corylos venio tibi, hic mihi primos
Amplexus, Amarilli, dabis, dabis oscula prima.
Lenta lego ad cerasum duo succina quae tibi servo.
Altera celatum culicem stridentibus alis
Includunt; tenui sub cortice murmurat ales.

And fed myself among the nursing kids;
And the pups know their master and come when they
are called.
Besides all this, I have special furnishings for the
bedchamber,
A garment. Lyrineia did the spinning, Alcon was the
weaver,
Alcon dear to Pallas; and he attached to it a twisted
ivory collar,
And a new pin of smooth boxwood fastens it.
Blue wool threads run down the sheer sleeves,
Wool threads, in whose midst a peacock gleams,
interwoven,
And variegated threads are mingled in a purple fringe.
This is kept for you, Amaryllis, for festive days,
An exquisite mantle, exquisite token, a marvelous
textile,[184]
So that even Lalage might envy you, and Olcas burst
with jealousy,
So that the wood nymphs might come to look at these
gifts,
So that Maeonian Arachne might admire such an
adornment.
I will come to meet you at the hazel wood; here,
Amaryllis,
You will give me the first embraces, you will give the
first kisses.
At the cherry tree I gathered two pieces of pliant
amber that I keep for you;
One holds inside a gnat with whirring wings,
Under the thin covering the winged one buzzes;

Altera nutantem sub iniquo pondere celant
Formicam; illa honeri incumbens trahit horrida farra.
Haec primo pro complexu tibi munera sunto.
Quid moror? en coryli iam summa cacumina motant,
Iam strepitant virgulta, Lycas latrat, eia, age, Thyrsi.
(Ipsa venit) propera, miserum me, num strepit aura?

104 *Herr.* Plenos voluptatis nos relinquis ac bonae spei, suavissime homo; nam quanquam multum tibi aetas debet nostra, qui ex agresti illa musica sic emerseris, debituri tamen plura multo sunt posteri, si qui te volent imitari. Fore enim speramus, si quos tui similes reliqueris, uti pristinam in dignitatem excellentiamque restituatur; tametsi quantum ipse hac in re profeceris non ignoramus.

Lyr. Si quid profeci, gaudeo; quamvis quid profecisse potuit homo tantis tum, suis tum alienis impeditus curis? Voluntas certe non defuit, defuere ocia, quodque paucos admodum novimus qui studiis his delectarentur; qua e re voluntas ipsa non parum pertepuit et, ut verius loquar, refrixit. In magnis tamen occupationibus et saeculorum iniquitate, si quid aetati nostrae attulimus ornamenti, laetamur, nec laborum poenitet, quos gravissimos ab adolescentia ipsa suscepisse non diffitemur, qui minus quidem apparent propter castrenses molestias, quae optimam vitae partem studiis eripuere. Sed desinam de iis dicere, ne de me ea ipse praedicem quae ab aliis coram praedicari non paterer. Satis enim et olim habui si perpaucis et nunc habeo si vobis gravissi-

The other covers an ant drooping under too great a load.
Leaning into her burden, she drags the prickly grain.
Let these be gifts to you for our first embrace.
Why do I delay? See—the hazels are nodding their tops now,[185]
Now the bushes are rustling, Lycas barks. Up now! Come, Thyrsis.
(She is coming) Hurry! Alas! Surely that wasn't the breeze rustling?

Enrico. You leave us full of pleasure and good hope, most delight- 104
ful man; for although our generation owes much to you for getting clear of the barbarous music of the past, posterity will have a much greater debt if you have any imitators. For we hope that if you leave any like yourself, music will be restored to its ancient greatness and perfection; all the same, we are well aware how much progress you have made in it yourself.

Lutenist. I am happy if I have accomplished anything; although what could a man accomplish when he was hampered by both his own great cares and those of others? Certainly, the will was there, but not the time; and because we know very few who take pleasure in these studies, the will itself grew not a little lukewarm—to tell the truth, it grew cold. Yet in great tasks and difficult times we are pleased if we have brought some distinction to our age, and we do not regret the labors—very great ones—which we do not deny having undertaken since our youth. These are less evident, indeed, because of the difficulties of military life, which took the best part of my life away from study. But I will stop talking of these matters, lest I say things about myself that I would not allow others to say in my presence. For I once considered it sufficient if my muse pleased just

mis senibus Musa nostra non displicet. Nec est quod ullas a vobis expectem gratias; tantum oro ut abire me quamprimum postquam aliqua ex parte vobis satisfeci, aequo animo feratis; invitatus enim ad amici nuptias propero, hymeneum decantaturus.

Herr. Et abire te quam aequissimo animo patimur, quamvis utinam nobiscum esse te et saepius et diutius liceret, et gratias etiam quantas possumus maximas agimus, qui animos nostros tam suaviter varieque delinieris.

Lyr. Valete igitur, continentissimi senes.

105 *Herr.* Et tu, lepidissime homo, abi quam auspicatissime. Admiraris, bone hospes, homuntionis huius canendi, ut video, suavitatem ac sub tam remisso incessu ingenii nobilitatem tantam. Scias velim usurpare solitum Antonium coeteros fere omnes huiusce artis studiosos ingenii sui ostentatores esse, hunc autem dissimulatorem et, quod ipsi saepe audivimus, cum aliis plurimum tribueret, sibi ipsi vel acerrime detrahentem.

106 Sed, quaeso, utorne ego recte oculis? quaenam haec pompa est? Dii boni, qui grex personatorum! Et hoc quoque recens Cisalpina e Gallia allatum est. Deerat unum hoc civitatis nostrae moribus tam concinnis! Praegreditur tubicen. Sequitur hedera coronatus, quasi populo recitaturus? Quis novus hic vates, tantum secum adducens personatorum? O larvatorum urbem, o fanatica ingenia! Quid quod pulpitum ac subsellia extruunt? an sibi audientiam parant? O iucundissime Antoni, ubi nunc es? ubi risus ille tuus leposque tam salsus? Ascendit vates pulpitum, auditores consedere. Canit iam tubicen, audiant ocio qui

a few, and I consider it sufficient now if it is not displeasing to you most venerable elders. Nor is there any reason that I should expect any thanks from you. I ask only that you not take it amiss for me to leave as soon as possible after I have satisfied you to some degree, for I have been invited to a friend's wedding, and I am hurrying off to sing the wedding song.

Enrico. We cheerfully let you go even though we wish you could be with us oftener and longer, and we give you the greatest possible thanks for soothing our spirits so pleasantly and with such variety.

Lutenist. Good-bye, then, most temperate elders.

Enrico. And you, most charming man, farewell and the best of good luck. As I see, good visitor, you are admiring the sweetness of this good man's singing and the nobility of his nature under such a mild demeanor. You should know that Antonio used to say that almost all other students of this art ostentatiously displayed their talent, but he alone concealed it, and, as we ourselves have often heard, most forcefully disparaged himself while giving great credit to others. 105

But, I ask you, am I seeing things? What is this parade? Great gods, what a crowd of people in masks! This thing too is a new import from northern Italy.[186] This was the only thing lacking to the elegant customs of our state! A trumpet player is leading the way. Then here comes someone crowned with ivy, as if he means to recite to the populace. Who is this new bard, bringing with him so many people in masks? O city of the bewitched! O frantic natures! Why are they erecting a platform and benches? Are they getting ready to be heard? O delightful Antonio, where are you now? Where is that laughter of yours and that facetious wit? The bard is ascending the platform, the 106

abundant. Me satis quidem fuerit in adolescentia delirasse, aetati huic compositiores sunt mores induendi; atque, ut video, experrectus somno Iovianus nos per puerum ad se vocat. Licet et te, Sicule hospes, nobiscum ad amicum et perhumanum hominem ingredi.

Hosp. An est quod magis cupiam? Vos praecedite, ego sequor.

[Metrum VIII]

Istrio Personatus

Tacete atque silete atque animum advortite,
Novam afferimus vobis quae vetus est fabulam.
Muti tacete, mutos tam diu volo
Silentium dum rumpat plausus, editus
Lingua, manu, pedibus quam clarissimus.
Hoc qui faciet plausum post editum bibet.
Tacent: nimirum sitiunt omnes maxime.
Atqui licet potare plausum ante editum;
Adest cadus, caupo, guttum[22] atque urceus.
Caveat tamen qui bibit, ebrius ne cubet;
Silentium non somnum mutamus mero.
Illi promito, caupo, sedet qui ultimus;
Vinosum eum esse non somniculosum indicat
Productus nasus, eminens, tuber, rufus.
Ipse hoc fatetur, ridet: habent hoc ebrii,
Rident libenter, risus nam sitim excitat,
Novum tamen poetam ridere abstine.
Coenabis post silentium, precium hoc erit,
Imo potabis large, abunde, Gallice;
Ridere sed iam desinas postquam satis

audience is seated. Now the trumpeter is blaring; let those with time on their hands pay attention. It is enough for me to have been crazy in my youth; my present time of life must adopt more sensible ways; and, as I see, Gioviano has wakened from his sleep and sent a boy to call us. You, too, Sicilian visitor, may come with us to see a friendly and kindly man.

Visitor. Is there anything more I could want? You go ahead; I'm right behind you.

[Poem VIII][187]

Masked Actor

Be quiet and keep silence and pay attention.
We're bringing you a new story that's old.
Keep still, I want you to be still a long time
Until applause breaks the silence, very loud applause
Produced by tongue, hands, and feet.
Anyone who applauds like this will drink afterward.
They are silent: they must all be very thirsty.
But it's allowed to drink before applauding.
Here are a cask, wine seller, flask, and jug.
But if you drink, careful! don't get pissed and pass out;
We're bargaining wine for silence, not slumber.
Now, wine seller, take some down to the guy in the
back;
That he's a wine bibber and not just a sleepyhead
Shows his nose—long, sticking out, bulbous, red.
He confesses it himself: he laughs. Drunks do that;
They like to laugh: laughing makes them thirsty.
Nevertheless, keep from laughing at the new poet.
You'll dine after your silence; this will be your reward.
No—you'll drink, a lot, very much—like a Frenchman;
But now you must stop laughing after you have drunk

Potasti, nasum emunge, atque aures arrige,
Novum dum vates carmen pulpito intonat.
Prius tamen argumentum hoc explico tibi:
Dum castra haberet ultimis in finibus
Ispaniae Sertorius dumque aggredi
Parat Pompeius ex improviso eum,
Fit per exploratores ipse certior.
Cogit in campis copias; committitur
Ab equitatu certamen saevum, atrox, dubium,
Equi virique hinc illinc confossi cadunt.
Duces accurrunt propere instructo agmine,
Pugnatur vi, dolo, fraude, audacia.
Nox proelium ac Dianae nuntia dirimit.
Habetis argumentum veteris fabulae.
Heus, tu, qui dexter assides, subrigito
Oculos ac mentulum; quid spectas humum?
Paulatim sic, ut video, somnum provocas.
Ridetis? dixi mentulum, non mentulam;
Nec est peccatum; a mento, non menta editum est
Vocabulum. Novus sed vates incipit,
Demulsit barbam, hederam capiti implicuit.
Tacete atque silete atque animum advortite.

[Metrum IX]

Poeta personatus

Ipse autem auratis fulgens Sertorius armis
Agmina cogebat campis; huic filius astat
Hernicus Ispanaque satus de matre Marullus.

Enough. Wipe your nose, and prick up your ears
While the bard thunders out his new song on the platform.
But first I will tell you the plot.
While Sertorius was encamped
In the remotest territory of Spain, and Pompey
Was preparing to attack him by surprise,
He heard about it from his scouts.
He assembled his troops on the field; the cavalry
Engaged in savage, fierce, indecisive struggle;
Horses and men on every side were run through and fell.
The leaders ran up, lining up their ranks in a hurry.
They battled with violence, guile, deceit, and daring.
Night and Diana's messenger put an end to the fight.
You have the plot of the old story.
Hey! You there, sitting on the right, raise up your eyes
And your little chin; why do you stare at the ground?
Little by little, as I see, you are inviting sleep that way.
Are you laughing? I said, "little chin" [*mentulum*], not "prick" [*mentulam*];
And I didn't do wrong. The word comes from *mento*,
Not *menta*.[188] But the new bard is beginning,
He has stroked his beard and twined ivy around his head.
Be quiet and keep silence and pay attention.

[Poem IX][189]

Masked Poet

Sertorius himself in his golden arms gleaming
Drew up his ranks on the plain.[190] Hernicus his son
Stood beside him, and Marullus, born of a Spanish mother.[191]

Hic peditem, ille equitem addensat, sua signa tribuni
Expediunt, portis ruit indignata iuventus
Praevenisse hostem et montis iuga celsa teneri.
Non aciem campo statui aut dare signa maniplis
Pompeianus eques patitur, volat agmine facto
Praecipitans. Primi Mariusque acerque Severus
Occultam nacti vallem, qua proxima ducit
Semita, limosumque ferunt vestigia ad amnem.
Astitit in ripa Marius prior; hunc vada nantem
Accipiunt tranquilla, ferox sed flumina servat
Mallius. Hic duro traiecit pectora conto
Percussitque ferum saxo; caput abdidit alveo
Attonitus sonipes, Marium rapit unda dehiscens
Atque hastae rotat infixum. Fortuna Severo
Haud melior fuit; acta manu cava tempora quassat
Funda levis cerebroque lapis compactus adhaesit;
Decidit exanimis vitamque effudit in undis.
Ter fluvio emersit iuvenis, ter gurges anhelum
Hausit hians, mox et trunco suffixit acuto.

Marullus rallied the infantry, Hernicus the cavalry; tribunes
Brought up the standards; soldiers charged from the gates, outraged
That the enemy, coming first, held the mountain's high ridge.
Pompey's cavalry did not wait to be lined up on the plain
Or for signs to be given the companies. In a column, it flew
Headlong. Marius[192] and fierce Severus were the first
To come upon a secret valley, where the nearest path
Led, and they made their way toward the muddy stream.
Marius stood first on the bank; the quiet waves took him
As he swam; but savage Mallius was guarding the river.
He pierced Marius' chest with his pitiless spear
And struck his horse with a rock. The terrified steed
Hid his head in the channel, and the gaping wave[193] seized Marius
And whirled him, stuck to the lance. Severus' luck
Was no better; a light sling whirled in the hand shattered
His hollow temples,[194] and the stone shot into his brain stuck there;
Unconscious, he fell, and poured out his life in the waves.
Thrice the youth emerged from the flood, thrice the yawning surge
Swallowed him gasping, and soon it impaled him on a sharp snag.

At Catulus Catulique genus Quintillus et asper
Tertullus patriique haeres cognominis Oscus,
In levam flexere; comes simul additur illis
Ispanus Bicia exclamans: 'Quo vertitis? huc vos,
Huc, iuvenes, ite ad pontem, dux ipse viarum
Praecedo.' Dixitque et per vestigia nota
Delatus, pontem ingreditur; tum coetera pubes
Insequitur, furit immissis equitatus habenis.
  Obvius his equitumque ciens peditumque catervas
Fit Rutilus Rutilique gener Veranius et qui
Prima puer Musis dedit ocia, moxque secutus
Arma, tulit meritum primae legionis honorem,
Pontius, a quo etiam ducta est Pontana propago;
Quem sequitur volucerque Melas alacerque Metiscus,
Et Pardus gladio melior, Chariteius hasta,
Insignes hederis meritaque ad tempora fronde,
Et cui casta comas tegit infula, certus et arcu
Et certus conto pugnax Corvinus acuto.
  Primus in adversum torquet Veranius hastam
Quintillum, quae praecipiti delapsa ruina
Per clypeumque femurque viri penetravit ad imum

But Catulus and Quintillus, Catulus' son, and violent
Tertullus and Oscus, named for his homeland,
Turned to the left; and at the same time gained a companion,
The Spaniard Bicia, who shouted: "Where are you going? This way,
This way, young men, go to the bridge; I will go first,
Leading the way." He spoke, and moving along the familiar track
Stepped onto the bridge; then the rest of the company
Followed; the horse soldiers rushed wildly, giving free rein.
Opposing them and rousing the troops of horse and foot
Were Rutilus and Rutilus' son-in-law Veranius and one
Who in boyhood gave his first leisure to the Muses, and soon following
Arms, won the well-deserved honor of the first legion,
Pontius, from whom is descended the line of Pontanus;[195]
Swift Melas and eager Metiscus followed him,
And Pardus, more skilled with the sword, Chariteius with the spear,[196]
Conspicuous with ivy and well-earned garlands on their temples;
And one whose hair a chaste fillet covered, a sure shot with the bow
And sure with the sharp lance, warlike Corvinus.[197]
Veranius, facing him, first hurled his spear against
Quintillus. In a violent arc it flew down and went through
The shield and the thigh of the man, to the inmost part

Pectus equi; gemuit sonipes, dumque excutit illam
Innitens, dum ferratis hic calcibus auras
Verberat, excussa Quintillus labitur hasta.
Accurrit pater ac, telo per tempus adacto,
Deturbat Rutilum. Inde Melas dum fervidus instat,
Dum Catulo cadit avulsus de pectore thorax,
Exegit medium praecordia ad intima ferrum.
Labenti dum ferrum iterumque iterumque coruscat,
Sensit praecipitem vento stridente sagittam;
Quam dum declinat iuvenis, forte ilia in Oscum
Obvertit, lateri et telum crudele recepit.
Extraxit telum obnitens ac talibus infit:
'Non tibi mentitum, Osce, genus veteresque parentes
Profuerint, Fauno aut mater dilecta petenti.'
Tum clypeo assiliens ensem quatit et ferit ora
Nuda Osci, cum forte levis cervice reflexa
Cassis hiat; cruor auratis diffunditur armis.
Ingeminat perque ora Melas perque ilia ferrum;
Ipse iterum lateri accepit moribundus acutum
Ensem, auratum ensem; mox corruit, acer et una

Of the horse's chest. The steed screamed, and while it was shaking it out,
Struggling, and beating the air with iron-shod hooves,
The lance was expelled and Quintillus fell.
His father ran up, and driving a spear through his temples,
Beat down Rutilus. Then while Melas was furiously attacking,
As Catulus' cuirass fell off, torn from his chest,
He drove his sword to the hilt deep into his belly.
While he was swinging the sword again and again at the falling man,
He sensed a swift arrow whistling through the air;
While the youth was dodging it, he happened to turn his flank
Toward Oscus, and took a cruel spear in his side.
He pulled out the spear with an effort and spoke in these words:
"May your false lineage not help you, Oscus, and your ancestors
Or your mother held dear by amorous Faunus."
Then leaping at his shield, he swung his sword and struck
Oscus' unprotected face when by chance the light helmet
Gaped open as he bent his neck. Blood spread over his golden armor.
Melas again struck the blade through his face and his flank;
In turn, he himself, near death, took a sharp sword in the side—
A sword of gold. Soon he fell to the ground; and at the same time

Corruit Oscus et ingenti premit arva fragore.
Attonitae stupuere acies. At Pontius instat:
'Ite, viri, mecum ite, viri, succidite pontem
Dum trepidant, nullo et liber custode tenetur.'
Haec ait, et rapta primus volat ipse securi,
Desiliitque pedes. Sequitur cuneata iuventus.
Tum Bicia increpitans: 'Quo nunc, Tertulle? quid haeres?
In ferrum, Romane, rue!' Atque hinc talia fatus
In medium incurrit peditem; nec defuit illi
Tertullus, volat aurato conspectus in ostro,
Nunc iaculo, nunc ense micans, fit vi via. Saevit
Effera vincentum rabies rabiesque cadentum.
Forte ut erat prolapsus equo Veranius, alte
Sustulit attollens oculos telumque vibrantem
Suspexit Biciam. 'Quo tu, quo, pessime, telum,
Carpetane, vibras? en hoc,' ait, 'accipe.' Et armos
Una haurit, simul abreptas detruncat habenas
Bellatoris equi, tum cominus ense reducto

Fierce Oscus fell and hit the earth with a great crash.
The stunned ranks were appalled. But Pontius pressed on:
"Come, men, come with me, men; cut down the bridge
While they're confused and it's open, held by no guard."
He spoke, and grabbing an axe, flew ahead himself, dismounting
To fight on foot. The young men followed, massed in a wedge.
Then Bicia said in reproach: "Where now, Tertullus? Why so slow?
Rush into the fray, Roman!" And that said, he dashed
Into the midst of the foot soldiers; and Tertullus did not
Fail him; he sped, a rare sight in purple set off with gold.
Darting now with his javelin, now with his sword, he fought his way through.
Madness raged, wild madness of victors and dying alike.
Veranius, falling by chance from his horse, raised his eyes
And looked up and saw Bicia above him, shaking his spear.
"Why do you shake your spear, you no-good,
Why, Carpetanan?[198] Here, take this!" he said. At once he tore open
The shoulders of the man's warhorse, and grabbing the reins
Lopped them off; then drawing back his sword, at close quarters

Perforat ingentemque alta prosternit in haerba.
In Biciam se cuncta cohors stipata ferebat;
Pro Bicia ferus assurgit Tertullus. At illi
Succidit iugulum, Parca indignante, Metiscus;
Concidit, ut tenuis cum flos enectus aratro est,
Insignis facie puer et florentibus annis.
Nec mora sive aliquis, dubium, milesne deusne
Sustuleritque manum iaculumque intorserit; intrat
Loricam galeamque inter ferratilis ornus,
Qua cervix commissa humeris, nam fata Metisco
Nec sua non properant Biciae seu cana senectus,
Cui caput avulsum collo Maurisius Atlas
Atque hastae infixum ostentat; quo territa retro
Pompeiana acies pontem turbata petebat.
Urgebat fugientem hasta Chariteius, ut se
Proripit e specula; simul et clamore premebat
Iuncta cohors; illi abruptis referuntur habenis.
Saevit at hic gladio incumbens Corvinus et harpe,
Ut quondam lupus in pecudes furit; omnis ab uno
Grex fugit, ille atrox et dente cruentat et ungui.
  Pontius, ut sensit strepitum, ac nutantia vidit

He stabbed the huge beast and laid him low in the tall grass.
The whole cohort advanced against Bicia en masse;
Fierce Tertullus rose up to defend him. But Metiscus
Cut his throat, offending Fate.
He fell, like a delicate flower slain by the plow,[199]
A boy fair of face in his blossoming years.
At once someone (no one knows who), whether soldier or god,
Raised his hand and hurled a lance. The iron-covered wood
Went in between the cuirass and helmet
Where the neck is joined to the shoulders. Indeed, fate
Did not come slow for Metiscus or hoary old age for Bicia,
Whose head the Moor Atlas[200] tore from his neck and displayed,
Put up on a spear. Thrown into panicked retreat by the sight,
Pompey's line in confusion ran for the bridge.
Chariteius dashed from his post and closed in on a runner,
Shaking his spear. At the same time the massed cohort
Pressed on with a shout. Their opponents turned back pell-mell.
But Corvinus now raged, driving with sword and scimitar,
As a wolf sometimes rages against sheep, and the whole flock
Flees from just one, and he savagely sheds blood with fang and claw.
Pontius, hearing the clamor and seeing the timbers

Robora et attrahere immanem tabulata ruinam,
'Cede, inquit, generosa phalanx, fugientibus, ipsi
Ferratis ad ripam hastis incumbite, qua se
Volvit agens retroque vagus convertitur amnis.'
Hic vero turbatus eques clamante tribuno
Constitit. Instaurata acies; tum Pardus et Actor
Sulpitiusque Aniusque et aviti nominis Arunx
Incumbunt, Variusque et Poeno e sanguine Hiensal,
Marmaridesque Mahar Atlantiadesque Maharbal,
Et Bostar Barceus et Pyreneus Hierus
Androclidesque Maron Antenoridesque Boriscus,
Atque alii, decus egregium quos traxit in arma,
Quique repostus equo Veranius aegra trahebat
Corpora, sed vincit famae generosa cupido.
Maeoniae nunc plectra, deae, cantusque ciete
Et bello decus et decori longam addite famam.
Non alias equitum maior seu maior equorum
Ardor, utrinque duces stimulant, utrinque tribuni:
'State, viri, pugnate, viri,' clamatur utrinque,
'Quo ruitis? Pompeius adest, incumbite fessis.'

Sagging and the platform on the verge of collapse,
Said, "Give way to those in flight, noble phalanx! You yourselves
Push on with your iron spears to the bank, where
The wandering stream rolls along and bends back in its course."
Here, at the shout of the captain, the excited cavalry
Pulled up. The line was re-formed; then Pardus and Actor[201]
And Sulpitius and Anius and Arunx, named for his grandfather,
Pressed on, and Varius and Hiempsal of Carthaginian blood,
And Mahar of Marmarica[202] and Maharbal of Atlas' line,
And Barcean Bostar and Pyrenean Hierus
And Maron son of Androcles and Boriscus of the line of Antenor,
And others whom excellent glory drew to arms,
And Veranius, seated again on his horse, his body
Wounded and dragging, but the noble desire for fame won out.
Now, Maeonian goddesses,[203] stir your lyres to song
And add glory to war and to glory long-lasting fame.
Never was there more fervor of horsemen, more of steeds.
On both sides leaders and captain spurred them on:
"Stand and fight, men!" The shout came on both sides.
"Where are you fleeing? Pompey is here. They're beaten; keep after them!"

'Impiger adventat Sertorius.' Arma cruore
Sparsa madent crepitantque enses, clypeique resultant
Impacti clypeis fractaeque hastilibus hastae;
Tum varius clamorque equitum atque hinnitus equorum.
Dissultant ripae et voces nemora alta remittunt;
Non aliter quam cum bello flagrante gigantum
Aeoliam ad Liparen sudat Vulcania pubes;
Fit strepitus, ferrique fluunt aerisque metalla;
Antra sonant validis incudibus itque cavernis
Immistus fumo sonitus; cava murmurat Aetna
Vicinaeque fremunt valles, maria ipsa resultant,
Ac longe fragor ingeminans defertur ad auras.
Hic Pardo suffossus equus, cadit impiger Actor
Androclidesque Maron, traiectus et ilia conto
Corruit infelix Arunx Bostarque Maharque,
Ense Mahar, iaculo Bostar per pectus adacto.
Sulpitius dextra execta levaque Maharbal
Inviti excedunt pugna. Veranius hastam
Crure trahit, dumque illam Anius convellere tentat,
Accipit aeratam per colla exerta bipennem.

"Tireless Sertorius is coming!" Their arms were drenched, dripping
With gore,[204] and swords clashed, and the clatter resounded[205]
Of shields struck by shields and spears broken by spears;
Then rose the mingled shouting of horsemen and neighing of horses.
The stream banks leapt in alarm and the deep woods reechoed,[206]
Just as when, during the blazing war of the giants,
Vulcan's workmen toiled hard near Aeolian Lipari.[207]
There was a din, and the iron and bronze ran molten;
The caves echoed with the mighty anvils, and noise
Mixed with smoke went through the caverns; hollow Etna groaned
And the nearby valleys roared, the very seas recoiled,
And the far echoing crash rose up to the sky.
Now Pardus' horse was stabbed; tireless Actor fell,
And Maron, son of Androcles; and with a spear piercing his loins
Poor Arunx came to grief, and both Bostar and Mahar—
Mahar by a sword, Bostar with a javelin thrust into his chest.
Sulpitius with his right hand cut off, Maharbal with his left,
Against their will withdrew from the fight. Veranius dragged a spear
Stuck in his leg, and while Anius tried to wrench it loose,
He exposed his neck and was hit with a bronze double axe.

Tum vero turbata phalanx cedente Borisco,
Quem clypeo exutum et galea Catilina premebat,
Syllanum genus et rara virtute tribunus,
Vociferans: 'En qui Hesperiam sua praemia poscunt,
Oceano et regnare parant!' Simul exigit harpen
Ore tenus dictisque ferox insultat amaris:
'Hesperiam quam quaeris habes; Patavina colebas
Rura, miser, nunc auratis occumbis in arvis.'
Tum Fabium Titiumque ferit flavumque Libyscum
Fonteiumque et quos Elice de matre gemellos
Sustulit Eleis praetor Vipsanius oris,
Almonem Andronemque et Cumanum Labeonem.
Dat leto Laufenum et amicum Nerea Musis,
Nerea praestantem forma et puerilibus annis,
Quem liquidis Sebethos aquis, quem cerula flevit
Parthenope, quem Nereidum chorus omnis et hudae
Sirenes conturbatis flevere sub antris.
Has inter strages Variusque et fortis Hiensal
Stabant invicti ferro, truduntque trahuntque,
Vulnera dant sternuntque. Prior sic fatur Hiensal:

Then the phalanx fell into confusion as Boriscus gave way.
He had lost his shield and helmet and Catilina[208] was chasing him,
Sulla's kinsman and a captain of unusual courage,
Shouting: "So these are the ones claiming Hesperia[209] as their prize,
And all set to rule Ocean!" At the same time he thrust
His scimitar in his face and uttered cruel taunting words:
"You have the Hesperia you seek; once you tilled a Paduan farm,
Poor wretch; now you meet your death in golden fields."
Then he smote Fabius and Titius and blond-haired Libyscus
And Fonteius and the twins the praetor Vipsanius
Received from their mother Elice on the shores of Elis,
Almo[210] and Andron, along with Cumaean Labeo.
He sent to their deaths Laufenus and Nereus, friend to the Muses,
Nereus outstanding in beauty and only a boy,
Whom Sebethos with his clear waters wept, and sea blue
Parthenope, and the whole chorus of Nereids[211] and the sea-drenched
Sirens wept under their grief-stricken caves.
  Amid this slaughter Varius and stouthearted Hiempsal[212]
Stood unbeaten by the sword; they pushed forward and pulled back,
Gave wounds, and laid low. Hiempsal spoke first:

'Macte, Vari, virtute, vides qua sorte ruat res?
Fraude opus est, hunc ipse locum cape, dum mihi segnis
Fit fuga.' Vix haec effatus, vestigia vertit.
Insequitur Catilina, fugam celerabat Hiensal,
Itque reditque iter inceptum, fallitque sequentem,
Dum Varius iaculum incoctum post terga sub ipsum
Infigit femur et dictis ferus increpat; ille
Saucius ingemuit vixque ad sua signa recepit;
Incumbunt tum victores victique facessunt.
Pontius interea positis vada ad ipsa maniplis,
Hos cogebat et hos, ut quem fors ipsa ruentem
Obtulerat tumulumque levis delatus in altum.
Eventum pugnae ut vidit, turbatus et amens:
'Huc, iuvenes,' simul ad pontem vestigia vertit.
Insequitur pedes atque eques, agglomeratur eodem
Cuncta manus. Simul ecce etiam fulgentia signa
Cernere erat, volat admissis Sertorius alis.
Parte alia de colle procul Romana ferebat
Se legio, volitant aquilae; Petreius ante

"Be blessed for your courage, Varius, do you how see it goes?
We need a trick. You hold this position, while I run away
Slowly." The words hardly out of his mouth, he turned on his heel.
Catilina pursued. Hiempsal was speeding up.
He went back and forth, this way and that, and tricked his pursuer,
While Varius behind thrust an untempered spear
Below his thigh and taunted him fiercely. The wounded
Man groaned and barely made it back to his lines;
Then the victors pressed on and the vanquished retired.
  Pontius meanwhile had stationed his troops at the ford
And was gathering them one after another as chance brought
Each one rushing his way, carried swiftly to the high mound.
When he saw the outcome of the fight, upset and frantic, he cried:
"This way, men!" and at the same time turned his steps to the bridge.
The foot and horse followed, and the whole troop joined forces
In the same place. At the same time—suddenly—gleaming standards
Came into view; Sertorius was hastening, his troops at full speed.
On the other side, at a distance, the Roman legion was moving
Down the hill, standards flying.[213] Petreius[214] in front

Agmen agit primusque vias et flumina monstrat.
Ut ventum ad ripam, stetit impiger et monstrato
Ponte, iubet primam confestim anteire cohortem.
Ingemuere trabes succisaque robora nutant
Assultu peditum vario. Tum pulsus ad amnem
Cedebat Catilina omnisque equitatus habenas
Laxabat; praemissa cohors tabulata tenebat
Ultima; per medium raptat vestigia pontem
Pulsus eques; ruit ecce trahens peditemque equitemque
Pons secum praecepsque cavo devolvitur alveo.
Substitit amnis: tum ripae intumuere profundae,
Conversusque nigras fluvius ructabat arenas.
  Attonitus casu tanto Petreius amnem
Spectabat: volat[23] acta manu Corybantis arundo,
Atque ocreis illapsa femur penetravit ad imum.
Pontius e ripa exclamat: 'Nunc vadite, segnes,
Et ripam tentate dolo.' Cum talia fatur,
Diffundit sese in partes ripasque relaxat

Led the column and first pointed out the paths and the river.
When they came to the bank, he stopped eagerly, and pointing to
The bridge, ordered the first cohort at once to advance.
The planks groaned and the timbers, cut from below, buckled
As the soldiers haphazard jumped on. Then Catilina, forced to the stream,
Was falling back and all his cavalry ran at full rein;
The advance cohort was reaching the end of the platform;
The routed cavalry dashed through the mid part
Of the bridge. It suddenly fell, dragging down foot soldiers
And troopers, and tumbled headlong into the deep channel below.
The stream stopped; then the banks were deep under water,
And the river, reversing its course, belched black sand.
  Thunderstruck by the disaster, Petreius was watching
The stream: a dart sent by the hand of Corybas came flying,
And sailing into his greaves sank into the lower part of his thigh.
From the bank Pontius shouted: "Now go ahead, sluggards;
Be clever and try for the bank." As he was saying these words,
The swollen stream flowed into separate channels and broke up the banks

Turgidus amnis aquis volvitque ad litora fluctu
Arma, viros, tabulas et corpora quadrupedantum.
Stant pedites innisi hastis versantque ruuntque
Semineces, spoliant alii, passimque secundum
Flumina suspendunt alte spolia indita ramis.
Exanimem implicitumque ulva fluctusque vomentem
Eructant undae Catilinam; ille aera ut almum
Hausit et accepit gratae spiramina vitae,
Apprendit ramum dextra tenuitque prehensum.
Hinc illinc oritur clamor; pugna aspera surgit,
Fundarum crepitat lapidosis ictibus amnis
Turbidus et multo sub verbere dissilit aer.
Exceptus tandem a sociis conamine magno
Curvatis trahitur contis ripaque locatus
Ulteriore vomit madidas de pectore arenas,
Cum subito rapidum affertur Sertorius amnem,
Et pugnam tuba terribili ciet horrida cantu.

[Metrum X]

Istrio personatus

Quievit, ut videtis, vates istricus;
Sitim pati non potest, quod Homericum

With its waters and cast up on the shores in its flood
Arms, men, planks, and corpses of four-footed beasts.[215]
The foot soldiers stood, weight on their spears, and they turned
And harried the drowning men; others despoiled them, and all
Along the river they hung high their spoils, fastened to branches.
Unconscious and tangled in sedge and spitting out water,
Catilina was belched out by the waves: as he drank in the reviving
Air and took in the breaths of life he had longed for,
He caught a branch with his right hand and held on.
Men shouted on this side and that. A violent battle ensued,
The roiling stream crackled with stones hurled from slings,
And the air jumped under many a sling-thong.
At last his comrades took him up with a great effort;
Pulled up by their bending lances and placed on the opposite
Bank, he was spitting out wet sand from his chest
When suddenly Sertorius came up to the rapid stream
And the harsh trumpet stirred battle with a terrible blast.

[Poem X][216]

Masked Actor

The theatrical poet, you see, is now silent;
He cannot bear thirst—a Homeric trait,

Ait fuisse seque similem illius
Mero potando noctu atque interdius.[24]
Bonum poetam nisi vinosum neminem
Ait, et id recte et quod ait re comprobat.
Heus, tu, cui nasus, ora, labra, guttura
Rubescunt, vin potando hoc experirier?
Taces, fateris victum, nunc hoc accipe.
Vides fortuna variet ut hominum vices?
Pugnabant illi de virtute et gloria,
Nos de mero; pugnabant ferro, hastilibus,
Nos vitro, nos argenteis carchesiis.
Hoc nunc agite, spectatores optimi,
Duces decoris pictos armis noscite
Et gesta Marte dubio certamina
Ac saevientes campis ignium globos
Vento rotatos et flamarum[25] turbinem
Agros, nemora peditumque ambusta corpora
Una absorbentem et coelo labentis faces.
   Audire pulchrum est strages et cadentium
Acervos ac cruore stagnantis agros,
Ipsum tranquillo et tuto sistere in loco.
   Illuc redeat unde est digressa oratio.
Prius quievit noster hic vates siti,
Nunc somno, vinum ut edormiscat scilicet.
Homeri hoc tantum habet, quod persaepe ebrius,
Maronis unum, nimio marcet ocio;
Sentitis ut apertis stertit faucibus?
Hiat, muscas venatur. Sane hoc est novum
Aucupium! Os aperit, stringit iam, tene, tene
Lepidam aviculam. Heus, vitule, heus, marina belua,

So he says, and that he is Homeric
In drinking unwatered wine night and day.
The only good poet's a drunk one, he says,
And quite rightly, proving the word with the deed.[217]
You there, with your nose, face, lips, and gullet
All glowing red, do you want to test this by drinking?
You're quiet and confess yourself beaten; now listen.
Do you see how fortune changes the lots of men?
They were fighting about courage and glory,
We about wine; they fought with sword and spear,
We with the glass, we with silver wine beakers.
Come now, do this, excellent spectators;
Learn about the leaders adorned with glorious arms
And the contests waged with Mars undecided
And the raging balls of fire in the fields,
Tossed by the wind, and the whirlwind of flames
Swallowing fields, woods, and the burned bodies
Of men all together, and comets dropping out of the sky.
It's fine to hear about slaughter and heaps
Of the dying and fields flooded with gore
Sitting in a quiet and safe place yourself.
Let the narration go back to where it left off.
First this poet of ours was quiet from thirst,
Now from dozing, no doubt to sleep off his wine.
He has only one trait of Homer, that he's often drunk,
Only one of Maro, that he flags with too much rest;
Do you see how he snores open mouthed?
He yawns, he's catching flies. This must be a new
Kind of fowling! He opens his mouth, now he touches—hold it,
Hold it!—a tiny winged creature. Hark, calf! Hark, sea monster,[218]

Deliciae Oceani, surge atque expergiscere,
Postquam venatus. Euge, iam erigit caput,
Iam defricat oculos, iam ascendit pulpitum.
Taceo, vos, spectatores, animum advortite.

[Metrum XI]

Poeta personatus

Constitit hic lustrans oculis loca, mox ita fatur:
'Haud parvo fraus haec steterit tibi, Magne'; nec ultra
Cunctatus vocat armatos ad signa tribunos.
Vos, Musae, memorate, etenim memorare potestis,
Vobis Pyrene, arcitenens dea rettulit illi.
Vos memori egregium facinus producite fama,
Quod iuvet et meminisse et commemorasse minores.
Altilius fraterque Lycon prima agmina ducunt,
Praestantes animis iuvenes, quos Nursia mater
Marte satos furtim patriis mandarat alendos
Montibus et succis haerbarum et lacte lyciscae;
Testatur nutricem auro galea alta lyciscam,
At clypeo quatit ingentem Mars efferus hastam.
Proxima Silvano clarus patre, clarior armis

Darling of Ocean, rise and wake up
Now that you've hunted. Excellent! now he lifts his head,
Now he rubs his eyes, now he ascends the platform.
I am quiet. You, spectators, pay attention.

[Poem XI][219]

Masked Poet

He stood surveying the scene, and then spoke:
"This ploy, Magnus,[220] will come at a cost." No delay,
At once he calls the armed captains to the standards.
You, Muses, tell the story, for you have the power to tell it,[221]
Pyrene[222] told it to you, the bow-wielding goddess to her.
You Muses, while fame remembers, bring forth the great deed—
A deed pleasing later generations to remember and tell.
Altilius[223] and his brother Lycon led the first columns,
Young men outstanding in courage, whom their mother Nursia
Conceived in Mars' secret embrace and entrusted to their father's
Mountains to be nursed on juices of plants and the milk of a wolf-dog.
Their high helmets bore witness in gold that their nurse was a wolf-dog,
But on their shields savage Mars shook his huge spear.
Famous for his father Silvanus, but more famous for arms,

Agmina agit Marsus; clypeo lacus enatat ingens,
Ipse antro fundit liquidas et Fucinus undas,
Pandit se cono advolitans argenteus anser,
Addictus puero custos, cum parvus ad amnem
Ludit avi puer et vitreos maris innatat aestus.
Hinc iaculo bonus, ense bonus, melior tamen arcu
Actius insequitur, argento auroque coruscus.
Nevit acu chlamidem coniunx, quam lucus opacat
Hesperidum pendentque suis poma aurea ramis.
Argento serpens riget et trahit horrida cauda
Septem orbes, micat et linguis furiata trisulcis.
Sub levam vagina auro viridique smaragdo
Irradiat distincta et iaspide fulgidus ensis
Ad capulum, nitet et nexu nova fibula eburno.
Aurea mandebat sonipes frena, aurea cassis
Emicat, auratos spargit sol aureus ignes,
Ac serpunt hederae per laevia tempora nigrae.
Lunat Amazonium in morem pelta horrida monstro
Lernaeo septemque illi capita alta tumescunt,

Marsus[224] led the next column. A huge lake floated over his shield,
And Fucinus himself poured clear waters out of his cave.
A silver goose flying up to the peak of his helmet spread its wings,[225]
Assigned as the child's guardian while the little boy played
By his grandfather's stream and swam in its glassy waves.
Next followed Actius,[226] good with javelin, good with sword,
But better with the bow, and shining with silver and gold.
His wife embroidered his cloak,[227] which the grove
Of the Hesperides shaded, branches fruited with gold.
The snake stood out in silver, and her scaly tail behind
Dragged seven coils; enraged, she sent flicks with her triple tongue.[228]
Under his left hand gleamed a scabbard, embellished with gold
And green emerald, and a sword shining with jasper
Up to the hilt, and a new buckle with its ivory clasp glowed.
His steed was champing a golden bit,[229] his golden helm
Glittered, a golden sun scattered its gilded flames,
And dark ivy twined around his smooth temples.
His shield curved in a crescent, Amazon-fashion, bristling
With the Lernaean Hydra, seven heads swollen high.

Et latos pandit rictus fera; defluit atrox
Virus et effuso livescit parma veneno.
At dorso pugnacis equi terga aspera pendent
Illa boum, tegit et crudus genua ultima pero.
Haec variat nemus Idaeum atque ad pocula raptus
Dardanius puer et cupido praeda acta Tonanti.
Ter puerum invadit praepes, ter praepetis alas
Evadit puer; hinc rostro sacer ales adunco
Abreptum implicitumque ungui multumque sub ala
Percussum, frustra auxilium divosque vocantem
Ante Iovem coelo statuit; mox versus in astrum
Inter sidereos ales micat aureus ignes.

Quem post venatore satus patre, maximus armis
Compater; huic apri clypeo riget horrida pellis,
Incoctumque ursi tergus; latrat aspera cassis
Ora canum duraque horrent venabula dextra.
Lartius hunc pater, amissa genitrice, lupina
Pelle fovet tectum foliis, subque hubera adactum
Lactantis quam cum catulis deprenderat ursae.

She fiercely opened her jaws wide; ghastly poison
Ran down, and the shield turned black with the venomous discharge.
But over the back of his warhorse hung a rough
Cow skin, and rawhide boots covered his leg to the knee.
The grove of Ida adorned these, and the Dardanian boy snatched
To be cupbearer and booty for the lusty Thunderer.[230]
Three times the bird went after the boy, three times he escaped
The bird's wings; then with hooked beak the sacred eagle
Snatched him up, and set the boy, caught in his talon
And repeatedly beaten beneath his wings, and calling in vain for help
On the gods, before Jupiter in heaven. Then, changed into a constellation,
The bird flashed golden among the starry fires.
After him came a hunter's son, mighty in arms,
Compater.[231] On his shield bristled the shaggy skin of a boar,
And the untanned hide of a bear; the cruel baying of hounds came
From his helmet, and hunting spears stuck out from his hard fist.
Since he had lost his mother, his father Lartius wrapped him warm
In a wolf skin, covered him with leaves, and set him down
Under the dugs of a nursing bear he had caught along with her cubs.

Mox puer exagitare feras assuevit et acto
Venatu tolerare famem atque inhiare cruori.
Qualis mane novo cum fulgidus igne nitenti
Lucifer irradiat coelo, mirantur et illum
Pastores, gaudet caro Venus aurea signo,
Aeratam sic ante aciem nitet ora Camillus,[26]
Insignisque coma puer et fulgentibus armis,
Miranturque ut tela manu atque ut torqueat hastam,
Ut gladium stringat dextra. Sertorius ipse
Concipit optatae iamdudum gaudia palmae.
Tum vates Phoebo carus Saxonius Astur,
Idem augur, cui vox avium pennaeque patebant,
Et curare manu doctus cantuque levare
Vulnera, non tamen ense minor, minus utilis hasta;
Laurea cingebat galeam, tegit infula crines,
Serpebant hederae clypeo, viret hasta corymbis
Et capulo insignis radiabat acinacis aureo.
Hinc Aspar Garamas, quo non praestantior alter
Aut torquere manu iaculum aut dare vulnera funda.

Soon the boy grew accustomed to driving game from its cover and
Supporting his hunger by hunting and having a thirst for blood.
Just as at daybreak[232] when bright Lucifer with his glowing fire
Lights up the sky and the shepherds marvel to see him,
And golden Venus rejoices in her dear star,
So before the bronze-armored battle line glowed Camillus,[233]
A boy who stood out for his hair and bright-shining arms,
And they marveled at how he hurled the lance and the spear,
How he drew the sword with his right hand. Sertorius himself
Took joy in anticipating his palm as a victor.
Then came Saxonian Astur,[234] a seer dear to Phoebus,
And also an augur, to whom the cry and flight of birds were revealed,
And with the skill to cure wounds with his hand and soothe them
With chant, and yet just as useful with sword or with spear;
Laurel wreathed his helmet, a fillet covered his hair,
Ivy twined over his shield, his spear green with ivy berries,
And his distinctive short saber with its golden hilt gleamed.
Next came Garamantian Aspar, none better
At hurling the javelin with his hand or giving wounds with the sling.

Ceruleus capiti trifido micat ore cerastes,
Ter caudam collo implicitans; puer Aspar et illi
Assuevit, cantata daret cum pabula, et aspis
Luderet infantis manibus, cum lambit et ora,
Ora genasque simul et collo lubricus errat.
Horret et insutus cetrae leo, cruda draconum
Terga humeros crudumque tegit thoraca elephantus.
Ipse arcum pharetramque humeris clavamque trinodem
Incoctamque sudem dextra gerit et quatit acer,
Marmaricoque subinde hululans vocat agmina cantu.
  Ecce decus belli rarum, Tritonia Birse,
Ipsa pedes quamvis, equites tamen eminet inter
Vertice iam toto et passu praevertit euntis.
Nodosam lateri clavam fert, dextera pinum,
Ingentem quassat pinum, quam fulva bipennis
Asperat. Ipsa exerta humeros et brachia et ipso
Poplite nuda tenus; non illi pectora thorax,
Non galea abscondit crines, sed tornulus aureus
Circuit ingentem lato curvamine frontem
Et multo pectus communit balteus aere,

On his head a cerulean horned serpent sent flicks from his mouth
Three-forked; his tail twined thrice around his neck. As a boy Aspar
Tamed him, giving him food that he'd charmed,
And the snake played in the child's hands, licking his face—
His face and cheeks at once, sinuously sliding around his neck.
A shaggy lion was sewn to his shield; rough snakeskins
Covered his shoulders and elephant hide his rough breastplate.
He wore a bow and quiver on his shoulders, and his fierce hand
Brandished a club with three knots and an untempered stake.[235]
Yelling, he called his troops again and again with his Mamarican cry.
  Look! the rare jewel of warfare, Tritonian Birse—
A foot soldier, but she towered over the troopers, taller
By a head, and she outpaced the riders with her step.[236]
She bore a gnarled club at her side; her right hand shook a pine—
A huge pine tree, hacked down with her bronze double axe.
She had unclad shoulders and arms and was bare
Right up to the knee. No cuirass hid her chest,
No helmet her hair, but a neat golden band
Encircled her mighty forehead in a broad arc
And a heavy bronze baldric went round her chest,

Palladis armisonae donum fatale, quod illi
Ferre dedit, tutum armatos munimen in hostes.
Hanc Fauno et nympha genitam Garamantide mater
Dum partum celat, tergo bovis indit et aspris
Sentibus impositam nymphis nemorique relegat.
Quam dum forte lavat Tritonide Pallas in unda,
Oblatam ut tenuit gremio, miratur et ora
Et latos humeros et membra ingentia; quodque
Nec vagit fertque aspectum non territa divae,
Quodque hastam galeamque oculis atque aegida lustrat,
Commendat matri Tritonidi; sedula mater
Educat. Illa, ut primum aetas tulit, ire per altas
Nuda genu silvas latebrasque intrare ferarum,
Sectari cervum cursu, venabula in aprum
Dirigere et fulvum iaculo attentare leonem.
Finitimis etiam bellis assueta, nigrantem
Gerionistheniden clava abstulit; hunc tremit omnis
Aegyptus, tremit extremi domus abdita Nili,
Egregium ac coeli columen Maurisius Atlas.

The fatal gift of Pallas of the ringing armor,[237] given
Birse to wear for protection against her armed foes.
She was the child of Faunus and a Garamantian nymph.[238] Her mother,
Concealing the birth, covered her with a cowhide and set her
In the rough bushes, consigned to the nymphs and the forest.
While by chance Pallas was bathing her in the Tritonian waters,
Picking her up and holding her in her arms, she marveled
At her face and broad shoulders and huge limbs; and because
She did not cry, and without fear bore the sight of the goddess,
And because the child cast her eyes on her spear and helmet and aegis,
She entrusted her to her own mother Tritonis; the mother reared her
With care. The girl, when she was old enough, went bare legged
Through the deep woods and got into the animals' lairs;
She ran in pursuit of the stag, aimed her spears
At the boar, and hunted the tawny lion with her lance.
Even getting practice in nearby wars, she demolished
Swarthy Gerionisthenides with her club. All Egypt
Trembled before him, the remote home of the farthest Nile
Trembled, and Moorish Atlas, splendid prop of the sky.

Accipit ob meritum donum immortale Minervae
Auratam fronti vittam atque ad pectora balteum,
Exultat quibus in bellis invicta virago.
Hernicus extremas acies atque ultima claudit
Agmina; nam iussus properare in castra Marullus,
Communire manu vallum portasque tueri.
Ipse ostro chlamidem intextam argentoque nitentem,
Aurea quam lato percurrit linea tractu,
Insignis fulvoque comam nodante pyropo
Irradiat, veluti roseo cum solis in ortu
Percussum radiis splendet mare, iam tremit unda
Iam feriunt sese radii, iam dissilit ardor
Huc illuc, nequeunt tum lumina nostra tueri.
Quin etiam auratos spargit de casside fluctus
Oceanus, splendet cano sub marmore Triton,
Fluctuat et clypeo per cerula concita delphin,
Argento assurgunt undae. Tum litora gemmis
Sparsa nitent, micat adverso sub lumine pontus.
Hos Arno genitus nymphaque Evarchide vates,
Quem Musae Aonio puerum fovere sub antro,

She took as reward the immortal gift of Minerva,
A fillet of gold for her forehead and the belt for her chest,
And rejoiced in them, a maiden heroic, unconquered in war.
  Hernicus stood at the end of the line and brought up
The rear; for Marullus was hastening to the camp under orders
To fortify the ramparts himself and put guards on the gates.[239]
Resplendent in a cloak woven with purple and gleaming
With silver, a wide stripe of gold running its length,
And his hair tied back with yellow gold-bronze,
He shone radiant, just as when at the rosy rising of the sun
The sea glitters, struck by its rays: now the water shimmers,
Now the rays collide, now the flashing brilliance shatters
This way and that, then our eyes are dazzled.
From his helmet Ocean sent gold billows streaming,
Triton gleamed under the sea's grey surface, and on his shield
A dolphin swam through roiled dark blue waters,
The waves rose up in silver. Then the shore gleamed,
Sprinkled with gems; the sea flashed, struck by the light.
  Puttius,[240] a bard born of Arno and the nymph Evarchis,
Whom in boyhood the Muses cherished in their Aonian cave,

Puttius ad pugnam vocat atque hortatur euntis:
'Di vobis sint tela, viri, Mars dextera cuique est;
Vicimus ipsa suas victoria concutit alas,
Pax parta, Hesperius nobis regnabitur orbis.'
Ut ventum est sub signa, ducem sua quemque secuta
Est legio, ac densis cogit se exercitus armis.
Intenti expectant signum moraque omnis iniqua est.
Oceano veluti in magno cum cerula Proteus
Agmina agit stabulis, coeunt immania monstra
Sub duce quaeque suo, fervent freta, pastor ad ipsas
Stat caulas baculoque greges et voce coercet;
Non casses, ipsi nequeunt retinere magistri.
Interea caesos equites primamque cohortem
Haustam undis ripasque et flumen ab hoste teneri
Nuntius attulerat Magno, famulique ferebant
Impositum clypeo Petreium. Aegerque dolensque
Substitit ad medium collem, secum ipse volutans,
Incertus casu tanto, pugnamne retractet
Paulatim colle excedens, an flumina tentans

Called men to battle, giving them heart on the way:
"Let the gods be your weapons, men; Mars is each one's right hand.
We are victors, victory herself is beating her wings.
Peace has been won, we will rule the Hesperian land."
When they came up under the standards, each legion
Followed its leader, and the army lined up in close ranks.
Eagerly they looked for the sign, and hated every delay,
Just as when in great Ocean Proteus drives his sea-dark herds
From their pens, and the great monsters assemble,
Each under its leader, the sea boils, and their shepherd stands
By the fold and checks the flock with his staff and his voice;
Not nets, not even their keepers can hold them back.
Meanwhile a messenger had bought Magnus the news
Of his slain troopers and the first cohort sucked down by the waves and
The banks and river held by the foe; and attendants were bearing
Petreius[241] laid out on his shield. Grieving and heartsick,
He stopped midway up the hill, turning it over in his mind,
Unsure in such a disaster, whether to give up the fight and little
By little withdraw from the hill, or to make an attempt on the river,

Implicitum eliciat ripis fluvialibus hostem
Fidentemque equite atque recenti caede tumentem.
Haec secum; mox accito iubet arma Cetego
Inferri ripis peditemque ad signa vocari.
Ipse invectus equo: 'Nunc, o fortissima bello
Pectora, nunc certate manu; tot flumina nando
Emensos torrens tenet atque ignobilis amnis?
Vincite iam victos unaque absolvite pugna
Relliquias tot bellorum.' Dum talia fatur
Magnus, ab impigro pugna est commissa Cetego.
Nanque ultra adversam ripam vada nota secutus
Pontius institerat, campo congressus iniquo,
Dum fossas et saxa inter versatur, equesque
Confossus cadit et pediti pedes additus instat.
   Quod postquam longe aspexit Sertorius et quae
Sit fortuna videt, nulla est mora, protinus agmen
Ire iubet, dictis stimulans. 'Nunc, lecta iuventus,
Nunc, victrix manus, ad ripas, vada pervia! Et ipse

Enticing the enemy when they were hemmed in by the banks
And confident in their cavalry and puffed up by fresh slaughter.[242]
He thought it over. Then summoning Cetegus,[243] he ordered an attack
On the banks and had him call infantry to the standards. He himself
Mounted his horse and spoke: "Now, O hearts bravest in battle,
Now put your backs into it. You have swum across so many rivers;
Does the rushing water of an obscure stream hold you back?
They're already beaten. Defeat them, and in one battle finish off
The dregs of so many wars." While Magnus was speaking
These words, energetic Cetegus joined battle.
Pontius had made for the well known ford and taken his stand
On the opposite bank, joining battle on unfavorable ground
While the fight went on between ditches and rocks, and cavalry fell
Wounded, and new foot troops attacked foot troops.
 Sertorius, watching it all from afar and seeing
How it was going, straightway commanded his line
To advance, urging them on in these words. "Now, chosen men,[244]
Now, victorious band, to the banks, the passable ford!

Pontius insultat campo, non audet et hostis
Aut conferre gradum aut descendere montibus altis.
Hesperiam dextra gerimus; spes omnis in armis.'
  Altilius fraterque Lycon trans flumina primi
Consistunt sequiturque hastis innisa iuventus.
Pars capiti scuta alta gerunt, pars insita pilis,
Pone trahunt alii; sistunt et flumina cursum
Mole virum atque undis[27] illisa remurmurat unda.
Tum ripae clamore sonant collesque resultant,
Offensa et nemorum assultu respondet imago.
Vix alias tantis animis in proelia ventum est;
Successus certamen alit, dum cedere neutris
Decretum est, urgetque ducum praesentia et ardor.
Ingeminant[28] vires, crescit certamine virtus.
Crudescit gladio Mavors, nec iam eminus hasta,
Cominus ense agitur; humescunt sanguine campi,
Caede natant fossae. Tum territa terra cadentum
Corporibus tremit et gladiis micat aereus aether.
  Tercentum clipeata phalanx, hinc sub duce Hiarba

See! Pontius is prancing on the field,[245] and the enemy does not dare
Either to engage or to come down from the high hills.
We have Hesperia in our power; our whole hope is in arms."[246]
Altilius and his brother Lycon,[247] first across the river,
Took a stand; their men followed, using lances for walking sticks.
Some bore their tall shields on their heads, some stuck on their spears;
Others dragged them behind; the river's course stopped, dammed up
By men, and wave dashing against wave resounded.[248]
Then the banks rang with shouting and the hills sent back the sound,[249]
And struck by the assault, the echoing woods replied.
Seldom has battle been joined with such courage;
Success fed[250] the struggle, with both sides resolved not to yield,
And the presence and zeal of their leaders spurred them on.
Their strength redoubled, their courage grew with the fight.
Mars' blade grew more savage; no longer with spears at a distance
They fought, but now with the sword, hand to hand; the field ran
With blood,[251] the trenches swimming in gore. Then the earth shook in fright
As the bodies fell; the sky gleamed bronze with their swords.
On this side a phalanx of three hundred with shields under Hiarbas,[252]

Illinc Suffeno, stabilis pedes, arma manusque
Contulerant, ut forte alnus radice revulsa
Conciderat ramisque ingens iter occupat, ut nec
Aut his aut illis pateat via. Saevit utrinque
Effera vis, durique crepant per scuta molares,
Ut cum se Orionis iniquo sidere grando
Praecipitat, vasto crepitant sub verbere tecta.
Hinc Tacio Lepidoque caput cervice revulsum
Ense Tagi ; cadit ense Remi Turnusque Ligusque;
Nam Liguri femur exectum, Turno ilia et ipsas
Traiecit costas ac pectora fervidus ensis.
Per galeam cerebrumque ac tempora guttur ad ipsum
Assaracum secat Ufentis sullata bipennis.
Illinc et Marus et Basso cum fratre Faliscus
Thessalicusque Maroniades et Lydius Hypseus
Conciderant, Siculusque Corax et Maurus Iopas:
Idem omnes eodem gladio ferus abstulit Ancus.
Hic genitus Vulcano atque Aetnea Cyanea
Fatiferum a patre ensem atque immedicabile ferrum
Accepit, Stygia genitor quod tinxerat unda.
    Dumque alnum truncosque super levis insilit Anser,

On that, steady infantry led by Suffenus, had engaged in the fight
Where by chance a great alder had fallen, torn up by the roots,
Blocking the way with its branches, leaving no space
For either force to pass through. On both sides wild violence
Raged, and the hard boulders clattered on their shields,
As when hail rushes down under the harsh sign of Orion
And the roofs keep up a clatter under its awful lashing.
On this side Tacius and Lepidus had their heads torn off their necks
By Tagus' sword; by Remus' sword fell both Turnus and Ligus;
Ligus' leg was cut off; Turnus had his flanks and ribs
And breast run through by the raging sword.[253]
Through helmet and brain and temples down to the throat
The raised double axe of Ufens[254] cut Assaracus in two.
On the other side, Marus and Faliscus with his brother Bassus
And Thessalian Maroniades and Lydian Hypseus
Had fallen, and Sicilian Corax and Moorish Iopas:
The same man, fierce Ancus, with the same sword, killed them all.[255]
This man, son of Vulcan and Etnaean Cyane,
Had from his father the deadly sword and the blade that gave
Incurable wounds, dipped by his sire in the water of Styx.
As Anser was leaping nimbly over the tree and the tree trunks,

Accipit aeratam infelix per guttura cornum;
Spiramenta animae clausit telum; ille volutus
Singultantem animam pronus vomit: 'Eia age,' Hiarbas
Exclamat, 'spolia illa viri!' Cum talia fantem
Ora per increpitans alis penetravit arundo;
Insultans cui Suffenus: 'Spolia accipe, victor,
Ista tibi,' iaculumque quatit; suffigitur hastae
Dextera, dum excusso properat torquere lacerto.
Hic caedes miseranda oritur super Ansere tracto,
Dum spolia exuviasque viri cupit hostis et hostis
Pro decore haud timet adversis incurrere telis.
Huc omnis legio versa, huc sua signa Cetegus
Inferri iubet, huc contra Altiliusque Lyconque
Accurrunt paribusque animis certatur utrinque.
Dum primam ferus ante aciem movit arma Cetegus
Ac iaculo ferit Iasium sternitque Volenum,
Murano clypeum avellit, transfigit utrunque
Quercenti femur, ingeminat per viscera ferrum
Quintilio atque huda morientem extendit in haerba.
Interea per scuta virum, per tela, per enses
Altilius ruit infrendens, caput amputat Istro,
Brachia Segnitio, nares et labra Mecillo,

The poor fellow took a bronze-fitted cornel spear in the throat;
The shaft choked his windpipe; pitching forward,
He panted out his life in gasps. "Come on!" shouted
Hiarbas, "the man's armor as spoils!" As he spoke,
A winged shaft in censure drove through his mouth.
Suffenus taunted him: "Take your spoils, victor;
They're yours!" And he brandished his javelin; a spear drove
Into his hand while he thrust out his arm in a hurry to throw.
Now a pitiful slaughter arose over the plundering of Anser,
While one foe lusted after the man's spoils and armor, and one,
Seeking glory, dashed intrepid against the opposing spears.
The whole legion turned this way; here Cetegus[256] ordered his
Men to advance, here Altilius and Lycon ran up to face them,
And they fought on both sides with equal courage.
While fierce Cetegus was leading the first line into battle,
He struck Iasius with a javelin and laid low Volenus,
Tore away the shield from Muranus, pierced Quercens
In both thighs, sent his steel again and again into Quintilius'
Entrails and laid him out dying on the damp grass.[257]
Meanwhile Altilius dashed raging through men's shields,
Through weapons and swords. He cut off Ister's head,
Segnitius' arms, the nose and lips of Mecillus;

Tempora diffringit Catio, prosternit Omasum,
Umbritioque haurit iugulum, forat ilia Cosso,
Praecipitemque inter fossas dat Amintora saxo.
  Tum leva de parte Lycon furiatus et amens
Quintilio extincto: 'Quid tu, generose Cetege,
In plebem furis?' exclamat. Cui talia contra
Ille refert: 'O Mavortis praeclara propago,
Mentitum genus in silvis, quid proelia differs?
Est clypeus, sunt tela tibi.' Simul iniicit hastam;
Avertit venientem umbone; ea lapsa pependit
Marmarici clypeo; contra venabula torquet
Dura Lycon; saltu devitat tela Cetegus;
Illa ocreis illapsa Tagi femora ultima et inguen
Extremum rupere; cadit Tagus, advolat Ammon
Elatamque alte subigit per colla securim
Et caput affigit conto; clamore secuta est
Laeta cohors; tum tela Lycon, tum saxa Cetegus
Ingeminat, stringunt acres et cominus enses.
  Interea paulatim acies ac signa movebat
Pompeius seque ad ripas non segnis agebat.

He crushed Catius' temples, laid low Omasus,
Cut Umbritius' throat, pierced Cossus' loins,
And with a rock sent Amintor headlong into the ditch.
Then on the left Lycon was thrown into frenzy
When Quintilius was slain. "Why, O noble Cetegus," he shouted,
"Do you rage against the rank and file?" The other replied
In these words: "O distinguished offspring of Mars,
Your birth in the woods is a lie. Why do you put off the fight?
You have a shield, you have spears." And he threw his lance.
Lycon turned it aside with his shield boss as it came; falling,
It hung in his Marmarican shield. In return he threw hard
Hunting spears; Cetegus dodged the missiles, jumping aside;
They slipped into Tagus' greaves and broke into the end of
His thigh and the tip of his groin. Tagus fell. Ammon flew up,
Raised his double axe in the air, drove it right through his neck,
And stuck his head on a pike. With a shout the cohort followed
Exultant. Then Lycon and Cetegus were at it again, Lycon with spears,
Cetegus with rocks. Keen swords drawn, they fought hand to hand.
Meanwhile, little by little Pompey was advancing
And steadily making his way up to the banks.

Ipse ostro insignis humeros auroque coruscus
Fertur equo, quem Neptunni de gente crearat
Mater ab adversi conceptum flatibus euri.
  Forte ut erat de caede equitum, de caede virorum
Fessus et extremum servabat Pontius amnem,
Vidit ut incensa stipula, exagitantibus auris,
Haeserat arenti trunco vapor; ille volutus
Per frondes urgente euro conceperat ignes
Et late ramos flamma crepitante cremabat.
Admovit dextram trunco avulsitque trahendo
Pontius et campo rapidus iacit atque ita fatur:
  'Eure pater, cui pars coeli pulcherrima servit,
Cui parent aurae Oceani, cui regia solis
Ampla vacat quique et terris pelagoque sonanti
Imperitas, quate nigrantem, rex magne, procellam,
Nunc exerce auras et pennis aera verre,
Ac mecum insidias hostemque ulciscere victor;
Sacra tibi ante aras statuam votiva quotannis
Candentis foetus ovium intactamque iuvencam.'
  Annuit excussitque alas deus. Illicet ingens

All agleam, his shoulders conspicuous in purple and gold, he rode
On a stallion brought forth by its dam from the stock of Neptune,
Conceived from the gusts of Eurus, the east wind blowing against her.
By chance Pontius, grown weary of the slaughter of troopers
And slaughter of men,[258] and guarding the edge of the stream,
Saw how, when the stubble was burning and the gusts drove it,
The heat had clung to a dry trunk. It had traveled
Through the leaves with Eurus spurring it on, starting fires,
Everywhere setting the branches alight with crackling flame.
Pontius put his hand on the trunk, pulled and tore it,
And quickly hurled it onto the plain with these words:
"Father Eurus, master of the fairest part of heaven,
Whom the breezes of Ocean obey, to whom the great palace
Of the sun is spread open, and who rule the lands and
The sounding sea, great king, let loose a darkening gale;
Now stir the breezes and sweep the air with your wings,
And with me, victorious, punish the tricks of the foe.
I will put before your altars votive offerings each year,
White offspring of sheep and a heifer untouched."
The god nodded and shook out his wings. All at once

Tempestas coelo exoritur, fremit arduus aether;
Dant silvae sonitum ingentem cavaque antra resultant;
Pulvereus sequitur confusa per agmina nimbus
Dispergitque undas flammarum atque omnia late
Involvit iactatque furens incendia ventus.
Tolluntur coelo fumi glomerataque flamma
Pervolitat, simul absorbens stirpesque virosque;
Et quamvis trepidum canerent iam signa receptum
Telaque proiicerent dextris clypeosque sinistris,
Flammatas tamen ante acies evadere non est.
Varenum Iasiosque duos, Liguremque Labullum,
Cretensemque Gian, Gaditanumque Liertem,
Assyriumque Naban, Pyreneumque Biantem,
Tris Alcmeonidas et clarum Hypsenora cantu
Erumpens atra primum de subere fumus
Involvit, mox flamma rubens una hausit, et alte
Iactati, mox flagranti cecidere ruina.
Constiterat forte ad saxum tardante sagitta
Narnius Himbrasius, dumque illam avellere tentat,
Exanimum exustumque alta suspendit in ulmo
Fulmineus globus, inde euro torquente rotatus

A great tempest rose in the sky, the upper air howled aloft,
The forests gave a great roar and the hollow caves reechoed;[259]
A cloud of dust chased through the disordered ranks,
And scattered torrents of flames and swallowed everything
Far and wide, and the raging wind hurled fire.
Smoke rose up in the sky and the massed flame
Flickered, at the same time engulfing vegetation and men;
And although they were already sounding a hasty retreat,
And throwing down spears with their right hands and shields
With their left, they could not outrun the army of flames.
Varenus, and the two Iasi, and Ligurian Labullus,
And Cretan Gyas, and Liertes of Cadiz,
Assyrian Naban, and Bias from the Pyrenees,
Three sons of Alcmeon, and Hypsenor, famous for song,
First were engulfed by the black smoke that burst
From the oak trunk, then all were swallowed at once by the red blaze.[260]
They were thrown high in the air, then fell down in flames.
  Narnian Himbrasius had stopped by a rock, slowed down
By an arrow, and while he was trying to pull it out,
A ball of fire killed and burned him and hung him high
In an elm, and then whirled as Eurus spun it around

Alconem rapit; huic barba crinisque reluxit,
Sullatumque alte coelo intulit, inde nigrantem
Ructantemque ignes medium deturbat in amnem.
Perstridere undae attactu fumumque dedere,
Ut cum versatum ardenti fornace metallum
Canduit exceptumque tenaci forcipe tingit
Ipse lacu faber, effervit lacus, obstrepit unda
Et fumus petit advolitans nigrantia tecta.
Tercentum huic capita hirta boum totidemque iuvencae
Pascebant Sila in magna; famam ipse secutus
Deseruit patriam et dulcis cum coniuge natos.
Bisseptem Aufidio nati, praeclara iuventus,
Surrenti domus ampla, Aequano in litore turris,
Felices Baccho colles, tot iugera campi
Totque greges Sarnusque fluens per florida rura.
Et natos tamen et patriam dulcisque recessus
Sirenum (potuit tantum ambitiosa cupido)
Posthabuit. Cui primum oculos flamma abstulit, inde

And seized Alcon;[261] it set fire to his beard and hair, picked him up
And carried him high in the sky, and then threw him, black
And belching flames, down into the stream at its midpoint.
The waves hissed at the touch and gave off smoke,
As when metal, turned in the glowing furnace, is white hot
And the smith picks it up, holding it fast with his tongs,
And plunges it into his trough;[262] the trough boils, water spills
Over, and the steam flies up to the blackening roof.
Three hundred head of shaggy cattle and as many heifers
He used to have that grazed in great Sila;[263] seeking glory
He left his country behind and his sweet children and wife.
Aufidius[264] had fourteen sons, splendid young men,
A great house in Sorrento, towers on the shore of Aequana,[265]
Hills fertile for wine, so many acres of land, so many flocks,
And the Sarno flowing through the flowering countryside.
And yet he discounted his sons and his home and the sweet haunts
Of the Sirens[266] (so great was the power of eager desire).
First the flame took his eyes, then ashes blown by the wind

Torruit ambustam dextram vento acta favilla;
Post tortus iaculante euro per viscera truncus
Candiut, ipse atros spirans de vulnere fumos
Et Sarni fontem et liquidos reminiscitur amnes.
Fatidica Ursidio mater praedixit eunti
In bellum, 'Fuge, nate, ignes, incendia vita.'
Correptus flammis queritur matremque deosque
Veriloquos quodque humentem liquisset et Arnum
Et Fesulas, natale solum florentiaque arva.
Tercentum sub rupe cava, sub sentibus aspris,
Deliterant[29] simul, insidiis delecta iuventus,
Tercentum simul absumpsit glomerata favillis
Aura novis; ut cum frondosa in valle sub astrum
Pleiadum tacta alta Iovis de fulmine quaercus;
Uno omnis simul afflatu per pascua circum
Grex cadit exitioque ruunt armenta sub uno.
Ter flammam pedibus pernix evaserat Ufens;
Infelix ora obvertit, videt aegra trahentem
Crura patrem exanguemque metu; vestigia retro
Praecipitat prensumque manu ac cervice reclina

Burned and scorched his right hand; after that Eurus hurled
A white-hot timber and sent it spinning into his belly.
As he breathed black smoke from the wound,
He thought of Sarno's water and clear-flowing streams.
Ursidius' mother, a prophetess, gave him a warning
As he went off to war: "Flee fires, my son, keep far from the flames."
Snatched up by the flames, he lamented leaving his mother behind
And the gods who spoke truly and the moist river Arno
And Fiesole his birthplace and the flowering fields.[267]
Three hundred under a hollow cliff, under prickly brush,
The young force chosen for ambush,[268] hid together.
Three hundred were destroyed together by a gust of wind
Packed with fresh ash; as when in a leafy valley just before
The constellation of the Pleiades a tall oak is struck by Jupiter's
Thunderbolt; the whole flock in the pasture by a single blast
Falls dead together, and herds perish in a single disaster.
Three times nimble Ufens[269] had outrun the flames.
He turned his head, poor fellow, and saw his father, weak legged
And dragging along, pale with fear. Quickly he turned on his heel,
Took his hand, bent his head, and draped him over his back.[270]

Impositum trahit et labens incendia vitat;
Improvisum anguem pressit gravis. Ille repente
Implicuit plantae agglomerans; dum se explicat Ufens,
Dum saevit coluber squamosa volumina torquens,
Exiliit fumosa vomens incendia turbo
Absorpsitque Ufentem una colubrumque patremque,
Ufentem, quem ceruleis Feronia in antris
Nutrirat, puer et viridi consueverat umbrae.
Hunc sacrum nymphae nemus, hunc flevere Napeae,
Circaeique sinus, hunc Anxuris ora lacusque
Setini et tacitae rupere silentia Amyclae.
Pervolitat turbo involvens silvasque ferasque;
Densatur coelum fumo, caligine montes
Conduntur fluitantque atrae per summa favillae;
Mox saevi erumpunt ignes, flammaeque coruscant,
Et coelum lambit rutilans et sidera vortex.
Hinc rursus torquente euro per inane volutus
Incumbit campis, truncosque ambustaque versat
Robora, candentemque rapit sese ante procellam.
Suffenum armigerosque duos eadem aura peremit
Cum geminis Vargunteiis Libicoque Gulussa.
Umbronem, Hisponemque, Lacetanumque Biorem,
Hastatosque Numantinos, Nomadumque cohortem,
Cetratamque manum, praeerat cui Turdulus Iscon,

He dragged him along and, stumbling, avoided the fire;
He never saw the snake, and stepped on it hard.[271]
Quickly
It tangled his foot in its coils; while Ufens untangled
himself,
While the snake raged and its scaly coils writhed,
A whirlwind burst forth spewing smoke and flame
And swallowed Ufens and the snake and the father at
once—
Ufens, whom Feronia had reared in a sea-blue cave,
Who as a boy had been used to green shade.
The sacred grove of the nymph wept for him, the
Napaeae wept,
And the bay of Circeo, the shore of Terracina, and the
lake
Of Sezze, and mute Amyclae broke its silence.[272]
The whirlwind roared on, engulfing forests and beasts;
The sky thickened with smoke, the mountains were
covered
In darkness, and black ash floated over the peaks;
Soon raging fires broke out, and the flames flashed,
And the whirling red column licked the sky and the
stars.[273]
Then as Eurus spun it again, it rolled through the void
And fell on the plains, and whirled trunks and burnt
Timbers, sweeping along before the hot-glowing gale.
The same wind snuffed out Suffenus and his two
squires,
Along with the twin Vargunteii and Libyan Gulussa.[274]
Umbro[275] and Hispo and Lacetanan Bior,
And the Numantine spearmen and the Numidian
cohort,
And the shield-bearing force led by Turdulan Iscon—

Iscon, avis atavisque genus qui ducit ab Orco;
Una omnis rapit unda, rapit Varumque Macrumque
Gisconemque Siracusium Garamantaque Bocchum,
Mox raptos flammarum hausit circum acta[30] vorago.
Ut cum Trinacriae campis de vertice summo
Aetna vomit rapidos aestus, it turbine denso
Sullatus coelo fumus, mox rumpit in auras
Flamma furens, volitant rutilae per inane favillae,
Post iactante noto agglomerans flectitque rotatque
Huc illuc; ea lapsa faces iaculatur et altis
Illisa arboribus silvas saltusque vagatur
Incensos; ruit interea, mirabile visu,
Flammarum torrens rapidus liquefactaque saxa
Praecipitat, simul involvens stirpesque ferasque
Tectaque pastoresque; furit Vulcanius amnis
Per valles, per culta; ingens metus urget agrestes
Vicinaeque suis diffidunt moenibus urbes;
Haud aliter pavor invasit, fuga coepta per omnis
Est acies. 'Ite,' exclamat Sertorius, 'ite,
Ite citi, vada nota citi pervadite'; et amnem

Iscon, who traced the ancient line of his fathers back to Orcus—
A single surge seized them all, seized Varus and Macer
And Gisco of Syracuse and Garamantian Bocchus;[276]
Then a wheeling chasm of fire swallowed them up.
As when on the Trinacrian plains Etna pours out
scorching heat[277] from its summit, and in a thick whirlwind
Smoke is carried up to the sky, then raging flame
Bursts into the air, and red ash flies through space; next,
Flung by Notus the south wind, the massing flame turns and spins
This way and that; as it falls, it shoots out firebrands, and hitting
The tree tops, ranges through forests and valleys, setting them
Ablaze; meantime, the rushing torrent of flames runs wild—
An amazing sight!—and brings down molten rock
Headlong, at the same time catching up vegetation and beasts,
Houses and shepherds; the Vulcanian river rages
Through valleys and farms; great terror drives the country folk,
And the cities nearby distrust the walls that protect them;
Just so, fear attacked; all through the battle lines they
Started to flee. "Go!" cried Sertorius. "Go!
Go quickly, quickly cross at the well-known crossing!" and he

Primus obit. Sequiturque ducem sua quemque iuventus
Et circumstetit armatus trans flumina miles.
Forte sub annosa quaercu in convalle silenti
Arcitenens dea saevarum de caede ferarum
Lassa quiescebat, trepido cum excita tumultu
Surgit et ascendit summi iuga pinea montis.
Constitit hic lustrans oculis loca, cernit utramque
Effusam campis aciem, videt agmina et ipsos
Hinc illinc instare duces, saevire protervum
Eurum atque in mediis volitare incendia silvis,
Tot strages, tot fumantes et corporum acervos.
Ingemuit traxitque alto suspiria corde:
Adventare diem quo dux Nursinus acerbo
Casurus fato Hesperiis occumberet arvis.
Nam puerum templo admotum cum sedula mater
Commendat Triviae atque adytis dea grata recondit,
Consuluit fratrem; frater fata abdita pandit:
Ingentem fore et Ispanis per bella, per enses
Regnaturum oris, tamen illum haud tarda manere
Funera, cum pariter flammaeque undaeque faverent

Was first to get to the stream. Each troop followed its leader,
And the men stood in their armor on the opposite bank.
By chance, under an ancient oak, in a quiet glen,
The bow-wielding goddess[278] was resting, weary from slaying
Savage beasts, when roused by the confusion and uproar,
She rose and went up the high mountain's pine-covered ridge.
Here she stood surveying the scene, made out the two
Armies spread out on the plain, saw the hosts and their leaders
Positioned on this side and that, and violent Eurus
Run mad, and flickering fires in the heart of the woods,
So much havoc, so many heaps of dead men clouded with smoke.
She groaned and sighed deep in her heart:
The day was at hand when the Nursian leader[279] would fall
By a bitter fate and lie dead in the fields of Hesperia.
For when his devoted mother brought the boy to her temple,
Commending him to Trivia, and the pleased goddess hid him away
In her shrine, she consulted her brother, who revealed the secrets of fate:
He would become great, and by the swords of war he would rule
On Spanish shores, but no late death awaited him
When flames and water alike came to his side in the fight

Pugnanti armatumque eurus prosterneret hostem.
Fatorum dea facta memor de valle propinqua
Pyrenen iubet acciri; haec nam fida ministra,
Haec comes, huic omnis thalami quoque credita cura.
Illa volat, dictis cui sic dea fatur amicis:
'Nota, soror, tibi fata ducis, quae certa propinquant;
I, propera, fac signa retro, fac agmina vertat;
Pugnatum satis est.' Nec plura effatur; at illa
In cervam conversa noto non segnior ibat.
Ipsa arcum leva stringens dextraque sagittam
Lunavit, simul ut capita accurvata coirent;
Laxavit, simul ut flammas elapsa sagitta
Conciperet. Fulxere aurae, tractu illa corusco
Emicat, et ducis ante pedes affixa reluxit.
Obstupuit tanto monitu Sertorius. Ecce
Cerva per attonitas penetrat non cognita turmas.
Agnovit Triviae famulam dux ac prior inquit:
'Nota venis, nec me fallit dea;' quadrupedemque

And Eurus laid low the armed foe.
Reminded of his destiny, the goddess had Pyrene[280] called
From a valley nearby; for she was her faithful handmaid,
Her companion, to her she entrusted every care of her chamber.
She hastened, and the goddess addressed her in kindly words:
"Sister, you know the fate of the leader, which is fixed and draws near.
Go, hurry, give the sign for retreat, turn back the lines.
The battle has been fought long enough." She said no more.
The other, changed into a deer, went as fast as Notus the south wind.
She herself, bow drawn with her left hand and an arrow with her right,
Made a crescent,[281] so that the curved points came together;
She loosed it, and at the same time the arrow caught fire as it slid away.
The air flashed, the arrow gleamed in its glittering path,
And glowed bright, stuck fast at the feet of the general.
Sertorius was thunderstruck by so great a warning. Suddenly
An unknown doe ran through the astonished throng.
The leader recognized Trivia's servant and addressed her:
"I knew you would come, and the goddess does not disappoint me."

Convertit ripae approperans; praecedit euntem
Pyrene pedibusque micans et cornibus aureis.
Signa canunt reditum. Sequitur tum ferrea pubes,
Oceanoque egressa polum nox occupat atra.

IOANNIS IOVIANI PONTANI
DIALOGUS QVI ANTONIVS INSCRIBITUR
FINIT FELICITER

He turned his four-footed steed to the bank, and
before him
Ran Pyrene with flashing feet and golden horns.
The retreat was sounded. Then the iron-hard soldiery
followed,
And rising from Ocean, black night took over the sky.

THE DIALOGUE ENTITLED ANTONIUS
OF GIOVANNI GIOVIANO PONTANO
ENDS SUCCESSFULLY

Note on the Texts

The texts of *Charon* and *Antonius* in this volume are based on the edition of Carmelo Previtera, *Giovanni Pontano: I Dialoghi* (Florence, 1943), which has been corrected against that of the first edition of 1491 (see below). Since the 1491 edition was printed in Pontano's lifetime and under his supervision, it is the most authoritative source of the text. Following Previtera, I refer to the edition as *Mo* (for the name of its printer, Moravus). I have also consulted the 1501 Venice edition and several modern discussions, noted in the Abbreviations below. Variations from Previtera's edition are signaled in the Notes to the Texts.

I have broken the text into numbered paragraphs. Since so many poems are interspersed in the dialogues, especially in *Antonius*, I have numbered them separately and added line numbers. I have silently corrected misprints in Previtera, and I have also occasionally changed his punctuation.

Pontano's orthography presents a particular problem for editors. Throughout his life Pontano took a serious interest in orthography; but he sometimes changed his mind about what was correct, and he often missed inconsistencies even in manuscripts and editions that he supervised. Previtera was well aware of the difficulty of determining Pontano's preferred spelling. Sometimes he tried to divine Pontano's intentions from his treatise *De aspiratione*; very often, although not consistently, he regularized the orthography of the *Dialogues* to conform to classical usage. In this edition, I have taken a different path, generally following the orthography in *Mo*. *Mo* is not perfectly consistent, but when in doubt I have used the preponderant spelling. I have also been guided by the texts and prefaces of de Nichilo (*Meteororum Liber*), Monti Sabia (*Hendecasyllaborum libri*), and Tateo (*I trattati delle virtù sociali*) for Pontano's spelling preferences.

ABBREVIATIONS

A	*Ioannis Ioviani Pontani opera omnia soluta oratione composita*. Vol. 2. Venice, 1518–19.
B_1	*Ioannis Ioviani Pontani, Librorum omnium, quos soluta oratione composuit, Tomus secundus*. Basel, 1538.
B_2	*Ioannis Ioviani Pontani, Librorum omnium, quos soluta oratione composuit, Tomus secundus*. Basel, 1556.
Mariotti	Scevola Mariotti. "Per lo studio dei dialoghi del Pontano." *Belfagor* 2 (1947): 332–44. Reprinted in his *Scritti medievali e umanistici*, ed. Silvia Rizzo, 261–84. Second edition. Rome, 1994.
Mo	[*Dialogi qui Charon et Antonius inscribuntur*]. Naples: Mathias Moravus. January 31, 1491.
Monti Sabia 1996	Liliana Monti Sabia. "Un ignoto codice del *Charon* di Pontano." In *Studi latini in ricordo di Rita Cappelletto*, 285–309. Urbino, 1996.
Ponte	Giovanni Ponte, ed. *Il Quattrocento*. Bologna, 1966.
Prev	Carmelo Previtera, *Giovanni Pontano: I Dialoghi*. Florence, 1943.
S	*Pontani Actius de numeris poeticis et lege historiae. Aegidius multiplicis argumenti. Tertius dialogus de ingratitudine qui Asinus inscribitur*. Naples, 1507.
Santo	Luigi Santo. "Hirquitulus, hirquiculus, e pisatilis. Nota pontaniana." *Quaderni dell' Istituto di filologia latina* 3 (1971): 79–127.
Terzaghi	Nicola Terzaghi. "Attorno al Pontano." Annali della Scuola Normale Superiore di Pisa: Lettere, storia e filosofia 16 (1947): 200–210.
Ve	*Ioannis Ioviani Pontani opera*. Venice, 1501.

Notes to the Texts

CHARON

1. maximum *Mo*: maximus *Prev*

2. charo *Mo*: caro *Prev*

3. contingit *Mo*: contigit *Prev*

4. septuennes (*see Monti Sabia 1996, 294 n. 33*): septennes *Mo Prev*

5. sint *Mo (see Monti Sabia 1996, 300)*: sunt *Prev*

6. quis *Mo*: quid *Prev*

7. disce *is my emendation*: addisce *Mo Prev*

8. fuit Mo: *omitted by Prev*

ANTONIUS

1. perspectior *is my emendation*: prospectior *Mo Prev. Cf. Cicero In Pisonem* 1.2: 'Homini ille honorem non generi, moribus non maioribus meis, virtuti perspectae non auditae nobilitati deferebat.'

2. concubinarios *is my correction*: concubitarios *Mo Prev*

3. Hosp. *added by Prev*: *omitted in Mo*

4. plenioris morbo *S Prev*: levitate *Mo Ve. Cf. Summonte in S, L4r*: 'Laborabat ex intestini plenioris morbo. Quae quidem loca sic Pontani ipsius manu emendata in eius archtypis leguntur.'

5. ne quidem vidit *Mo*: ne vidit quidem *Prev. (See n. 15 below.)*

6. quod *Quintilian 8.3.11*: qui *Mo Prev*

7. dicetur *Mo*: diceretur *Prev*

8. conflictione causarum *Mo*: causarum conflictione *Prev*

9. *Prev wrongly attributes this speech to the Hospes. Mo reads* Hos, *which Prev has taken for* Ho. *or* Hosp.

10. exuberantia *emendation of J. Hankins*: exuperantia *Mo Prev*

11. *Sc.* exanhelatis

12. *The 1477 edition of Gellius' text, as well as that in modern editions, reads* nimis opimam.

13. videtur *Mo*: videatur *Prev*

14. hyperbolen *Mo*: hyperbolem *Prev*

15. ne quidem nisi *Mo*: ne nisi quidem *Prev. Mariotti 276 points out that the same word order appears in Vat. Lat. 2843 in* Actius: ne quidem cum ipse ait *(and cf. n. 5 above).*

16. Tullio *is my correction*: Tullo *Mo Prev*

17. perreptat *is Ponte's correction (p. 139)*: perrectat *Mo Prev. See also Santo 119–20.*

18. exclamare B_1 B_2: ex . . . exclamare *Mo Prev. But* ex . . . exclamare *is defended by Santo 121.*

19. hirquiculi *Santo 101–2*: hirquituli *Mo Prev*

20. mammae *A*: mamae *Mo Prev*

21. dextram: *Terzaghi 208 n. 1, metri gratia*: dexteram *Mo Prev*

22. guttum *Mo Prev. Pontano has used* guttum *(sc.* guttus*) metri gratia.*

23. volat: *Mariotti 283, metri gratia*: volabat *Mo Prev*

24. interdius *Mo*: interdiu *Prev*

25. flamarum *Mo*: flammarum *Prev*

26. Camillus *Mo*: Miroldus *Ve Prev*

27. undis *Mo Prev*: vadis *Mariotti 283, adducing Vergil,* Aeneid *10.291*

28. ingeminant *Mariotti 283*: ingeminat *Mo Prev*

29. deliterant *Mo*: delituerant *Prev. Deliterant is pluperfect of deliteo, but the perfect stem* delit- *seems unattested elsewhere.*

30. circum acta: *Terzaghi 209, metri causa*: circumacta *Mo Prev*

Notes to the Translations

CHARON

1. Compare Cicero's characterization of Scipio Africanus (*De officiis* 3.1.1): *et in otio de negotiis cogitare* ("even in his free time he thought about the business of the state").

2. "Hoop" (*trochulus*): apparently a coinage by Pontano. For "knowledge of the best things," cf. Cicero, *De oratore* 3.16.60: *rerum optimarum cognitio.*

3. After the people of Aeacus' city had all died of plague, his father, Jupiter, replaced them, transforming ants (Greek *myrmices*) into a new population, the Myrmidons. Ovid tells the story in *Metamorphoses* 7.614–57.

4. Minos is referring to the greatest earthquakes ever to shake the Italian peninsula, the multiple shocks from December 1456 to mid-January 1457. A first-person account is given by Angelo de Tummulillis, *Notabilia temporum,* ed. C. Corvisieri (Livorno, 1980), 69–70. See also Monti, "Ricerche," 261–63. Pontano himself seems to have had a narrow escape, as he relates in *Meteororum liber* 978–81:

> Ut quondam infelix valido Campania motu
> oppressit miseras ipsis cum civibus urbes,
> cum vatem fessae vix eripuere Camoenae
> labenti e thalamo ac tecti minitante ruina.

("As unfortunate Campania once with a powerful earthquake buried wretched cities with their citizens, when the exhausted Muses barely snatched the poet from his falling chamber and the impending collapse of the house.")

5. The setting under the cypresses beside the Styx is an underworld counterpart of the setting under the plane trees beside the Ilissus in Plato, *Phaedrus* 229, but Pontano is probably also thinking of Cicero, *De legibus* 1.14 and fr. 4; *De oratore* 1.28.

6. The sophist's syllogism puns on *Charon* and *caro* ("flesh"), illustrating the logical fallacy of equivocation. The following three syllogisms illustrate the same fallacy.

7. The sophist is punning on the homonyms *palus* ("marsh") and *palus* ("stake" or "post").

8. Charon uses both hands to row; the oar blade (*palma*) makes three. His boat is often pictured as a sort of punt, propelled and steered with a pole — as in a manuscript of *Charon* in the Vatican Library: Urb. lat. 225, fol. 132v (illustrated in Kidwell, *Pontano,* 68).

9. *superstitiosulus* ("superstitious fellow") cf: *superstitiosulae,* (*Antonius* 91): apparently a Quattrocento neologism rather than a coinage by Pontano as Sabbadini suggested (*Storia del Ciceronianismo,* 79). Johann Ramminger's *Neulateinische Wortliste: Ein Wörterbuch des Lateinischen von Petrarca bis 1700, online at http://www.lrz.de/~ramminger/neulateinische_wortliste.htm,* lists the adverbial form *superstitiosule* as appearing in Bruni.

10. I.e., logical discussions and theological discussions, respectively.

11. Pontano seems to be recalling a story of Pythagoras' death in Diogenes Laertius, *Lives of the Philosophers* 8.39. He is apparently using another version in paragraph 9. See Monti Sabia, "Un ignoto codice," 304–6.

12. The reference is to the early Christian doctrine of the harrowing of Hell, Christ's descent into the Underworld after his death, where he released Adam and Eve and other righteous persons who lived before the time of Christ.

13. The "well known Stagirite" is Aristotle, from the town of Stagira in Macedonia. His teacher was Plato. Aristotle was often seen as the proverbial *ingratus discipulus* for having misrepresented and disagreed with Plato's doctrine.

14. A broad summary of the doctrine of Aristotle's *Nicomachean Ethics,* where morality is conceived as rational control of appetites, achieved by holding to a virtuous mean between extremes of vice.

15. "puppy, quail, or jackdaw" (*catellus, coturnix, monedula*): cf. Plautus, *Captivi* 1002–3, *patriciis pueris aut monerulae / aut anites aut coturnices dantur, quicum lusitent* ("patrician boys are given jackdaws or ducks or quails to play with"). Cappelletto, "*lectura Plauti*", 76, 171.

16. A stade is a unit of linear measurement, equivalent to an eighth of a Roman mile. Whether the number of the stars was odd or even was proverbial as an irresolvable question; cf. Cicero, *Lucullus* 32.

17. Illyrians: inhabitants of the western part of the Balkan peninsula, modern Albania.

18. Celtiberians: a mixed Celtic and Iberian people inhabiting the northeastern part of central Spain.

19. The Catalan Pere de Besalú (d. before 1470), conservator general or treasurer for Alfonso the Magnanimous, was widely regarded as extortionate. Pontano treats him harshly also in *Amores* 1.34.16–19 and in *De oboedientia*. (*Opera omnia soluta oratione composita* 1:34r–v). For his duties and powers see Ryder, *Kingdom of Naples*, 205–10.

20. The two cardinals are Lodovico Trevisan (ca. 1401–March 22, 1465) and Juan de Mella (1397–October 13, 1467). Trevisan, a papal chamberlain who was cardinal of San Lorenzo in Damaso as well as patriarch of Aquileia, negotiated the treaty of Terracina (1443) between Alfonso and Pope Eugenius IV. His portrait by Mantegna is in the Gemäldegalerie in Berlin. De Mella was first bishop, then cardinal of Zamora. See Monti, "Ricerche," 265–67.

21. Charon is recalling a famous aphorism of the Greek wise man Solon from Cicero's paraphrase (*De senectute* 26): *qui se cotidie aliquid addiscentem dicit senem fieri* ("he said that he grew old learning something new every day").

22. Mercury is engaging in some untranslatable word play: the shade, like a *mergus* ("gull"), is seen to dive (*mergere*) and then to emerge (*emergere*) from the stream.

23. Crates the Theban was a Cynic philosopher and a follower of Diogenes the Cynic. According to a source in Diogenes Laertius (*Lives of Eminent Philosophers* 6.87), he threw his money into the sea and embraced a life of poverty. Both Diogenes and Crates were known in the Renaissance primarily owing to the pseudonymous letter collections that circulated under their names; both collections were published in Latin around 1475. A scene depicting Crates emptying his wealth into the sea was laid out in

the mosaic pavement of the cathedral in Siena, following a design of Pinturicchio made around 1504.

24. "On the Greek Calends": i.e., never; dating by Calends was only a Roman convention. Cf. Suetonius, *Augustus* 87.

25. A point argued by Leonardo Bruni in his popular *Life of Aristotle* (1428/29). Pontano in general follows Bruni's view of the relative merits of Plato and Aristotle.

26. Philosophy and especially theology in Renaissance Italy was dominated by members of religious orders, particularly the Dominicans and Franciscans.

27. On Apuleius' braying (*subrudebat*) cf. Lorenzo Valla (*In errores Antonii Raudensis adnotationes* in *Opera omnia* [Basel, 1540; repr. Turin 1962], 1:414): *Quid dicam de Apuleio, in eo praesertim opere, cuius nomen est de asino aureo? Cuius sermonem si quis imitetur, non tam auree loqui, quam nonnihil rudere videatur.* ("What shall I say about Apuleius, especially in the work entitled the *Golden Ass?* If anyone were to imitate its language, he would seem not so much to speak golden words as to bray.")

28. *deambulatiuncula* ("brief stroll"): apparently a Renaissance coinage. It appears in Bruni, *Ep.* 4.12; Poggio, *Ep. fam.* 2.8.13. See Ramminger, *Neulateinische Wortliste* s.v.

29. Pontano would have known the Clitumnus well, for it runs near his native Cerreto.

30. *roratilis* ("dewy"): perhaps a coinage by Pontano. He uses it again in *Hesperides* 1.444.

31. *moerentiolum* ("mourning flower"): perhaps a coinage by Pontano.

32. Ovid tells how Apollo mistakenly killed his lover Hyacinth, whose blood he transformed into the flower that bears his name, inscribing the letters AI AI ("woe! woe!") on its petals (*Metamorphoses* 10.210–16).

33. The ancients marked happy days with a white pebble (see Catullus 68.148). Porphyrio in his commentary on Horace, *Odes* 1.36.10 says that it was a Cretan custom; a white stone was dropped into the quiver for a fortunate day, a black stone for an unlucky one. Cf. also *Baiae* 1.12.7 (*candidis lapillis*).

34. Mercury uses the word "lictor" in its precise technical sense: "an officer whose functions were to attend upon a magistrate, bearing the fasces before him, and to execute sentence of judgement upon offenders" (*Oxford English Dictionary*).

35. See n. 4 above.

36. Mercury is referring to Halley's comet, which appeared in June 1456. Pontano recalls it in his *Commentary on Ptolemy*: "Nobis adolescentibus insignis etiam cometes ad orientem in Cancri Leonisque regionibus multis diebus fulsit, tantae longitudinis ut amplius quam duo coeli signa comae suae tractu occuparet. Eum secuta est Alphonsi regis mors quae Aemiliam, Sabinam, Campaniam, universumque regnum Neapolitanum et longo et gravi bello implicavit. Secuta est etiam pestilentia aliquanto diuturnior." See *Commentationes in Centum Sententiis Ptolemaei*, 2.100. In *Opera omnia soluta oratione composita* (Venice, 1518–19) 3:91v. ("When I was young, a notable comet shone for several days in the east in the area of Cancer and Leo. It was long enough to take up more than the space of two constellations. It was followed by the death of King Alfonso [June 27, 1458], which involved Emilia, Sabina, Campania, and the whole kingdom of Naples in a long and grievous war. A somewhat longer pestilence also followed.") See Monti, "Ricerche," 263–64. See also Tummulillis, *Notabilia temporum*, 63.

37. Horace, *Epistles* 1.2.14. When Achilles and Agamemnon quarreled and Achilles withdrew from the fighting, the Greeks (Achaeans) were beaten back and slaughtered by the Trojans.

38. Pontano perhaps refers either to the phenomenon of May 28, 1456, or to that of September 1456, both described by Tummulillis (*Notabilia temporum*, 70, 135).

39. November 11. Since St. Martin's Day was followed by forty days of fasting, it was celebrated with a burst of proleptic eating and drinking. Pontano refers to the alcoholic aspects of the celebration much more enthusiastically in his poetry. *Eridanus* 1.35 begins: *Martinum conviva saturque et potus adoret* ("Let the guest adore Martin sated and drunk"); see also *Hendecasyllabi* 1.17.

40. *lagenatus* ("drunk as a lord") may be a coinage by Pontano. Its meaning seems to be "bottled," i.e., "completely drunk" (René Hoven, *Lexique de la prose latine de la Renaissance* [Leiden-Boston, 2006], s.v.).

41. Early in May the Neapolitans celebrated their patron saint, San Gennaro, with processions through the city and masses in the cathedral that is dedicated to him.

42. I have slightly mistranslated Pontano's *campanis* ("bells") as "campaniles" to preserve Charon's pun with "Campanians." Rabelais, no doubt remembering this passage, attributed the hatred of bells to Pontano himself: "C'estoyt Pontanus poete seculier—qu'il desyroit qu'elles [cloches] feussent de plume, et le batail feust d'une queue de renard: pource qu'elles luy engendroient la chronique aux tripes du cerveau quant il composoyt ses verses carminiformes." ("It was the secular poet Pontano who wanted bells made of feathers and the clapper of a fox's tail because they made his head throb when he was writing his poetic verses."), *Gargantua*, ed. Ruth Calder (Geneva, 1970), chapter 18.

43. The anecdote of Timon and the fig tree appears in Plutarch's *Life of Antony* (70.4–5) and was picked up by Shakespeare (*Timon of Athens* v.i.210–17). Timon, a famous misanthrope, lived in voluntary isolation. One day he announced to his fellow Athenians that he had a fig tree on which many had hanged themselves and offered prospective suicides the chance to use it before he cut it down. Pontano has Charon give an underworld twist to the story.

44. The ancient philosopher Diogenes was called "cynic" (i.e., "doglike" in Greek) because of his shameless behavior. Hence the name Cynic for his brand of philosophy.

45. *piscicanis* ("dogfish"): an apparent coinage by Pontano.

46. Pontano is recalling the story that Diogenes, responding to Plato's definition of man as an "animal, biped and featherless," plucked a chicken and brought it into Plato's school, saying, "this is Plato's man" (Diogenes Laertius, *Lives of the Philosophers* 6.40). But in his telling, as Monti Sabia points out ("Un ignoto codice," 303–4), the biped is feminine and feathered (*pennatam*), not masculine and plucked. Pontano's Diogenes presents Plato with a hen, and one possibly still alive. Plato's comment on Diog-

enes' muscles and the detail about Diogenes as a gladiator seem to be Pontano's inventions.

47. Diogenes is supposed to have lived in a tub (Diogenes Laertius, *Lives of the Philosophers*, 6.23); various stories are told about his meeting with Alexander (e.g., in *Lives of the Philosophers* 6.38 and 68; Cicero, *Tusculan Disputations* 5.92; Plutarch, *Life of Alexander* 14); and he was renowned for his coarse behavior. But the story of his powerful fart may be an invention by Pontano.

48. Charon and Mercury saw Crates in paragraphs 20–21. He is still looking for the money he threw into the sea.

49. "May you enjoy better fortune:" i.e., in the search for his money. This is presumably ironic, since according to Diogenes Laertius 6.87, Diogenes the Cynic convinced Crates to throw his wealth into the sea so as to make himself independent of fortune. In the same vein, perhaps, is Diogenes' desire for mullet, since in the letters of pseudo-Crates (no. 14, ed. Hercher, p. 210), Crates advises his disciples to accustom themselves to bread and water and to avoid wine and fish, lest they become bestial or soft.

50. After taking Constantinople (1453), the Turks conquered Greece; Athens fell in 1458. The "lament for Greece" was a common theme of humanist eloquence of the 1450s.

51. The region of Epiros in northwest Greece is now part of Albania. The Liburnians inhabited the area between Dalmatia and the Istrian peninsula. By the mid-1460s most of the Balkan Peninsula was under Turkish control. See Monti, "Ricerche," 267–69.

52. I.e., Rhadamanthus, mentioned as being on duty by himself in paragraph 2.

53. Mercury's words (*phaselus ille . . . vectoribus*) imitate both the phrasing and the meter (iambic trimeter) of Catullus 4.1: *phaselus ille quem videtis, hospites* ("that bark you see, my friends"). But Catullus' poem is in *pure* iambic trimeter, which allows no substitutions.

54. Maia, the daughter of Atlas, was Mercury's mother. His father was Jupiter.

55. Cf. *Aeneid* 1.195–96: *vina bonus quae deinde cadis onerarat Acestes / litore Trinacrio* ("the wine that good Acestes had stowed in jars on the coast of Sicily"). The number of wine jars and some trivia in Pedanus' next speech are indebted to Juvenal's ironic list of details that the *grammaticus* should know: *dicat / nutricem Anchisae, . . . / . . . dicat quot Acestes vixerit annis, / quot Siculi Phrygibus vini donaverit urnas* (*Satire* 7.233–36). ("Let him identify the nurse of Anchises . . . let him say how many years Acestes lived, how many jars of Sicilian wine he gave to the Trojans.")

56. Oenosios: Pontano has coined the name from Greek *oinos* ("wine").

57. Hipparchus was a famous Greek astronomer of the second century BCE.

58. Vergil says that the Italian town Gaeta took its name from Aeneas' nurse Caieta, who died on the site: *Tu quoque litoribus nostris, Aeneia nutrix, / aeternam moriens famam, Caieta, dedisti* (*Aeneid* 7.1–2). ("You, too, nurse of Aeneas, in your death gave eternal fame to our shores.") The death and burial of Misenus are related at *Aeneid* 6.158–235.

59. The Greek hero Palamedes (whose name means "the contriving one") is best known for tricking Odysseus into joining the Greek expedition against Troy and his subsequent destruction by Odysseus' own cleverness, but he is also supposed to have invented some of the letters of the Greek alphabet (Hyginus, *Fabulae* 277.1).

60. Naucis: the rower's name is coined from Greek *naus* ("ship").

61. "descendant of Atlas": Mercury's mother, Maia, was a daughter of Atlas. The schoolmaster is showing off.

62. Cf. Caesar, *De bello gallico* 1.1: *Gallia est omnis divisa in partes tres*.

63. Theanus was too ignorant to realize that Caesar was referring to Gallic wagons (*carros*), not Roman chariots (*curros*).

64. Pedum was an ancient town not far from Rome. Horace places Tibullus in a country seat there in *Epistle* 1.4.2: *quid nunc te dicam facere in regione Pedana?* ("what shall I say you are doing in the district of Pedum?").

65. Tibullus 1.6.82.

66. According to Jerome, Lucretius wrote *De rerum natura* in the intervals of madness caused by a love potion and ultimately committed suicide.

67. Lucretius 5.719. Modern texts read not *quod* ("a thing that"), but *quia* ("because"): "nor is it possible for it to be seen because it moves without light."

68. Recalling his own schooldays, Juvenal says (*Satire* 1.15): "Well then, we too put our hand under the rod" (*et nos ergo manum ferulae subduximus*).

69. Pedanus had addressed Mercury (pedantically) as "Arcadian God." Mercury returns the favor with "Arcadian schoolmaster"—unkindly, since the Arcadians were proverbially rustic and stupid. He is probably also alluding to Juvenal, *Satire* 7.160, where a doltish schoolboy is called *Arcadico iuveni* ("Arcadian youth").

70. The scene between Theanus and Pedanus parodies the grammatical dispute between Valla and Poggio. (Ferraù, *Pontano critico*, 13–14 note 1). The argument about the use of *debeo* echoes the exchange of Poggio and Valla over a passage in Terence. Valla: *scribi debet* (*Elegantie* 2.15, in *Opera omnia* 1:54); Poggio: *scribi debuisse* (*Oratio* 1, in *Opera omnia*, ed. R. Fubini, 4 vols. [Turin, 1964–69], 1:198); Valla: *non enim dixi scribi debuisse, sed scribi debere* (*Antidotum Primum: La prima apologia contro Poggio Bracciolini*, ed. Ari Wesseling [Amsterdam, 1978], 1.38).

71. Priscian (fifth-sixth century CE) was a prominent and influential grammarian.

72. *grammaticunculi* ("foolish little grammarians"): probably Pontano's coinage. It is a diminutive of the diminutive *grammaticulus* ("little grammarian").

73. The explanation of *lapis* depends on a false etymology from Isidore of Seville: *Lapis autem dictus quod laedat pedem* (*Etymologiae* 16.3.1). Pontano has Menicellus create an etymology for *petra* on the same principle. Isidore derived the components of *lapis* from the first syllables of *laedit* ("harms") and *pedem* ("foot"); Menicellus derives *petra* from the first syllables in *pede* ("foot") and *teratur* ("is ground"). The focus on grammatical gender is the starting point for a series of *doubles entendres* continuing into the next exchange. *Lapis* is masculine because it plays the active role; *petra*

is acted upon, hence feminine and passive. The joke depends on the frequent use of *tero* to describe the sexual act (cf. the pun in Plautus, *Captivi* 888: *Boius est, boiam terit*) and the fact that the term "passive" can be used of sex as well as grammar.

74. Menicellus' joke depends on the sexual senses of "doing a job" (*faciendo opere;* cf. Plautus, *Asinaria* 873) and "is passive" (*patitur*).

75. More innuendo. Among the Romans, *manus* represented the legal power a man had over his wife, hence my translation "marriage." *Coeo* ("come together"; cf. English "coitus") and various words meaning "beat" are often used of the sexual act; see J. N. Adams, *The Latin Sexual Vocabulary* (London, 1982), 178–79, 145–49. *Coeo* is also used in a sexual sense in sections 54, 55.

76. "Naples among the Oscans": since the Oscans (early inhabitants of Campania) were proverbial for stupidity, Menicellus is insulting Pontano and his friends. One of the humanists' favorite meeting places was in the area called *ad Arcum* from its proximity to a medieval tower built on four arches at the intersection of via Nilo, via Atri, and via Tribunali. Both Pontano and Panormita lived nearby. For the tower, see Ferdinando Ferrajoli, *Napoli monumentale* (Naples, 1981), 162.

77. Antonio Panormita (Antonio Beccadelli, 1394–1471) is the subject of *Antonius.* He was Pontano's mentor and predecessor as head of the Neapolitan academy. His neologism *epistolutia* is apparently coined on Italian *epistoluccia.* See Sabbadini, *Storia del Ciceronianismo,* 79; Mariotti, "Per lo studio dei *Dialoghi* del Pontano," 261.

78. Pontano has Mercury coin *grammaticonem* ("grammaticone") from Italian, using the stem *grammatic-* + the disparaging suffix *-one,* denoting excessive size. See ibid., 261 n.

79. The harlot may be from Cyprus, but prostitutes were often called Cyprians since the island was famous in antiquity for its cults of Aphrodite.

80. The story of the girl deceived by the priest has important elements in common with that told by Pontano's friend Masuccio Salernitano (1410–75) in *Il Novellino* 1.2, ed. A. Mauro (Bari, 1940; repr., ed. S. Nigro, Bari and Rome, 1975). The strongest parallels are in the seduction scene, presented as a blasphemous travesty of religious ritual by both authors.

Masuccio dedicated *Il Novellino* 1.3 to Pontano, and Pontano commemorated Masuccio's death in *Tumuli* 1.36.

81. In coining *castigatulum* Pontano was perhaps thinking of Ovid's description of his mistress at *Amores* 1.5.21: *quam castigato planus sub pectore venter* ("how flat her belly under her *taut* chest").

82. Plowing is an ancient and common sexual metaphor, but *ager* ("field") is much more frequent in such contexts than *fundus* ("farm"). Pontano is probably thinking of a line in the same passage from Plautus' *Asinaria* that he used in paragraph 52 (a wife's complaint about her adulterous husband): *fundum alienum arat, incultum familiarem deserit* ("he tills someone else's farm, and leaves his own untilled"; *Asinaria,* 874). See n. 74 above.

83. The shade embodies views like those of the "laughing philosopher" Democritus, as portrayed, for example, by Seneca (*De tranquillitate animi* 15.2–5; *De ira* 2.10.5) and Lucian, (*Philosophies for Sale,* 13). But his views are those of a generic Hellenistic philosopher rather than those of the historical Democritus, the pre-Socratic philosopher of the fifth century BCE. Democritus as the "laughing philosopher" was traditionally paired with Heraclitus, the "weeping philosopher," perhaps alluded to in §62. On the history of the legend, see Thomas Rütten, *Demokrit, lachender Philosoph et sanguinischer Melancholiker: Eine pseudohippokratische Geschichte* (Leiden, 1992).

84. If this shade represents Heraclitus, he is depicted very unsympathetically. For Heraclitus, see Diogenes Laertius 9.1.

85. Cf. Plautus, *Mercator,* 361: *muscast meu' pater, nil potest clam illum haberi* ("my father is a fly; nothing can be kept from him"). Pontano both marked the phrase *musca est* in his manuscript of Plautus (Vienna, Österreiches Nationalbibliothek MS lat. 3168) and wrote it in the margin; see Cappelletto, *"lectura Plauti" del Pontano,* 92–93, 175.

86. The old man was an alchemist.

87. The Umbrian shade defines happiness in ethical terms ("right action" and "correct understanding"), alluding to and correcting the purely intellectual and philosophical visions of Lucretius (see especially *De rerum natura* 1.62–79) and Vergil (*Georgics* 2.490–92):

felix qui potuit rerum cognoscere causas
atque metus omnis et inexorabile fatum
subiecit pedibus strepitumque Acherontis avari.

("Happy the man who has been able to learn the causes of things and has cast beneath his feet all fears and relentless fate and the uproar of greedy Acheron.") The shade's speech contains elements of Aristotelian and Stoic ethics but does not indicate clear dogmatic commitments to any one school.

88. The meter is a mixture of dactyls and spondees. The first and third verses of each stanza consist of a dactylic hemiepes (– ∪ ∪ – ∪ ∪ –) followed by an adonic (– ∪ ∪ – –); the two segments are separated by diaeresis, and substitutions of spondees for dactyls are allowed in the first segment. The second and fourth verses consist of two spondees (– – – –), followed by an adonic, with diaeresis between the two segments.

89. The meter in the first three verses of each stanza is trochaic dimeter; that of the fourth verse is a hemiepes followed by an adonic, with diaeresis between the segments.

ANTONIUS

1. Compater (Petrus Compater): Pietro Golino (1431–1501), a close friend of Pontano's for over fifty years. He is also an interlocutor in *Actius*, and his death is lamented in *Aegidius*. He is the dedicatee of both books of *Tumuli* and of *Commentationes super centum sententiis Ptolemaei* and the addressee of *Baiae* 1.9; he is celebrated in *Tumuli* 2.19 and mentioned in *Parthenopeus* 1.26, *Baiae* 1.1, 1.10, 2.28.

2. Antonio: Antonio Beccadelli, called Panormita (1394–1471), Pontano's mentor and predecessor as head of the group of Neapolitan humanists who frequently gathered under the arcades of a portico on Via dei Tribunali. The name "Porticus Antoniana" was regularly used for both the arcades and the group. See Hankins, "Humanist Academies," 36. Panormita is the dedicatee of *De laudibus divinis* 1, celebrated in *Tumuli* 1.20, the addressee of *Parthenopeus* 1.27, and mentioned in *Tumuli* 2.34.

3. Panormita lived on Via Nilo, around the corner from the portico on Via dei Tribunali. For his house, see Ferrajoli, *Napoli monumentale,* 156–62.

4. Enrico Poderico (Erricus or Herricus Pudericus, died between 1472 and 1475), a Neapolitan aristocrat and courtier. He is celebrated in *Tumuli* 1.28, *De sermone* 4.3.12, and *De beneficentia* 7. See C. Minieri Riccio, *Biografie degli accademici alfonsini detti poi Pontaniani dal 1442 al 1543* (Naples, 1991; repr. Bologna, 1969), 152–56; Monti Sabia, "*Bellum Sertoriacum* di Giovanni Pontano," 725 n.61.

5. A legendary fourth-century Sicilian martyr, invoked against various diseases, including epilepsy, and against dog bites and snake bites.

6. The meter of lines 1–8 is glyconic; line 9 is a hexameter. See Mariotti, "Per lo studio," 283–84.

7. *pellicanus* ("dog averter"): a coinage by Pontano.

8. Polignano: Polignano a Mare, an ancient town on the east coast of Apulia.

9. The Oscans were an Italic people who lived in the territory around Naples in Roman times. The phrase "Osce loqui," speak like an Oscan," meant to use foul or lewd language according to Festus' popular etymological dictionary.

10. Branca (whom Pontano calls Blancas) has been identified by Monti ("Ricerche," 283 n. 126) as the physician mentioned by Elisio Calenzio (*Opuscula* 1503, 63v): "Orpiane, si tibi nasum restitui vis ad me veni. Profecto res est apud homines mira Branca Siculus ingenio vir egregio didicit nares inserere quas vel de brachio reficit vel de servis mutuatas impingit." ("Orpianus, if you want your nose restored, come to me. Indeed, people are amazed at the thing; the gifted Sicilian Branca has learned how to insert nostrils that he either fashions from an arm or borrows from slaves and fastens on.") For Calenzio see section 17 and n. 27 below. For Branca de'Branca of Catania and his high reputation in the history of rhinoplasty, see William Eamon, *The Professor of Secrets: Mystery, Medicine and Alchemy in Renaissance Italy* (Washington, D.C., 2010), 94. Branca's arrival in Naples around 1450 was noted by the historian Pietro Ranzano.

11. "See to it that, etc.": the language is that of the ancient *senatus consultum ultimum* ("ultimate decree of the senate"), passed by the Roman senate in times of extreme emergency and granting magistrates extraordinary powers, including summary execution of those thought to be dangerous to the state. Cf. Cicero, *In Catilinam* 1.2.4; Caesar, *De bello civili* 1.5.3.

12. Pontano's house was on Via dei Tribunali. It is the setting for *Aegidius*. See Ferrajoli, *Napoli monumentale*, 162–75.

13. *pilleatulus* ("little fellow in the felt hat"): a coinage of Pontano's. See Sabbadini, *Storia del Ciceronianismo*, 79.

14. As in section 7, the text refers to the speaker as PER (i.e., *peregrinus*, "stranger" or "traveler"), but this Greek speaker is clearly not the same person as the agitated traveler above.

15. "The best is water," Pindar, *Olympian* 1.1.

16. "But gold, like fire blazing in the night, outshines haughty wealth," Pindar, *Olympian* 1.1–2.

17. *suffarcinatulus* ("puffed-up fellow"): a coinage of Pontano's. See Sabbadini, *Storia del Ciceronianismo*, 79.

18. Ladislas, king of Naples (ca. 1376–1414), one of the last Angevin rulers of the Regno.

19. Cf. Cicero, *Cat.* 1.1.2: *O tempora, o mores!*

20. The meter is elegiac couplet.

21. The Old Man reverses the argument made by the swarthy lover in Vergil (*Eclogue* 2.17–18): *O formose puer, nimium ne crede colori: / alba ligustra cadunt, vaccinia nigra leguntur* ("O beautiful boy, don't pay too much attention to color; / white privet blossoms fall, dark violets are gathered").

22. *asserenascit* ("evening is near"): a coinage of Pontano's. See Sabbadini, *Storia del Ciceronianismo*, 79.

23. Cf. Vergil, *Aeneid* 6.417–21, and especially the phrase *offam/obicit* (420–21). The phrase became proverbial, meaning "to lull a monster to sleep," or "keep a monster quiet."

24. Both Cicero (*De divinatione* 1.24.49) and Livy (21.22.8) report Hannibal's dream, which foretold that Italy would be laid to waste by his in-

vasion. Pontano's version is closer to Cicero's: *tum visam beluam vastam et immanem circumplicatam serpentibus, quacumque incederet, omnia arbusta, virgulta, tecta pervertere* ("then he saw a great wild beast twined round with serpents, and wherever it went it overturned all bushes, vegetation, houses").

25. In fact, Pontano uses new words in the description, coining *dentitono* and *hinnifremo* (and probably *candelabror*). See Sabbadini, *Storia del Ciceronianismo*, 79.

26. Father Dis: Pluto. Pontano is misquoting: the claim was made by the Gauls. Cf. Caesar, *Bellum Gallicum* 6.18.1: *Galli se omnes ab Dite patre prognatos praedicant* ("The Gauls claim that they were all spung from Father Dis").

27. Elisio Calenzio (Elisius Gallutius, Luigi Gallucci, 1430–1502/3), a poet and tutor of Federico, the future king of Naples. He is the dedicatee of *Parthenopeus* 2.10 and *Baiae* 2.2, mentioned in *Baiae* 1.10, and mourned in *Aegidius*. Andrea Contrario, a peripatetic and polemical humanist. He was born in Venice, but settled in Naples in the 1470s. He is celebrated as a philosopher in *Baiae* 2.3.

28. "This college": the Accademia Pontaniana.

29. To wish someone "opulent health" would be regarded by a strict grammarian as a fault of style, a catachresis or use of a word (wealth) in an inappropriate context (wishing someone health).

30. *oscitatius* ("yawn-making"): probably a coinage by Pontano.

31. Andrea is quoting from Quintilian, *Institutio oratoria* 10.1.109 and 112. Modern editions of 10.1.109 read *in quo totas vires*, not *in quem totas virtutes*. Since Lorenzo Valla was known for praising Quintilian at the expense of Cicero as a teacher of Latin eloquence, he is perhaps the target of Pontano's attack. Valla would count as a "grammarian" for Pontano owing to his well-known work, *De elegantiis linguae Latinae* (begun 1443, first printed 1471). Another possible target is Giuniano Maio, a student of Valla who taught grammar and rhetoric at the Neapolitan Studio. For Pontano's debts to Valla, however, see Nauta, "Philology as Philosophy."

32. Cicero, *De inventione* 1.5.6, quoted by Quintilian, *Institutio oratoria* 2.15.5; cf. Cicero, *De oratore* 1.31.138. Andrea will conflate Cicero's position with that of Boethius in *De topicis differentiis* 4 (see below). Cicero distinguishes between the orator's task or duty (*officium*) and his end (*finis*). It is his *officium* to speak in a persuasive manner, his *finis* to persuade with speech (*De inv.* 1.5.6). Boethius sees two ends, the one internal to the orator (performing his task of speaking in a persuasive manner) and the other external (actually persuading).

33. Andrea is paraphrasing Boethius, *De topicis differentiis* 4.1206C–D. For a translation and commentary, see E. Stump, *Boethius's De topicis differentiis* (Ithaca, 1978), 80.

34. Cf. Boethius, *De topicis differentiis* 4.1208D–1209A.

35. Cf. Quintilian, *Institutio oratoria* 2.15.38: *nam si est ipsa bene dicendi scientia, finis eius et summum est bene dicere.*

36. "to persuade by speech" (*persuadere dictione*): Cicero, *De inventione* 1.5.6.

37. Cf. Quintilian, *Institutio oratoria* 2.15.6–9.

38. Cicero, *De inventione* 1.5.6. Modern editions read *quod in officio, quid fieri, in fine, quid effici conveniat, consideratur* ("In duty one considers what should be done; in purpose, what should be accomplished").

39. See Aristotle, *Nicomachean Ethics* 1.2, 1094a.

40. Quintilian, *Institutio oratoria* 2.14.2. Modern editions read *effertur,* not *efferetur.*

41. Quintilian, *Institutio oratoria* 8.3.11–13.

42. *Status:* a rhetorical term meaning the point at issue.

43. *labyrinthiplexia:* "labyrinthitis" or "being tied up in knots." A coinage, whether by Panormita or Pontano himself. The paternity of its second element, *plexia,* is appropriately confusing, simultaneously suggesting both a parallel with *apoplexia* ("apoplexy") and a connection with complexity (cf. *plecto,* "tie, twine") and recalling (more remotely, given the initial "p") *lexis* ("language").

44. Either Pontano or the text is in error. The passage appears in Livy 3.63.10.

45. Livy 5.28.4.

46. Livy 3.68.1.

47. Enrico ends with a little word play, using another form of "fill" (*expleo*), here with the ablative.

48. Cicero, *De inventione* 1.8.10.

49. Quintilian, *Institutio oratoria* 3.6.4–5.

50. Quintilian, *Institutio oratoria* 3.6.6.

51. A standard example of definition; e.g., Quintilian, *Institutio oratoria* 7.3.15, or Porphyry, *Isagoge* 2.4.

52. Pontano is struggling to express in humanist Latin the logical ideas of extension and inversion. In a true definition, the inverse is also true because both terms of the proposition have the same extension, i.e., they refer to the same number of objects. Quintilian's definition is defective because one term denotes more objects than the other. Boethius, *De topicis differentiis* 1.1178A, explains the reversibility of a true definition using the same example (the definition of man as a rational mortal animal).

53. Antonio was a fellow Sicilian, having been born in Palermo.

54. *Virgiliocarpos* ("Vergil-shredders") seems to be a coinage by Pontano. *Vergiliomastix* ("Vergil-scourger"), used by Servius at *Eclogue* 2.23 and *Aeneid* 5.521, is modeled on *Homeromastix,* used of the Alexandrian critic Zoilus.

55. Claudian, *De raptu Proserpinae* 1.163–65.

56. Vergil, *Aeneid* 3.570–77.

57. Favorinus' comparison of the descriptions of Etna by Pindar and Vergil in Aulus Gellius, *Noctes Atticae* 17.10 was a staple in discussions of Vergil. For this sentence, cf. Gellius 17.10.10 (*Audite nunc inquit Vergilii versus, quos inchoasse eum verius dixerim, quam fecisse*) and 17.10.5–6 (*Nam quae reliquit perfecta expolitaque quibusque inposuit census atque dilectus sui supremam manum, omni poeticae venustatis laude florent; sed quae procrastinata sunt ab eo, ut post recenserentur, et absolvi, quoniam mors praeverterat, nequiverunt, nequaquam poetarum elegantissimi nomine atque iudicio digna sunt*). See also Macrobius, *Saturnalia* 5.17.7–11.

58. Cf. Gellius, *Noctes Atticae* 17.10.18. In Gellius this criticism is ascribed to Favorinus.

59. Vergil, *Aeneid* 7.187–88.

60. The name "Fabarinus," which can be translated as "little prick," is a bilingual jest. One of the meanings of Italian *fava* ("bean") is membrum virile; but *fava* in Latin is *faba,* hence *Fabarinus.* The jest gains additional point from the fact that Favorinus was a congenital eunuch; see Maud W. Gleason, *Making Men: Sophists and Self-Presentation in Ancient Rome* (Princeton, 1995), 3–8.

61. Gellius quotes Pindar's Greek without translating it. The Latin translation is found in early editions of Gellius, e.g., in the edition printed in Venice in 1477, fol. t8v.

62. Cf. Pindar, *Pythian* 1.21–26; Gellius 17.10.9; Macrobius, *Saturnalia.* 5.17.9. According to Leofranc Holford-Strevens, *Aulus Gellius: An Antonine Scholar and His Achievement* (Oxford, 2003), 172 n. 50, Gellius' text lacked Pindar's *petras* as the object of *pherei* (*fert*).

63. *glomeratus:* perhaps a coinage by Pontano.

64. I.e., *bocca* (*volcanica*). A *crater* in Latin is a shallow mixing bowl.

65. Vergil, *Georgics* 1.472–73.

66. *fabulosum commentum:* cf. Martianus Capella 8.817, *fabulosisque commentis Grai complevere caelum* ("And the Greeks filled the sky with mythological fictions"). Pontano uses the phrase again in paragraph 57.

67. Vergil, *Aeneid* 3.578–82. Modern editions read *mutet* rather than *motet.*

68. Cf. Gellius, *Noctes Atticae* 17.10.8: *eiusmodi sententias et verba molitus est, ut Pindaro quoque ipso, qui nimis opima pinguique esse facundia existimatus est, insolentior hoc quidem in loco tumidiorque sit.* ("He piled up thoughts and words of such a kind that at least in this passage he is even more extravagant and bombastic than Pindar himself, whose eloquence was considered excessively luxuriant and rich.") Pontano omits Gellius' *nimis* ("excessively") before *opimam.*

69. Cf. Gellius, *Noctes Atticae* 17.10.13–15. Pontano's *fluxum fumi calidi* and *ignis fluenta* are based on glosses of Gellius' Greek (*rhoon kapnou aithona, id*

est fluxum fumi calidi; kronous, id est fluenta) in early editions; cf. Venice 1477, fol. t8v. Pontano takes *crasse* ("inartistically") and *duriter* ("awkwardly") from Gellius 17.10.14–15; *improprie* ("incorrectly") translates ἀκύρως in 17.10.15.

70. Pontano's dating here is very loose: according to the Global Volcanism Program of the Smithsonian Institution, the most recent eruption in Ischia occurred in 1302. Pontano refers to this eruption also in *Eclogue* 1.5.30–32, *Meteororum liber* 998–1002, and *De bello Neapolitano* 6 (*Opera omnia*, 1518–19, vol. 3, 310v).

71. Carlo II d'Angiò (1248–1309).

72. Macrobius, *Saturnalia* 5.17.1–4. He uses the words "trivial and childish" (*leve nimisque puerile*) at *Sat.* 5.17.2. In Vergil the war is started when the Trojans kill a stag treated as a pet by the Latins (*Aeneid* 7.475–539).

73. *praesumptonem* ("a great presumptuous fellow"): a coinage of Pontano's; see Sabbadini, *Storia del Ciceronianismo*, 79. Previtera, *Giovanni Pontano: I Dialoghi*, 315, notes that it makes a jingle with *nebulonem* in the preceding line.

74. *praedocinium* ("brigandage") seems to be a coinage by Pontano; it is modeled on *latrocinium*. See Previtera, 315.

75. The "woman" is Silvia, who especially treasured the stag. Cf. *Aeneid* 7.503–4: *Silvia . . . / auxilium vocat et duros conclamat agrestis.*

76. *Aeneid* 7.386–600. Juno summons the greatest of the Furies (Allecto), who inflames Amata with madness and calls the Latins to war against the urgings of king Latinus.

77. For "Atina renews its arms," cf. *Aeneid* 7.629–31: *quinque adeo magnae positis incudibus urbes / tela nouant, Atina potens Tiburque superbum, / Ardea Crustumerique et turrigerae Antemnae.* For "Mezentius is first to come to war," cf. *Aeneid* 7.647–48: *primus init bellum . . . / . . . Mezentius.* The women not refusing weapons are the Amazons, led by Camilla (on whom see esp. 7.803–17; 11.498–596, 648–867).

78. Allecto's snaky locks play an important part in *Aeneid* 7 (see 7.329, 346–53, 447–51).

79. Juvenal, *Satire* 7.70–71. Allecto sounds a war trumpet at *Aeneid* 7.513–25.

80. Macrobius, *Saturnalia* 5.17.4.

81. Most of these examples are taken from *Saturnalia* 1 *praef.*:

"to process into digestion" and "to go into the memory and intellect": *Idem in his quibus aluntur ingenia praestemus, ut quaecumque hausimus non patiamur integra esse, ne aliena sint, sed in quandam digeriem concoquantur: alioquin in memoriam ire possunt, non in ingenium* (*Sat.* 1 *praef.* 7).

"to grow into an increment": *Homerus* Ἔριν, *hoc est contentionem, a parvo dixit incipere, et postea in incrementum ad caelum usque subcrescere* (*Sat.* 5.13.31).

"I wish this present work such a thing": *Tale hoc praesens opus volo* (*Sat.* 1 *praef.* 10).

"native elegance of the Roman accent": *si in nostro sermone nativa Romani oris elegantia desideretur* (*Sat.* 1 *praef.* 12).

"to promise a heap of things worth knowing": *praesens opus non eloquentiae ostentationem sed noscendorum congeriem pollicetur* (*Sat.* 1 *praef.* 4).

82. Cf. Macrobius, *Saturnalia* 1 *praef.* 11: *nos sub alio ortos caelo Latinae linguae vena non adiuvet.*

83. Cf. Cicero, *Tusculanae disputationes* 1.1.1.

84. For "mythological fictions" (*commentis fabulosis*) see n. 66. The Renaissance generally accepted the attribution of the late ancient epic poem called the *Argonautica Orphica* (not to be confused with the epic of the same name by Apollonius Rhodius) to the legendary poet and musician Orpheus, supposed to have been an approximate contemporary of Moses, Hermes Trismegistus, and Zoroaster.

85. Vergil, *Aeneid* 4.176–77. From the description of *Fama.*

86. Cf. Macrobius, *Saturnalia.* 5.13.31–32. Modern texts read *augmenta* ("growth"), not *argumenta* ("subjects").

87. For the mixing of true and false by *fama,* Pontano paraphrases *Aeneid* 4.188–90. Cf. especially *facta atque infacta nuntiare* ("reports things done and not done") with *Aeneid* 4.190: *pariter facta atque infecta canebat.* For the physical appearance of *fama,* see *Aeneid* 4.180–85.

88. Pontano is paraphrasing Vergil, *Aeneid.* 2.604–6 (Venus' words to Aeneas).

89. Pontano is about to commit some verbal sleight of hand here. Macrobius (and Vergil) were using *fama* in the sense of "rumor"; in what follows Pontano will use it in the sense of "fame" or "renown," as well as "report" and "reputation."

90. Sallust, *Bellum Catilinae* 8.2. Modern texts read *aliquanto* ("somewhat") rather than *aliquando* ("sometimes").

91. Cf. Cato, *Monosticha: consulendum famae existimavi.*

92. Quintus Curtius Rufus, *Historiae Alexandri Magni,* 8.8.15: *fama enim bella constant.*

93. Theodore of Gaza (ca. 1398–1475).

94. Cf. Macrobius, *Saturnalia* 5.13.35; Homer, *Iliad* 5.1–8.

95. *Aeneid* 9.732–33.

96. *Aeneid* 10.270–71.

97. Cf. Macrobius, *Saturnalia* 15.13.35.

98. Cf. *Aeneid* 10.262–64, 276.

99. Cf. *Aeneid* 10.260–62: *Iamque in conspectu Teucros habet et sua castra / stans celsa in puppi, clipeum cum deinde sinistra / extulit ardentem.*

100. Macrobius, *Saturnalia* 5.13.36; *Aeneid* 8.620.

101. Cf. *Aeneid* 8.619: *miraturque interque manus et bracchia uersat.*

102. Cf. *Aeneid* 8.616: *arma sub aduersa posuit radiantia quercu.*

103. Macrobius, *Saturnalia* 5.13.36; *Aeneid* 7.785–88.

104. *Aeneid* 7.783–84.

105. *Aeneid* 7.793–94: *insequitur nimbus peditum clipeataque totis / agmina densentur campis.*

106. Macrobius, *Saturnalia* 5.13.38. Jupiter speaks at *Aeneid* 1.254–96 (prophecy to Venus), 4.222–37 (instructions to Mercury), 9.94–106 (reassurance to Cybele).

107. *Aeneid* 10.101–3.

108. Paraphrased from Macrobius, *Saturnalia* 5.13.38.

109. Cf. *Aeneid* 10.96–97: *cunctique fremebant / caelicolae adsensu uario.*

110. *Aeneid* 10.112, 10.114, 10.115.

111. *Aeneid* 6.365–66; Aulus Gellius, *Noctes Atticae* 10.16.1–5.

112. Aulus Gellius, *Noctes Atticae* 10.16.11–13; *Aeneid* 6.122–23; *Aeneid* 6.617–18.

113. *Aeneid* 6.838–40.

114. Aulus Gellius, *Noctes Atticae* 10.16.14–18. Pontano's paraphrase follows Gellius' summary of Hyginus almost verbatim.

115. Propertius 4.11.39–40. Propertius' text is corrupt. Pontano quotes it as it appears in his own manuscript (Berlin, Deutsche Staatsbibliothek Preussischer Kulturbesitz [Haus Zwei], MS lat. fol. 500, fol. 65v), where he has corrected his first reading *proavos* (4.11.40) to *proavus*, glossing it "Pa<ulus> Emilius."

116. *Aeneid* 6.836–37.

117. Turnus' allies are catalogued at *Aeneid* 7.641–817, Aeneas' at *Aeneid* 10.163–214.

118. Macrobius, *Saturnalia* 5.15.1–15. Homer's catalog appears in *Iliad* 2.484–877.

119. Cf. *Aeneid* 10.201–3: *Mantua diues auis, sed non genus omnibus unum: / gens illi triplex, populi sub gente quaterni, / ipsa caput populis.*

120. Suetonius, *Divus Iulius* 57.

121. Cf. *Aeneid* 10.655 (modern texts read *Osinius*).

122. For the Stoics and other ancient philosophers, the heart, not the brain, was considered the seat of intelligence and judgment. Here and in the next two exchanges Pontano plays on the double sense of *cor* ("heart" and "intelligence") and the fact that the related words *cordatissime* and *cordate* (translated here as "as heartily as possible" and "with your heart") are used primarily of intelligence. The wordplay leads into a jesting contrast of "heart" and "head."

123. "A thing you might call old (*senile*)": Suppazio puns here and throughout the sentence on the popular (but false) etymology deriving the name Siena (Latin *Sena*) from *senex* ("old").

124. "Given over to their hide": leatherworking was a principal industry in Pisa. In calling Pisa "an old city and a Greek one," Suppazio refers to the tradition that it was founded by citizens of the Greek city of the same name; see Servius' *Commentary on the Aeneid* 10.179, Strabo 5.222, Justinus 20.1.11, and n. 168 below on *Pisatiles*.

125. Pisa, weakened by internal strife, was conquered by the Florentines in 1406.

126. Suppazio is perhaps referring to the *Volto Santo di Lucca*, a medieval wooden statue of the crucified Christ, especially venerated for its face, said to have been sculpted by an angel.

127. The *sacra cintola* of Mary in Prato Cathedral is still shown on several feast days.

128. Florence in the Renaissance was known for sumptuousness of female costume as well as for sodomy.

129. Lorenzo de' Medici, the de facto ruler of Florence, was credited with maintaining the balance of power in Italy.

130. Pontano is probably referring to the coup attempt of 1488 against the tyrant of Bologna, Giovanni II Bentivoglio, which ended in the hanging or exile of the conspirators.

131. Genoa in the Renaissance was famous for its political instability.

132. Talamone, after a flourishing period as the port of Florence in the mid-fourteenth century, was largely depopulated by the end of the fifteenth.

133. Cicero, *Paradoxa Stoicorum, proemium* 3; Vergil, *Eclogue* 8.80–81, *Eclogue* 4.28; Columella, *De re rustica* 2.17; Pliny, *Naturalis historia* 11.238.

134. Cicero, *Philippics* 12.4.9 (not in *Philippics* 3); *De amicitia* 21.78.

135. Perhaps an allusion to the sixteen *Savi* (wise men) who formed part of the governing Collegio.

136. The discussion of *frictio* paraphrases and corrects Valla's argument for *fricatio* in *De linguae latinae elegantia* 1.2.5–6. For this and some other corrections to Valla in Suppazio's speech, see David Marsh, "Grammar, Method, and Polemic in Lorenzo Valla's *Elegantiae*," *Rinascimento* 19 (1979): 91–116.

137. For the discussion and examples, cf. Priscian, *Institutiones grammaticae* in *Grammatici latini*, ed. Keil, 2.122.3. The example of *internetio* (from *in-ternecto,* "bind up") is taken nearly verbatim from Priscian: '*internectus' autem 'internecti internecio' fecit euphoniae causa abiecta t.*

138. The wordplay on *verba* and *verbera* is impossible in English.

139. The rule of bears and lions exemplifies savage tyranny in Antonio Beccadelli's *De dictis et factis Alphonsi regis* (Basel, 1538), 2.49 (following Seneca, *De clementia* 1.26.3). For Pontano's "I thought I was dealing with a bear or a lion, not a man," cf. Beccadelli's "clemency is the quality of a man, ferocity of wild beasts" (*hominis sane clementiam, beluarum feritatem*).

140. Caesar, *Bellum Gallicum* 7.30.1; 7.80.5.

141. Caesar, *Bellum Gallicum* 7.30.3.

142. Caesar, *Bellum Gallicum* 7.26.4; 5.41.4; 5.3.5.

143. Caesar, *Bellum Gallicum* 1.32.2; 4.7.5; 6.5.4; *Rhetorica ad Herennium* 3.20.1.

144. Caesar, *Bellum Gallicum* 5.44.1.

145. Caesar, *Bellum Gallicum* 7.32.5.

146. Quintilian, *Institutio oratoria* 10.1.87.

147. Caesar, *Bellum Gallicum* 4.14.3.

148. Sallust, *Bellum Catilinae* 5.7.

149. Caesar, *Bellum Gallicum* 1.53.4. Modern editions give the king's name as Voccio, not Boctio, and print *utraque* rather than *utraeque*.

150. Lactantius, *Divinae institutiones* 1.6.14; Caesar, *Bellum Gallicum* 4.3.3; Pliny, *Epistulae* 2.17.15; 9.33.4. Pontano's texts of Caesar and Pliny *Ep.* 2.17.15 differ slightly from those in modern editions. Pontano is correcting Valla, who had criticized Lactantius in *De linguae latinae elegantiae* 1.13: "the correct thing to say was 'most celebrated and famous'" (*celeberrima et nobilissima dicendum erat*). Marsh, "Grammar, Method, and Polemic," 113.

151. Quintilian, *Institutio oratoria, Prooemium* 23. Modern texts read *scientia, quibus solis quidam.*

152. Quintilian, *Institutio oratoria* 2.5.1.

153. Caesar, *Bellum Gallicum* 7.71.1.

154. *Rhetorica ad Herennium* 3.8.15. Modern texts do not include the words *rhetoricae orationis*.

155. Sallust, *Bellum Catilinae* 4.1; *mihi* does not appear in modern texts of Sallust.

156. Quintilian, *Institutio oratoria* 3.6.9.

157. Quintilian, *Institutio oratoria* 3.6.10.

158. *conspicatissimus* ("wonderfully clear") is perhaps a coinage by Pontano.

159. "Gullible" (*superstitiosulae*). For the word, a Renaissance neologism, see *Charon* 5 and n. 9 (*Charon*).

160. Probably referring to the notorious passage in *Republic* 5.457B–66D where Plato's Socrates argues in favor of a polity where wives are held in common.

161. At the beginning of the *Annales* (fragments 1–13) Ennius relates a dream in which he met Homer on Mt. Helicon (Lucretius, *De rerum natura* 1.117–19). (Pontano perhaps found the reference to Parnassus in the scholia to Persius, *Prol.* 2.3.).

162. The contrast is between the newfangled theology of the scholastics and the theology of ancient Christianity.

163. Pontano discusses Frater Franciscus Hispanus in *De sermone* 2.17.7, describing him as an ignorant and inflammatory charlatan obsessed with the idea that the Jews should be expelled from Naples. He claimed first that the message of his preaching was directed by an angel and then that he had found it on secret tablets buried by Saint Cataldus.

164. The ass story is an old fable that exists in several versions, including those in Petrarch (*Ep. fam.* 16.13) and San Bernardino ("Racconto III. Come si dè fare il bene e lassare ch'altri dica a sua posta, non remanendosene," in *Novellette, Esempi morali, e Apologhi di San Bernadino da Siena*, disp. 97, in *Libro di Novelle antiche tratte da diversi testi del buon secolo della lingua* [Bologna, 1868; repr. Bologna, 1968], vol. 20, 5–9). Suppazio's pro-

tagonists are himself and his young servant, Petrarch's a father and a son, San Bernardino's two monks (a man and a boy).

165. The phrase "so to speak" perhaps hints that Pontano has coined *excachinno* ("guffaw at").

166. Porta Capuana was built in 1484 on the northeast edge of Naples at the end of Via Tribunali, the major east-west street bisecting the old city. Pontano's house was several blocks down Via Tribunali from the gate. See Ferrajoli, *Napoli monumentale*, 162–75 and fig. 87.

167. Luciolo: i.e., Pontano's son Lucio (1469–98).

168. The old friend is Suppazio, who went to see Pontano at the end of the previous scene and returns at the beginning of the next, complaining of his encounter with an angry woman. See Spitzer, "Zu Pontans Latinität," 914 n. 1.

169. Santo argues that in saying "Pisatiles," Pontano's wife confuses the names of the inhabitants of the Italian and Greek Pisas ("Pisatilis," attested in Festus, refers to the latter); see Santo, "Hirquitulus, hirquiculus, e pisatilis," 109–112. But there may also be a double entendre, for it is possible that Pontano is playing with *pinso* ("beat, grind") and its derivatives. J. N. Adams does not specifically mention *pinso*, but he notes that words with this meaning are commonly used in a sexual sense (*The Latin Sexual Vocabulary* [London, 1982], 145–49). If there is a such a word play, *pisatilis* would mean something like "for banging."

170. *evomius* ("spewing") is a coinage by Pontano. See Sabbadini, *Storia del Ciceronianismo*, 79.

171. The meter of lines 1–3 is a twelve-syllable pattern with diaeresis: ∪ – – – ∪ – || – ∪ ∪ – ∪ –. Line 4 is dactylic hexameter.

172. This was a common subject of debate among fifteenth century humanists; typical texts include Poggio Bracciolini's *An seni sit uxor ducenda* (Whether an Old Man Should Marry, 1435) and Bartolomeo Scala's *Ducendane sit uxor sapienti* (Whether the Wise Man Should Marry, 1457/9).

173. See n. 181, below.

174. The following song is well chosen to please Enrico Poderico, whose son Francesco is celebrated with a mistress named Telesina in *Eridanus* 2.30, "De Telesina et Puderico." See Monti Sabia in *Poeti latini del Quattrocento,* 537.

175. The meter is elegiac couplet.

176. Pontano likes to contrast the roles played by simplicity and adornment in female beauty. In *Eridanus* 2.8 he assures Telesina that her blushes make her beautiful; cf. 2.8.4 (*Ipse pudor formae iuraque vimque tenet*) with line 6 here (*ipse pudor veri iura decoris habet*). But in *Eridanus* 2.13 he advises her to dress up; contrast 2.13.1 (*Et faciem, Telesina, cole, et cole, dia, capillum*) with line 1 here (*Ne faciem, Telesina, colas, neu finge capillum*). See also *Eridanus* 2.9 and 2.15.

177. The meter is hendecasyllabic.

178. The meter is Sapphic strophe.

179. For "frolics sweetly" (*dulce . . . ludit*), cf. Catullus 51.5 and Horace, *Odes* 1.22.23 (both also in Sapphics): *dulce ridentem* ("laughing sweetly").

180. Cf. Polyphemus' songs to Galatea at *Lyra* 13 and 16 (both also in Sapphics).

181. Pontano is probably referring to the "new art" of performing extemporaneous Latin verse to the accompaniment of the lute or lira da braccio. The verses were often sung in the volgare, but also in Latin, especially in humanist and court circles. Two such performers that we know worked in Naples were Aurelio Lippo Brandolini and Pietrobono del Chitarino, both of whom visited the Aragonese court in Naples in 1473. Pietrobono was much praised by humanists who accorded him the ultimate accolade (echoed by Enrico at §104, below) of having revived ancient music after the barbarous Middle Ages. See F. Alberto Gallo, *Music in the Castle: Troubadours, Books and Orators in Italian Courts of the Thirteenth, Fourteenth and Fifteenth Centuries* (Chicago, 1995), chapter 3; Allan W. Atlas, *Music at the Aragonese Court of Naples* (Cambridge, 1985), 108.

182. Cf. Horace, *Satire* 1.3.2: *ut numquam inducant animum cantare rogati.*

183. The meter is dactylic hexameter.

184. For "a marvelous textile" (*mirabile textum*) cf. Statius, *Thebaid* 10.56.

185. Cf. Vergil, *Eclogue* 6.27–28: *uideres / . . . rigidas motare cacumina quercus*.

186. The celebration of Carnival, a day (or days) of license and celebration after Epiphany and preceding Lent in Catholic countries, is first recorded in Venice and the Veneto in the thirteenth century, but began to spread to southern Italy at the end of the fourteenth.

187. The meter is iambic senarius in the manner of Plautus and Terence, but with some substitutions. The speech of the Masked Actor is modeled on that of the Prologus in Roman comedy. His speech begins and ends (lines 1 and 42) with a close imitation of Plautus, *Poenulus* 3: *siletque et tacete atque animum advortite*. See Monti Sabia, "Il *Bellum Sertoriacum*," 707, 716–17.

188. A play on the false etymology of *mentula* playfully suggested by Cicero, *Epistulae familiares* 9.22.3: *"Ruta" et "menta," recte utrumque: volo mentam pusillam ita appellare, ut "rutulam;" non licet* ("'Rue' [*ruta*] and 'mint' [*menta*] are both all right; but if I want to say 'little mint' [*mentula*] as I do "little rue" [*rutula*], it won't do").

189. The meter is dactylic hexameter.

190. For Sertorius see Plutarch, *Sertorius*. Pontano's poem is an epic account of the indecisive battle of Sertorius and Pompey at the river Sucro in 75 BCE. Pontano refers to the poem in the account of his poetic accomplishments at the end of *Urania* (5.959–62):

Instruxitque alas equitum, ac sertoria signa
Extulit Hesperiae in campis, tinxitque cruore
Arva super; tumuitque amnis, dum gurgite mersat
Arma, viros, phalerasque, et corpora quadrupedantum.

("And he drew up the wings of the cavalry and displayed
Sertorius' standards on the Hesperian plains, and dyed
The fields with gore; and the river swelled, drowning
Arms, men, and trappings, and the bodies of steeds.")

191. Pontano gives Sertorius two sons. Hernicus is of Italian stock, as his name suggests (*Hernicus*, "Hernician," refers to a region of Latium). The half-Spanish Marullus, like several heroes in Sertorius' army, is named

after one of Pontano's friends in the Neapolitan academy. His namesake is the famous poet Michele Marullo (1453–1500).

192. The name Marius appears in Lucan 2.92, etc.; Silius, *Punica* 9.401, etc.

193. "gaping wave" (*unda dehiscens*); cf. Vergil, *Aeneid* 1.106.

194. "hollow temples" (*cava tempora*): cf. Vergil, *Aeneid* 9.633, etc. Ovid, *Metamorphoses* 7.313; Lucan 3.711.

195. Like some characters in the *Aeneid*, Pontius is the ancestor of a famous lineage with a similar but not identical name (here Pontanus). Pontius will emerge as the principal actor in the epic. His exploit at the bridge (*pons, pontis*) suggests a connection with his name.

196. The name Melas appears in Lucan 6.374 and Statius, *Thebaid* 7.273; Metiscus appears in Vergil, *Aeneid* 12.469, etc., Silius 1.437. Pardus and Chariteius are named after members of the Academy. Giovanni Pardo (d. after 1512) was a Spanish priest, scholar, and poet and secretary in the royal chancellery. He was an interlocutor in *Actius, Aegidius,* and *Asinus;* speaker in *De fortuna* 3; dedicatee of *De rebus coelestibus* 3 and *De conviventia;* named in *Eridanus* 1.31; *Baiae* 2.6, 2.10, 2.23: *De sermone* 1.30. Chariteius is a slightly altered form of Chariteus (i.e., Benet Gareth or Benedetto Cariteo; 1450?–1514; the academy name Chariteus or Cariteo means "dear to the Graces"); a Catalan poet; secretary of state to King Ferrandino; interlocutor in *Aegidius* and *Asinus;* dedicatee of *De splendore* 1; celebrated in *Eridanus* 1.37 and *Baiae* 1.30; mentioned in *Tumuli* 2.35.

197. Corvinus is named for Leonardo Corvino (died before March 16, 1502), a humanist, priest, and Latin poet. He is the dedicatee of *Baiae* 2.27. Here and in line 99 below, Pontano seems to have substituted him for Aurelius (Aurelio Bienato), another Neapolitan humanist. See Monti Sabia, "Il *Bellum Sertoriacum,*" 712–14.

198. Carpetanan: i.e., Spaniard. The Carpetani were a people of northeastern Spain.

199. For the image, cf. Catullus 11.22–24; Vergil, *Aeneid* 9.435–37.

200. The name "Atlas" appears at Silius 5.271, 16.378, etc.

201. Pontano has borrowed several names in this sentence from Vergil's *Aeneid* or Silius' *Punica.* From Vergil: Actor (*Aeneid* 9.500, etc., but also Statius, *Thebaid* 8.152, etc.); Anius (*Aeneid* 3.80); Arunx (Arruns, *Aeneid* 11.759, etc., but also Lucan 1.106, etc.). From Silius: Hiempsal (1.408, but also Sallust *Iugurtha* 1.5.7, etc.); Maharbal (4.562, but also Livy 22.46, etc.); Bostar (Silius 3.6, etc.).

202. Marmarica is a region of north Africa. *Marmarides* appears in Lucan 9.893, etc., and Silius 2.165, etc.

203. I.e., epic or Homeric Muses. Homer is often called *Maeonius.*

204. For "arms . . . with gore" (*arma cruore*), cf. Vergil, *Aeneid* 10.907, 12.308.

205. For *clipeique resultant,* cf. Vergil, *Aeneid* 10.330 (*clipeoque resultant*).

206. For "banks leap apart in alarm" (*dissultant ripae*), cf. Vergil, *Aeneid* 8.240; for "the deep woods echo" (*voces nemora alta remittunt*), cf. *Aeneid* 12.929 (*vocem late nemora alta remittunt*).

207. Cf. Vergil, *Aeneid* 8.417–22.

208. Catilina is named for the infamous L. Sergius Catilina, who was one of Sulla's lieutenants (Pontano makes him a kinsman of Sulla). He has an *aristeia* in 144–70 and is nearly killed in 186–208.

209. I.e., Spain, the "western land."

210. The name "Almo" is taken from Vergil, *Aeneid* 7.532 and 575.

211. For "whole chorus of Nereids," cf. Silius Italicus *Punica* 3.412–13: *fluit omnis ab antris / Nereidum chorus.*

212. Varius and Hiempsal were introduced at line 110 above.

213. Pontano seems to be thinking of multiple pennants and not of the single silver eagle of a Roman legion.

214. Petreius is an appropriate name for Pompey's lieutenant since his namesake, Marcus Petreius, served under Pompey in Spain after 55 BCE and supported him against Caesar. See Sallust, *Bellum Catilinae* 60.1, etc; Caesar, *Bellum Civile* 1.38, etc.; Lucan 4.5, etc.

215. Compare *Urania* 5.962, quoted in n. 190 above.

216. The meter is iambic senarius, as in Poem VIII.

217. For poets and wine cf. Horace, *Epistle* 1.19.1–11, especially: *laudibus arguitur uini uinosus Homerus* (1.19.6 "because of his praises of wine Homer is charged with being bibulous"). To drink wine unmixed with water in antiquity was the mark of a drunkard.

218. Sea calves (seals) were proverbially sleepy. See Pliny, *Historia Naturalis* 9.42: *nullum animal graviore somno premitur* ("no animal is overcome by heavier sleep"). Cf. Seneca, *Apocolocyntosis* 5.3; Juvenal 3.238.

219. The meter is dactylic hexameter, as in Poem IX.

220. I.e., Pompey (Pompeius Magnus).

221. Cf. Vergil, *Aeneid* 7.645: *et meministis enim, divae, et memorare potestis* ("for you remember, goddesses, and you are able to tell"). Vergil's verse also introduces a catalog of heroes.

222. Pyrene is the nymph after whom the Pyrenees were named. Pontano makes her the servant of Sertorius' divine patron Diana ("the bow-wielding goddess"). At the end of the poem she changes herself into a doe to warn Sertorius of his impending death. For the importance of Diana and the doe in Sertorius' self-created legend, see Plutarch, *Sertorius* 11.3–12.1; 20.

223. Altilius is named after a member of the Academy, Gabriele Altilio (ca. 1440–1501); poet, tutor and later political secretary of Ferrandino, and bishop of Policastro. Altilio is an interlocutor in *Actius* and *Asinus*, dedicatee of *Tumuli* 1.18 and *De magnificentia*, addressee of *Baiae* 1.25, mentioned in *Baiae* 1.10.12, 21.

224. Possibly a reference to Pietro Marsi or Paolo Marsi, both humanist scholars belonging to Pomponio Leto's Roman academy. The Fucine Lake (Fucinus), an important source of water for ancient Rome, was situated in the territory of the Marsi, near modern Avezzano.

225. For "a silver goose flying" (*advolitans argenteus anser*), cf. Vergil, *Aeneid* 8.655: *volitans argenteus anser*.

226. Actius is named after the great poet Jacopo Sannazaro (1455/6–1530), whose academic name was Actius Syncerus. Sannazaro is the

principal interlocutor in Pontano's *Actius,* as well as the dedicatee of *Eclogue* 5 and *Baiae* 1.11.

227. For "his wife embroidered his cloak" (*nevit acu chlamydem coniunx*), cf. Vergil, *Aeneid* 10.818: *et tunicam molli mater quam neuerat auro.*

228. For "she sent flicks *with her triple tongue*" (*micat et linguis . . . trisulcis*), cf. line 72 below (*trifido micat ore cerastes*), and Vergil, *Georgics* 3.439 and *Aeneid* 2.475: *linguis micat ore trisulcis* ("he sent flicks from his mouth with his triple tongue").

229. For "his steed was champing at a golden bit" (*Aurea mandebat sonipes frena*), cf. Vergil, *Aeneid* 4.135: *stat sonipes ac frena ferox spumantia mandit.*

230. For Pontano's ecphrasis of Ganymede, cf. Vergil, *Aeneid* 5.250–57.

231. Compater is named for Pontano's friend Pietro Golino (called Compater in the Academy), a principal interlocutor in the dialogue. See n. 1 above.

232. For "at daybreak" (*mane novo*), cf. Vergil, *Georgics* 3.325: *dum mane novum.*

233. For "bronze-armored battle line" (*aeratam . . . aciem*), cf. Vergil, *Aeneid* 9.463: *aeratas acies.* Camillus: Pontano has borrowed the name of a fourth-century BCE general (Marcus Furius Camillus), invoked as an example of old Roman virtue by Vergil (*Aeneid* 6.825); Lucan 5.28, etc.; Silius 1.626, etc.

234. The name "Astur" appears in Vergil, *Aeneid* 10.180, 181 (Astyr); Lucan 4.8; Silius 1.231, etc. His epithet "Saxonian" perhaps recalls the surname of Pontano's wife (Adriana Sassone); see Benedetto Soldati, "Improvvisatori, Canterini e Buffoni in un Dialogo del Pontano," in *Miscellanea di studi critici pubblicati in onore di Guido Mazzoni dai suoi discepoli,* ed. Arnaldo della Torre (Florence, 1907), 342.

235. For "club with three knots" (*clavam . . . trinodem*), cf. Ovid, *Heroides* 4.115 (*clava . . . trinodi*); *Fasti* 1.575 (*clava trinodis*). For *incoctus* ("untempered"), see Poem IX, 168.

236. The female warrior Birse has features of both Vergil's Camilla (*Aeneid* 7.803–17, 11.532–96, 648–847) and Silius' Asbyte (*Punica* 2.56–88), as well as Vergil's Turnus (*Aeneid* 7.783–92). She is Tritonian because of her

association with Tritonian Pallas and Lake Tritonis in Africa, but also to recall Silius' Asbyte, descended from the nymph Tritonis (2.65). Like Vergil's Camilla, she has a divine patroness (Birse's is Pallas, Camilla's Diana) and is swift footed; cf. "outpaces the riders with her step" (*passu praevertit euntes,* 85) with Vergil's *cursuque pedum praevertere ventos* ("outpaces the winds with her running feet," *Aeneid* 7.807). Like both Camilla and Asbyte, she is a huntress. Like Turnus, she is huge, higher by a head than the rest (*eminet . . . / vertice iam toto,* 83–84; cf. *toto vertice supra est, Aeneid* 7.784).

237. For "Pallas of the ringing armor" (*Palladis armisonae*), cf. Vergil, *Aeneid* 3.544.

238. For "Garamantian nymph" (*nympha . . . Garamantide*), cf. Vergil, *Aeneid* 4.198 (*Garamantide nympha*).

239. The brothers Hernicus and Marullus were introduced in Poem IX, 2–3.

240. Puttius must also be named for a member of the Academy, Francesco Pucci (1463–1512). Pucci, an early pupil of Angelo Poliziano, arrived in Naples in 1485 or 1486, becoming a professor in the university and librarian of the royal library. He is an interlocutor in *Aegidius,* addressee of *Baiae* 2.9, mentioned in *Baiae* 2.25 and *De sermone* 4.3.38 and 5.3.60.

241. Petreius was introduced in Poem 9.181.

242. For "fresh slaughter" (*recenti caede*), cf. *recenti/caede:* Vergil, *Aeneid* 8.195–96; Ovid, *Metamorphoses* 4.96–97.

243. The name "Cetegus" (Cethegus) is found in Vergil, *Aeneid* 12.513; Lucan 2.543, etc; Silius 8.575. Cetegus appears again in lines 219–47 below.

244. For "chosen men" (*lecta iuventus*), cf. Vergil, *Aeneid* 8.606; Lucan 9.478. See also *delecta iuventus* at line 319 below.

245. For "is prancing on the field" (*insultat campo*), cf. Vergil, *Georgics* 3.117: *insultare solo.*

246. For "our whole hope is in arms" (*spes omnis in armis*), cf. Sallust, *Iugurtha* 14.10.

247. The brothers Altilius and Lycon were introduced in line 8 above. They will appear again at line 220.

248. For "wave resounded" (*remurmurat unda*), cf. Vergil, *Aeneid* 10.291.

249. For "and the hills sent back the sound" (*collesque resultant*), see Vergil, *Aeneid* 8.305.

250. For "success fed" (*successus . . . alit*), cf. Vergil, *Aeneid* 5.231 (*successus alit*).

251. For "the field ran with blood" (*humescunt sanguine campi*, 183), cf. Catullus 64.344: *manabunt sanguine <campi>*.

252. Hiarbas: the name "Iarbas" appears in Vergil, *Aeneid* 4.36, etc; Silius 8.54.

253. Tagus is also the name of a river in Spain (the Tajo), mentioned in the epics of Lucan (7.775) and Silius (1.155, etc.). He is killed in lines 242–45 below. The name "Remus" is used not only of Romulus' brother, but also for heroes (Vergil's *Aeneid* 9.330; Lucan 1.424). Turnus is the name of Aeneas' great adversary (*Aeneid* 7.56, etc.); the name "Ligus" appears at *Aeneid* 11.715; Silius 4.591, etc.

254. The name "Ufens" is found in both Vergil and Silius: *Aeneid* 7.745, etc; Silius 4.337, etc. Ufens appears again in lines 325–39. Assaracus was an ancestor of the Trojans (see *Aeneid* 6.560).

255. Some names in this sentence appear in ancient epic: Marus (Silius 6.74, etc.); Hypseus (Ovid, *Metamorphoses* 5.98; Statius, *Thebaid* 7.723, etc.); Iopas (Vergil, *Aeneid* 1.740); Ancus (*Aeneid* 6.815, an early king of Rome). Two others are the academic names of friends of Pontano. Faliscus is Francesco Colocci; see Federico Ubaldini, *Vita di Mons. Angelo Colocci*, ed. Vittorio Fanelli, Studi e Testi 256 (Città del Vaticano, 1969),18, n.20. Bassus is Francesco's nephew, the Roman humanist Angelo Colocci (1474–1549). The much younger Angelo met Pontano in Rome in 1486, became his great admirer, and sponsored the publication of several of his works after his death. In the dedication of *De magnanimitate*, Summonte addresses him as A. Colotius Bassus and refers to the use of his name in *Antonius*: "Tu vero quo exquisita haec otiosius legas, intermissa paulum Sertoriana illa militia, ad quam ipse a Pontano es haud immerito vocatus,

depositisque hasta, ac clipeo ad notas te aliquando Musas refer (You may read these choice words at your leisure, when you are off duty for a while from that Sertorian military service to which you were justly called by Pontano; setting down spear and shield betake yourself at last to the well-known Muses)." Pontano, *Opera omnia* 1518, vol. 2, fol. 226b.

256. Cetegus was introduced at line 152 above. His *aristeia* extends from 220 to 247.

257. The name "Iasius" appears at Vergil, *Aeneid* 3.168; Statius, *Thebaid*, 2.219. Muranus (Murranus): *Aeneid* 12.529, etc.; Silius 4.529, etc. Quercens: *Aeneid* 9.684; Silius 10.151.

258. For "slaughter of men" (*caede virorum*), cf. Vergil, *Aeneid* 11.634; Silius 11.519.

259. The phrase "and the hollow caves reechoed" (*cavaque antra resultant*) appears again at *Meteororum liber* 850.

260. The name "Varenus" appears in Silius 4.543. Gias (Gyas) appears in Vergil, *Aeneid* 5.116, etc.; Silius 1.439; Statius, *Thebaid* 6.610, etc.

261. Alcon appears in Statius, *Thebaid*, 6.606, etc.

262. For "plunges it into his trough" (*tingit / ipse lacu*), cf. Vergil, *Georgics* 4.172–73 (*tingunt / aera lacu*).

263. For "heifers grazed in great Sila" (*iuvencae / pascebant Sila in magna*), cf. Vergil, *Georgics* 3.219: *pascitur in magna Sila formosa iuuenca.*

264. Aufidius is perhaps to be identified with Marino Correale (died 1499); see Monti Sabia, "Il *Bellum Sertoriacum*," 709, n. 9. For Correale, see Petrucci, "Correale, Marino."

265. Modern Vico Equense.

266. One ancient tradition located the Sirens on the coast near Sorrento. Strabo mentions a nearby temple of the Sirens (*Geography* 5.4.8).

267. I.e., the land of Florence (*Florentia*).

268. The phrase *delecta iuventus* ("picked force of young men, chosen youth") is a favorite cadence in ancient epic: Vergil, *Aeneid* 4.130, etc.; Lucan 7.270; Silius 16.174. Cf. *lecta iuventus* above at line 166.

269. Ufens was introduced at line 199 above.

270. The scene recalls Vergil's description of Aeneas carrying his father Anchises from burning Troy. Cf. Pontano's *cervice reclina/impositum* and Aeneas' instructions to Anchises: *cervici imponere nostrae* (*Aeneid* 2.707).

271. Cf. Vergil, *Aeneid* 2.379–80: *improuisum aspris ueluti qui sentibus anguem /pressit* ("just as one who does not see a snake and steps on it in the rough brambles").

272. For "mute Amyclae" (*tacitae . . . Amyclae*), cf. Vergil, *Aeneid* 10.564: *tacitis . . . Amyclis*.

273. Cf. Vergil's description of Etna discussed in paragraphs 39–53 above, and especially *Aeneid* 3.574: *sidera lambit* ("licks the stars").

274. Gulussa has the name of a son of the Numidian king Masinissa, who was active on behalf of the Romans in the third Punic War. See Livy 42.23–24, 43.3; Sallust, *Iugurtha* 5.6, 35.1.

275. The name "Umbro" appears in Vergil's *Aeneid* 7.752, etc.

276. The name "Gisco" appears in Silius 2.111, etc. Bocchus has the name of the king of Mauretania who was the father-in-law of Jugurtha; the name appears in Silius 3.285: Sallust, *Iugurtha*, passim.

277. For "scorching heat" (*rapidos aestus*), cf. Vergil, *Eclogue* 2.10: *rapido . . . aestu*. Cf. also Vergil's description of Etna (*Aeneid* 3.570–87) and the discussion in paragraphs 39–53.

278. The "bow-wielding goddess" is Diana, called Trivia in line 388 below. Her brother (line 389) is Apollo, god of prophecy.

279. The "Nursian leader" is Sertorius, born in Nursia (modern Norcia). He was assassinated by some of his followers in 73 BCE.

280. Pyrene was introduced at line 5 above.

281. *Lunavit* ("made a crescent") appears in classical Latin only at Ovid, *Amores* 1.1.21 (where Cupid shoots his arrow at Ovid).

Bibliography

EDITIONS OF PONTANO'S *DIALOGUES*

[*Dialogi qui Charon et Antonius inscribuntur*]. Naples: Mathias Moravus, January 31, 1491.

Ioannnis Ioviani Pontani opera. Venice: Bernardinus Vercellensis, 1501.

Pontani Actius de numeris poeticis et lege historiae. Aegidius multiplicis argumenti. Tertius dialogus de ingratitudine qui Asinus inscribitur. Naples: Sigismund Mayr, 1507.

Opera. . . . Dialogus qui Charon inscribitur. Dialogus qui Antonius inscribitur. Venice: Joannes Rubeus and Bernardinus Vercellensis, 1512.

Opera Ioannis Ioviani Pontani. Lyon: Bartolomeus Troth, 1514.

Ioannnis Ioviani Pontani opera omnia soluta oratione composita. 3 vols. Venice: Heirs of Aldus, 1518–19.

Ioannis Ioviani Pontani opera omnia soluta oratione composita. 6 vols. Florence: Heirs of Philippus Iunta, 1520.

Ioannis Ioviani Pontani opera quae soluta oratione composuit omnia, in tomos tres digesta. Basel: Andreas Cratander, 1538–40.

Ioannis Ioviani Pontani opera a mendis expurgata et in quattuor tomis digesta. Basel: Heinrich Petri, 1556.

Actius. In *Johannis Bodini Methodus historica, duodecim eiusdem argumenti scriptorum tam veterum quam recentiorum commentariis adaucta*. Basel: Petrus Perna, 1576.

Actius. In *Artis historicae penus octodecim scriptorum tam veterum quam recentiorum monumentis . . . instructa*. Basel: Petrus Perna, 1579.

Charon. In *Equitis Franci et adolescentulae mulieris Italae Practica artis amandi. . . . Cui . . . alia quaedam huic materiae non inconvenientia iam primum accesserunt,* edited by Hilarius Drudo [pseud.]. Oberursel: Cornelius Sutorius, 1606. Repr. Amsterdam: Georgius Trigg, 1651.

Charon dialogus. In Carlo Maria Tallarigo, *Giovanni Pontano e i suoi tempi,* 2:687–744. 2 vols. Naples: D. Morano, 1874.

L'Asino e il Caronte. Edited by Marcello Campodonico. Lanciano: G. Carabba, 1918.

"Antonius" di Giovanni Pontano. Edited by Vincenzo Grillo. Lanciano: G. Carabba, 1939.

Giovanni Pontano: I Dialoghi. Edited by Carmelo Previtera. Florence: Sansoni, 1943.

Dialoge. Translated by Hermann Kiefer and others. Introduction by Ernesto Grassi. Munich: W. Fink, 1984. With Previtera's Latin text.

OTHER WORKS BY PONTANO CITED

Baiae. Translated by Rodney G. Dennis. Cambridge, MA: Harvard University Press, 2006.

Carmina. Ecloghe, Elegie, Liriche. Edited by Johannes Oeschger. Bari: Laterza, 1948.

Hendecasyllaborum libri. Edited by Liliana Monti Sabia. Naples: Associazione di studi tardoantichi, 1978.

I trattati delle virtù sociali. De liberalitate, De beneficentia, De magnificentia, De splendore, De conviventia. Edited by Francesco Tateo. Rome, 1965.

Meteororum liber. Edited by Mauro de Nichilo. In Mauro de Nichilo, *I poemi astrologici di Giovanni Pontano: storia di testo, con un saggio di edizione critica del Meteorum liber*. Bari: Dedalo libri, 1975.

[*Urania seu de stellis*]. *Quae in hoc enchyridio contineantur: Ioannis Ioviani Pontani Urania seu de stellis libri quinque. Meteororum Liber unus. De hortis Hesperidum libri duo. Eiusdem pompae septem, quibus titulus Lepidina, nec non Meliseus, Maeon, Acon, carmina pastoralia*. Florence: Filippo Giunta, 1514.

MODERN LITERATURE

Bentley, Jerry H. *Politics and Culture in Renaissance Naples*. Princeton: Princeton University Press, 1987.

Cappelletto, Rita. *La "lectura Plauti" del Pontano*. Urbino: QuattroVenti, 1988.

Cox, Virginia. *The Renaissance Dialogue. Literary Dialogue in Its Social and Political Contexts, Castiglione to Galileo*. Cambridge: Cambridge University Press, 1992.

Ferrajoli, Ferdinando. *Napoli monumentale*. Adriano Gallina Editore. Naples, 1981.

Ferraù, Giacomo. *Pontano critico*. Messina: Università degli studi di Messina, Facoltà di lettere e filosofia, Centro di studi umanistici, 1983.

Furstenberg-Levi, Shulamit. "The Fifteenth-Century Accademia Pontaniana: An Analysis of Its Institutional Elements." *History of Universities* 21.1 (2006): 33–70.

Gaisser, Julia Haig. *Catullus and His Renaissance Readers*. Oxford: Oxford University Press, 1993.

Hankins, James. "Humanist Academies and the 'Platonic Academy' of Florence." In *On Renaissance Academies*, edited by Marianne Pade, 31–46. (Proceedings of the International Conference, "From the Roman Academy to the Danish Academy in Rome." The Danish Academy in Rome, October 11–13, 2006.) Rome: Danish Institute, 2010.

Kidwell, Carol. *Pontano. Poet and Prime Minister*. London: Duckworth, 1991.

Ludwig, Walther. "Catullus Renatus." In *Litterae neolatinae: Schriften zur neulateinischen Literatur*, 162–94. Munich: W. Fink, 1989.

Mariotti, Scevola. "Per lo studio dei dialoghi del Pontano." *Belfagor* 2 (1947): 332–44. Reprinted in *Scritti medievali e umanistici*, edited by Silvia Rizzo, 261–84. Second edition. Rome: Edizioni di Storia e Letteratura, 1994.

Marsh, David. *The Quattrocento Dialogue: Classical Tradition and Humanist Innovation*. Cambridge, MA: Harvard University Press, 1980.

Monti, Salvatore. "Ricerche sulla cronologia dei *Dialoghi* di Pontano." *Annali della Facoltà di Letteratura e Filosofia, Università di Napoli*, 10 (1962–63): 247–305. Reprinted in Monti Sabia and Monti, *Studi su Giovanni Pontano*, 2:757–826.

Monti Sabia, Liliana. "Il *Bellum Sertoriacum* di Giovanni Pontano." In *Synodia. Studia humanitatis Antonio Garzya septuagenario ab amicis atque discipulis dicata*, edited by Ugo Criscuolo and Riccardo Maisano, 707–26. Naples, 1997. Reprinted in Monti Sabia and Monti, *Studi su Giovanni Pontano*, 1:729–56.

——. "Giovanni Gioviano Pontano." In *Poeti Latini del Quattrocento*, edited by Francesco Arnaldi, Lucia Gualdo Rosa, and Liliana Monti Sabia, 307–14. Milan: Riccardo Ricciardi Editore, 1964.

———. "Un ignoto codice del *Charon* di Pontano." In *Studi latini in ricordo di Rita Cappelletto*, 285–309. Urbino: QuattroVenti, 1996. Reprinted in Monti Sabia and Monti, *Studi su Giovanni Pontano*, 2:947–72.

———. *Un profilo moderno e due vitae antiche di Giovanni Pontano*. Quaderni dell'Accademia Pontaniana 25. Naples: Accademia pontaniana, 1998.

Monti Sabia, Liliana, and Salvatore Monti. *Studi su Giovanni Pontano*. Edited by Giuseppe Germano. 2 vols. Messina: Centro Interdipartimentale di Studi Umanistici, 2010.

Nauta, Lodi. "Philology as Philosophy: Giovanni Pontano on Language, Meaning and Grammar." *Journal of the History of Ideas* 72.4 (2011): 481–502.

Petrucci, F. "Correale, Marino." *Dizionario biografico degli Italiani* 29 (Rome: Instituto della Enciclopedia italiana, 1983), 421–22.

Resta, Gianvito. "Beccadelli, Antonio." *Dizionario biografico degli Italiani* 7 (Rome: Istituto della Enciclopedia italiana, 1965), 400–406.

Ryder, Alan. "Antonio Beccadelli: A Humanist in Government." In *Cultural Aspects of the Italian Renaissance. Essays in Honour of Paul Oskar Kristeller*, edited by Cecil H. Clough, 123–40. Manchester: Manchester University Press, 1976.

———. *The Kingdom of Naples under Alfonso the Magnanimous. The Making of a Modern State*. Oxford: Oxford University Press, 1976.

Sabbadini, Remigio. *Storia del Ciceronianismo e di altre questioni letterarie nell'età della Rinascenza*. Turin: E. Loescher, 1885.

Santo, Luigi. "Hirquitulus, hirquiculus, e pisatilis. Nota pontaniana." *Quaderni dell' Istituto di filologia latina* 3 (1971): 79–127.

Spitzer, Leo. "Zu Pontans Latinität. (*hirquituli?*)." In *Romanische Literaturstudien 1936–1956*, 913–22. Tübingen: M. Niemeyer, 1959.

Index

Publication of this volume has been made possible by

The Myron and Sheila Gilmore Publication Fund at I Tatti
The Robert Lehman Endowment Fund
The Jean-François Malle Scholarly Programs and Publications Fund
The Andrew W. Mellon Scholarly Publications Fund
The Craig and Barbara Smyth Fund
for Scholarly Programs and Publications
The Lila Wallace–Reader's Digest Endowment Fund
The Malcolm Wiener Fund for Scholarly Programs and Publications